Praise for Dorian Lynskey's

THE MINISTRY OF TRUTH

"Dorian Lynskey's *The Ministry of Truth* manages, against all odds, to find many original points to make about the dystopian classic."
—*New Statesman* (London)

"Thoroughly researched and wear[s] its scholarship lightly.... This astute study locates the origins of the novel and its life within pop culture." —*The Guardian*

"Dorian Lynskey's book amounts to a comprehensive survey of the history of utopia and dystopia, centring on Orwell's immensely influential novel, and it is full of connections that make the reader's mind spin off in all directions and search the bookshelves and the internet.... This thought-provoking book explores the many possibilities of what [Orwell] may have meant by 'it.'"
—Margaret Drabble, *The Times Literary Supplement* (London)

"Perhaps the best book of its kind that I've ever read. The portrait it provides of Orwell is sharp, nuanced, and moving, and its capsule histories of the major and minor planets in orbit around *1984* are surprising and deeply informative. Above all, it's just flat out fun to read. With *The Ministry of Truth*, Dorian Lynskey has done anyone who loves literature a great service." —Tom Bissell, author of *Apostle* and coauthor of *The Disaster Artist*

"*The Ministry of Truth* is a fantastic and important read, and I know I will be reading it again in the coming months and years."
—Greg Lukianoff, president of the Foundation for Individual Rights in Education and coauthor of *The Coddling of the American Mind*

"Gaslighting, doublespeak, the horror of a crowd of human 'gramophones...playing the same tune' at frenzied rallies where mob and demagogue crescendo together in an orgasm of hate: Orwell saw our future and sent us a time capsule to be opened in case of emergency. That moment is now. Briskly written and brilliantly argued, *The Ministry of Truth* delves deep into the cultural impact—and terrifying relevance—of a book that, seventy years on, still delivers the jolt of a torturer's electrodes."
—Mark Dery,
author of *Born to Be Posthumous: The Eccentric Life and Mysterious Genius of Edward Gorey*

"A deeply researched and highly readable intellectual history, providing a wealth of information and anecdotes about Orwell's life and work. Lynskey skillfully weaves together literary and political histories to create a rich tapestry, full of context, color, and insight into one of the most important books of the last century—and thus far, this century as well. *The Ministry of Truth* is an illuminating and entertaining companion to *1984*, a novel whose relevance and necessity are more evident than ever, at a time when the very concept of objective reality is under attack."
—Charles Yu,
author of *How to Live Safely in a Science Fictional Universe*

"[A] vibrant, spirited story of a man and his book....Lynskey does a superb job analyzing the young Orwell's political beliefs, his hatred of fascism, and his 'vision of common sense radicalism.'...[A] fascinating literary history."
—*Kirkus Reviews*

"The defining book of 2019 focuses on *1984*, or more properly, on *Nineteen Eighty-Four*, by George Orwell. Dorian Lynskey's *The Ministry of Truth*, a biography of the novel, has the zest and momentum of a Stephen King novel, and the piercing clarity and dark sensibility of Orwell himself."
—Cass Sunstein, *Bloomberg*

DORIAN LYNSKEY

THE MINISTRY OF TRUTH

Dorian Lynskey has been writing about music, film, and politics for more than twenty years for publications including *The Guardian*, *The Observer*, *GQ*, *Q*, *Empire*, *Billboard*, and the *New Statesman*. His first book, *33 Revolutions Per Minute: A History of Protest Songs, from Billie Holiday to Green Day*, was published in 2011.

www.dorianlynskey.com

ALSO BY DORIAN LYNSKEY

*33 Revolutions Per Minute: A History of Protest Songs,
from Billie Holiday to Green Day*

THE
MINISTRY
OF
TRUTH

The Biography of
George Orwell's *1984*

DORIAN LYNSKEY

ANCHOR BOOKS
A Division of Penguin Random House LLC
New York

For Lucy, Eleanor and Rosa

FIRST ANCHOR BOOKS EDITION, MAY 2020

Copyright © 2019 by Dorian Lynskey

The Library of Congress has cataloged the Doubleday edition as follows:
Name: Lynskey, Dorian, author.
Title: The ministry of truth : the biography of George Orwell's 1984 / Dorian Lynskey.
Description: First American edition. | New York : Doubleday
2019. | Includes bibliographical references and index.
Identifiers: LCCN 2019937137
Subjects: LCSH: Orwell, George, 1903–1950. | Nineteen eighty-four. | Science fiction,
English—History and criticism. | Dystopias in literature. | Totalitarianism in literature.
LC record available at https://lccn.loc.gov/2019937137

Anchor Books Trade Paperback ISBN: 978-0-525-56372-3
eBook ISBN: 978-0-385-54406-1

Author photograph © Alexandra Dao
Book design by Michael Collica

www.anchorbooks.com

Printed in the United States of America
10 9 8 7 6 5 4 3 2 1

It's a sad commentary on our age that we find Dystopias a lot easier to believe in than Utopias: Utopias we can only imagine, Dystopias we've already had.

—Margaret Atwood

There was truth and there was untruth, and if you clung to the truth even against the whole world, you were not mad.

—George Orwell, *Nineteen Eighty-Four*

Contents

Introduction

December 1948. A man sits at a typewriter, in bed, on a remote island, fighting to complete the book that means more to him than any other. He is terribly ill. The book will be finished and, a year or so later, so will the man.

January 2017. Another man stands before a crowd, which is not as large as he would like, in Washington, DC, taking the oath of office as the forty-fifth president of the United States of America. His press secretary later says that it was the "largest audience to ever witness an inauguration—period—both in person and around the globe." Asked to justify such a preposterous lie, the president's adviser describes the statement as "alternative facts." Over the next four days, US sales of the dead man's book will rocket by almost 10,000 per cent, making it a number-one best seller.

When George Orwell's *Nineteen Eighty-Four* was published in the United Kingdom on June 8, 1949, in the heart of the twentieth century, one critic wondered how such a timely book could possibly exert the same power over generations to come. Thirty-five years later, when the present caught up with Orwell's future and the world was not the nightmare he had described, commentators again predicted that the book's popularity would wane. Another thirty-five years have elapsed since then, and *Nineteen Eighty-Four* remains the book we turn to when truth is mutilated, language is distorted, power is abused, and we want to know how bad things can get, because someone who lived and died in another era was clear-sighted enough to identify these evils and sufficiently talented to present them in the form of a novel that Anthony Burgess, author of *A Clockwork Orange,* called "an apocalyptical codex of our worst fears."

Nineteen Eighty-Four has not just sold tens of millions of copies; it has infiltrated the consciousness of countless people who have never read it. The phrases and concepts that Orwell minted have become essential fixtures of political language, still potent after decades of use and misuse: Newspeak, Big Brother, the Thought Police, Room 101, the Two Minutes Hate, doublethink, unperson, memory hole, telescreen, $2 + 2 = 5$, and the Ministry of Truth. Its title came to dominate a calendar year, while the word *Orwellian* has turned the author's own name into a capacious synonym for everything he hated and feared. The book has been adapted for cinema, television, radio, theatre, opera and ballet. It has prompted a sequel (György Dalos's *1985*), a postmodern rewriting (Peter Huber's *Orwell's Revenge: The 1984 Palimpsest*) and innumerable retorts. Even the *writing* of the book has inspired a 1983 BBC drama, *The Crystal Spirit: Orwell on Jura,* and two novels: Dennis Glover's *The Last Man in Europe* and Norman Bissell's *Barnhill. Nineteen Eighty-Four* has influenced novels, films, plays, television shows, comic books, albums, advertisements, speeches, election campaigns and uprisings. People have spent years in jail just for reading it. No work of literary fiction from the past century approaches its cultural ubiquity while retaining its weight. Dissenting voices such as Milan Kundera and Harold Bloom have alleged that *Nineteen Eighty-Four* is actually a bad novel, with thin characters, humdrum prose and an implausible plot, but even they couldn't gainsay its importance. As Orwell's publisher Fredric Warburg observed, its success is extraordinary "for a novel that is not designed to please nor all that easy to understand."

For any artist, the price of immense popularity is the guarantee that you will be misunderstood. *Nineteen Eighty-Four* is more known about than truly known. This book is an attempt to restore some balance by explaining what Orwell's book actually is, how it came to be written, and how it has shaped the world, in its author's absence, over the past seventy years. The meaning of a work of art is never limited to its creator's intentions but in this case Orwell's intentions, too often distorted or ignored, are well worth revisiting if the book is to be understood *as a book* and not just a useful cache of memes. It is both a work of art and a means of reading the world.

This, then, is the story of *Nineteen Eighty-Four.* There have been several biographies of George Orwell and some academic studies of his book's intellectual context but never an attempt to merge the two streams into one narrative, while also exploring the book's afterlife. I am interested in Orwell's life primarily as a means to illuminate the experiences and ideas that nourished this very personal nightmare in which everything he prized was systematically destroyed: honesty, decency, fairness, memory, history, clarity, privacy, common sense, sanity, England, and love. This means starting with his decision to fight in the Spanish Civil War in 1936, because Spain was where he first became acutely conscious of the ways in which political expediency corrupts moral integrity, language and truth itself. I'll follow him, via the Blitz, the Home Guard, the BBC, literary London and post-war Europe, to the island of Jura, where he finally wrote his novel, so as to explode the myth that *Nineteen Eighty-Four* was a protracted wail of despair issuing from a lonely, dying man who couldn't face the future. I want to draw attention to what he was actually thinking, and how he came to think it.

One reason it took Orwell so long to write *Nineteen Eighty-Four* is that it synthesised ideas that he had been developing for most of his writing life. The book was the consummation of years of thinking, writing and reading about utopias, super-states, dictators, prisoners, propaganda, technology, power, language, culture, class, sex, the countryside, rats and more, often to the point where it becomes impossible to attribute a particular phrase or idea to a single source. Although Orwell said little about the evolution of the novel, he left a paper trail thousands of pages long. Even if he had lived decades longer, *Nineteen Eighty-Four* would have been the end of something: as a writer, he would have needed to start again.

In Part One, I will be telling the story of Orwell and the world he inhabited: the people he met, the news he followed and the books he read. I will also devote three chapters to crucial influences on *Nineteen Eighty-Four:* H. G. Wells, Yevgeny Zamyatin's *We,* and the genre of utopian (and anti-utopian) fiction. Every book, play or film cited is one that Orwell was familiar with, unless otherwise noted. Part Two will follow the political and cultural life of *Nineteen Eighty-Four* from Orwell's death to the present day. Along the way, we will encounter Aldous Huxley and E. M. Forster; Winston Churchill and Clement Attlee; Ayn Rand and Joseph McCarthy; Arthur Koestler and Hannah Arendt; Lee Harvey Oswald and J. Edgar Hoover;

Margaret Atwood and Margaret Thatcher; the CIA and the BBC; David Bowie and *The Prisoner; Brazil* and *V for Vendetta; A Clockwork Orange* and *Children of Men;* Edward Snowden and Steve Jobs; Lenin, Stalin and Hitler. Throughout, connections to the current political situation are sometimes stated and sometimes implied. I'd rather not repeatedly dig the reader in the ribs but do keep our present rulers in mind.

A few words about terminology. *Orwellian* has two opposing definitions: either work that reflects Orwell's style and values, or real-world developments that threaten them. To avoid confusion, I will use only the latter meaning and substitute *Orwell-like* for the former. I will also use the novel's British title, *Nineteen Eighty-Four,* rather than *1984,* except when quoting others. It carries more weight, I think.

"Orwell was successful because he wrote exactly the right books at exactly the right time," wrote the philosopher Richard Rorty. Prior to *Animal Farm* and *Nineteen Eighty-Four,* Orwell was a man to watch in British political and literary circles but he was far from a household name. Now all of his books, even those that he dismissed as failed experiments or hack work, are never out of print, and it is possible to read every surviving word he wrote, thanks to the Herculean scholarship of Professor Peter Davison, whose twenty-volume *The Complete Works of George Orwell* runs to almost nine thousand pages and two million words. Readers of the first edition of *Nineteen Eighty-Four* in 1949 knew only a fraction of what is now available.

Knowing how carefully Orwell chose what to share with the public, I haven't been able to read it all without the occasional shiver of guilt. He would have been mortified to see most of his journalism republished, let alone his private letters, yet almost none of it is worthless. Even when he was sick, or overworked, or desperate to be writing something else, his brain was actively engaged with big problems and small consolations, many of which fed into *Nineteen Eighty-Four.* Because he refused to outsource his judgement to an ideology or party line, even when he was wrong, which was quite often, he was wrong in a sincere and interesting way. He possessed what he praised Charles Dickens for having: a "free intelligence." He was by no means a unique genius (I also want to shine a light on some

of his less celebrated contemporaries) but he was the only writer of
his era to do so many things so well.

Orwell's schoolfriend Cyril Connolly remembered that "something shone through about him which made you want him to like
you a little bit better." That same quality shines through his writing
and makes his admirers crave his imagined approval. But I have no
desire to sanctify a man who was sceptical of saints, utopias and
perfection in general. Only by being frank about his errors and
shortcomings—as he usually was—can I explain both the man
and the book. Although his prose created the illusion that he was a
decent, commonsensical chap telling you an obvious truth that you
knew in your gut but just hadn't acknowledged yet, Orwell could
be rash, hyperbolic, irritable, blinkered and perverse. We value him
despite his flaws because he was right about the defining questions
of fascism, communism, imperialism and racism at a time when so
many people who should have known better didn't.

Orwell felt that he lived in cursed times. He fantasised about
another life in which he could have spent his days gardening and
writing fiction instead of being "forced into becoming a pamphleteer,"
but that would have been a waste. His real talent was for analys-
ing and explaining a tumultuous period in human history. Written
down, his core values might seem too vague to mean much—honesty,
decency, liberty, justice—but nobody wrestled more tirelessly, in
private and in public, with what those ideas meant during the darkest
days of the twentieth century. He always tried to tell the truth, and
admired anyone who did likewise. Nothing built on a lie, however
seductively convenient, could have value. Central to his honesty was
his commitment to constantly working out what he thought and why
he thought it, and never ceasing to reassess those opinions. To quote
Christopher Hitchens, one of Orwell's most eloquent disciples: "It
matters not what you think, but *how* you think."

I want to give the reader an accurate picture of where Orwell
stood on the vital issues of his time, and when and why some of
those positions changed, without claiming to know what he would
have thought about, say, Brexit. Such claims can only be achieved
by selective quotation which often verges on fraud. I remember in
1993 hearing Conservative prime minister John Major quote Orwell's
line about "old maids bicycling to Holy Communion through the

morning mist," as if it had not come from *The Lion and the Unicorn*, a passionate argument for socialism. When the hosts of InfoWars, the website notorious for disseminating outrageous conspiracy theories, routinely cite Orwell, you know that doublethink is real.

A novel that has been claimed by socialists, conservatives, anarchists, liberals, Catholics, and libertarians of every description cannot be, as Milan Kundera alleged, merely "political thought disguised as a novel." It is certainly not a precise allegory like *Animal Farm*, where every element slots into the real world with a neat click. Orwell's famously translucent prose conceals a world of complexity. *Nineteen Eighty-Four* is usually described as a dystopia. It is also, to varying and debatable degrees, a satire, a prophecy, a warning, a political thesis, a work of science fiction, a spy thriller, a psychological horror, a gothic nightmare, a postmodern text, and a love story. Most people read *Nineteen Eighty-Four* when they are young and feel bruised by it—it offers more suffering and less reassurance than any other standard high-school text—but don't feel compelled to rediscover it in adulthood. That's a shame. It is far richer and stranger than you probably remember, and I urge you to read it again. In the meantime, I've briefly summarised the plot, characters and terminology in the appendix to this book.

I first encountered *Nineteen Eighty-Four* as a teenager in suburban south London. As Orwell said, the books you read when you're young stay with you forever. I found it shocking and compelling, but this was circa 1990, when communism and apartheid were on the way out, optimism reigned, and the world didn't feel particularly Orwellian. Even after 9/11, the book's relevance was fragmentary: it was quoted in reference to political language, or the media, or surveillance, but not the whole picture. Democracy was on the rise and the internet was largely considered a force for good.

While I was planning and writing *The Ministry of Truth*, however, the world changed. People took to talking anxiously about the political upheavals of the 1970s and, worse, the 1930s. Bookshop shelves began filling up with titles such as *How Democracy Ends*, *Fascism: A Warning*, *The Road to Unfreedom* and *The Death of Truth*, many of which quoted Orwell. Hannah Arendt's *The Origins of Totalitarianism* merited a new edition, pitched as "a nonfiction bookend to *Nineteen Eighty-Four*"; so did Sinclair Lewis's 1935 novel about American fascism, *It Can't Happen Here*. Hulu's television adaptation of Margaret Atwood's 1985 novel *The Handmaid's Tale* was as alarming as a documentary. "I was asleep before," said Elisabeth Moss's character Offred. "That's how we let it happen." Well, we weren't asleep anymore. I was reminded of something Orwell wrote about fascism in 1936: "If you pretend that it is merely an aberration which will presently pass off of its own accord, you are dreaming a dream from which you will awake when somebody coshes you with a rubber truncheon." *Nineteen Eighty-Four* is a book designed to wake you up.

Nineteen Eighty-Four was the first fully realised dystopian novel to be written in the knowledge that dystopia was real. In Germany and the Soviet bloc, men had built it and forced other men and women to live and die within its iron walls. Those regimes may be gone, but Orwell's book continues to define our nightmares, even as they shift and change. "For me it's like a Greek myth, to take and do with what you will—to examine yourself," Michael Radford, the director of the 1984 movie adaptation, told me. "It's a mirror," says a character in the 2013 stage version by Robert Icke and Duncan Macmillan. "Every age sees itself reflected." For singer-songwriter Billy Bragg, "Every time I read it, it seems to be about something else."

Still, the fact that the novel speaks to us so loudly and clearly in 2019 is a terrible indictment of politicians and citizens alike. While it's still a warning, it has also become a reminder of all the painful lessons that the world appears to have unlearned since Orwell's lifetime, especially those concerning the fragility of truth in the face of power. I hesitate to say that *Nineteen Eighty-Four* is more relevant than ever, but it's a damn sight more relevant than it should be.

To paraphrase Orwell's disclaimer in *Homage to Catalonia*, his book about the Spanish Civil War: I warn you of my biases but I have tried to tell the truth.

PART ONE

CHAPTER 1

History Stopped

Orwell 1936–1938

We are living in a world in which nobody is free, in which hardly anybody is secure, in which it is almost impossible to be honest and to remain alive.

—George Orwell, *The Road to Wigan Pier,* 1937

Shortly before Christmas 1936, George Orwell stomped into the office of *The New English Weekly* in London, dressed for an expedition, bearing a heavy suitcase, and declared, "I'm going to Spain."

"Why?" asked Philip Mairet, the magazine's urbane French editor.

"This fascism," said Orwell. "Somebody's got to stop it."

Who was this thirty-three-year-old man in Mairet's office? What kind of impression did he make? He was around six foot three, with size-twelve feet, large, expressive hands, and gangling limbs that he seemed unsure where to place. He had a pale, gaunt, prematurely worn-out face with deep grooves around the mouth, creating an impression of noble suffering that reminded friends of Don Quixote or an El Greco saint. His pale blue eyes conveyed a mournful, compassionate intelligence. His mouth was prone to twists of ironic amusement and, if you were lucky, a rusty growl of laughter. His hair sprouted vertically like the bristles of a brush. He dressed shabbily, his clothes not so much fitting his body as hanging off it, a thin moustache his only concession to neatness. He smelled of burnt tobacco and, some said, an indefinable tang of sickness. He spoke in a dry, rasping monotone whose aspiration to classlessness was thwarted by a stubborn residue of Eton. On first encounter, he could seem standoffish and detached: a dry old stick. Those who got to know him soon unearthed his generosity and good humour but still bumped up against his emotional reserve. He was a firm believer in hard work and modest pleasures. Newly wed, to a bright, bold Oxford graduate named Eileen O'Shaughnessy. Politically engaged but not ideological. Well-travelled and multilingual. Going places.

Just as important are the things he wasn't. He was not yet a major figure, a committed socialist, an expert on totalitarianism, nor a writer whose prose was a windowpane. He was barely George Orwell. Spain was to become the great rupture in his life: his zero hour. Years later, he would tell his friend Arthur Koestler, "History stopped in 1936." Meaning totalitarianism. Meaning Spain. History stopped, and *Nineteen Eighty-Four* began.

"Until I was about thirty," Orwell wrote in middle age, "I always planned my life on the assumption not only that any major undertaking was bound to fail, but that I could only expect to live a few years longer."

He was born Eric Arthur Blair in India on June 25, 1903. His mother, Ida, who brought him to England the following year, was a sharply intelligent woman, half-French, who mixed with suffragettes and Fabians. His father, Richard Blair, was a mid-ranking civil servant for the British imperial government's Opium Department who didn't re-enter his son's life until 1912, at which point he appeared "simply as a gruff-voiced elderly man forever saying 'Don't.'" In *Nineteen Eighty-Four*, Winston Smith is haunted by his childhood betrayal of his mother and sister, but he can barely remember his father.

Orwell was thus born into what he called the "lower-upper-middle-class," a troubled stratum of the English class system that had the pretensions and manners of the wealthy but not the capital, and therefore spent most of the money it did have on "keeping up appearances." He later regarded his younger self, with embarrassment, shame and no small amount of contempt, as the kind of "odious little snob" that his class and education were designed to breed. "Your snobbishness, unless you root it out like the bindweed it is, sticks by you till your grave." Between the ages of eight and thirteen, he was a pupil at St. Cyprian's, a small private school in Sussex that he loathed with alarming passion for the rest of his life. "Failure, failure, failure—failure behind me, failure ahead of me—that was by far the deepest conviction that I carried away."

In the short autobiography that Orwell contributed to *Twentieth Century Authors* in 1940, he wrote, "I was educated at Eton, 1917–1921, as I had been lucky enough to win a scholarship, but I did no work there and learned very little, and I don't feel that Eton has been much of a formative influence in my life." While he probably exaggerated the contempt the fee-payers felt for the scholarship boys, it's true that he was a mediocre student with a profound sense of unbelonging. Although he was known as a "Bolshie," his alleged socialism was more of a fashionable pose than a deep conviction. One fellow pupil remembered him as "a boy with a permanent chip on the shoulder, always liking to find everything around him wrong, and giving the impression that he was there to put it right." Another said, "he was more sardonic than rebellious, and standing aside from things a bit, observing—always observing."

After Eton, Orwell rejected the chance to attend university and joined the Indian Imperial Police in Burma, where his mother had grown up: a surprising decision which he never tried to explain to his readers or friends. Orwell shelved his writing ambitions, but his five years in Burma did furnish him with the material for one decent novel (*Burmese Days*) and two very good essays ("A Hanging" and "Shooting an Elephant") and a lifelong belief in the value of lived experience. Orwell disliked intellectuals, a word he tended to suspend in scare quotes, who relied on theory and speculation; he never truly believed something until he had, in some way, lived it. "In order to hate imperialism you have got to be part of it" is a fallacious generalisation, but it was true for him. In Orwell's writing, *you* often meant *I*.

Burma functioned as aversion therapy. Through seeing how members of the ruling class were corrupted and confined by their abuse of power and the hypocrisy that cloaked it, Orwell developed a disgust for oppression of every stripe and briefly became a kind of anarchist before deciding that this was "sentimental nonsense." He returned to England in 1927 (on leave, but he never went back) with "an immense weight of guilt that I had got to expiate." This manifested as a masochistic desire to thrust himself into uncomfortable and even life-threatening situations. "How can you write about the poor unless you become poor yourself, even if it's temporary?" he asked a friend. A librarian who met him during this period astutely noticed that he was a man "in the process of rearranging himself."

With, by his own admission, "no interest in Socialism or any other economic theory," he sought to submerge himself in the netherworld of the oppressed—those who, by having no jobs, property or status whatsoever, had transcended, or rather sunk below, the class system—by becoming a tramp in England and a dishwasher in Paris in the late 1920s. "It is a sort of world-within-a-world where everyone is equal, a small squalid democracy—perhaps the nearest thing to democracy that exists in England," he wrote. Richard Rees, editor of *The Adelphi,* thought that Orwell chose this path "as a kind of penance or ablution to wash himself clean of the taint of imperialism." This *nostalgie de la boue,* which foreshadowed Winston Smith's expeditions into the prole district in *Nineteen Eighty-Four,* led him to write his first book, the memoir *Down and Out in Paris and London.*

Published in 1933, the book marked the birth of "George Orwell." One reason he gave for using a pseudonym was a desire to spare his family any embarrassment if the book's contents shocked them, or if his career as a writer fizzled out, but then he always disliked the name Eric and was hungry for reinvention. Taken from the River Orwell in Suffolk, this quintessentially English name squeezed out his alternative ideas, Kenneth Miles, P. S. Burton and H. Lewis Allways. And a good job, too: *Allwaysian* would not have been a graceful adjective.

By 1936, Orwell was the author of three novels, one non-fiction book, a few weak poems, and a trickle-to-a-stream of journalism, all of which did not yet add up to a viable career. He could only keep his head above water by taking on work as a teacher and a bookseller. That year, he painted a grimly exaggerated self-portrait in his third novel, *Keep the Aspidistra Flying.* Gordon Comstock is a hard-up fugitive from the "shabby-genteel" middle classes who nurses unfulfilled literary ambitions and works in a bookshop to make ends meet. He is "not thirty yet, but moth-eaten already. Very pale, with bitter, ineradicable lines." His self-pity, pessimism and misanthropy are so claustrophobic that his final surrender to the bourgeois conformity symbolised by the aspidistra house plant comes as a merciful release. Comstock is a gargoyle of Orwell: the man he might have become had he succumbed to bitterness and gloom.

In January 1936, Orwell accepted a commission from his publisher Victor Gollancz, a bullish, energetic Jewish socialist, to explore the plight of the industrial working class in the north of England. Published the following year, Part I of *The Road to Wigan Pier* is a sterling example of campaigning journalism, eliciting the reader's empathy by interleaving hard data with a vivid sense of the sights, sounds, tastes and smells of working-class life. The image of a woman kneeling to unclog a waste pipe struck Orwell as such an indelible tableau of drudgery that he restaged it years later in *Nineteen Eighty-Four.* He was captured by the look on her face: "She knew well enough what was happening to her." Orwell wrote frequently about the power of the face to reveal personality in a profound way, whether it was Dickens, Hitler, a Spanish militiaman or Big Brother. In Airstrip One, *Nineteen Eighty-Four*'s version of Britain, the danger of physically betraying one's true feelings is called "facecrime," and the torturer O'Brien's metaphor for tyranny is "a boot stamping on a human face—for ever."

Although he seriously downplays the pleasures of working-class life in order to emphasize the hardships, in Part I of *The Road to Wigan Pier* Orwell gives his subjects their due as human beings, not merely statistical units or emblems of the struggling masses. So when he told the working-class writer Jack Common, "I am afraid I have made rather a muck of parts of it," he presumably meant the more essayistic Part II, which he later said wasn't worth reprinting.

The opening stretch of Part II is a kind of memoir, tracing the evolution of his political consciousness with punishing honesty. By saying that he was trained from birth to "hate, fear and despise the working class," he implicitly makes the book a means of both education and penance. The rest, however, is a confused polemic. Orwell thought that if socialism was clearly necessary, then its unpopularity must be down to its image, which "drives away the very people who ought to be flocking to its support" by obscuring its fundamental ideals of justice, liberty and common decency. He identifies two major obstacles. One is socialism's cult of the machine, which creates an unappetising vision of "aeroplanes, tractors and huge glittering factories of glass and concrete." The other is middle-class crankishness. Barely noting the existence of working-class socialists or the trade union movement, Orwell launders his own eccentric prejudices through the imagined mindset of the common man, excoriating all the fetishes and foibles that allegedly make socialism unattractive to them (i.e., him), including vegetarians, teetotallers, nudists, Quakers, sandals, fruit juice, Marxist jargon, the word *comrade,* pistachio-coloured shirts, birth control, yoga, beards and Welwyn Garden City, the Hertfordshire town custom-built on utopian principles. Although Orwell claims in the book that he is only playing devil's advocate, it is hard to escape the feeling that he has more fun insulting a kooky minority of socialists than defending other forms of socialism. After such a performance, for him to conclude the book by calling for "left-wingers of all complexions to drop their differences and hang together" is a bit rich.

Orwell made life difficult for Victor Gollancz, who had recently founded the Left Book Club with the Labour MP John Strachey and the political scientist Harold Laski in order to promote socialism. Laski, Britain's most influential socialist intellectual, called Part I of *The Road to Wigan Pier* "admirable propaganda for our ideas" but Gollancz felt compelled to write a preface to the Left Book Club edition which distanced the club from the harsh judgements of Part II. In the preface, Gollancz put his finger on Orwell's torturously paradoxical nature: "The truth is that he is at one and the same time an extreme intellectual and a violent anti-intellectual. Similarly he is a frightful snob—still (he must forgive me for saying this), and a genuine hater of every form of snobbery." Until the end of his life, Orwell acknowledged that microbes of everything he criticised existed in himself. In fact, it was this awareness of his own flaws that inoculated him against utopian delusions of human perfectibility.

Gollancz also accused Orwell of never defining his preferred version of socialism, nor explaining how it might come about. According to Orwell's bookshop colleague and subsequent editor Jon Kimche, Orwell was a "gut socialist": "very decent but not attuned, I would say, to complicated political or military situations." Yet however patchy and perverse his critique of socialism may have been, Orwell's intentions were sincere. He believed that "nothing else can save us from the misery of the present or the nightmare of the future," and if it failed to persuade ordinary Britons, then their discontent would surely be exploited by someone like Hitler. Socialism in Britain, he wrote, "smells of crankishness, machine-worship and the stupid cult of Russia. Unless you can remove that smell, and very rapidly, Fascism may win."

Even as he wrote those words, Orwell was making plans to fight fascism more directly. *Adelphi* editor Richard Rees had known Orwell since 1930, but it was only when his friend went to Spain that Rees "began to realize he was extraordinary."

"The Spanish Civil War is one of the comparatively few cases when the most widely accepted version of events has been written more persuasively by the losers of the conflict than by the winners," wrote the historian Antony Beevor. What's more, the most widely read memoir of the conflict, Orwell's *Homage to Catalonia,* was written by a man who fought with the losers of the losers: the Partido Obrero de Unificación Marxista (Workers' Party of Marxist Unification), known as the POUM. That is a very particular point of view. The POUM were small in size and influence, militarily weak and politically unpopular. So when contemporaries and, later, historians claimed that Orwell's book gave a distorted picture of the war, they were not wrong, but it did tell the truth about Orwell's war.

In February 1936, while Orwell was in Wigan, voters in the turbulent, five-year-old Spanish Republic narrowly elected a Popular Front coalition of anarchists, socialists, communists and liberal republicans, thus horrifying the church and the army, the twin pillars of reactionary monarchist sentiment. On July 17, after five months of instability, General Francisco Franco mounted a coup in Spanish Morocco and the Canary Islands which initiated a brutal civil war that split the country in two and became a proxy for the decade-defining struggle between fascism and communism. Germany and Italy immediately furnished Franco's rebels with arms and personnel while Russia, thanks to Britain and France's misguided arms embargo, became the Republic's key ally, with dire consequences.

Orwell followed events in Spain very closely; the final pages of *The Road to Wigan Pier* include a reference to the battle for Madrid that November. He went to Spain with the expectation of fighting fascism and defending "common decency" but found himself plunged into a boiling alphabet soup of political acronyms which, for some people, would spell the difference between life and death. Explaining what Orwell called "a plague of initials" is a necessary evil, so I'll be brief. The PSUC (Unified Socialist Party of Catalonia) was the Catalan affiliate of the fast-growing Spanish communist party, by far the wealthiest and most well-armed faction thanks to Russian support. The anarchists were represented by the FAI (Iberian Anarchist Federation) and the CNT (National Confederation of Labour). The socialist UGT (General Union of Workers) had produced Spain's latest prime minister, Francisco Largo Caballero. Then there was the POUM, led by forty-four-year-old Andrés Nin: a renegade working-class Marxist party in the lonely and vulnerable position of opposing Stalin while falling out with Trotsky. These left-wing factions came to wage a civil war within the civil war. The communists, following Moscow's new Popular Front strategy of an anti-fascist alliance with capitalists, insisted that winning the war had to take priority over revolution. The anarchists and the POUM felt that victory without revolution was unacceptable, and even impossible. The two positions could not be reconciled.

Orwell's allegiance to the POUM feels, in retrospect, characteristically quixotic. In fact, he admitted later, "I was not only uninterested in the political situation but unaware of it." Had he known more, he told Jack Common, he would have joined the anarchists, or even the communist-backed International Brigades, but the decision was effectively made for him. Seeking a letter of recommendation to smooth his passage to Spain, he had first approached Harry Pollitt, the devoutly Stalinist general secretary of the Communist Party of Great Britain. Pollitt thought him politically unreliable (which of course he was, and proud of it) and turned him down. Orwell had better luck with Fenner Brockway of the Independent Labour Party (ILP), a small, maverick socialist party aligned with the POUM, and so the die was cast. Both the POUM and the ILP had proven their honesty and courage, in Orwell's eyes, by denouncing the ongoing show trials in Moscow.

Orwell's brew of idealism, ignorance and grit was not unusual among the foreigners who flocked to Spain in 1936. The great left-wing cause of the day attracted all sorts: adventurers and dreamers, poets and plumbers, doctrinaire Marxists and frustrated misfits. One volunteer called it "a world where lost and lonely people could feel important." Up to 35,000 men from fifty-three countries served in the International Brigades and another five thousand in militias affiliated with anarchists and the POUM. Over a thousand journalists and authors went, too, including Ernest Hemingway, Martha Gellhorn, Antoine de Saint-Exupéry and the poet Stephen Spender, who later wrote, "It was in part an anarchist's war, a poet's war." Few, if any, foreigners understood the complexity of the political situation before they arrived, but still, said the journalist Malcolm Muggeridge, "it seemed certain that in Spain Good and Evil were at last joined in bloody combat."

Orwell left London on December 22 and travelled to Spain via Paris. There he visited the American novelist Henry Miller, who considered risking one's life for a political cause an absurd folly and tried to talk him out of it. "Though he was a wonderful chap in his way, Orwell, in the end I thought him stupid," Miller said decades later. "He was like so many English people, an idealist, and, it seemed to me, a foolish idealist." Orwell crossed the border into Spain and reached Barcelona on Boxing Day.

Catalonia was a proudly quasi-independent region with a long history of anarchism. Franco's July coup had sparked an anti-clerical revolution there, with many churches burned and clergy executed. The bourgeoisie were largely spared, but banks, factories, hotels, restaurants, cinemas and taxis were appropriated by the working-class parties and blazoned with the initials of the CNT and FAI. Franz Borkenau, an Austrian writer Orwell came to know and admire, visited Spain in August and caught the tail end of the revolutionary fervour. "It was overwhelming," he wrote. "It was as if we had been landed on a continent different from anything I had seen before." Orwell's schoolfriend Cyril Connolly had witnessed it, too, and it had momentarily knocked the snobbery out of him. "It is as if the masses, the mob in fact credited usually only with instincts of stupidity and persecution, should blossom into what is really a kind of flowering of humanity."

It is unclear whether Orwell went to Spain to fight and ended up writing as well, or vice versa. John McNair, the ILP's man in Barcelona, remembered Orwell walking into his office and declaring, "I have come to Spain to join the militia to fight against Fascism," but in *Homage to Catalonia* Orwell suggests that the journalism came first. Either way, within only a few days he had decided to do both.

What he found was "a bad copy of 1914–18, a positional war of trenches, artillery, raids, snipers, mud, barbed wire, lice and stagnation." He spent most of the next four months with the POUM's 29th Division in the trenches of the Aragón front, which divided the Republican-held town of Alcubierre from the fascist strongholds of Saragossa and Huesca. Orwell's major concerns were, in descending order, "firewood, food, tobacco, candles and"—a distant last—"the enemy." Starved of Russian arms and equipment, the POUM militias were incapable of mounting an assault on the fascists. Among other things, they lacked uniforms, helmets, bayonets, binoculars, maps, torches and modern weaponry. Orwell's own rifle was a Mauser dating back to 1896. He was infuriated by a sense of paralysis and futility and damned the front with the same verdict he passed on the dreary inertia of the Comstock family in *Keep the Aspidistra Flying:* "Nothing ever happened." Georges Kopp, the maverick Belgian commander of Orwell's battalion, told his men, "This is not a war. It is a comic opera with an occasional death." Yet Orwell found in the trenches a superior version of the cleansing egalitarianism that he had found among the tramps, and it made him a socialist at last. He "breathed the air of equality." It was this localised experience that enabled him to say later, despite everything, that he had left Spain with "not less but more belief in the decency of human beings."

Another, less spiritual consolation was the supply of chocolate, cigars and Fortnum & Mason tea that Orwell began receiving from his wife Eileen after she followed him to Spain in February to work as McNair's secretary in Barcelona. The couple had married eight months earlier, having met at a party in 1935, and in many respects they were an excellent match. Both were emotionally reticent, with a tendency towards gloom enlivened by an ironic sense of humour and a spirit of generosity. They shared a passion for nature and literature, frugal tastes, and a carelessness about their health and appearance, rarely seen without a cigarette dangling from their lips. Both had strong principles and the courage to act on them. The difference was ambition. Eileen was a highly intelligent Oxford graduate, universally well-liked, but she subordinated her own aspirations to Orwell's, dropping out of a master's degree programme in educational psychology to live with him in a cottage-cum-shop in the Hertfordshire village of Wallington. One friend said, "She caught George's dreams from him like measles."

Orwell finally saw action in April, when the militia advanced towards the fascist trenches. He displayed genuine mettle by braving enemy fire while shouting, "Come on, you bastards!," to which one fellow volunteer responded, "For Christ's sake, Eric, get down!" During the long weeks of stalemate, however, his eccentric side emerged. This is a man who refused to shoot a retreating fascist because the man was struggling to hold up his trousers after a toilet visit and was therefore "visibly a fellow creature, similar to yourself, and you don't feel like shooting at him," yet was so alarmed by a rat that he blasted it with his rifle, thus alerting the enemy and triggering a fierce firefight which ended up destroying the militia's cookhouse and two of their buses. "If there is one thing I hate more than another it is a rat running over me in the darkness," he wrote, a dozen years before the rodents broke Winston Smith's spirit. Rats are mentioned in all but one of Orwell's nine books.

For all the camaraderie, Orwell had not yet come to love the POUM. This was partly due to his contrarianism: "The political side of the war bored me and I naturally reacted against the viewpoint of which I heard most." But he also thought the communists were making more of a difference. His romantic affection for the underdog was overtaken by his pragmatic desire to get things done. Even years later, he believed that the POUM's insistence that a successful revolution would have led to victory was misguided.

Due a few days' leave with Eileen in Barcelona in late April, Orwell therefore planned to quit the militia and join the International Brigades in Madrid, where the action was. His fellow militiamen told him he was a fool and that the communists would kill him, but Orwell was adamant. Only later did he realise how fortunate he was to be allowed to challenge the party line without being denounced or threatened. He had no idea how dangerous Barcelona had become for people like him. He was about to find out.

—

Shortly before Orwell returned to Barcelona, Richard Rees passed through town on his way to Madrid to serve as an ambulance driver for the Republican army. When Rees met Eileen at the POUM office, he initially interpreted her dazed, distracted manner as concern for her husband, until he realised what was really unsettling her: "She was the first person in whom I had witnessed the effects of living under a political terror."

Franz Borkenau had revisited Barcelona in January and found a city already very different from the one he had left in September. Whereas previously he had been able to travel Republican Spain unmolested, now all doubts and criticisms were taboo. "It is an atmosphere of suspicion and denunciation," he wrote, "whose unpleasantness it is difficult to convey to those who have not lived through it." The POUM, "liked by nobody," had been designated "Trotskyists," a label that Stalin's show trials had transformed into a death sentence. The fact that Trotsky had disowned them, Borkenau noted, was irrelevant: "A Trotskyist, in communist vocabulary, is synonymous with a man who deserves to be killed." In February, Yan Berzin, Russia's chief military adviser to the Republic, sent a report to Moscow about the POUM. "It goes without saying," he wrote, "that it is impossible to win the war against the rebels if these scum within the republican camp are not liquidated."

Orwell sensed immediately "an unmistakable and horrible feeling of political rivalry and hatred" in the city. The revolutionary solidarity had evaporated, with food queues for some and black market–fuelled nightclubs and restaurants for others. Everyone he spoke to thought that violence was inevitable. In the lobby of the Hotel Continental one morning, Orwell introduced himself to the celebrated American novelist John Dos Passos, who had come to Spain to make a propaganda documentary with Ernest Hemingway and was now searching for news of his missing translator José Robles. Dos Passos noticed that Barcelona had "a furtive, gutted look, stores shuttered, people glancing over their shoulders as they walked." Drinking vermouth in wicker chairs, the two men compared notes on the importation of Stalinism to Spain. Dos Passos was relieved, at last, "to be talking to an honest man." They were not easy to find.

"The match that fired an already existing bomb," in Orwell's words, was lit on May 3, when the city's Assault Guards, under communist orders, stormed the anarchist-controlled Telephone Exchange and set off five days and nights of street fighting that came to be known as the May Days. Orwell spent three of them stationed in the rooftop observatory of the Poliorama cinema with a rifle to help defend the POUM headquarters across the road. From his eyrie, he could see that the communists controlled the streets to the east of the Ramblas and the anarchists the west. Rival flags fluttered from the hotels, cafés and offices that had been transfigured, overnight, into armed strongholds.

Only the Hotel Continental at the head of the Ramblas was considered neutral ground, so it became a surreal community of fighters, reporters, foreign agents and some stranded French lorry drivers, all seeking food and shelter. It was there that Orwell spotted the fat Russian known only as "Charlie Chan." This alleged agent for the NKVD, Stalin's secret police, told anyone who would listen that the violence was an anarchist putsch designed to undermine the Republic and aid Franco. "It was the first time I had seen a person whose profession was telling lies," Orwell wrote, "unless one counts journalists."*

After the violence subsided, leaving hundreds dead, those lies were plastered to the walls in the form of posters reading "Tear the mask." They depicted a mask, bearing the hammer-and-sickle, being wrenched away to reveal a snarling, swastika-tattooed maniac: allegedly the true face of the POUM. In *Burmese Days* the innocent Dr. Veraswami is turned into a Trotsky (or an early version of *Nineteen Eighty-Four*'s arch-heretic Emmanuel Goldstein) by the corrupt magistrate U Po Kyin: "To hear what was said about him, anyone would have imagined the doctor a compound of Machiavelli, Sweeney Todd and the Marquis de Sade." This was now the fate of the "Trotskyist-fascists" of the POUM. Their Radio Verdad used the pointed slogan "The only broadcasting service that uses reality in preference to make-believe." But make-believe was winning.

---

* Over the last century, the Russian secret police has had many names, including the Cheka, OGPU, the NKVD, the KGB and the FSB. The mentality of the organisation has remained remarkably consistent.

Orwell was not surprised that the tension between the factions had boiled over into armed combat. What he did not foresee, and could not forgive, was the subsequent deceit. The communists claimed to have exposed a vast network of traitors communicating with the fascists via secret radio stations and invisible ink, and plotting to assassinate Republican leaders—lies so outrageous that people assumed they had to be true because nobody would dare fabricate them. Franco, who benefitted from the idea that the Republic was riddled with his spies, endorsed the claim. A Special Tribunal for Espionage and High Treason was established. Newspapers were censored. Thousands of anarchists and union members were arrested. The streets writhed with fear and distrust.

To Orwell's dismay, foreign communist newspapers such as Britain's *Daily Worker* were in accord with Charlie Chan. "One of the dreariest effects of this war has been to teach me that the Left-wing press is every bit as spurious and dishonest as that of the Right," he wrote, making an honourable exception for *The Manchester Guardian*. It would take a book to set the record straight, and he wrote to Gollancz to tell him so: "I hope I shall get the chance to write the truth about what I have seen. The stuff appearing in the English papers is largely the most appalling lies." It was even worse in Franco territory, where the press claimed that Republican militias were raping nuns, feeding prisoners to zoo animals, and letting stacks of corpses rot in gutters. One American journalist observed that the scale of deceit in Salamanca, the nationalist capital, was "almost a mental disease." For Stephen Spender, whose idealism evaporated so fast that he left the Communist Party after a matter of weeks, the war triggered a fundamental revelation about human nature: "This was simply that nearly all human beings have an extremely intermittent grasp on reality. Only a few things, which illustrate their own interests and ideas, are real to them; other things, which are in fact equally real, appear to them as abstractions." He did not exempt himself. "I gradually acquired a certain horror of the way in which my own mind worked."

After the shock of the May Days there was no way that Orwell could abandon the POUM, so he went straight back to the Aragón front. He didn't last long. Orwell was so much taller than the average Spaniard that his head protruded over the trench's parapet. Every morning he liked to stand up to enjoy his first cigarette of the day.

When an American militiaman, Harry Milton, asked him one day if he was worried about snipers, Orwell shrugged it off: "They couldn't hit a bull in a passage." At dawn on May 20, one marksman proved him wrong, with a well-aimed bullet that hit him in the throat beneath his larynx. Orwell assumed he was dying. Another millimetre and he would have been, but the bullet missed the carotid artery and only temporarily paralysed the nerve controlling one of his vocal cords.* Lying in the trench, blood pouring from his throat, Orwell's first thought was for Eileen; his second "a violent resentment at having to leave this world which, when all is said and done, suits me so well . . . The stupid mischance infuriated me. The meaninglessness of it!"

Orwell was hospitalised for the next three weeks. Clearly, his war was over, but he needed to get his discharge papers signed by a doctor on the front line. By the time he returned to Barcelona on June 20, the hammer had come down. As soon as he walked into the Hotel Continental, Eileen took him by the arm and whispered, "Get out."

The May Days crisis had led to the removal of Prime Minister Largo Caballero, and thus the last roadblock to a complete crackdown on the POUM. The party was now illegal, as any militiaman coming back from the front soon discovered. Orwell's battalion commander Georges Kopp was arrested. Young ILP member Bob Smillie ("the best of the bunch," said Orwell) died in jail in the Republican capital Valencia. James McNair and Stafford Cottman of the ILP were in hiding. Andrés Nin was missing, and his fate would soon become another lie. He was brutally tortured by Russian NKVD agents ("his face was no more than a formless mass," a report found), then killed, but some German members of the International Brigades dressed up as Gestapo agents and staged a "rescue," so that the communists could claim that Nin was still alive and residing with his true masters in Salamanca or Berlin, much as Snowball in *Animal Farm* is rumoured to be with Mr. Frederick of Pinchfield Farm.

Barcelona during the crackdown was Orwell's first and only taste of

---

* It may even have saved his life by removing him from the front before the Republican assault on Huesca a few weeks later, a bloody fiasco that wiped out around nine thousand anarchists and POUM members.

the "nightmare atmosphere" that would envelop *Nineteen Eighty-Four*. In that poisonous broth of rumours, smears and paranoia, "however little you were actually conspiring, the atmosphere forced you to feel like a conspirator." Even when nothing bad was happening, the threat of *something* happening tore at the nerves. Orwell and Eileen's hotel room was raided and a warrant was issued for their arrest. Reports by NKVD agents and their Spanish counterparts, discovered in the 1980s, falsely described the couple as "pronounced Trotskyists," conspiring with dissidents in Moscow.

After three fearful days and nights, which Orwell spent wandering the streets as unobtrusively as possible and sleeping rough, he, Eileen, McNair and Cottman managed to obtain their travel documents from the British consulate and catch the morning train to France and freedom. "It was a queer business," Orwell wrote to his friend Rayner Heppenstall. "We started off being heroic defenders of democracy and ended by slipping over the border with the police panting on our heels. Eileen was wonderful, in fact actually seemed to enjoy it." Fenner Brockway, travelling the other way to try to secure the release of imprisoned ILP members, met Orwell at Perpignan, just over the French border. "It was about the only time I saw him really angry," Brockway recalled.

Orwell had been driven to Spain by his hatred of fascism, but he left six months later with a second enemy. The fascists had behaved just as appallingly as he had expected they would, but the ruthlessness and dishonesty of the communists had shocked him. According to Jack Branthwaite, an ILP comrade, "He said he used to take what people said about the communists as capitalist propaganda, but he said, 'You know, Jack, it's true.'"

"Almost every journalist assigned to Spain," wrote the American reporter Frank Hanighen, "became a different man sometime or other after he crossed the Pyrenees." Orwell certainly did. At various points, he found his time in Spain thrilling, boring, inspiring, terrifying, and, ultimately, clarifying. "The Spanish War and other events in 1936–7 turned the scale and thereafter I knew where I stood," he wrote a decade later, just prior to starting work on *Nineteen*

Eighty-Four. "Every line of serious work that I have written since 1936 has been written, directly or indirectly, *against* totalitarianism and *for* democratic Socialism, as I understand it."

Orwell's final act of naivety was to believe that his old colleagues would publish his conclusions. Instead, Gollancz turned down his book and Kingsley Martin, editor of *The New Statesman & Society,* rejected not just his essay about the war but a review of Borkenau's *The Spanish Cockpit* in which he attempted to smuggle the gist of that essay. When Orwell did finally get the chance to tell his story, in Philip Mairet's *New English Weekly,* it was under the pointed title "Spilling the Spanish Beans." "There has been a quite deliberate conspiracy . . . to prevent the Spanish situation from being understood," he wrote. "People who ought to know better have lent themselves to the deception on the ground that if you tell the truth about Spain it will be used as Fascist propaganda."

It was not so much the crime that enraged him—war breeds lies as surely as it produces lice and corpses—as the cover-up. In Orwell's vocabulary, *swindle, racket* and *humbug* were the dirtiest words. The *realpolitik* of Gollancz and Martin struck him as a dire precedent. Suppressing the truth for short-term gain is like declaring a state of emergency: a temporary suspension of freedom too easily becomes permanent. Reporting the messy reality of the war within a war was a test, and Britain's pro-communist left failed it by loyally recycling totalitarian propaganda. He had expected better.

For Orwell, the truth mattered even, or perhaps *especially,* when it was inconvenient. In his earlier non-fiction, he had finessed anecdotes and omitted awkward facts for literary purposes, but *Homage to Catalonia* was written with a new commitment to accuracy as a moral virtue. Without a consensus reality, he argued, "there can be no argument; the necessary minimum of agreement cannot be reached." Orwell was clear-eyed enough to know that one can't always get to the objective truth but that if one doesn't at least accept that such a thing exists, then all bets are off. "I found myself feeling very strongly that a true history of this war never would or could be written," he wrote years later. "Accurate figures, objective accounts of what was happening, simply did not exist." This is what he meant by "History stopped," a phrase that recurs in *Nineteen Eighty-Four.* When the only arbiter of reality was power, the victor could ensure that the lie became, to all intents and purposes, the truth.

Well, up to a point. The deceit of the Ingsoc regime in *Nineteen Eighty-Four* appears impregnable. In reality, however, lies tend to backfire sooner or later. Borkenau noticed that communists in Spain who began lying to fool others often ended up deceiving themselves. Paranoia bred blame-shifting, purges and plunging morale, while the exaggerations of communist propaganda led to military errors. In Russia, the liars soon became the lied about. Most of the leading Russian officials in Spain were executed or sent to the gulag. Berzin, the military adviser who had recommended "liquidating" the POUM, was accused of espionage and shot in Moscow's Lubyanka prison.

Thanks to Fenner Brockway, Orwell eventually found a publisher for *Homage to Catalonia* in Secker & Warburg, a fledgling company with an anti-Stalinist reputation and an open mind. "It was my purpose to find and support those writers who wished to put forward a programme for Utopia and outline the road to it," co-director Fredric Warburg wrote in his memoir. "But which programme and what road were the ones that led to the promised land, I was far from certain, and this should be counted in my favour."

Homage to Catalonia is Orwell's finest non-fiction book. Published on April 25, 1938, only a year after *The Road to Wigan Pier*, it is wiser, calmer, more humble and more generous. "It shows us the heart of innocence that lies in revolution; also the miasma of lying that, far more than the cruelty, takes the heart out of it," wrote Philip Mairet. Posterity has transformed it into an essential document of the Spanish Civil War, but at the time it was one of a glut of accounts, and sold around half of its print run of fifteen hundred. British communist critics dismissed the book as at best confused, at worst a treacherous gift to Franco. Orwell was phlegmatic about bad reviews, filing even the stinkers under good publicity, and he didn't deny that his book was a partial account. "I warn everyone against my bias, and I warn everyone against my mistakes," he wrote. "Still," he added, "I have done my best to be honest." Because he felt that the distinction between truth and lies was real and worth preserving, he wrote letters of complaint about reviews which smeared his old comrades. If he exaggerated his pro-POUM sympathies in the book, then it was only because nobody else would stand up for the falsely accused. "If

I had not been angry about that," he later wrote, "I should never have written the book."

One compliment that meant a great deal was a letter from Borkenau, who was now living in England: "To me your book is a further confirmation of my conviction that it is possible to be perfectly honest with one's facts quite irrespective of one's political convictions." The respect was mutual. Orwell praised *The Spanish Cockpit* with a typically technophobic metaphor ("It is a most encouraging thing to hear a human voice when fifty thousand gramophones are playing the same tune") and later called Borkenau's *The Communist International* "a book that has taught me more than any other about the general course of the Revolution." Borkenau had resigned from the German Communist Party in 1929 in opposition to Stalin, funnelled aid to an anti-Nazi party, and developed an early theory of totalitarianism. "Civilisation is bound to perish," Borkenau wrote, "not simply by the existence of certain restrictions on the expression of freedom of thought . . . but by the wholesale submission of thinking to orders from a party centre."

Only one person has suggested that Orwell ever approved of communism. While Orwell was slumming in Paris in the late 1920s, he sometimes enjoyed the hospitality of his aunt, Nellie Limouzin, and her partner, Eugene Adam. Adam and his friend Louis Bannier were ex-communists and champions of Esperanto, the idealistic international language that managed to draw the ire of both Hitler and Stalin. Bannier later claimed to remember a fierce argument between Adam and the young Orwell, who "continued to proclaim that the Soviet system was the definitive socialism." It's a curious anecdote, at odds with everything Orwell wrote, but true or not, his uncle was probably his introduction to the fervour of the former communist.

Many of Orwell's favourite writers in the years after Spain were ex-communists: Borkenau and Koestler from Austria; Ignazio Silone from Italy; Victor Serge from Russia; Max Eastman and Eugene Lyons from the US; André Gide, Boris Souvarine and André Malraux from France. They had learned about communism in the same way that he had come to understand imperialism: from inside the belly of the beast. Testimonials such as Gide's *Retour de l'U.R.S.S.* and

Souvarine's *Cauchemar en U.R.S.S.* supplied Orwell's first insight into the operation of Stalin's regime. Many of the details and anecdotes he discovered there fed into *Nineteen Eighty-Four:* the cult of personality; the rewriting of history; the obliteration of freedom of speech; the contempt for objective truth; the echoes of the Spanish Inquisition; the arbitrary arrests, denunciations and forced confessions; above all, the suffocating climate of suspicion, self-censorship and fear.

To take just one example, in Orwell's novel Winston Smith discovers a photograph which proves that the alleged traitors Jones, Aaronson and Rutherford were actually in New York on the date that they had confessed to being in Eurasia. Orwell had read about such cases, in which scripted confessions were contradicted by hard evidence. One alleged conspirator was photographed at a conference in Brussels on the very same day he had "confessed" to plotting in Moscow. Another was alleged to have met Trotsky in a Copenhagen hotel that, it transpired, had been torn down fifteen years earlier.

Orwell didn't just respect these writers for the information they provided. Their attacks on Stalin were nourished by personal shame and a visceral need to exorcise their credulity and complicity through what Orwell called a "literature of disillusionment." Former communists in that terrifying, exhilarating first flush of heresy wrote with compelling urgency. Orwell also found their loneliness heroic. Many were ostracised by old friends and snubbed by publishers. Silone, he wrote approvingly, "is one of those men who are denounced as Communists by Fascists and as Fascists by Communists, a band of men which is still small but steadily growing."

Why did Orwell criticise communism so much more energetically than fascism? Because he had seen it up close, and because its appeal was more treacherous. Both ideologies reached the same totalitarian destination but communism began with nobler aims and therefore required more lies to sustain it. It became "a form of Socialism that makes mental honesty impossible," and its literature "a mechanism for explaining away mistakes." He didn't personally know any fascists and had contempt for those in the public realm such as the poet Ezra Pound and Oswald Mosley, the leader of the British Union of Fascists whom he had seen speak in Barnsley in 1936: "his speech though delivered with an excellent platform technique was the most unutterable bollox."* But he knew plenty of communists. Among the literary intelligentsia, fascism was a mucky vice, while communism "had an almost irresistible fascination for any writer under forty." He was still angered by their hypocrisy years later, when he wrote in *Nineteen Eighty-Four* that the atrocities of the 1930s were "tolerated and even defended by people who considered themselves enlightened and progressive."

The ex-communists had broken out of the syllogism that bound so much of the left to Stalin: I believe in socialism; the USSR is the only socialist state; therefore I believe in the USSR. Orwell's rebuttal was twofold: firstly, no ends, however utopian, can be justified by such grotesque means; secondly, Stalin's Russia was not truly socialist because it denied liberty and justice. But then he had never invested himself, intellectually, emotionally and socially, in the Soviet experiment. Those who had were thrown into an existential crisis.

One of them was Eugene Lyons, a Russian Jewish immigrant who had grown up in the seething tenements of New York's Lower East Side and become a campaigning journalist for socialist newspapers. In 1922, he became a communist and disowned his more moderate friends. Between 1928 and 1934 he was the United Press's man in Moscow, explaining the USSR to American readers. At first a staunch defender of Stalin, and the first Western journalist to interview him, he became horrified by the propaganda, persecution and industrial-scale dishonesty in which he had participated. Orwell reviewed Lyons's epic *mea culpa* in June 1938, and it's safe to assume that his attention was grabbed by this account of Stalin's efforts to complete the first Five Year Plan in just four years:

> The formula $2 + 2 = 5$ instantly riveted my attention. It seemed to me at once bold and preposterous—the daring and the paradox and the tragic absurdity of the Soviet scene, its mystical simplicity, its defiance of logic, all reduced to nose-thumbing

* That didn't mean Orwell thought Mosley was harmless: "Mosley will bear watching, for experience shows (*vide* the careers of Hitler, Napoleon III) that to a political climber it is sometimes an advantage not to be taken too seriously at the beginning of his career."

arithmetic . . . 2 + 2 = 5: in electric lights on Moscow house-
fronts, in foot-high letters on billboards, spelled planned error,
hyperbole, perverse optimism; something childishly headstrong
and stirringly imaginative.

Within a few months, Orwell was using the unreal equation
himself. In a generally positive review of Bertrand Russell's *Power:
A New Social Analysis,* he challenged the assumption that common
sense would win out: "The peculiar horror of the present moment is
that we cannot be sure that this is so. It is quite possible that we are
descending into an age in which two and two will make five when the
Leader says so . . . One has only to think of the sinister possibilities
of the radio, State-controlled education and so forth, to realize that
'the truth is great and will prevail' is a prayer rather than an axiom."

Orwell must also have appreciated Lyons's description of the
personal cost of apostasy. When he returned to New York, Lyons
agonised over whether to be honest about what he'd seen. Telling the
truth was both a moral obligation and social suicide. Having made
his choice, Lyons quickly found himself excommunicated and vilified
by his old comrades. To the true believers, his exposure of Stalin's
crimes was an almost spiritual affront, and therefore unforgivable. "I
was guilty of the most heinous offence: puncturing noble delusions,"
he wrote. The gates of their mythical Russia had to be protected
at all costs from the barbaric reality. "So many weary or bored or
panicky Americans had made their spiritual homes in its wonder-
chambers that anyone who threatened to undermine its foundations
was treated as a shameless vandal. Perhaps he was."

The bitterly ironic title of Lyons's book was *Assignment in Utopia.*

CHAPTER 2

Utopia Fever

Orwell and the Optimists

What fun it must have been, in those hopeful days back
in the 'eighties, working away for the best of all possible
causes—and there were so many causes to choose from.
Who could have foreseen where it would all end?

—George Orwell, *The Adelphi*, May 1940

A map of the world that does not include Utopia is not worth
even glancing at," wrote Oscar Wilde in his 1891 essay "The
Soul of Man Under Socialism." "Progress is the realization
of Utopias." Orwell's response was effectively "Yes, but . . ." He liked
the idea of utopia as an inspiring antidote to pessimism and caution
but he found any attempt to describe it tedious, and any effort to build
it sinister. In the Christmas 1943 issue of *Tribune*, using the pseudonym John Freeman, Orwell wrote an essay called "Can Socialists Be
Happy?," which contrasted the palpable joy at the end of Dickens's
A Christmas Carol with the unconvincing "permanent happiness"
of utopias. The reason people argued and fought and died for socialism, he said, was for the idea of brotherhood, not "some central-
heated, air-conditioned, strip-lighted Paradise." Of course the world
could, and should, be improved, but never perfected. "Whoever tries
to imagine perfection simply reveals his own emptiness."

Historically, utopia preceded dystopia the same way that heaven
came before hell. Perhaps it's a credit to humanity that people were
designing the ideal society long before they imagined the opposite.
The earliest blueprint was Plato's *Republic*, a Socratic dialogue that
was an acknowledged precursor to Thomas More's 1516 book *Utopia*.

More's coinage derived from the Greek *ou* (not) and *topos* (place): utopia is a place that doesn't exist. But *ou* was easily confused with *eu* (good) and whether or not More's word was an intentional pun, utopia acquired a more specific meaning: an earthly paradise. In politics, the latter interpretation took over, but in literature the ambiguity remained, which is how Orwell could describe *Nineteen Eighty-Four* as "a Utopia." He made a distinction between "favourable" and "pessimistic" utopias because it would not have occurred to him to call the latter dystopias. Even though the word *dystopia* (literally "the not-good place") was used by John Stuart Mill in 1868, it lay dormant for close to a century, eclipsed by Jeremy Bentham's *cacotopia* ("the bad place") or by *anti-utopia*, until it was revived in 1962 by the poet and scholar Chad Walsh. Orwell's novel has become synonymous with a word he never used.

Orwell was well-versed in utopian literature. He wrote more than once about Samuel Butler's 1872 satire *Erewhon*, William Morris's 1890 socialist fantasy *News from Nowhere*, and the many contributions of H. G. Wells, but was rarely convinced that utopian ideas made for satisfying fiction. "Happiness is notoriously difficult to describe," he wrote in his essay on *Gulliver's Travels*, "and pictures of a just and well-ordered society are seldom either attractive or convincing." As early as *Down and Out in Paris and London*, he considered the promise of "some dismal Marxist Utopia" an obstacle to socialism. At root, he thought utopias sounded boring and joyless and didn't believe people really wanted them. "On the whole human beings want to be good," he wrote in his 1941 essay "The Art of Donald McGill," "but not too good, and not quite all the time."

Given Orwell's interests, the most puzzling lacuna in his writing is any reference to the book that turned the practice of designing ideal societies into a cultural phenomenon that swept the final years of the nineteenth century. In the entirety of his collected works, there is not a single reference to Edward Bellamy.

In August 1887, Edward Bellamy was a little-known author and journalist from Massachusetts. He was an earnest, sensitive thirty-seven-year-old with a doleful expression, a tremendous moustache and a burning sense of moral conviction. The suffragist Frances Willard described him as "quiet, yet observant, modest but perfectly self-poised, with mild and gentle tones, yet full of personality, and vibrating with purposes." When he looked around at the United States of America in the Gilded Age Bellamy saw a "nervous, dyspeptic, and bilious nation," wracked by grotesque inequality. Millionaire dynasties controlled the industrial economy, while the labouring classes worked sixty-hour weeks for low pay in unsafe factories and sweatshops, and lived in foul slums. The march of technology produced miracles—the electric lightbulb, the phonograph, the telephone—while poisoning rivers and blackening the sky. The economy staggered under the blows of panics and recessions. An epidemic of labour strikes swept the country from sea to sea.

To Bellamy, the status quo was not just unjust; it was untenable. He believed that he was living in critical times and that a great transformation was surely imminent, for good or ill. The fate of America would decide the fate of the world. "Let us bear in mind that, if it be a failure, it will be a final failure," he wrote. "There can be no more new worlds to be discovered, no fresh continents to offer virgin fields for new ventures."

That August Bellamy finished a novel which reframed the turbulence of the 1880s as the painful but necessary precursor to a peaceful socialist utopia. "I am particularly desirous that it should see the light as quickly as possible," he wrote to his publisher. "Now is the accepted time, it appears to me, for a publication touching on social and industrial questions to obtain a hearing."

Looking Backward 2000–1887 certainly did that. Published in 1888, it became the most widely read novel in the United States since *Uncle Tom's Cabin* and the most imitated since *Jane Eyre*. Like many surprise bestsellers, Bellamy's book synthesised extant trends, capitalising on the popularity of utopian visions such as W. H. Hudson's *A Crystal Age* and radical tracts like Henry George's phenomenally successful *Progress and Poverty* by merging the two forms. In America, according to the journalist Henry Demarest Lloyd, it was "debated by all down to the boot-blacks on the curbstones." In Britain, it became such a talking point that it was considered an oversight in intellectual circles not to have read it. "I suppose you have seen or read, or at least tried to read, '*Looking Backward*,'" the socialist writer and designer William Morris wrote to a friend in 1889. In Russia, where it sold briskly, it was praised by Chekhov, Gorky and Tolstoy, who called it "an exceedingly remarkable book." Its American admirers included Jack London, Upton Sinclair, Elizabeth Gurley Flynn, and two future leaders of the Socialist Party. Mark Twain dubbed it "the latest and best of all the Bibles."

Like the Bible, *Looking Backward* attracted apostles, compelled to spread the good news about Bellamy's middle-class, respectable, distinctly American form of socialism, which he called Nationalism. "Bellamy is the Moses of today," wrote one convert. "He has shown us that the promised land exists." Bellamy's admirers formed the first Nationalist Club in Boston in 1888; within three years there were more than 160 across the nation, attracting journalists, artists, lawyers, doctors, businessmen and reformers, among them the crusading attorney Clarence Darrow and the feminist Charlotte Perkins Gilman. In rural areas, travelling salesmen sold the book door to door. The newly formed Populist Party, which won five states in the 1892 presidential election, drew much of its progressive platform from Bellamy's ideas. Residents of downtown Los Angeles can still see for themselves the life-changing power of *Looking Backward*. Architect George Wyman based the Bradbury Building, later the location for the final act of Ridley Scott's *Blade Runner*, on Bellamy's description of the department store of the future.

Just as Orwell was beginning his journalistic career, the Great Depression revived interest in Bellamy's cheering prophecy. President Roosevelt read and discussed Bellamy, and his New Deal administration included the author's biographer, Arthur E. Morgan. In 1935, *The Atlantic Monthly* named *Looking Backward* the second most important book of the past fifty years, claiming that only *Das Kapital* had done more to shape the world. The Labour leader Clement Attlee derived his enthusiasm for a "cooperative commonwealth" from *Looking Backward* and told the writer's son Paul that his post-war government was "a child of the Bellamy ideal." The book was still so well-known in America in 1949 that Harry Scherman, president of the Book-of-the-Month Club, described *Nineteen Eighty-Four* as "Bellamy's *Looking Backward* in reverse."

It might seem strange that one of the most culturally influential books in the history of literature is now so little-known—until you read it. Stories endure; manifestoes thinly disguised as novels become slaves to history.

Julian West is a feckless aristocrat living in complacent luxury in Boston in 1887, preparing to marry his saintly fiancée. Suffering from insomnia, he is mesmerised by a quack doctor and falls into a trance in a soundproof subterranean vault. Like Rip Van Winkle, he oversleeps, and wakes up over a century later in the home of one Doctor Leete, who proceeds to explain how society has attained perfection based on "the solidarity of the race and the brotherhood of man." Narrated by Julian, the novel is little more than a series of conversations about policy. Bellamy later admitted that he added a romance subplot "with some impatience, in the hope of inducing the more to give it at least a reading." Considering that the only women Julian meets are Doctor Leete's wife and his daughter Edith, the reader is not exactly on tenterhooks.

Although Bellamy predicted, in passing, such innovations as the debit card and the clock radio, he was no Jules Verne. In order to make his utopia appealing to "the sober and morally-minded masses of American people," Bellamy had to make it accessible. Like Louis-Sebastién Mercier's *The Year 2440: A Dream If Ever There Was One*, a publishing sensation in pre-Revolutionary France, Bellamy's utopia had a date and a map reference.* Bellamy originally planned to describe "a cloud palace for an ideal humanity" but "stumbled over the destined cornerstone of the new social order." In a postscript to the second edition he said that it was "intended, in all seriousness, as a forecast."

Doctor Leete is a tireless exposition machine. In each chapter Julian, as a surrogate for the nineteenth-century reader, asks how this or that development could be possible, and Leete blandly replies that nothing could be simpler: it is all "the logical outcome of the operation of human nature under rational conditions." This was a common view among socialists in the 1880s. In his 1946 essay "What

* Verne wrote a similar tale, *Paris in the Twentieth Century*, in 1863 but his publisher rejected it, saying, "You have taken on an impossible task."

is Socialism?," Orwell wrote that until the Russian revolution, "all Socialist thought was in some sense Utopian," because it had not yet been tested in the real world. "Only let economic injustice be brought to an end and all other forms of tyranny would vanish too. The age of human brotherhood would begin, and war, crime, disease, poverty, and overwork would be things of the past."

In Doctor Leete's world, equality is the skeleton key that unlocks everything. The new system, which conscripts every citizen into an "industrial army," does away with the need for lawyers, lawmakers, soldiers, clergymen, taxmen and gaolers. Women are equal, albeit segregated into a separate industrial army. The air is clean, work is painless, lying is almost obsolete, and life expectancy exceeds eighty-five. People are fitter, kinder, happier and better in every way. Here are all the standard fixtures that Orwell mocked in his review of Herbert Samuel's 1942 utopia *An Unknown Land:* "the hygiene, the labour-saving devices, the fantastic machines, the emphasis on Science, the all-round reasonableness tempered by a rather watery religiosity . . . There is no war, no crime, no disease, no poverty, no class-distinctions, etc., etc." *Looking Backward* is a very etcetera kind of book.

Bellamy's vision suffers from one extraordinary omission. Not long after Julian wakes up, Doctor Leete takes him to the roof of his house and shows him the view. Julian sees miles of boulevards, buildings, trees, parks and fountains, arranged in exquisite harmony, but no human beings. It is like an architect's diorama before the miniature figurines have been inserted. When the masses do at last appear, the prose convulses with horror. So effectively has Bellamy acclimatised the reader to the placid efficiency of 2000 that when Julian wakes up to find himself back in the Boston of 1887, the grimy hubbub shocks the senses. Designed to defamiliarise the present and jolt the reader into political action, the sequence also reveals that Bellamy was the kind of paternalistic socialist who loved the working man in theory but struggled with the actuality. Before Julian wakes up yet again to find that 1887 is a nightmare and 2000 the reality, he recoils from the "festering mass of human wretchedness" before him. Sadly observing their "brutish masks," he says, "They were all quite dead." If there is hope, it does not lie in the proles.

—

"The only safe way of reading a utopia," William Morris wrote in his wary review of *Looking Backward,* "is to consider it as the expression of the temperament of its author."

Ironically for a reformer, Bellamy confessed to a "deep-seated aversion to change." One of four sons of a popular Baptist minister and a puritanical Calvinist, he spent almost his entire life in Chicopee Falls, Massachusetts, a formerly idyllic town transformed into an industrial powerhouse. From the windows of the Bellamys' two-storey house beside the Connecticut River, young Edward could see it all: the smoke-belching mills and foundries, the shabby tenements crammed with immigrant labourers, and the grand mansions of the factory owners, who reminded him of feudal barons. When he was fourteen he had a religious epiphany and "saw the world with new eyes."

As a precocious student at Union College in Schenectady, New York, Bellamy first encountered the utopian socialism of the late French thinkers Henri de Saint-Simon and Auguste Comte. In 1868, he spent a year in Germany with his cousin William Packer. There he became hideously aware of "the inferno of poverty beneath our civilization" and spent long hours with William earnestly pondering "some plan for equalising human conditions." Back home in Chicopee Falls, Edward passed the bar but promptly quit the law after he was hired to evict a widow for non-payment of rent, and turned to journalism. He spent 1872 exposing parlous living conditions and political chicanery for the *Evening Post* in New York, a tough, seething city under the thumb of wealthy power broker Boss Tweed and his outrageously corrupt Tammany Hall Democratic Party machine. "Hard to live," Bellamy wrote in his notebook. "Sees lots of suffering, becomes a Nationalist."

Witnessing poverty at home and abroad shook Bellamy's faith in God and made him determined to solve the "mystery" of life for himself with a universal theory which would unite politics, economics, society, art and religion. Bellamy laid out his mystical species of socialism in his 1873 essay "Religion of Solidarity," in which each human being is a manifestation of the infinite "not-self" and true happiness is only attainable by putting the interests of the common-weal before individual desires. He wanted to make others see the world with new eyes.

Bellamy's essay coincided with the financial panic of 1873. During industrial capitalism's first depression, ten US states, hundreds of banks, thousands of businesses and more than one hundred railroads went bankrupt. The Great Railroad Strike of 1877 was America's first nationwide labour dispute, suppressed only after forty-five days of riots and bloodletting. There were street battles in Chicago and Baltimore, a massacre in Pittsburgh, martial law in Scranton. Even once the economy rallied in 1879, American capitalism felt unnervingly fragile. In the first chapter of *Looking Backward,* Julian observes that some of his gilded contemporaries fear "an impending social cataclysm." This anxiety, mirrored across the Western world, inspired a vogue for post-apocalyptic novels like Richard Jefferies's *After London* and Joaquin Miller's *The Destruction of Gotham*—the 1880s equivalent of disaster movies.

During the depression, Bellamy wrote wonkish editorials for *The Springfield Union,* a Massachusetts newspaper, and several novellas and short stories driven by ideas rather than persuasive characters. In 1880, Edward and his brother Charles launched the *Daily News,* "the people's newspaper," which diligently covered labour disputes. Edward was sympathetic to the strikers' plight but thought that the unions didn't aim high enough. The goal should be an entirely new system, not just a better deal for particular interest groups. Marriage and parenthood spurred Edward to imagine the better world which, he hoped, his children might inhabit. "When I came to consider what could be radically done for social reorganization," he confided to his notebook, "I was helped by every former disgust with the various socialist schemes."

Bellamy started writing *Looking Backward* in the midst of his country's first Red Scare. On May 4, 1886, a dynamite bomb killed seven police officers during a workers' rally in Chicago's Haymarket Square. Most of the era's violence was committed by the state or the bosses' armed thugs—the police shot dead several protesters at Haymarket—but the conviction, on outrageously flimsy evidence, of eight anarchists enabled a crackdown on anarchists, socialists and labour unions. Any successful prospectus for socialism would therefore need to be as unthreatening as possible.

To Bellamy, like Orwell fifty years later, socialism was a tremendous product with terrible salesmen. "In the radicalness of the opinions I have expressed I may seem to outsocialize the socialists," he wrote to his friend and fellow utopian William Dean Howells, "yet the word socialist is one I never could well stomach. In the first place it is a foreign word in itself and equally foreign in all its suggestions. It smells to the average American of petroleum, suggests the red flag, with all manner of sexual novelties, and an abusive tone about God and religion." (Orwell, too, complained of the "smell" of socialism.) In *Looking Backward*, Doctor Leete explains that "the followers of the red flag" in the 1880s "so disgusted people as to deprive the best considered projects for social reform of a hearing." In fact, he reveals, they were secretly paid by the capitalist monopolies to discredit radical ideas with violent rhetoric, leading Julian to raise the popular conspiracy theory that the real Haymarket bomb-thrower was a capitalist stooge.

In such a tense climate, Bellamy proposed evolution rather than revolution. Just as in his journalism he advised reformers to be clear, direct and polite, in his novel he tidied up and smoothed out socialism until it no longer appeared remotely dangerous. He reassured his wealthier readers that they need not feel nervous or guilty, because they, too, were blameless victims of "a hideous, ghastly mistake, a colossal world-darkening blunder," i.e., capitalism. Once that has been removed, without a drop being shed, in *Looking Backward*, so too has all tension between social classes, sexes, races and regions, for all time. This kind of utopian assumption confounded Orwell, who thought that one of the left's great fallacies was "the belief that the truth will prevail and persecution defeats itself, or that man is naturally good and is only corrupted by his environment."

Bellamy's dramatisation of exactly that belief made *Looking Backward* a flat novel but a seductive political argument. America in 1888 was eventful to a fault; by comparison, a future in which all our hero has to do is sit in a nice house while Doctor Leete explains things to him must have seemed very attractive. Heaven is a place where nothing ever happens.

—

The publication of *Looking Backward* transformed a provincial journalist into one of the most celebrated thinkers in the world. Nationalist Clubs launched dozens of newspapers, two of which Bellamy edited himself, and gave the nascent Populists an intellectual framework, although he disapproved of their fiery rhetoric. In his preamble to the Populists' manifesto in the 1892 election, Ignatius Donnelly fulminated, "A vast conspiracy against mankind has been organised on two continents, and it is rapidly taking possession of the world. If not met and overthrown at once it forebodes terrible social convulsions, the destruction of civilization, or the establishment of an absolute despotism."

Donnelly, a Minnesota congressman who was variously known as "the Tribune of the People" and "the Prince of Cranks," was one of the people responsible for injecting conspiracy theories into the bloodstream of American politics. He wrote his own hair-raisingly lurid utopian novel, *Caesar's Column,* in which paradise is carved out in a Swiss-owned Uganda while American capitalism perishes in blood and fire; the titular column consists of a quarter of a million corpses, piled high in New York's Union Square and covered in cement. In the 1896 election, the Populists endorsed the Democratic candidate William Jennings Bryan, whose rabble-rousing style was too salty for Bellamy's palate. When Bryan was soundly defeated, the Nationalist moment was over.

Bellamy's influence, however, transcended the movement. Among American socialists, he was more widely read than Marx. Eugene Debs, co-founder of the Socialist Party of America, claimed that Bellamy "not only aroused the people but started many on the road to the revolutionary movement." Britain's fledgling Fabian Society, whose Beatrice Webb toyed with writing her own Bellamyite utopia, *Looking Forward,* asked Bellamy to write the introduction to the American edition of *Fabian Essays in Socialism.* He had fans among the women's movement, too. Frances Willard joked that perhaps Edward was secretly "Edwardina": "a big-hearted, big-brained woman."

Bellamy died of tuberculosis in 1898, at the age of forty-eight. His swansong was the 1897 novel *Equality,* a diligent exercise in filling in the gaps left by *Looking Backward,* while responding to his critics.

Bellamy took pains to respect personal liberty, empower women and emphasise America's founding values, claiming that economic equality was "the obvious, necessary, and only adequate pledge of these three birthrights—life, liberty, and happiness." For many of Bellamy's later admirers, *Equality* was even more significant than its predecessor. Its best chapter, "The Parable of the Water Tank," was extracted as a pamphlet, selling hundreds of thousands of copies in Russia. Peter Kropotkin, the world's most famous anarchist, exclaimed, "What a pity that Bellamy has not lived longer!"

In literary terms, *Looking Backward* was a dandelion clock, each scattered seed producing a bloom. The utopian template that Bellamy popularised proved extremely attractive to first-time novelists, removing the need for psychologically rich characters or dynamic narratives. All writers had to do was transport their curious observer to another land, by airship or shipwreck, dream or trance, locate a helpful guide with time on his hands, and describe the society that dramatised their political beliefs. They came in their scores: serious thinkers and obsessive eccentrics, dry pragmatists and wild-eyed prophets, dreamers and cranks, covering every conceivable fin-de-siècle obsession, from vegetarianism and electric lighting to eugenics and imperialism. There were more than 150 responses to Bellamy in the United States alone, many of which were direct homages or ripostes with titles like *Looking Forward, Looking Ahead, Looking Further Backward* or *Mr. East's Experiences in Mr. Bellamy's World.* Some were essentially fan fiction by virtue of reusing Julian West for their own ends. Even the Wizard of Oz was a Bellamyite, to judge by L. Frank Baum's description of his egalitarian society in *The Emerald City of Oz.*

As early as 1890, a writer for *The Literary World* was complaining that "books on the twentieth or twenty-first century are getting to be so numerous that the whole subject will soon be a deadly bore," and the craze was only getting started. As the United States raced feverishly towards the new century, its upheavals continued to nourish wild imaginations. The Panic of 1893 knocked the economy off its feet for another four years. More cheeringly, the World's Fair in Chicago that year introduced millions of Americans to such futuristic novelties as the dishwasher, the travelator, the zipper and the Ferris wheel. It was at the fair that Baptist minister Francis Bellamy—Edward's cousin—launched the Pledge of Allegiance into national life and the celebrated historian of the American West Frederick Jackson Turner declared, "The frontier has gone, and with its going has closed the first period of American history." New frontiers—social, political, spiritual, technological—were required.

Scores of writers were inspired to delineate a golden future which reflected their own political priorities. William Morris told a friend that his utopia *News from Nowhere* was conceived as "a counterblast" to the "cockney paradise" of *Looking Backward*. Set in 2102, Morris's ideal society is agrarian rather than urban, anarchistic rather than centralised, and motivated by pleasure, not duty. It became an international bestseller and inspired Ebenezer Howard to start the garden city movement, but its many fans did not include Orwell, who called it "a sort of goody-goody version of the Wellsian Utopia." "Everyone is kindly and reasonable, all the upholstery comes from Liberty's, but the impression left behind is of a sort of watery melancholy."

Like the Austrian economist Theodor Hertzka's *Freeland* and Bellamy's friend William Dean Howells's trilogy about the pastoral utopia of Altruria, *News from Nowhere* gained a substantial following, but most of the post-Bellamy novels made only a modest impact.

In *The Human Drift*, King Camp Gillette, the razor magnate, relocated every American to one giant city, Metropolis, powered by Niagara Falls; each copy of the book optimistically included a certificate of membership for the United People's Party, a real-life organisation of which no more was heard. Maine businessman Bradford C. Peck used *The World a Department Store* to promote the cooperative movement. For J. McCullough, author of *Golf in the Year 2000, or, What We Are Coming To*, utopia meant uninterrupted golf. Sutton E. Griggs, a Baptist minister and son of a former slave, self-published the first black utopia, *Imperium in Imperio*, about a secret underground government of African-Americans in Waco, Texas. Feminist utopias such as Elizabeth Corbett's *New Amazonia: A Foretaste of the Future* and Charlotte Perkins Gilman's more successful 1915 novel *Herland* were absent of men, and therefore of violence. Such utopias made readers believe that fundamental change was possible, however helpless they might feel in real life.

One person's utopia was, of course, another's anti-utopia. As

Clement Attlee wrote, "We should most of us be very unhappy in each other's paradises." For New York lawyer Arthur Dudley Vinton, Bellamy's imaginary future was closer to hell than to heaven. In Vinton's fiercely bigoted sequel, *Looking Further Backward*, Nationalism and feminism have reduced America to a decadent, frivolous, emasculated nation that is easily invaded by China, and a disillusioned Julian must draw on his Gilded Age wits to fight the yellow peril. A much funnier riposte came from Jerome K. Jerome, the British author of *Three Men in a Boat*, whose short story "The New Utopia" was a droll spoof of both Bellamy's ideas and his prose. "Have they got it all right by this time?" Jerome's unflappable narrator asks after waking up one thousand years later. "Is everybody equal now, and sin and sorrow and all that sort of thing done away with?" "Oh yes," his Leete-like guide replies. "You'll find everything all right now . . . Nobody is allowed to do anything wrong or silly." Jerome gave citizens of his drably uniform world ("one language, one law, one life") numbers instead of names: a joke that would become a science-fiction cliché. In Orwell's novel Winston Smith is also known as "6079 Smith W."

Conservative utopias dreamed of less regulation, weaker unions, a stronger police force and military, and more imperialism: manifest destiny on steroids. John Jacob Astor, one of the richest men in the world, set *A Journey in Other Worlds: A Romance of the Future* in 2000, when the United States, having dominated half the planet, sets out to colonise the solar system and renames Jupiter Kentucky. Many of these novels now make for terrifying reading. In Addison Peale Russell's *Sub-Coelum: A Sky-Built Human World*, the "unfit" are sterilised while "unchaste" women are jailed for such crimes as drinking, whistling and bad grammar. In *A.D. 2050: Electrical Development at Atlantis* by John Bachelder, refugees from Bellamy's failing Nationalist society flee to Atlantis, which they turn into a proto-Orwellian police state under constant surveillance. William Harben came to a comparable scenario from the left in *The Land of the Changing Sun:* in the underwater society of Alpha a government of eugenicists uses television scanning devices to identify dissidents, and psychological torture to crush them.

There was even a foretaste of Orwell's Oceania in Bellamy's own work. In his 1880 novella *Dr. Heidenhoff's Process* the eponymous scientist has discovered how to wipe painful memories and erase guilt: "Memory is the principle of moral degeneracy. Remembered sin is the most utterly diabolical influence in the universe." The happy race of mind readers in his 1889 short story "To Whom This May Come," whose telepathy has eliminated crime and deceit by "rending the veil of self, and leaving no spot in darkness in the mind for lies to hide in," make Orwell's Thought Police look like amateurs.

It is a mark of Bellamy's unwavering faith in human nature and common sense that he failed to see the dystopian implications of unanimous obedience to a one-party state that will last forever, nor the possibility that his *not-self* would eliminate what Orwell called *ownlife*. The late-nineteenth-century idealist had a thoroughly pre-totalitarian mind. Orwell was to skewer that generation's naivety in the voice of O'Brien in *Nineteen Eighty-Four:* "Do you begin to see, then, what kind of world we are creating? It is the exact opposite of the stupid hedonistic Utopias that the old reformers imagined."

Orwell critiqued and mocked utopian writing on numerous occasions. By the late 1940s, however, he had developed a pitying fondness for nineteenth-century visions of a better world, however bland or naive they may have been. Writing about Oscar Wilde's "The Soul of Man Under Socialism" in 1948, he found that Wilde's rosy predictions of a populace liberated by technology and the abolition of private property to enjoy a life of individual fulfilment under the benevolent eye of a minimal state made "rather painful reading." Wilde was, it seemed to him, extraordinarily wrong. And yet Orwell also saw great value in being reminded that socialism did not have to mean labour camps, food queues and secret police. The nineteenth-century utopias, he wrote, "may demand the impossible, and they may—since a Utopia necessarily reflects the aesthetic ideas of its own period—sometimes seem 'dated' and ridiculous; but they do at least ... remind the Socialist movement of its original, half-forgotten objective of human brotherhood."

Orwell had seen too much to be an idealist but he was not above feeling tenderness, and perhaps a little envy, towards those dreamers who had lived in more hopeful times.

CHAPTER 3

The World We're Going Down Into

Orwell 1938–1940

The future, at any rate the immediate future, is not with the "sensible" men. The future is with the fanatics.

—George Orwell, *Time & Tide,* June 8, 1940

On May 22, 1938, Orwell wrote to his friend Jack Common to say he was planning to start his fourth novel, although the historical circumstances were less than ideal. "As it is if I start in August I daresay I'll have to finish it in the concentration camp," he joked darkly.*

He was writing from Preston Hall, a sanatorium in Aylesford, Kent, because two months earlier he had begun coughing up blood. Eileen's beloved older brother Laurence "Eric" O'Shaughnessy, one of Britain's leading experts on tuberculosis, diagnosed a lesion on Orwell's left lung and recommended the sanatorium, where O'Shaughnessy was a consultant surgeon. During his three-month stay, Orwell received visitors from all corners of his unusual, class-hopping life. Nurses could hear the fluting voices of literary friends such as Richard Rees and Cyril Connolly one day and the working-class accents of his ILP comrades from Spain the next. Henry Miller sent him a friendly letter advising him to "stop thinking and worrying about the external pattern," which was rather like Orwell telling Miller to stop thinking about himself.

Once a fortnight, Eileen travelled from their home in Wallington,

---

* Orwell meant *concentration camp* in its original sense of an internment camp, in this case a British one.

where they kept a grey poodle. "We called him Marx to remind us that we had never read Marx," she told a friend, with typically dry humour, "and now we have read a little and taken so strong a personal dislike to the man that we can't look the dog in the face when we speak to him." The couple could tell a lot about a visitor from whether they assumed the animal was named after Karl, Groucho or the Marks & Spencer department store.

The doctors at Preston Hall advised Orwell to spend the winter in a more congenial climate. Funded by an anonymous £300 donation from the novelist L. H. Myers, the Orwells decided on Morocco, arriving in Marrakech on September 11. Despite his best efforts to fill a diary with typically precise observations about local customs, Orwell found Morocco "rather a dull country." It was, therefore, a good place to write a novel.

For roughly two years, between fighting in one war and attempting to fight in another, Orwell was a pacifist. The British establishment's version of anti-fascism struck him as "a thin disguise for jingo imperialism." Furthermore, he was convinced that war would have a "fascising" effect on the British people: "wage-reductions, suppression of free speech, brutalities in the colonies, etc."* One of his favourite quotations around this time was Nietzsche's argument that those who fight dragons risk becoming dragons themselves. "Fascism after all is only a development of capitalism, and the mildest democracy, so-called, is liable to turn into Fascism when the pinch comes," he wrote to his friend Geoffrey Gorer in 1937. He put it more bluntly in a letter to a reader: "Fascism and so-called democracy are Tweedledum and Tweedledee." So he signed an anti-war manifesto in the *New Leader*, officially joined the ILP, and was writing ferocious anti-war essays as late as July 1939. He even planned to organise illegal protests. He told Richard Rees and his agent Leonard Moore in 1938 that he was writing an anti-war pamphlet called "Socialism and War," but it was never published, so the clearest public expression of

---

* This belief was not unusual at the time. The novelist E. M. Forster thought "that if Fascism wins we are done for, and that we must become Fascist to win."

Orwell's pacifism, and the reasons behind it, was the novel he wrote in Morocco.

Coming Up for Air was about the very thing Orwell thought might prevent him from finishing it. The Munich Agreement was signed shortly after he arrived in Morocco, but that was merely to postpone the inevitable. Orwell later claimed that he had known since 1931 that "the future must be catastrophic" and since 1936 that England would go to war with Germany. Later, he remembered "the feeling of futility and impermanence, of hanging about in a draughty room and waiting for the guns to begin to shoot." His pessimism amused Eileen, who wrote to Orwell's sister Marjorie about his plans to build a bomb shelter at Wallington when he got home. "But the dugout has generally been by way of light relief; his specialities are concentration camps & the famine."

Some of Orwell's friends later attributed the despondency of *Nineteen Eighty-Four* to his failing health, but the ghastly sensation of individual helplessness was in his novels all along. Orwell was as merciless in his fiction as he was compassionate in his journalism. His typical protagonist is a plain, mediocre individual who finds their role in society intolerable, attempts to resist or escape, and ends up back where they began, minus the hope that a better life is possible. All of his plots have this baleful circularity. In *Burmese Days, A Clergyman's Daughter, Keep the Aspidistra Flying* and *Coming Up for Air,* his characters are not only defeated but broken and alienated, and by forces less extreme than electric shocks and Room 101.

In 1934's *Burmese Days,* for example, the teak merchant John Flory is a tormented imperialist, who lives in "a stifling, stultifying world . . . in which every word and every thought is censored . . . Free speech is unthinkable." The lie the colonisers tell themselves, that their role is to elevate Burma rather than to exploit it, poisons them, while Flory's hidden dissent condemns him to a lonely, sterile life: "It is a corrupting thing to live one's real life in secret." In *Keep the Aspidistra Flying,* everything is dismal, tasteless and grey, except when it is lurid and hellish. Its protagonist Gordon Comstock's poem (which Orwell had already published in *The Adelphi*) turns 1930s London into a sketch for Airstrip One, with its torn posters fluttering in a cruel wind, and the malign authority "Who spies with jealous, watchful care, / Our thoughts, our dreams, our secret ways, / Who picks our words and cuts our clothes, / And maps the pattern of our days." This tyrant is "the money-god," his "money-priesthood" is the Party, and his "thousand million slaves" are the proles. Where Winston is oppressed by propaganda posters, Comstock is tormented by advertising hoardings: his Big Brother is Roland Butta, the character who promotes a hot drink called Bovex. The name of the ad agency where Comstock "packs a world of lies into a hundred words" even sounds like a fascist movement: New Albion.

As a writer of fiction, Orwell had both a limited imagination and a hoarder's impulse. His first four novels were junk shops piled to the rafters with miscellaneous preoccupations for which he couldn't find a more suitable home. In 1946, the writer Julian Symons told Orwell that, while it was fine as a veiled autobiography, *Coming Up for Air* barely qualified as a novel. Orwell did not put up a fight. "Of course you are perfectly right about my own character constantly intruding on that of the narrator," he wrote back. "I am not a real novelist anyway." He considered *A Clergyman's Daughter* and *Keep the Aspidistra Flying* "silly potboilers which I ought not to have published in the first place." What makes his early novels worth reading is not plot or character but voice: the lively flow of opinions, observations, anecdotes and jokes; the persuasive expression of a world view; the sense of a writer getting something off his chest.

Coming Up for Air is equal parts nostalgia and dread, each emotion sharpening the flavour of the other. Its narrator is George Bowling, a chubby, middlebrow suburbanite with a family and a solid job in the insurance business. Walking through London one day, Bowling is so haunted by premonitions of war that he decides to visit Lower Binfield, his idyllic childhood home in the Thames Valley, and go fishing. His long, rhapsodic reminiscences of a rural paradise simultaneously anticipate Winston Smith's "Golden Country" and constitute a stock clearance of Orwell's childhood memories, giving weight to Cyril Connolly's pointed quip that Orwell was "a revolutionary in love with 1910." But nostalgia, which is not necessarily reactionary, feels justified here. If ever there was a time when one could fairly claim that the past was looking better than the future, then it was 1938. And memory matters; in *Nineteen Eighty-Four*, it's both sword and shield. Bowling admits that society was harsher and more unequal in his youth but "people then had something that we haven't got now. What? It was simply that they didn't think of the future as something to be terrified of."

Bowling doesn't just fear the world to come; he can actually *see* it. Strolling through London, "as if I'd got X-rays in my eyes," he has startling visions of food queues, propaganda posters and machine guns blurting from bedroom windows. Even worse, he imagines the "after-war":

> The world we're going down into, the kind of hate-world, slogan world. The coloured shirts. The barbed wire. The rubber truncheons. The secret cells where the electric light burns night and day, and the detectives watching you while you sleep. And the processions and the posters with enormous faces, and the crowds of a million people all cheering for the leader till they deafen themselves into thinking that they really worship him, and all the time, underneath, they hate him so that they want to puke.

This grisly premonition of Airstrip One is underlined by the same warning as *Nineteen Eighty-Four:* "the things that you tell yourself are just a nightmare or only happen in foreign countries" can happen here.

Bowling even witnesses a dress rehearsal for the Two Minutes Hate when he attends a meeting of the Left Book Club and hears an anti-fascist speaking in mechanical slogans. "It's a ghastly thing, really, to have a sort of human barrel-organ shooting propaganda at you by the hour. The same thing over and over and over again. Hate, hate, hate. Let's all get together and have a good hate." It's not the politics that makes Orwell recoil—he, too, was an anti-fascist—but the language and tone. Even after he rejected pacifism, he never lost his suspicion of brutalising rhetoric. *Nineteen Eighty-Four* springs a nasty surprise on the reader when O'Brien, an Inner Party official, posing as a member of the underground Brotherhood, asks Winston and his lover Julia if they are prepared to murder, sabotage, plant bombs, and even "throw sulfuric acid in a child's face" in the cause of defeating Big Brother's Ingsoc regime. Yes, they say without hesitation. Yes. Later, O'Brien reminds Winston of that moment when he endorsed the idea that the ends justify the means. The fact that the opposition to Big Brother is called the Brotherhood suggests that they are not as different as Winston would like to believe.

Bowling's sojourn to Lower Binfield is a washout. His erstwhile childhood paradise is now all noise and concrete. Modernity is a plague in Bowling's eyes, and his language bridges the gap between democracy and totalitarianism. The "new kind of men from eastern Europe ... who think in slogans and talk in bullets" are "streamlined," but then so is modern Britain.* In Orwell's 1930s lexicon, *streamlined* was as pernicious a word as *hygienic, sterile* or *slick*. This is capitalism as dystopia: "Celluloid, rubber, chromium-steel everywhere, arc-lamps blazing over your head, radios all playing the same tune, no vegetation left, everything cemented over . . ." It sounds a lot like Orwell's list of pet hates in *Twentieth Century Authors:* "I dislike big towns, noise, motor cars, the radio, tinned food, central heating and 'modern' furniture." Orwell's abstemious, old-fashioned tastes meant that, even as he valorised the common man, he disdained many of the things that the common man of the 1930s enjoyed.

So there are things that Bowling would not mind seeing succumb to the bombs. Likewise, Comstock in *Keep the Aspidistra Flying* both fears war and relishes it, as a terrible purge that will sweep away the tawdriest aspects of modern life: "Only a little while before the aeroplanes come. Zoom—bang! A few tons of TNT to send our civilisation back to hell where it belongs." This is the same petulant apocalyptic instinct that drove H. G. Wells to fantasise about Martians laying waste to Woking, or John Betjeman to invite bombs to rain on Slough: rip it up and start again. All of Orwell's first four novels, despite their significant differences, share a pungent sense of claustrophobia, corruption, and living death. Above all, there is the ozone smell of fear.

"We swim in it," says Bowling. "It's our element. Everyone that isn't scared stiff of losing his job is scared stiff of war, or Fascism, or Communism, or something."

---

* See Winston's estranged wife Katharine: "She had not a thought in her head that was not a slogan."

—

At 8 p.m. Eastern Time on October 30, 1938, CBS Radio inadvertently conducted a nationwide study in the psychology of fear. The Halloween episode of *The Mercury Theatre on the Air* was an adaptation of H. G. Wells's 1898 novel *The War of the Worlds* by twenty-three-year-old wunderkind Orson Welles and writer Howard Koch. Welles did not mean to fool anybody. "It was our thought that perhaps people might be bored or annoyed at hearing a tale so improbable," he said later. As if the prospect of Martian death machines making landfall in New Jersey were not implausible enough, he topped and tailed each half of the hour-long broadcast with an announcement clarifying that it was fiction. But the first half was convincingly presented as a series of emergency news bulletins and, so soon after Munich, nerves were frayed.

Some Americans tuned in to *The War of the Worlds* at exactly the wrong time, convinced themselves it was real, and flew into a panic. Reporters harangued a startled Welles with wild rumours of stampedes and suicides. Newspapers, radio stations and police precincts were swamped with phone calls seeking more information. A radio announcer in Cleveland was accused of "covering up the truth" after he told listeners there was no invasion. Such reactions were so extreme and unexpected that the story prompted more than twelve thousand newspaper articles over the next three weeks. Even Howard Koch was affected. Walking through Manhattan the next morning, he overheard talk of an invasion and assumed that Germany had declared war.

In his 1940 book *The Invasion from Mars: A Study in the Psychology of Panic*, Princeton psychologist Hadley Cantril hugely overestimated the number of people affected, but his intentions were sincere and his case studies revealing. His team found that the people most likely to believe the broadcast without checking other sources were the intensely religious, the anxious and the economically insecure, because it confirmed the fear and lack of control that they already felt. Cantril wrote, "The complexity of modern finance and government, the discrepancies shown in the economic and political proposals of the various 'experts,' the felt threats of Fascism, Communism, prolonged unemployment among millions of Americans—these together with a thousand and one other characteristics of modern living—create an environment which the average individual is completely unable to interpret." One interviewee said that the real news made it easier to believe incredible things, because "so many things we hear are unbelievable."

Orwell thought that Cantril's book shed useful light on totalitarian methods. For one thing, the incident demonstrated the power of radio to manipulate public opinion, even when it wasn't trying. Newspapers, he wrote, "cannot tell lies of more than a certain magnitude." The trade gazette *Editor & Publisher* warned, "The nation as a whole continues to face the danger of incomplete, misunderstood news over a medium which has yet to prove that it is competent to perform the news job."

Cantril's research also shed light on the public's irrationality and failure to check facts. "The evident connection between personal unhappiness and readiness to believe the incredible is its most interesting discovery," Orwell wrote. "It is a similar frame of mind that has induced whole nations to fling themselves into the arms of a Saviour." It's ironic, then, that Hitler, the master of the Big Lie, pounced on the *War of the Worlds* affair as proof of the decadence of democracy. The columnist Dorothy Thompson thought that the incident was "the perfect demonstration that the danger is not from Mars but from the theatrical demagogue."

If Welles could deceive so many people without even trying, what might a calculating liar do to the human mind? That was the theme of Patrick Hamilton's play *Gas Light*, which opened at London's Richmond Theatre on December 5, 1938. In Hamilton's hit Victorian melodrama, a bullying husband called Manningham attempts to convince his wife, Bella, that she is losing her mind, so that he can send her to an asylum, by fabricating evidence and telling her to disbelieve her own senses. "You are not going out of your mind, Mrs. Manningham, you are slowly, methodically, systematically being *driven* out of your mind," a police detective tells Bella. Orwell often compared the effects of organised lying to mental illness: Barcelona during the communist purge, for example, was "a lunatic asylum." In *Nineteen Eighty-Four,* Winston fights to affirm his own sanity in the face of O'Brien's insistence that he is "mentally deranged." In *The Woman Who Could Not Die,* a memoir of two years in the hands of

Stalin's secret police which Orwell owned but did not review, the Russian writer and diplomat's wife Iulia de Beausobre summarised the psychological effect of captivity in a totalitarian regime like so: "Am I really mad? Are they all mad? Is the whole world mad?" Mental disintegration was, of course, the desired effect.

The word *gaslighting* later made its way into clinical literature and, eventually, political discourse. Far too late to describe Hitler and Stalin, both of whom could gaslight a nation.

Orwell and Eileen returned to London on March 30, 1939, two days before the last of the Spanish Republicans surrendered to Franco. They dropped off the manuscript of *Coming Up for Air* with Victor Gollancz, spent three weeks with Laurence O'Shaughnessy in Greenwich, and visited Orwell's ailing father in Southwold, a small town near the River Orwell in Suffolk. Richard Blair died of cancer in June, aged eighty-two. Hours before he passed away, Orwell's sister Avril read their father a positive review of *Coming Up for Air;* he died knowing that his son had amounted to something after all. The couple moved back to Wallington to wait for the coming war, which Orwell saw as both a grand catastrophe and a personal affront. He had things he wanted to do, chiefly a three-part family saga called *The Quick and the Dead,* and "the idea that I've got to abandon them and either be bumped off or depart to some filthy concentration camp just infuriates me," he told Jack Common. "Eileen and I have decided that if war does come the best thing will be to just stay alive and thus add to the number of sane people."

The impression one gets from reading Orwell's work during this period is of a man urgently trying to clarify the relationship between fascism, communism and capitalism. He clearly preferred a fourth option—democratic socialism—but that didn't seem to be on the table. Just before he went to Spain, he had scorned "the vulgar lie, now so popular, that 'Communism and Fascism are the same thing.'" But when he read *Assignment in Utopia,* he felt that Stalinism, as described by Lyons, "does not seem to be so very different from Fascism."

Only one word could explain the puzzling affinity between two apparent enemies. The concept of totalitarianism was developed by its supporters in Italy during the 1920s—Mussolini defined it as "Everything within the state, nothing outside the state, nothing against the state"—but it translated into English with purely negative connotations. Borkenau's 1940 book *The Totalitarian Enemy* presented Nazism and Stalinism as two faces of the same monster: "Brown Bolshevism" and "Red Fascism." This radically contradicted the older theory, popularised by John Strachey's 1932 book *The Coming Struggle for Power,* that fascism was "simply the bludgeon of the capitalist class" and communism the only defence. "The two regimes, having started from opposite ends, are rapidly evolving towards the same system—a form of oligarchical collectivism," Orwell wrote in his review of Borkenau, anticipating the title of Emmanuel Goldstein's book in *Nineteen Eighty-Four: The Theory and Practice of Oligarchical Collectivism.* "The sin of nearly all leftwingers from 1933 onwards," he later wrote, "is that they have wanted to be anti-Fascist without being anti-totalitarian."

History couldn't explain what was happening; this was something quite new. "This book is subtitled 'Back to the Middle Ages,' which is unfair to the Middle Ages," Orwell wrote in a review of a book about Franco. "There were no machine-guns in those days, and the Inquisition was a very amateurish business. After all, even Torquemada only burnt two thousand people in ten years. In modern Russia or Germany they'd say he wasn't trying."

At 11:15 a.m. on September 3, 1939, Prime Minister Neville Chamberlain announced that the United Kingdom was at war with Germany. London's first air-raid drill took place minutes later. The evacuation of children to the countryside began. Gas masks were distributed. The skies over London filled with barrage balloons, the pavements with sandbags. The lights went out. "Groping along darkened streets," wrote journalist Malcolm Muggeridge, "dimly it was felt that a way of life was failing, its comfortable familiarity passing away never to reappear . . . Difficult to project any existing thing into the future, difficult to imagine its continuance."

Orwell was no longer a pacifist. A couple of weeks into the war, the novelist Ethel Mannin, who still was, wrote to Orwell praising the anti-war message of *Coming Up for Air.* She was "bitched buggered and bewildered" when he wrote back to say that he was now eager to sign up and do his bit. "I thought you thought it all crazy, this smashing in of Nazi faces," she protested.

It was the shock of the Nazi-Soviet Pact that changed his mind. On August 23, Nazi foreign minister Joachim von Ribbentrop was greeted at the Moscow airport by a fluttering swastika and the Red Army Band playing the "Horst Wessel Song." For Orwell, even an imperialist England was better than a totalitarian alliance. Unusually for such a rational man, he attributed his epiphany not to the pact itself but to a dream he had had the night before the news broke: "It taught me two things, first, that I should be simply relieved when the long-dreaded war started, secondly, that I was patriotic at heart, would not sabotage or act against my own side, would support the war, would fight in it if possible." He immediately quit the ILP and described pacifism as a form of appeasement—even "objectively pro-Fascist" (an allegation he later described as "dishonest"). "The intellectuals who are at present pointing out that that democracy and fascism are the same thing etc. depress me horribly," he told Gollancz. So much for Tweedledum and Tweedledee.

The British government had made plans for mass graves and cardboard coffins in anticipation of up to twenty thousand casualties from massive air raids. But the bombers did not come. Instead, September 3 marked the beginning of eight months of "phony war," which Orwell described, in a phrase he would later reuse with greater success, as a "cold war." It reminded him too much of the long, empty months on the Aragón front; Orwell hated the sensation of nothing happening. Reading a report by the social research body Mass Observation six months later, he found that most Britons were "bored, bewildered and a little irritated, but at the same time buoyed up by a completely false idea that winning the war is going to be an easy business."

Eileen immediately took a job at the Ministry of Information's censorship department and moved to London, while Orwell stayed in Wallington, feeling useless. He wanted to fight in "this bloody war," but his lungs put paid to that. Largely out of the swim of freelance journalism, he spent his phony war contemplating the world's plunge into the abyss.

It is hard to disentangle the true extent of Orwell's pessimism from his love of negative hyperbole. "I find that anything outrageously strange generally ends by fascinating me even when I abominate it," he wrote in *The Road to Wigan Pier*. From *Down and Out in Paris and London* to *Nineteen Eighty-Four*, his prose quickens its pulse whenever it veers towards catastrophe. It's therefore no surprise that Orwell enjoyed Malcolm Muggeridge's "brilliant and depressing" book *The Thirties*. Muggeridge, the former Moscow correspondent for *The Manchester Guardian*, was a flamboyant phrase-maker, and *The Thirties* was a bracingly harsh and witty account of a shameful decade. "He is looking only on the black side, but it is doubtful whether there is any bright side to look on," Orwell wrote in his review. "What a decade! A riot of appalling folly that suddenly becomes a nightmare, a scenic railway ending in a torture-chamber."

Of all Muggeridge's slashing insights, the most striking now is the unintended consequences of the decade's new obsession with accumulating data, in the form of documentaries, studies and surveys. "With this craving for facts and abundant provision of them, went, ironically, or it may be inevitably, a craving for fantasy and abundant provision of it . . . Never before, it may be assumed, have statistics been so greatly in demand, never before so extravagantly falsified." A cultural fetish for data incentivises the manufacture of bogus information and thus, far from cementing the truth, ends up producing more resilient lies. It happened in Russia and Germany and it happens in Oceania, where Winston Smith spends his days rewriting back copies of *The Times* for the Records Department. Facts do not actually matter in the Ministry of Truth, but they must be *seen* to matter, because vaporous, unreliable memory is no match for "evidence."

What should a writer do in such dire times? What is the decent response to the obscene calamity of war? During those lonely months in Wallington, Orwell was struggling for answers. In the title work of *Inside the Whale*, his first essay collection, he didn't manage to convince himself, let alone the reader, that the politically apathetic self-absorption of Henry Miller was admirable (he later dismissed it as "nihilistic quietism"), only that he preferred the American's rude humanity and lack of humbug to the "labels, slogans and evasions" of the pro-communist intelligentsia. "Good novels are not written by orthodoxy-sniffers, nor by people who are conscience-stricken about their unorthodoxy. Good novels are written by people who are *not frightened*." The bedrock of the essay was despair and an attempt to salvage integrity, if nothing else, from the wreckage of the 1930s. When all the options are bad, when the world is "moving into an age . . . in which freedom of thought will be at first a deadly sin and later on a meaningless abstraction," one should at least choose to be honest.

"Inside the Whale" should never be quoted without noting that Orwell wrote it during a period of emotional distress and intellectual flux. For example, "the literary history of the thirties seems to justify the opinion that a writer does well to keep out of politics" is an opinion that he spent the rest of his life ignoring. The collection's second essay was dedicated to a writer who refused to hide inside the whale. Charles Dickens, he wrote, was "always on the side of the underdog, on the side of the weak against the strong," and "always preaching a sermon . . . Because you can only create if you can *care*." His empathy with his subject was so intense that the essay amounted to a flood of self-analysis. As a literary critic, Orwell was less interested in close textual analysis than in individuals and ideas: What sort of people were Dickens, Shakespeare, Miller, et al., and how did they see the world? The essay ends with his famous description of Dickens's face, or at least the face Orwell imagined: "It is the face of a man who is always fighting against something, but who fights in the open and is not frightened, the face of a man who is *generously angry*—in other words, of a nineteenth-century liberal, a free intelligence, a type hated with equal hatred by all the smelly little orthodoxies which are now contending for our souls." It is the face of the man, and the writer, that Orwell aspired to be—a man in many ways out of time.

Orwell had no way of knowing that his points about Dickens's posthumous ubiquity would one day apply to his own: "I should doubt whether anyone who has actually read Dickens can go a week without remembering him in one context or another. Whether you approve of him or not, he is *there* like the Nelson Column [sic]." (The column held symbolic power for Orwell: in *Nineteen Eighty-Four*, the statue of Admiral Nelson has been replaced by one of Big Brother.) In a talk to the Dickens Fellowship in London in May 1940, Orwell went further. According to the fellowship's report, "To be a lover of Dickens, he felt, it was not necessary to know his work perfectly, as he was one of the very few writers who have a tradition that moves outside the realm of literature." Orwell mentioned the time he spent in Kent in 1931 working alongside hop-pickers who knew all about *Oliver Twist* without having read the novel, and felt that Dickens was on their side. Anyone who cites doublethink or Big Brother second-hand is fellow to those hop-pickers.

Orwell finally joined Eileen in London in May, the month that Winston Churchill replaced Chamberlain as prime minister, and the couple rented a top-floor flat at 18 Dorset Chambers, Chagford Street, near Regent's Park. Needing a regular pay cheque, he reluctantly became the theatre critic for *Time and Tide,* and his sense of impotence and irrelevance was very quickly brought home to him on the evening of May 29. He was reviewing Audrey Lucas's *Portrait of Helen* at the Torch Theatre when, during the interval, an usher announced that the British Expeditionary Force was being evacuated from Dunkirk. Eileen's brother was on that beach, treating the wounded. Orwell spent June 1 waiting at Victoria and Waterloo stations to see if O'Shaughnessy was among the men returning from the coast, but in vain. He had, the couple soon learned, been killed by a German bomb in the streets of Dunkirk on May 27. Eileen, who worshipped her brother, grew thin and careworn. For the next four years, she told her friend Lettice Cooper, she didn't really care if she lived or died.

On June 10, Italy entered the war on the side of Germany and rumours of a German invasion became commonplace. In Berlin, SS-Oberführer Walter Schellenberg began compiling the *Sonderfahndungsliste GB*, a list of almost three thousand British nationals and European exiles who should be arrested after a successful occupation. The list, discovered by British soldiers in 1945 and dubbed "the Black Book," included H. G. Wells, Aldous Huxley, Franz Borkenau, Kingsley Martin and Victor Gollancz but not Orwell. It was a kind of snub that the Nazis did not yet consider him worth arresting.

"Everything is disintegrating," Orwell wrote in his diary. "It makes me writhe to be writing book-reviews etc. at such a time, and even angers me that such time-wasting should still be permitted . . . At present I feel as I felt in 1936 when the Fascists were closing in on Madrid, only far worse."

At least he now had an opportunity to bear arms, in a manner of speaking. Under pressure from the press and public, the government had recently invited men who couldn't fight to sign up for the Local Defence Volunteers, later renamed the Home Guard, and prepare for an invasion. Orwell signed up on June 20. As Sergeant Blair, he recruited Fredric Warburg to his section, which included several European refugees. As if to illustrate how a national crisis united different political tribes, his commanding officer was a former member of Mosley's Blackshirts.

Far from fearing an invasion, Orwell hoped for one, recklessly banking on Britain's ability to repel it: "We shall at any rate get rid once and for all of the gang that got us into this mess." Quixotically, he saw the Home Guard as a serious potential militia and wrote a letter to *Time and Tide* with some street-fighting tips that he had picked up in Barcelona, calling for citizens to be armed with hand grenades, shotguns and radio sets. It must have been a jolt for readers to see their theatre critic crying "ARM THE PEOPLE" in the same issue that he reviewed Reginald Beckwith's play *Boys in Brown*. Walking through London, Orwell found himself studying windows and wondering which of them would make effective machine-gun nests. Like George Bowling with his X-ray vision, Orwell could see the skull behind London's face, waiting to be revealed. Warburg saw him as "an Ironside, austere, resolute, implacably determined to destroy his enemies without fear or mercy, if only they came within his reach." But of course they never did.

On August 20, Ramón Mercader, a Catalan NKVD agent masquerading as a French Trotskyist, talked his way into Trotsky's study in Mexico City, removed an ice axe from his raincoat, and plunged it into Trotsky's skull. The arch-heretic died in hospital the next day. The headline in the *Daily Worker* was "A Counter-Revolutionary Gangster Passes."

"How will the Russian state get on without Trotsky?" Orwell mused. "Or the Communists elsewhere? Probably they will be forced to invent a substitute."

—

That summer, Orwell gestured towards a canon of dystopian literature in a short article for the left-wing weekly *Tribune*. He took four novels published between 1899 and 1932—H. G. Wells's *When the Sleeper Wakes*, Ernest Bramah's *The Secret of the League*, Jack London's *The Iron Heel*, Aldous Huxley's *Brave New World*—and tested their prophecies against the reality of fascism, coming down in favour of London. Two readers wrote in to suggest that such novels were actually "cultural blue-prints" that gave Hitler and Mussolini dangerous ideas. Orwell wasn't convinced: "I don't think anyone need fear that by writing, for instance, a forecast of a British Fascist state he is 'putting ideas' into the head of some local Hitler. The ideas will get there of their own accord, so long as the class struggle is a reality."

Note that *Brave New World* was the only recent novel Orwell considered. As an ambitious but unsuccessful novelist, Orwell tended to caricature his peers as either irrelevant or tediously doctrinaire. In doing so, he overlooked a slew of speculative fiction from the British left. Novels written during the early 1930s, such as *Between Two Men* by Frederick le Gros Clark and *Purple Plague* by ILP leader Fenner Brockway, had an anti-capitalist emphasis. (It's worth noting that *To Tell the Truth*, a witty double-edged satire by John Strachey's sister Amabel Williams-Ellis, included minor characters called Big Brother and Julia.) As the decade darkened, the focus turned to home-grown strains of fascism in books including *London's Burning: A Novel for the Decline and Fall of the Liberal Age* by Barbara Wootton, *Minimum Man: or, Time to Be Gone* by Andrew Marvell, and *In the Second Year* by Margaret Storm Jameson.* "I could imagine an English Fascism," Storm Jameson explained, "the brutality half-masked and devious with streaks of Methodist virtue." When her book was accused of defeatism, the *Left Review* came to her defence: "The novel does not set out to be a prophecy, but a *warning to liberals.*"

None of these novels was as gripping or persuasive as Sinclair Lewis's vision of American fascism in *It Can't Happen Here*, but there were enough of them to make Orwell's silence surprising. He never

---

* H. G. Wells was ahead of the curve with *The Autocracy of Mr. Parham*, a patchy 1930 satire about a right-wing academic who falls asleep during a seance and dreams of becoming a world-conquering dictator. "Reality has outdone fiction since," he wrote in 1934, "and Mosley fooling it in the Albert Hall with his black shirts makes Parham's great dream-meeting there seem preposterously sane and sound."

wrote about the most remarkable example, Murray Constantine's *Swastika Night*, but it's unlikely that he missed it, considering that it was published by Gollancz in 1937 and reissued as a Left Book Club selection three years later. In his review of *Mein Kampf* that year, his vision of Nazism in 2040 as "a horrible brainless empire in which, essentially, nothing ever happens except the training of young men for war and the endless breeding of fresh cannon-fodder" is almost a précis of Constantine's novel.

In the "year of the Lord Hitler 720," the world is divided between the German and Japanese empires. The German Empire is rigidly stratified, with the "Knights" playing the role of the Inner Party and the Nazis the Outer Party. Below them are women, and lowest of all are the savages who persist in practising Christianity. The truth about Hitler and the "Twenty Year War" has been wiped out by a war on memory. According to the Hitler Bible—the only book, apart from technical manuals, that anyone is permitted to read—Hitler was a Thor-like blond god, seven feet tall, and Nazism his religion.

Decades later, the critic Daphne Patai discovered that Murray Constantine was a pseudonym for the feminist novelist Katharine Burdekin. Reading *Swastika Night* now, this seems obvious, because its misogynist theocracy makes Gilead in *The Handmaid's Tale* look half-hearted. Considered less than human, women are used solely for breeding and can be raped with impunity. But the German Empire has grown stagnant and sterile because men are committing suicide and girls, for some mysterious reason, are not being born. Unable to conquer one another, the Germans and Japanese are locked in a paralysing peace that proves toxic to societies founded on military glory: the inverse of *Nineteen Eighty-Four*'s endlessly warring super-states. "We can create nothing," complains the disillusioned Knight Friedrich Von Hess, "we can invent nothing—we have no use for creation, we do not need to invent. We are Germans. We are holy. We are perfect, and we are dead." In *Nineteen Eighty-Four*, Orwell gives Winston a variety of arguments against the endurance of dictator-ships in order for O'Brien to knock them down, and one of them is essentially Von Hess's. A society founded on fear, hatred and cruelty, Winston says, "would have no vitality. It would disintegrate. It would commit suicide."

The engine of the plot also points to *Nineteen Eighty-Four*. Von Hess tells Burdekin's hero, an English aviation engineer named Alfred, about an explosive family secret. His forbidden book, in which his ancestor wrote down the true history of Nazism, is as destabilising as Goldstein's. And just as Winston is shaken by finding the photograph of Jones, Aaronson and Rutherford, Alfred is rocked by a snapshot which shows that Hitler was no Aryan deity but "a little soft dark fat smiling thing," and that women were once confident, attractive and fully human. "There is not the whole width of the Empire between the falsification of history and its destruction," says Von Hess. Burdekin's secret resistance movement, like Orwell's, is called the Brotherhood.

We don't know what Orwell made of *Swastika Night*, but he did engage with at least one story about fascism in England. On August 24, 1940, he saw *Take Back Your Freedom*, a new play that he found "remarkable in its insight." Winifred Holtby, a feminist writer and ILP member, began writing the play (under the title *Dictator*) in 1934 but died of kidney disease before she could make the changes requested by her theatrical producer, so playwright Norman Ginsbury finished the job. Between them, Holtby and Ginsbury demonstrated a keen understanding of the appeal of populist demagogues. The play's main character, Arnold Clayton, is a junior minister, young, clever, charismatic, who resigns from the government and forms the British Planning Party, with a platform of "Action. Isolation. Order." Orwell interpreted him as "a more gentlemanly Hitler or a more intelligent Mosley." Clayton wins a shock victory by tapping into the irrational impulses of the public he despises. "We must have emotion," he tells his mother. "Reason divides men into a thousand parties, but passion unites them." As Muggeridge said of Hitler, "Many who had found thinking with their minds unprofitable were ready to follow him in thinking with their blood." Once in office, Clayton becomes a tyrant who conscripts men, bans women from the workplace, purges his rivals and imprisons his opponents in concentration camps.

Orwell admired the play for its depiction of Clayton as a "prisoner of power," who has gradually sacrificed his integrity to the Plan, the Plan to the Party, the Party to his friends, and his friends to himself. Perhaps he also enjoyed the play's most Orwellian exchange. During the election campaign, four of Clayton's Gestapo-like Grey Guards kill a Jewish protester and he defuses the scandal by claiming that the killers are agents provocateurs working for his enemies. His mother, initially supportive but increasingly horrified, is doubtful.

> Mrs. Clayton: "Is this true—about the *agents provocateurs*?"
> Clayton: "You heard what I said."
> Mrs. Clayton: "I repeat—is it true?"
> Clayton: "It is necessary. Therefore it will be true."

Orwell did not like London at the best of times, but he bonded with it at the worst of times. The Blitz began on September 7, 1940, and the truth is that Orwell found it rather exciting. The puritan in him appreciated the hardship; the socialist savoured the enforced solidarity; the man of action thrilled to the thunder of bombs, the burning sky, the barrage balloons blushing pink in the flames' glow, the strangely soothing rhythm of anti-aircraft fire. Cyril Connolly suspected that Orwell "felt enormously at home in the Blitz, among the bombs, the bravery, the rubble, the shortages, the homeless, the signs of rising revolutionary temper."

During the flight from Dunkirk, Orwell and Connolly had taken a stroll through the park and observed Londoners playing cricket and pushing prams as if nothing was wrong. "They'll behave like this until the bombs start dropping, and then they'll panic," Connolly predicted. Yet, as Orwell later noted, they didn't; "they preserved the ordinary pattern of their lives to a surprising extent." There were times when Orwell could walk through London and observe a stubborn normality, and others when it felt as if life had been broken into pieces and reassembled as an absurd mosaic. A deserted Oxford Street sparkling with shattered glass. A hillock of department store mannequins which looked, from a distance, like a mound of corpses. London Zoo selling off its animals because there was not enough food to feed them. Two dazed young women, their faces masked with dirt, asking Orwell, "Please sir, can you tell us where we are?" A city of fragments. One morning, his close friend Inez Holden found herself staring at a tree in Regent's Park that was draped with stockings, strands of silk and a brand-new bowler hat—colourful debris from a hotel that had been bombed the night before. She bumped into a friend who was a surrealist painter. "Of course we were painting this sort of thing years ago," he said, "but it has taken some time to get here."

Orwell thought Britain required radical transformation of a different kind. The sight of garish advertising posters on the tube just after Dunkirk sparked a flash of apocalyptic disgust worthy of Comstock: "How much rubbish this war will sweep away, if only we can hang on throughout the summer." Having tried pacifism and made a conflicted case for quietism, Orwell now alighted on revolutionary patriotism. In "My Country Right or Left," published that autumn, he painted a melodramatic picture of street fighting and socialist militias in the Ritz. In his diary, he was increasingly disgusted by the selfishness of the rich, whom he compared to the Russian aristocracy in 1916: "Apparently nothing will ever teach these people that the other 99% of the population exists." In two contributions to *The Betrayal of the Left*, the essay anthology that Victor Gollancz assembled in order to articulate his anguish over the Nazi-Soviet Pact, Orwell echoed the old POUM line: "We cannot beat Hitler without passing through revolution, nor consolidate our revolution without beating Hitler."

Orwell expanded on this idea in his remarkable pamphlet *The Lion and the Unicorn: Socialism and the English Genius*. In January, Warburg had introduced Orwell to the German-born Zionist writer Tosco Fyvel to discuss Britain's war aims. Fyvel raised the idea of commissioning a series of pamphlets "written in simple language without the rubber-stamp political jargon of the past," under the name Searchlight Books. Stephen Spender, *Daily Mirror* columnist William Connor (aka "Cassandra") and the socialist science-fiction writer Olaf Stapledon were among the contributors. So too, after some hesitation, was Orwell. *The Lion and the Unicorn* is unmistakably the product of a very peculiar year, but it was both his finest writing about England ("a land of snobbery and privilege, ruled largely by the old and silly," yet "bound together by an invisible chain") and his strongest argument for socialism: he proposed the nationalisation of industry, progressive taxation, the abolition of private education, and independence for India. Foreshadowing the horror of Airstrip One's surveillance state, Orwell celebrated "the *privateness* of English life . . . The most hateful of all names in an English ear is Nosey Parker." Fyvel called it "the only really positive, optimistic book he ever wrote." Eileen's assessment was typically droll and irreverent. "George has written a little book, explaining how to be a Socialist though Tory," she told a friend.

Orwell believed that the collapse in France had changed everything by exposing beyond doubt the weakness of capitalism. For the first time, an English form of socialism—no rallies, no uniforms, no blood in the streets—was not just possible but necessary. As he wrote in a *Tribune* piece urging readers to join the Home Guard, "We are in a strange period of history in which a revolutionary has to be a patriot and a patriot has to be a revolutionary." He had come so far from the "fascising" theory behind *Coming Up for Air* that he derided the "soft-boiled intellectuals" who declared that "if we fight against the Nazis we shall 'go Nazi' ourselves," as if he had never made that claim himself. The pacifist Orwell of 1938 was now an unperson.

When *The Lion and the Unicorn* was published in February 1941, it quickly sold more than twelve thousand copies. "Here was somebody who had never been accused of being a super-patriot or pro-imperialist suddenly arguing very cogently and very effectively that this was a war that had to be supported," remembered his friend Jon Kimche, who was inspired to quit the ILP. "It was a turning point for many people like myself." Warburg, meanwhile, thought that Orwell's vision of common-sense radicalism laid the ground for Labour's election victory in 1945. So Orwell was right to see the war as an agent of social transformation, eventually. He was of course wrong to predict that victory would be impossible without revolution, but he wasn't the only writer to smell radical change in the air. After Dunkirk, H. G. Wells, the aged colossus of Edwardian literature, declared, "The revolution in England has now begun."

While they were trying to get Searchlight Books off the ground, Orwell, Fyvel and Warburg made a pilgrimage to Wells's home at Hanover Terrace, on the fringes of Regent's Park. At seventy-four, Wells was a lion in winter, but in his day he had embodied better than anyone the ability to finesse literary success into political influence, so he seemed like a good man to ask for advice. Alas, the Searchlight trio found "a querulous man who was ailing," said Fyvel. "Orwell and I both felt the loss of a boyhood hero."

CHAPTER 4

Wells-World

Orwell and H. G.

> In the early twentieth century, the vision of a future society unbelievably rich, leisured, orderly and efficient—a glittering anti-septic world of glass and steel and snow-white concrete—was part of the consciousness of nearly every literate person.
>
> —George Orwell, *Nineteen Eighty-Four*

H. G. Wells loomed over Orwell's childhood like a planet—awe-inspiring, oppressive, impossible to ignore—and Orwell never got over it. "I doubt whether anyone who was writing books between 1900 and 1920, at any rate in the English language, influenced the young so much," he wrote in his 1941 essay "Wells, Hitler and the World State." "The minds of all of us, and therefore the physical world, would be perceptibly different if Wells had never existed."

At Eton, Orwell had shared a dog-eared copy of Wells's collection *The Country of the Blind and Other Stories* with Cyril Connolly, who recalled that Orwell enjoyed the stories' "fearful, moral, morbid questions." During his summer holidays with the Buddicom family in Oxfordshire, he was a keen reader of *A Modern Utopia;* Jacintha Buddicom remembered him saying that "he might write that kind of book himself." In fact, Orwell's very first published story, when he was at Eton, was "A Peep into the Future," a Wellsian tale of an uprising against a kind of scientific theocracy. He almost met the great man himself through his well-connected aunt Nellie, a member of the Fabian Society, but it was not to be. He looked, said Buddicom, "so disappointed that I wondered if he would ever smile again."

For an ambitious, questioning young man like Orwell, Wells's books were intellectual gelignite which blew the doors off the dreary, know-your-place conformity of a respectable Edwardian childhood. In the mind of Wells, who transcended origins far humbler than Orwell's own, there was nothing a writer couldn't do with enough hard work and willpower. He was a graphomaniac who published in his lifetime more than a hundred works of fiction, non-fiction, and uncategorisable hybrids of the two, as if he could shift the world on its axis through the sheer weight of his words. "I have to overwork, with all the penalties of overworking in loss of grace and finish, to get my work done," he wrote. And his work was never done. Known as "the Man Who Invented Tomorrow," Wells predicted space travel, tanks, electric trains, wind and water power, identity cards, poison gas, the Channel tunnel and atom bombs, and popularised in fiction the time machine, Martian invasions, invisibility and genetic engineering. He was the most mesmerising, infuriating writer of his era, occupying the minds of even those who couldn't stand him. It is no exaggeration to say that the genre of dystopian fiction evolved as it did because so many people wanted to prove H. G. Wells wrong.

Orwell appears to have read everything that Wells wrote, so there was an Oedipal hue to his irresistible urge to knock down "this wonderful man" who had towered over his youth. He wondered if his attacks constituted "a sort of parricide." Starting with *The Road to Wigan Pier*, he turned Wells into a straw man: the errant prophet whose grand schemes for human improvement, propelled by the almighty machine, were at best misguided and at worst repellent. "The Socialist world is to be above all other things an *ordered* world, an *efficient* world," he wrote contemptuously. "But it is precisely from that vision of the future as a sort of glittering Wells-world that sensitive minds recoil." At any rate Orwell's mind recoiled, and that is exactly the vision derided in Goldstein's book. In "Inside the Whale," Orwell was more woundingly personal, mocking "the 'progressives,' the yea-sayers, the Shaw-Wells type, always leaping forward to embrace the ego-projections which they mistake for the future."

It's not surprising that Wells met Orwell, because Wells met everybody: several British prime ministers, four US presidents, two Soviet premiers, Henry Ford, Charlie Chaplin, Orson Welles, and almost every writer that Orwell admired. Wells's hunger for life was maddeningly insatiable. If he achieved wealth and acclaim, he craved more. If he had the love of one woman, he needed (at least) one more. If he formed a friendship, more often than not he would stretch it until it snapped. Almost as soon as he joined a political group or alliance, he was desperate to quit. Wherever he was in his life, geographically, intellectually, emotionally, Wells longed to be elsewhere, hence his enthusiasm for utopias. The value of the form, he wrote, "lies in that regard towards human freedom, in the undying interest of the human power of self-escape, the power to resist the causation of the past, and to evade, initiate, endeavour and overcome." This was the story of Wells's life.

Herbert George "Bertie" Wells was a petulant, demanding child and, in some respects, remained one until his death at the age of seventy-nine. But his colossal egotism was tempered by a keen awareness, albeit usually retrospective, of his shortcomings and mistakes.

He was born on September 21, 1866, in Bromley, one of London's fast-growing suburbs, to a pair of servants-turned-shopkeepers. He came to see his father as a failure and his mother as a religious fanatic, and treated his older brothers with "vindictive resentment and clamorous aggression." As a boy, he fantasised about mighty battles in the fields of Kent, in which he played the benign dictator who could wrench the masses back onto the right path with his unparalleled wisdom and strength. In 1934, startlingly, he described Hitler as "nothing more than one of my thirteen year old reveries come real." Rejecting the paths laid out for him—religious conformity and the drapery business—he secured a scholarship to the Normal School of Science in South Kensington in 1884. It was his first feat of self-escape.

Studying under the evolutionary biologist Thomas Henry Huxley strengthened Wells's belief in both the potential of science to cure humankind's ills, and its fragility. Reading Henry George's *Progress and Poverty* sparked his curiosity about socialism. In one combination or another, these two interests would guide his thinking for the rest of his life. With his charm, wit, energy and bracing intolerance for orthodoxy and humbug, Wells became a star of the Debating Society. His talk "The Past and Present of the Future Race" explored ideas that would reappear in his novels. He began writing short stories about the future, too. But his strengths did not include exam performance, and he left South Kensington after three years with a crushing sense of rejection and panic. "I had done practically everything necessary to ensure failure and dismissal, but when these came they found me planless and amazed."

Wells became a schoolteacher. In 1891, he ventured into journalism with his essay "The Rediscovery of the Unique," describing science as "a match that man has just got alight"—one which, instead of illuminating a room full of wonders, draws attention to the vast darkness beyond its puny glow. This first Age of Anxiety afflicted Britain as well as America. During the last years of the century, many writers were consumed by the idea of decadence and decline. Before he became an apostle of progress, Wells tapped into the apocalyptic vein of his imagination, with spectacular success.

The New Review began serialising Wells's first novel, *The Time Machine*, in 1895, and immediately struck a nerve. *The Review of Reviews* declared, "H. G. Wells is a man of genius." For over a century, writers had been transporting characters to the future via a long sleep. It took Wells to come up with the time machine and therefore the concept of time *travel*. According to James Gleick in *Time Travel: A History*, "When Wells in his lamp-lit room imagined a time machine, he also invented a new mode of thought." His pessimism was just as innovative. The critic Mark Hillegas called *The Time Machine* "the first well-executed, imaginatively coherent picture of a future worse than the present." The word *Wellsian* came to mean belief in an orderly scientific utopia, but the four science-fiction landmarks he wrote between 1895 and 1898—*The Time Machine, The Island of Dr. Moreau, The Invisible Man* and *The War of the Worlds*—not to mention short stories such as "A Story of the Days to Come," are cautionary tales of progress thwarted, science abused and complacency punished. Wells was not yet Wellsian.

His career was up and running. "It's rather pleasant to find oneself something in the world after all the years of trying and disappointment," he told his mother. He quickly made literary friends, many of whom also had the restive insecurity of outsiders, and saw in the new century at a spectacular house party in Sussex, hosted by the American novelist Stephen Crane, in the company of Henry James, Joseph Conrad, George Gissing, H. Rider Haggard and Ford Madox Ford. "It did not take us long to realize that here was Genius," wrote Ford. "Authentic, real Genius . . . And all Great London lay prostrate at his feet."

Wells was often called England's answer to Jules Verne, but both writers rejected the comparison. "I make use of physics," said Verne. "He invents." Among other things, the much older man represented a more optimistic generation. Wells spoke to a time when everybody realised that immense change was happening but nobody knew whether it was leading to heaven or hell. Science could create celestial miracles or unspeakable monstrosities. Great men could be benevolent supermen or power-crazed maniacs. The future must lead, via entropy, to the icy black void but perhaps, before then, to paradise. Wells filled the reader's head with wonders: spacemen, beast-men and men who could not be seen; time machines, flying machines and death machines; a "world of cooling stars and battling dinosaurs," as Orwell put it.

Wells assimilated new material at terrific speed. He would seize on some new theory or invention, combine it with one of the latest fictional trends—lost worlds, double identities, foreign invasions, mad scientists—and ground it in reality by using some device—a machine, a door, a scientific experiment—to transport his protagonist from Victorian England to another time or place. "I had realised that the more impossible the story I had to tell, the more ordinary must be the setting," he wrote. He dreamed up *The War of the Worlds* while cycling around Woking, imposing Martian tripods onto the Surrey countryside, and taking great pleasure in "selecting South Kensington for feats of particular atrocity."

Wells's early science fiction was exhilarating because it swarmed with ideas rather than messages. His imagination was too large and conflicted to stiffen into didacticism. In a review of another writer, he offered some sound advice that he later forgot: "the philosopher who masquerades as a novelist, violating the conditions of art that his gospel may win notoriety, discredits both himself and his message." *The War of the Worlds* may contain an implicit critique of imperialism but that has no bearing on the reader's enjoyment, and the only character with a clear plan for the future is the Artilleryman, a proto-fascist blowhard who looks forward to building a new society of "able-bodied, clean-minded men." If Wells's hopes were outsized, then so were his fears, and his early work was a struggle to reconcile his reason with his nightmares.

That dissonance was particularly intense in his 1899 novel, *When the Sleeper Wakes*, the first time that politics overtook science in his fiction. As a gripping read, Wells later admitted, it fell short of its peers. Overworked, he rushed the conclusion and only fixed some of the structural problems when he rewrote it in 1910 as *The Sleeper Awakes*. But it still became one of the most enduringly influential anti-utopias. "Everyone who has ever read *The Sleeper Wakes* [*sic*] remembers it," Orwell wrote. "It is a vision of a glittering, sinister world in which society has hardened into a caste system and the workers are permanently enslaved." That word again: *glittering*. In *Nineteen Eighty-Four*, it describes both the Ministry of Truth and the Ministry of Love.

Wells was unapologetically inspired by Edward Bellamy, to the point of making his Sleeper, Graham, acknowledge that *Looking Backward* "oddly anticipated this actual experience." But when Graham wakes up from a trance after 203 years, he does not find a socialist paradise. London has evolved instead into a mega-city of thirty-three million souls: a "gigantic glass hive" where the privileged grow flabby in decadent "Pleasure Cities" while, far below them, the masses toil in squalor. Wells called it "our contemporary world in a state of highly inflamed distention."

The genealogy of *Nineteen Eighty-Four*, and indeed all dystopian fiction, starts here. The role of technology is to maintain control. The enslaved masses are uniformed in blue like Orwell's Outer Party, and kept in line by the Labour Police. Children are raised in state crèches. Books are burned, pornography rampant, and the English language crudely reduced, with print replaced by phonographs and "kinetotelephotographs," Wells's version of the telescreen. On every street, Babble Machines blurt propaganda, advertisements, and "idiotic slang," and hypnotists stand ready "to print permanent memories on the mind . . . conversely memories could be effaced, habits removed, and desires eradicated—a sort of psychic surgery was, in fact, in general use." The problem with Wells's "nightmare of capitalism triumphant" is that it is not fully a nightmare. "It suffers from vast contradictions," wrote Orwell, "because of the fact that Wells, as the arch-priest of 'progress,' cannot write with any conviction *against* 'progress.'"

While Graham sleeps, compound interest makes him the unspeakably rich, quasi-divine "Master of the Earth," and the world is ruled on his behalf by his trustees, the White Council. His awakening is no chance event but a plot to facilitate a coup led by Ostrog, a brutal Nietzschean strongman who rubbishes socialism and democracy as "worn-out dreams of the nineteenth century." Before Graham can talk himself into fighting Ostrog, he has to get over his admiration for the cruelly efficient rulers and their marvellous machines, and to develop some fellow feeling for the "monstrous crowds." Wells seems as disappointed as Graham to find that this hi-tech state is incompatible with liberty, describing his conflicted hero's revolt as "the impulse of passionate inadequacy against inevitable things." The author gives Ostrog a brilliantly villainous monologue:

> The hope of mankind—what is it? That some day the Overman may come, that some day the inferior, the weak and the bestial may be subdued or eliminated . . . The world is no place for the bad, the stupid, the enervated. Their duty—it's a fine duty too!—is to die. The death of the failure! That is the path by which the beast rose to manhood, by which man goes on to higher things.

Yet Ostrog is a baleful version of the kind of capable, antidemocratic elitist that Wells would spend the rest of his life valorising. The character's name alluded to Moisey Ostrogorsky, a Russian political scientist whose work Wells admired. So the writer could not decide whether Ostrog was merely a brutal tyrant or a visionary with a point.

As the new century drew near, Wells saw a gap in the market for a man who could describe the shape of things to come. "For this year," he told his agent in 1899, "I'm the futurity man." The world was entering the age of the motor car, the motion picture and the aeroplane; of socialism, feminism and free love (a cause in which Wells took an energetic personal interest); of upheavals in every area of life. "The old local order has been broken up or is now being broken up all over the earth," he wrote in 1905's *A Modern Utopia*, "and everywhere societies deliquesce, everywhere men are afloat amidst the wreckage of their flooded conventions." Just as he had articulated the fears of the 1890s, he now sought to express the high hopes of the 1900s, and fiction was no longer enough.

Wells called *Anticipations of the Reaction of Mechanical and Scientific Progress Upon Human Life and Thought* "the keystone to the main arch of my work." Unlike his scientific romances, it was to be an unprecedented work of "sober forecasting" based on contemporary trends: a discipline he called "Human Ecology." The technological soothsaying was merely the bait, he told a friend; *Anticipations* was "designed to undermine and destroy the monarch, monogamy, faith in God & respectability—& the British Empire, all under the guise of a speculation about motor cars & electrical heating."

Wells firmly believed that scientific progress was incompatible with existing social and political structures. Humankind's best hope, therefore, was a single World State governed by a meritocratic elite. In *Anticipations* this ruling clique was named the New Republic, after Plato; later, he called it the Samurai, then the Open Conspiracy. But while the fundamental idea remained intact, Wells kept changing his mind about who the members of this elite should be, how they should reorganise society, and whether they could be trusted not to abuse their power. Joseph Conrad was quick to spot Wells's fatal weakness: "Generally the fault I find with you is that you do not take sufficient account of human imbecility which is cunning and perfidious." It was not that Wells didn't recognise irrationality; more that he believed in the power of great men to conquer, and ultimately extinguish, it.

Wells's vision was impressive—his prediction of three multinational "coalescences" by the year 2000 anticipated Orwell's Oceania, Eurasia and Eastasia—but his conviction that the greatest obstacle to progress was overpopulation led him badly astray in his final chapter, which reads appallingly like a collaboration between Malthus, Ostrog and the Artilleryman. His solution to the problem of "inferior" people, whom he termed "the people of the Abyss," is matter-of-factly genocidal: "Well, the world is a world, not a charitable institution, and I take it they will have to go." The idea that the New Republic would "have an ideal that will make killing worth the while" drew sharp criticism from readers including G. K. Chesterton and Arthur Conan Doyle, and Wells went to great lengths to make amends in his later designs for the future. Still, to Wells, humanity was always a mess that needed tidying up.

Despite its disturbing conclusion, *Anticipations* was a remarkable success when it was published in 1901. Suddenly, Britain thought as highly of H. G. Wells's intellect as he did. When the novelist and critic Arnold Bennett, one of his closest friends, wrote to say that he must be either "one of the most remarkable men alive" or a superb confidence man, Wells replied: "There is no illusion. I *am* great." The book transformed him from a popular novelist into a respected public intellectual, and became his passport to the great and good. He joined both the Fabian Society and the Coefficients, an informal brains trust of politicians and philosophers. Beatrice Webb, a leading member of both groups, found this new arrival both exasperating and refreshing in his determination to throw aside orthodox thinking and become "an explorer of a new world."

While *Anticipations* established Wells as a prophet, it kneecapped him as a writer of scientific romances. On a mission to propagandise for a better world, he lost the pungent ambivalence that made his early stories so compelling and became increasingly pedagogic and emotionally chilly. Over the next decade or so, he tried out various fantastical routes to utopia in *The Food of the Gods and How It Came to Earth, In the Days of the Comet, The War in the Air* and *The World Set Free*, which predicted atomic bombs thirty-two years before the fact. "Heaven defend us from his Utopias!" cried *The Nation*'s reviewer. "But we like his explosions."

Wells was proudest of *A Modern Utopia,* in which two men hiking in the Alps stumble into a parallel-universe Earth ruled by the Samurai, a puritanical caste of "voluntary noblemen." On one level, the book was a running argument with everyone from More and Bacon to Bellamy and Morris, ribbing their "imaginary laws to fit incredible people." Wells attempted to reintroduce liberty, individuality, privacy and fun to a genre known for its "strange and inhuman" perfection, and to replace tedious serenity with dynamic change: a "kinetic" utopia rather than a "static" one. It was also an advance on *Anticipations*, introducing equality of sexes and races, and milder forms of population control. Wells's pleasantly efficient parallel Earth, "like a well-oiled engine beside a scrap heap," is not a perfect world, just a better one. "There will be many Utopias," he concludes. "Each generation will have its new version of Utopia, a little more certain and complete and real."

As a teenager, Orwell was entranced by *A Modern Utopia*, but you would never guess that from his later writing about Wells. "We all want to abolish the things Wells wants to abolish," he wrote in 1943. "But is there anyone who actually wants to live in a Wellsian Utopia? On the contrary, not to live in a world like that, not to wake up in a hygienic garden suburb infested by naked schoolmarms, has actually become a conscious political motive." Hitler, he thought, was proof of that. Instead of peace and pleasure, the Führer promised the German people "struggle, danger and death," and they drank it up.

Some of Wells's contemporaries grew frustrated with his utopias, too. Joseph Conrad fell out with him around this time, saying, "The difference between us, Wells, is fundamental. You don't care for humanity but think they are to be improved. I love humanity but know they are not!" Clement Attlee named Wells as the archetypal scientific reformer whose "besetting sin . . . is his failure to make allowance for the idiosyncrasies of the individual."

E. M. Forster, meanwhile, was moved to respond in the form of a short story. In 1909, between *A Room With a View* and *Howards End*, Forster published "The Machine Stops," an enduringly brilliant "counterblast to one of the heavens of H. G. Wells." The twentieth century filled him with dread, he wrote in his diary: "Science, instead of freeing man . . . is enslaving him to machines . . . God what a prospect! The little houses that I am used to will be swept away, the fields will stink of petrol, and the airships will shatter the stars."

A complete novice in science fiction, Forster pilfered most of his futuristic ideas from books like *A Modern Utopia, When the Sleeper Wakes* and *The First Men in the Moon,* turning Wells's imagination against him. The citizens of Forster's subterranean future state live in a hi-tech cocoon where everything they need—light, air, food, water, music, company—is delivered by the holy Machine. Reduced to weak, pasty lumps by inactivity, they can deliver lectures and speak to their "several thousand" friends around the world via video: a premonition of YouTube, Skype and Facebook. Some airships remain in service, but few bother to use them because the Machine has made everywhere the same: "What was the good of going to Pekin when it was just like Shrewsbury?" The more powerful the Machine becomes, the more people rely on it; the more they rely on it, the more powerful it becomes. Technology itself is the tyrant. "Progress had come to mean the progress of the Machine."

Finally, mysteriously, the Machine begins to fail, but the people are too enslaved to protest. They tolerate the stinking bathwater and rotting artificial fruit until the terminal day when civilisation collapses. Forster's fable about addiction to technology includes one strikingly proto-Orwellian idea. In a society where "terrestrial facts" are anathema, history is endlessly rewritten until perfection is achieved by the "absolutely colourless" generation "which will see the French Revolution not as it happened, nor as they would like it to have happened, but as it would have happened had it taken place in the days of the Machine."

Such an elaborate retort was proof of Wells's cultural impact. *A Modern Utopia* puffed him up with enough confidence to attempt a coup that would transform the gradualist Fabian Society into a revolutionary order of Samurai: a "confused, tedious, ill-conceived and ineffectual campaign" that he would come to consider the most embarrassing episode of his career. Working with other people was a skill Wells would never learn. Webb remarked, "He has neither the patience nor the good manners needed for cooperative effort—and just at present his conceit is possibly disabling." Like Bellamy and Orwell, Wells did not accept the prevailing version of socialism (he considered Marxism "an enfeebling mental epidemic of spite"), so he had to design his own "plan for the reconstruction of human life, for the replacement of a disorder by order, for the making of a state in which mankind shall live bravely and beautifully beyond our present imagining."

Wells's arrogance and impatience immunised him against the twin viruses of fascism and communism which infected so many of his contemporaries between the wars. Nobody else's ideology could compete with the wonderful plans in his head.

—

It is commonplace to wonder what Orwell's reputation would now be had he lived past forty-six, but it's just as interesting to ask what would have happened if Wells *hadn't*. "Many writers, perhaps most, ought simply to stop writing when they reach middle age," Orwell wrote. "Unfortunately our society will not let him stop." He thought that even the best writers only enjoy fifteen years of brilliance, and presented Wells's career as Exhibit A. Between *The Time Machine* in 1895 and *The Sleeper Awakes* in 1910, Wells wrote all of his lasting fiction: the scientific romances, the most persuasive utopias, the comic novels of middle-class frustration such as *Kipps* and *The History of Mr. Polly,* and the book he considered his masterpiece, *Tono-Bungay.** Had he lived precisely as long as Orwell, he would have died on April 19, 1913, his reputation impregnable. Instead, he had another thirty-three years in which to be wrong.

Wells had predicted world wars, including one initiated by Germany, in both *The War in the Air* and *The World Set Free.* Indeed when Ford Madox Ford joined the army and arrived at the Western Front, he had been so forewarned by Wells that he felt strangely underwhelmed. But on a fundamental level Wells did not believe that governments were imbecilic enough to actually let it happen. Once it did, he could not accept that such a disaster wouldn't shock humanity to its senses. On the evening of August 4, 1914, the day Britain declared war on Germany, he sat down to write an essay with the unfortunately memorable title "The War That Will End War."

The war unravelled Wells, physically (his hair began falling out) and mentally. "The return to complete sanity took the greater part of two years," he wrote. He became such a fierce jingo that some of his pacifist friends never forgave him. He then outraged his secularist admirers by undergoing a bizarre and short-lived religious conversion. He liked to claim he had invented the tank in his 1903 story "The Land Ironclads" (until he was eventually sued by the man who

---

* *Kipps* is the kind of novel Orwell meant when he referred to *Coming Up for Air* as "Wells watered down. I have a great admiration for Wells, i.e. as a writer, and he was a very early influence on me." Note "as a writer." Not as a thinker.

had), and was aggrieved that the army declined to make full use of his brilliance. Not until 1918 did Lord Northcliffe, owner of the *Daily Mail* and the new director of propaganda, draw Wells into the war effort, hiring him to write fake newspapers that would rain down on German soldiers to sap their morale. He lasted a few weeks.

Wells could predict machines but not how they would interact with human nature. He thought air war, for example, by obliterating the difference between combatant and civilian, would be so horrific that nobody would dare engage in it. In fact, nations proved to be remarkably comfortable with slaughtering the innocent from a great height. He then believed that such a cataclysmic war would surely lead to "a wave of sanity" that would bring down militarism, imperialism and aristocracy and lead to a worldwide confederation of socialist states. He therefore threw himself into the movement to form a post-war League of Nations, but grew predictably impatient with its poverty of vision. Once again, he felt like a giant surrounded by pygmies, and now he could feel his power and reputation waning. In a devastating essay called "The Late Mr. Wells," the critic H. L. Mencken concluded, "he suffers from a messianic delusion—and once a man begins to suffer from a messianic delusion his days as a serious artist are ended."

The war changed everything. In 1918, Orwell later remembered, "there was, among the young, a curious cult of hatred of 'old men.' The dominance of 'old men' was held to be responsible for every evil known to humanity." Wells, at fifty-two, qualified as an "old man." "My boom is over," he told Arnold Bennett. "I've had my boom. I'm yesterday."

Yet Wells always believed he could begin again, and he chose to wrench himself out of his post-war funk by writing nothing less than the entire history of the human race. What his 1920 epic *The Outline of History* lacked in historical rigour it made up for in vigour, propelling the reader, as Winston Churchill said, all the way "from nebula to the Third International." To Wells, history had a rhythm, a cycle. Nations were elevated by the creative energy of a Samurai-like caste, stagnated under the stewardship of an oppressive bureaucracy, and finally succumbed to barbarians. He thought that the world was now deep into the second phase and required a new generation of Samurai to start again.

The Outline sold two million copies in the UK and US alone. With both his bank account and his ego bulging anew, Wells was ready to take on the world again. He accepted an invitation from the Russian novelist Maxim Gorky, whom he had met in New York in 1906, to visit post-Revolutionary Russia, a trip which included a conversation with Lenin himself. To his surprise, he found Lenin to be an "amazing little man" whose pragmatism was "very refreshing"—for a Marxist. Alas, the admiration wasn't mutual. According to Trotsky, the Russian leader snorted, "What a narrow petty bourgeois! Ugh! What a Philistine!"

Even the success of *The Outline* could not rid Wells of the sickening sense that he was wasting his time and talent. Dipping his toe back into politics by joining the Labour Party and standing twice (unsuccessfully) for Parliament did nothing to relieve his dissatisfaction. His love life was untenable, as his inability to choose between his long-suffering wife, Jane, and long-standing mistress, Rebecca West, led West to break off their affair in 1923. On a trip to Geneva, Wells fell for a writer named Odette Keun and began spending time with her on the French Riviera, even when, later, Jane was dying of cancer. Boredom, his arch-enemy, had been vanquished yet again.

Tedium was, however, a growing problem for his readers, as Wells became fixated on the latest incarnation of his heroic elite, the Open Conspiracy. In *Men Like Gods,* an anxious, overworked journalist is rejuvenated by falling into a perfect parallel-universe Earth where the state has withered away. He returns to the 1920s determined to "never desist nor rest again until old Earth is one city and Utopia set up therein." In *The Dream,* a scientist in the year 4000 dreams the entire life of an ordinary man in the "fear-haunted world" of the early twentieth century. Wells remained dedicated to explaining his dreams—always a risky endeavour—but readers preferred his nightmares.

Orwell took against *The Dream* and *Men Like Gods* in *The Road to Wigan Pier.* He thought that Wells's comfortable, foolproof utopias, by removing all pain and danger, would diminish many of the human qualities that Wells admired. Wells thought that whether machines were used to liberate or enslave, to elevate or destroy, was a question of leadership. Like Forster, Orwell thought that Wells could not accept that the machine itself might be the problem: "a huge glittering vehicle whirling us we are not certain where, but probably towards the padded Wells-world and the brain in the bottle." In the same chapter, Orwell praised Aldous Huxley's *Brave New World* as "a memorable assault on the more fat-bellied type of perfectionism. Allowing for the exaggerations of caricature, it probably expresses what a majority of thinking people feel about machine-civilization."

Wells had a complicated relationship with the Huxley family. Thomas changed his life, Thomas's grandson Julian helped him write the 1929 biology textbook *Science of Life,* and now Julian's brother Aldous was making fun of his utopias. Decades later, Huxley told *The Paris Review* that *Brave New World* "started out as a parody of H. G. Wells's *Men Like Gods* but gradually it got out of hand and turned into something quite different from what I'd originally intended."

Brave New World and *Nineteen Eighty-Four* are awkward literary twins. Most readers discover them around the same age, in a kind of two-for-one deal on classic dystopias, and therefore see them as rival prophecies, as if both authors were, at the same point in time, given the same brief to predict the future, and now we have to decide which was the more accurate. Pleasure or punishment? Sex or death? A hit of soma or a boot in the face? Who got it right?

Huxley later attempted to retrofit *Brave New World* as a serious prophecy, making sure to inform Orwell: "I feel that the nightmare of *Nineteen Eighty-Four* is destined to modulate into the nightmare of a world having more resemblance to that which I imagined in *Brave New World*." But he wrote it as a Swiftian satire. While working on it in France during the summer of 1931, he revealed in a letter: "I am writing a novel about the future—on the horror of the Wellsian utopia and a revolt against it. Very difficult. I have hardly enough imagination to deal with such a subject." So he used someone else's imagination. *Brave New World* is full of Wellsian ideas made ludicrous or sinister. Huxley had previously poked fun at Wells's schemes in *Crome Yellow* and *Point Counter Point,* described him privately as "a rather horrid, vulgar little man," and written a sheaf of essays fretting about technological progress. "Men no longer amuse themselves, creatively, but sit and are passively amused by mechanical devices," he complained in "Spinoza's Worm." *Brave New World*'s epigraph is a quote from the Russian philosopher Nicolas Berdiaeff: "Utopias appear much more realizable than we had formerly supposed. And now we find ourselves faced with a question which is painful in quite a new way: How can we avoid their final realization?"

Huxley was writing in a different world from Orwell. Although Mussolini and Stalin were already in power, the totalitarian era was in its infancy. And Huxley was not really thinking about Europe. In 1926, he had sailed from Asia to California and spent a few weeks stoking the engines of his snobbery by exploring the American scene at the height of the Jazz Age. On the boat, he found a copy of Henry Ford's *My Life and Work*, which became the basis for *Brave New World's* mechanised religion, Fordism. He planned to return to America one day, "just to know the worst, as one must do from time to time."

Huxley's World State (the phrase a blatant dig at Wells) is kept in line not by the truncheon and the whip, but by drugs, hypnotism, entertainment, and a genetically engineered caste system, running from the Alpha-Plus elite down to the Epsilon-Minus labourers. With its skyscrapers, zippers, chewing gum, "sexophones" and "feelies" (a tactile version of the talkies), the novel drew heavily on his travels in America, where he called Los Angeles the "City of Dreadful Joy." Huxley would end up spending the last twenty-six years of his life in California, but his first impression was damning: "It is all movement and noise, like the water gurgling out of a bath—down the waste." Huxley's satire didn't stop at America. He also mocked Freud, Keynes, and, via his imagined "Savage Reservation," the romantic primitivism of his late friend D. H. Lawrence. By invoking famous industrialists, Marxists, atheists, scientists, psychiatrists and politicians in the names of his characters, Huxley implied that all great men, and all great movements, were tending in the same dire direction.

The book was further complicated by the fact that Huxley was attracted to some of the ideas he parodied. Like his brother Julian, he was intrigued by eugenics, and the economic crisis that wracked Britain while he was writing the novel led him to think that some loss of freedom might be a price worth paying to preserve order over chaos. As Mustapha Mond, the Resident World Controller for Western Europe, rather seductively puts it, "What's the point of truth or beauty or knowledge when anthrax bombs are popping all around you?"

Orwell admired *Brave New World,* up to a point. He had fond memories of being taught by Huxley at Eton in 1918; a classmate claimed Huxley had given Orwell a "taste for words and their accurate and significant use." But as someone who was fearful of pain and suspicious of pleasure, he was unconvinced by *Brave New World*'s tyranny of gratification. "There is no power-hunger, no sadism, no hardness of any kind," he complained in 1946. "Those at the top have no strong motive for staying at the top, and though everyone is happy in a vacuous way, life has become so pointless that it is difficult to believe that such a society could endure." Orwell's dystopia delivers neither freedom nor happiness. It does not glitter. So both writers found each other's version of a bleak future implausible. The similarities are negligible, the differences profound, but the two books do overlap in one area: the status of the proles.

Orwell's description of the proles is the least persuasive element of *Nineteen Eighty-Four.* It is hardly credible that a regime obsessed with absolute control would allow 85 per cent of the population to live beyond the reach of the Thought Police and telescreens, nor that the proles would be immune to doublethink. As Russia and Germany demonstrated, you can't have totalitarianism without the masses. What Orwell is doing is satirising two incompatible political systems. While the operation of the Party represents totalitarianism, the world of the proles is a caricature of capitalism which functions, albeit more shabbily, rather like the society in *Brave New World.*

In *The Road to Wigan Pier,* Orwell dismissed the "bread and circuses" theory that the British government was deliberately anaesthetising the masses with cheap food, mass media and consumer goods. It happened, he wrote, because of "the quite natural interaction between the manufacturer's need for a market and the need of half-starved people for cheap palliatives." In *Nineteen Eighty-Four,* however, it is both a deliberate tactic and an utterly effective one. The proles are lulled into apathy by a steady diet of movies, pulp fiction, pornography, horoscopes, football, beer, gambling and sentimental songs. This is their soma.

The success of this strategy makes the proles impotent but not contemptible. Orwell did not suffer from the same acerbic snobbishness as Huxley. Winston comes to believe that the proles are, in fact, superior to Party members—not because, as he initially imagines, they are a potential revolutionary army but simply because they "had stayed human. They had not become hardened inside." They are not the dead. When Winston watches a woman hanging out the washing, she may be singing a banal ditty vomited out by a versificator, but she suffuses it with humanity and a thrush-like purity. "The birds sang, the proles sang, the Party did not sing." And what is this supposedly meaningless song about? Love, dreams, and memories that do not fade. With this simple, human act, the woman unwittingly validates Winston's belief: "If there is hope, it lies in the proles."

Brave New World was the first bestselling anti-utopia, and its Shake-spearean title became famous enough to be widely referenced. Labour MP Hugh Dalton jokingly called an underwhelming 1939 speech by Clement Attlee "Vague New World." The following year, Malcolm Muggeridge described the clash between Nazism and communism as "a Brave New World and a Brave Old World facing one another and menacingly flourishing the same weapons." In *Keep the Aspidistra Flying,* Comstock imagines a socialist society as "some kind of Aldous Huxley *Brave New World:* only not so amusing." The novel's success inspired a fresh vogue for futuristic satires. Even Cyril Connolly weighed in with his playful short story "Year Nine," set in a totalitarian state where Our Leader's face looms down from neon signs and military censors roam the streets, eliminating "degenerate art" (like the novels of "Deadwells") left over from the old regime.

And what did Wells make of *Brave New World*? Huxley had dinner with him on the Riviera just after the book came out and wrote that the older man, "I fear, wasn't best pleased with it." Indeed not. Wells later called the novel "a great disappointment to me. A writer of the standing of Aldous Huxley has no right to betray the future as he did in that book."

Wells struck back in fiction, describing *Brave New World* as a "Bible of the impotent genteel" in *The New World Order,* and Huxley as "one of the most brilliant of the reactionary writers" in *The Shape of Things to Come,* the last book he wrote before his extravagantly entertaining autobiography. Wells framed his latest history of the future as a textbook from 2106, read in a dream by a diplomat from 1933. The "Age of Frustration," it transpires, descended into another world war, economic collapse and a virulent plague which brought civilisation to its knees. The world was rescued from chaos by an elite of airmen, who established a "Puritan Tyranny." Comrade Ogilvy, the war hero invented by Winston Smith, sounds rather like one of Wells's airmen: celibate, abstinent, obsessively athletic, utterly joyless. After a century of this necessary evil, the Dictatorship of the Air was gently overthrown by a peaceful utopia of middle-class intellectuals—every one an Alpha.

During the 1920s, Wells had mentally auditioned bankers and industrialists for roles in his Open Conspiracy, but the 1929 crash and subsequent depression had found them sorely wanting. He now considered himself "an ultra-left revolutionary" and, in 1934, set off to visit two of the potential architects of a socialist world state. In Washington, DC, he found President Franklin Delano Roosevelt to be "the most effective transmitting instrument possible for the coming of the new world order." In Moscow, he attempted for three hours to convince Stalin that Marxism was hogwash and what he was really building was a version of the New Deal's state capitalism. Wells is justly criticised for his conviction that he had "never met a man more candid, fair and honest," but he wasn't gulled as thoroughly as Beatrice and Sidney Webb or George Bernard Shaw.* He wrote that Soviet Russia was not the Cosmopolis he had hoped for and he grew tired of people telling him, "Come and see us again in ten years' time." They'd said that in 1920 as well. Ultimately, he thought, "Russia had let me down." The wording typifies Wells's sense that humanity was personally disappointing him, despite his best efforts to light the way forward. One friend compared him, in this exasperated mode, to "a disgruntled inspector-general of the universe."

During his travels, Wells was writing a scenario of *The Shape of Things to Come* (abbreviated to *Things to Come*) for film producer Alexander Korda. He liked the possibility of using cinema as a vehicle for his ideas. The cinema of science fiction was still in its infancy, the crowning example to date being Fritz Lang's *Metropolis.*† Although

---

* Malcolm Muggeridge told Orwell that the Webbs, his aunt and uncle by marriage, had withheld inconvenient facts about the USSR from their book *Soviet Communism: A New Civilization?*, a shameful whitewash.
† The phrase *science fiction* began to replace the earlier *scientifiction* in 1929.

it was based on a Wellsian novel by Thea von Harbou, Lang's wife, Wells was not flattered by the homage. In his *New York Times* review, he did to *Metropolis* what his Martians did to Woking: "It gives in one eddying concentration almost every possible foolishness, cliché, platitude, and muddlement about mechanical progress and progress in general served up with a sauce of sentimentality that is all its own." Identifying "decaying fragments" of *The Sleeper Awakes*, he thought Lang's vision of a vertical city built on slavery foolishly outdated.

Yet *Things to Come*, released in 1936, fell well short of *Metropolis*, notable more for its designs (including its prophetic image of bombers over London) than for its ideas, which managed to offend communists, fascists, liberals and Christians alike. Wells, blaming Korda, called it "a mess of a film." Orwell first attacked Wells in the year the film came out, so the chilly self-caricature of *Things to Come* was most likely what he meant when he complained about the glittering Wells-World.

Orwell never equated technology with progress. On the contrary, he wrote during the war, "every scientific advance speeds up the trend towards nationalism and dictatorship." It was in a review of Wells's scenario for *Things to Come* that he mocked what he called the author's false antithesis between the benign scientist and the bellicose reactionary. "It never occurred to Mr. Wells that his categories might have got mixed, that it might be the reactionary who would make the fullest use of the machine and that the scientist might use his brains chiefly on race-theory and poison gas." That wasn't fair at all. The creator of the Invisible Man and Doctor Moreau was no stranger to perverted science. But *Things to Come* did his reputation no favours.

Judging from *The Road to Wigan Pier*, if Orwell had written a dystopia in the 1930s it would probably have been an anti-machine satire along the lines of *Brave New World*, attacking what he envisioned in a 1933 letter as "all-round trustification and Fordification, with the entire population reduced to docile wage-slaves," mercilessly exploited "in the name of Progress." But notwithstanding a few futuristic elements, like the supersized Ministry of Truth, sordid, exhausted Airstrip One is a long way from Wells-World. In *Nineteen Eighty-Four*, white-coated scientists design telescreens and spy helicopters, invent new weapons, defoliants and torture devices, practise radical plastic surgery, and work on abolishing the orgasm, while doing nothing to improve the quality of life. For the most part, science, like history, has stopped. This, writes Goldstein, is "partly because scientific and technical progress depended on the empirical habit of thought, which could not survive in a strictly regimented society. As a whole the world is more primitive today than it was fifty years ago."

Orwell had been keeping a close eye on the corruption of science under Stalin, and especially on Trofim Lysenko, the Soviet agronomist whose pseudoscientific Marxist theory of genetic inheritance led to needless famines and a crippling purge of dissenting scientists. One of the last books Orwell ever read was *Soviet Genetics and World Science*, a demolition of Lysenko's junk science by Julian Huxley. Science in Oceania owes more to Lysenko than to Wells, who had yet again underrated human imbecility.

We are coming now to the Wells that Orwell met at Hanover Terrace: rewriting old ideas; searching ever more desperately for candidates to lead his new world order; plagued by ill-health, suicidal thoughts and a sense of ultimate defeat. The *New Statesman* editor Kingsley Martin speculated, "The failure of mankind in the Second World War he felt as his personal failure." During an unsuccessful US lecture tour in 1940 to promote his latest big idea, a "Declaration of the Rights of Man," Wells met the writer Somerset Maugham, who found him "old, tired and shrivelled," overtaken by events: "The river has flowed on and left him high and dry on the bank." Wells's declaration, which he redrafted several times between 1939 and 1944, would come to be seen as a pioneering contribution to the field of human rights, but not in his lifetime. For now he was an ex-prophet, pontificating into the void.

"I have no gang, I have no party," Wells had written to a friend as the war approached. "My epitaph will be 'He was clever, but not clever enough . . .' I write books, and it is like throwing gold bricks into mud." But his books weren't gold; they weren't even bricks. Most of his final works were slim, hasty volumes that only ended up between hard covers due to his vestigial prestige. He had been writing too long. Wells splashed his pessimism onto a wall at Hanover Terrace in the form of a mural representing evolution. Next to Man he painted three damning words: "Time to Go."

CHAPTER 5

Radio Orwell

Orwell 1941–1943

All propaganda is lies, even when one is telling the truth. I don't think this matters so long as one knows what one is doing, and why.

—George Orwell, diary entry, March 14, 1942

I n August 1941, Orwell and Eileen invited H. G. Wells to dinner. Several months earlier, Orwell's friend Inez Holden had lost her home to the Luftwaffe and Wells had offered her the use of his mews flat. A bohemian dropout from the aristocracy, Holden had made a dazzling first impression as a Bright Young Thing in the 1920s. Anthony Powell, whom she introduced to Orwell one night at London's Café Royal, described her as "excellent company," fizzing with opinions, gossip and witty impersonations. Now thirty-seven, she was a sharp chronicler of Britain at war in her novels and diaries, and a loyal friend to Orwell throughout the 1940s. Holden was happy to facilitate a proper meeting between two men she liked and admired. Two days before the dinner, however, Wells learned that Orwell had published an essay about him in Cyril Connolly's magazine *Horizon* and procured a copy. "Wells, Hitler and the World State" did not fill him with delight.

Orwell and Eileen lived on the fifth floor of Langford Court, an eight-storey 1930s tower block on Abbey Road in northwest London that probably inspired Victory Mansions in *Nineteen Eighty-Four*. Most nights, the camp bed in their front room hosted one or other of their bombed-out friends. That evening their guests were Wells, Holden and the celebrated young critic William Empson. Wells kept his powder dry until after they had eaten. Only when the dishes had been cleared away did he produce his copy of *Horizon* from his coat pocket with an ominous flourish. Orwell responded by grabbing his own copy and thwacking it down on the dinner table. The two men joined battle while Empson, who had only known Orwell for a day, sat in silence, drowning his embarrassment in whiskey.

Orwell separated politically engaged writers into two categories: those who understood the true nature of totalitarianism (none of them British) and those who did not. In the offending essay, he claimed that Wells's mind—rational, scientific, immune to the allure of blood and soil—was incapable of taking Hitler ("that screaming little defective in Berlin") seriously. "Wells is too sane to understand the modern world," he wrote, concluding on a peculiar blend of praise and condemnation: "since 1920 he has squandered his talents in slaying paper dragons. But how much it is, after all, to have any talents to squander."

Orwell was proud of his "intellectual brutality." He often befriended people he had previously insulted in print, including Stephen Spender, the crime writer Julian Symons, and the Canadian anarchist writer George Woodcock, who called him "one of those unusual beings who drew closer through disagreement." Orwell told Spender that as soon as he met somebody they became "a human being & not a sort of caricature embodying certain ideas," but the freedom to express himself without apology on the page was so fundamental that it didn't occur to him that some people might resent being caricatured and might express that resentment to his face. Kill your idols, yes, but don't let that stop you from inviting them to dinner.

The argument at Langford Court continued for some time before Wells's rage burned itself out. On the way home he told Holden it had been "an amusing evening." Seven months later, however, Wells read another Orwell essay, "The Rediscovery of Europe: Literature Between the Wars," and was infuriated by the claim that he believed that science could "solve all the ills that humanity is heir to." In a letter to the editor, he challenged Orwell's "foolish generalizations." In a private letter he was more direct: "I don't say that at all. Read my early works, you shit." And that was the end of that relationship.

The offending essay was a print version of one of Orwell's talks for the Indian Section of the BBC's Eastern Service, where he worked between August 1941 and November 1943. Like Wells in 1918, Orwell was now reluctantly writing for the state. He later described it as "two wasted years," but we shouldn't believe him. Day to day, the job introduced him to the mechanics of propaganda, bureaucracy, censorship and mass media, informing Winston Smith's job at the Ministry of Truth. What's more, his BBC output comprised hours of ruminations on the war, politics, totalitarianism and literature which prepared the ground for his two great works of fiction and his finest essays. For a mind as busy as Orwell's, there was no such thing as a wasted year.

For the first half of 1941, Orwell had been purposeless and adrift in the "strange boring nightmare" of wartime London. The year began with a new wave of rumours about a German invasion of Britain, inspiring the Ministry of Information to commission a pamphlet which dramatised the consequences. *I, James Blunt*, authored by travel writer H. V. Morton, describes German occupation through the eyes of an ordinary old man in an ordinary English village. After explaining how the Nazi regime of censorship, surveillance, indoctrination and persecution has taken hold in England, retired tradesman James Blunt discovers that a bitter former employee has joined the Gestapo and reported him for his earlier anti-fascist rhetoric. Morton dedicated his powerful short story to "all complacent optimists and wishful thinkers." In 1943, after the threat of invasion had evaporated, the barrister and soldier Robin Maugham used Morton's template—a diary which ends just before a knock on the door from the secret police—to write *The 1946 MS.*, in which a British war hero seizes power amid post-war turmoil and establishes a fascist state. Published by War Facts Press, which was connected to the MOI, Maugham's afterword was as explicit as Morton's: "Lord Murdoch and General Pointer do not exist. This story was written so that they never will exist and so that Britons never will be slaves."

Orwell reviewed *I, James Blunt* ("good flesh-creeper") and owned a copy of *The 1946 MS.* in his substantial collection of pamphlets, so he was familiar with didactic "It could happen here" literature, but he felt incapable of producing fiction himself. "Only the mentally dead are capable of sitting down and writing novels while this nightmare is going on," he wrote in April 1941. According to Cyril Connolly, this was a common paralysis: "We must remember that the life which many of us are now leading is unfriendly to the appreciation of literature; we are living history, which means that we are living from hand to mouth and reading innumerable editions of the evening paper."

That was good news, at least, for freelance journalism, which is how Orwell just about paid the bills. He used book reviews as an opportunity to explore the mechanics of totalitarianism from every possible angle. *An Epic of the Gestapo,* Sir Paul Dukes's vivid account of his investigation into a disappearance in Nazi-occupied Czechoslovakia, described a society in which, Orwell observed, "the practice of lying becomes so habitual that it is almost impossible to believe that anyone else can ever be speaking the truth." The vignettes of life under Hitler in Erika Mann's *The Lights Go Down* left him wondering how a regime that appeared "so unspeakable that no sane and decent person could possibly accept it" could command popular support. John Mair's hard-bitten conspiracy thriller *Never Come Back* appealed to Orwell as evidence that "the horrible political jungle, with its underground parties, tortures, pass-words, denunciations, forged passports, cipher messages, etc., is becoming sufficiently well-known to be suitable material for 'light' literature." Secrecy, deceit and betrayal were key ingredients of both totalitarian reality and page-turning fiction, as *Nineteen Eighty-Four* would demonstrate. The scenes in which Winston believes he is conspiring with O'Brien and the Brotherhood against the Party feel like fugitive episodes from a spy novel.

In addition to books, Orwell reviewed dozens of films for *Time and Tide* between October 1940 and August 1941, although it would be generous to call him a film critic. He had no appreciation of cinematic technique or screen acting and no respect for a job in which he was "expected to sell his honour for a glass of inferior sherry." In fact, he actively disliked American cinema: in his catalogue of contemporary plagues in "Inside the Whale," Hollywood films fall between aspirins and political murders. Anthony Powell said that Orwell was "easily bored. If a subject came up in conversation that did not appeal to him, he would make no effort to take it in." Clearly bored by cinema, he served several great movies with either faint praise or blunt contempt. *High Sierra,* now considered a classic film noir, struck him as merely a celebration of "sadism" and "bully-worship."

Orwell's curiosity was only ignited by films which said something about totalitarianism. He praised, for example, the parts of the forgettable Hollywood war movie *Escape* that captured "the nightmare atmosphere of a totalitarian country, the utter helplessness of the ordinary person, the complete disappearance of the concepts of justice and objective truth"—in other words, the parts that we would describe as Orwellian. As soon as the hero and heroine escape, he thought the film was nonsense. A plausible movie about Nazi Germany would not have a happy ending. It would not be called *Escape.* He had warmer things to say about Charlie Chaplin's *The Great Dictator.* Despite being a dogged defender of the Soviet Union in private, on the screen Chaplin stood, Orwell thought, for "a sort of concentrated essence of the common man, for the ineradicable belief in decency that exists in the hearts of ordinary people." Relishing the irony of Chaplin's physical resemblance to Hitler, Orwell reckoned that the British government would do well to subsidise and distribute the film as anti-fascist propaganda because of Chaplin's "power to reassert the fact, overlaid by Fascism and, ironically enough, by [Soviet] Socialism, that *vox populi* is *vox Dei* and giants are vermin."

By 1941, however, *vox populi* wasn't in great shape. The window of revolutionary opportunity that Orwell thought had been opened by the humiliation of Dunkirk had firmly closed. The rich cemented their privilege with black market treats, while everyone else dutifully chugged along. Orwell joked to a friend that within a year they would see "Rat Soup" on restaurant menus; a year after that it would be "Mock Rat Soup." In his war diary and his bimonthly "London Letter" for *Partisan Review,* an anti-Stalinist left-wing New York magazine run by Philip Rahv and William Phillips, Orwell documented life during wartime with cool precision. The air raids, he told *Partisan Review*'s readers, were "less terrifying and more of a nuisance than you perhaps imagine." It wasn't the prospect of a bomb crashing through the roof that bothered him so much as the kind of daily inconveniences that furnish the first chapter of *Nineteen Eighty-Four:* the power cuts, the shop closures, the dead telephone lines, the bus shortages, the piles of debris, the price of beer. Life became "a constant scramble to catch up lost time." It was all very aggravating. He filled his fireplace with year-old, pre-Dunkirk newspapers, "getting glimpses of optimistic headlines as they go up in smoke."

The Blitz lasted for eight months, but Orwell wasn't directly affected until its final hours. On the night of May 10, the Luftwaffe dropped eight hundred tonnes of bombs on the capital; he and Eileen were almost among the hundreds of casualties. At 2 a.m., they were woken by a monstrous crash. Langford Court had been hit; the corridors were filled with the stench of burning rubber and thick, blinding smoke. Their faces black with soot, they grabbed a few belongings and escaped to a friend's house, where they recovered with tea and chocolate. In *Nineteen Eighty-Four*, chocolate is a symbolic commodity: when Julia procures some for Winston, it's an act of love; when Winston steals some from his sister, it's a dire betrayal.

Even though London endured the German onslaught, the news from the Continent was grim. "By the middle of 1941," Orwell later wrote, "the British people knew what they were up against." The Wehrmacht took Greece and Yugoslavia, while Rommel's Afrika Korps pushed back the Allies in North Africa. In the early hours of June 22, Hitler broke the Nazi-Soviet Pact and three million German soldiers crossed the Russian border, forcing anti-war communists into a comically abrupt U-turn. Orwell enjoyed retelling an anecdote he'd heard about a party member who was in the toilet of a New York café when the news broke and returned to his friends to find that the line had already changed: a possible inspiration for the Inner Party orator in *Nineteen Eighty-Four* who "switched from one line to the other actually in mid-sentence."

The events of the summer plunged Orwell into despair: "Within two years we will either be conquered or we shall be a Socialist republic fighting for its life, with a secret police force and half the population starving."

Orwell desperately wanted to do something more than attend Home Guard meetings twice a week, but what? He was too unhealthy to fight, or even to be a war correspondent, and his application to work for the director of public relations at the Air Ministry had been rejected. Things had to get desperate before the British government would employ him in any capacity, not least because of his politics. In 1937, the India Office had studied his work and identified "not merely a determined Left Wing, but probably an extremist, outlook."

By 1941, though, the BBC needed Orwell's talent more than it feared his views. "The British Government started the present war," he later wrote, "with the more or less openly declared intention of keeping the literary intelligentsia out of it; yet after three years of war almost every writer, however undesirable his political history or opinions, has been sucked into the various ministries or the BBC." The political risk of hiring Orwell was minimal because every broadcast was censored twice: once for security, once for policy. Z. A. Bokhari, who ran the Indian Section, had already tested him out by commissioning four talks on literary criticism. In "Literature and Totalitarianism," broadcast that May, Orwell argued that literature derives from emotional truth and therefore cannot survive under a system that relies on mutilating truth.

> The peculiarity of the totalitarian state is that though it controls thought, it does not fix it. It sets up unquestionable dogmas, and it alters them from day to day. It needs the dogmas, because it needs absolute obedience from its subjects, but cannot avoid the changes, which are dictated by the needs of power politics. It declares itself infallible, and at the same time it attacks the very concept of objective truth.

Orwell joined the Indian Section as Empire talks assistant on August 18, on a generous starting salary of £640 a year, which dwarfed his freelance income. He spent two weeks at Bedford College in Regent's Park on an induction course with other new recruits, including William Empson, who called it "the Liars' School." While there, Orwell concluded his war diary for the time being, vowing not to resume it until something significant changed: "There is no victory in sight at present. We are in for a long, dreary, exhausting war, with everyone growing poorer all the time." On September 23, he arrived at Portland Place, the BBC's central London headquarters, to start work for Bokhari under the overall control of the director of talks, Guy Burgess. For a free agent like Orwell, working for a large bureaucracy in wartime was an invaluable education in the machinery of the state.

In recent years, the BBC has exploited its Orwell connection in ways that might have amused the man himself. To mark Orwell's centenary in 2003, it commissioned the artist Rachel Whiteread to produce a plaster cast of Room 101 in 55 Portland Place, revealing only how unremarkable and irrelevant to the novel it was. In 2017, it erected a bronze statue of Orwell outside its headquarters at Broadcasting House, beside an engraved line from the unpublished preface to *Animal Farm*—"If liberty means anything at all it means the right to tell people what they do not want to hear"—which is a good description of what Orwell's job in the Indian Section *wasn't*.

Empson described the early chapters of *Nineteen Eighty-Four* as practically a "farce" about the corporation. That's a serious overstatement, although Orwell used images, words, sounds and smells from his time there to give Winston's workplace a pungent authenticity. In June 1942, the Indian Section relocated from Portland Place to a requisitioned department store at 200 Oxford Street, where the staff worked in cubicles like the ones in the Ministry of Truth's Records Department. The subterranean staff canteen, with its distinctive aroma of boiled cabbage, resurfaced in the novel, as did the cleaners who sang to themselves every morning as they swept the corridors. The Ministry of Truth's building—"an enormous pyramidal structure of glittering white concrete"—was a Wellsian exaggeration of the Ministry of Information's HQ at the University of London's Senate House, where Eileen worked. Though one-fifth the size of the fictional Ministry, this sixty-four-metre-tall art deco tower was then the second highest building in London; the Orwells could see it from the windows of Langford Court. The Ministry's telegraphic address was MINIFORM, hence Minitrue in the novel. Other connections are far more tenuous. Room 101 was just one of the rooms that hosted meetings of the Eastern Service and not an especially unpleasant one. Brendan Bracken, Churchill's fearsome minister of information, was an enthusiastic supporter of C. K. Ogden's Basic English, a heavily simplified vocabulary of just 850 core words which H. G. Wells made the universal language of the twenty-first century in *The Shape of Things to Come*. Basic has often been called the model for Newspeak's even narrower lexicon ("to *diminish* the range of thought"), but the idea of a purer, clearer English didn't strike Orwell as necessarily malign. In fact, he thought that it might be beneficial. In 1944, he defended Basic from its myriad critics because in Ogden's language "you cannot make a meaningless statement without its being apparent that it is meaningless." As late as 1947 he wrote, "There are areas where a lingua franca of some kind is indispensable, and the perversions actually in use make one see what a lot there is to be said of Basic."

So the Ministry of Truth was by no means the BBC in disguise. The BBC was simply the only corporate environment that Orwell knew intimately. His job taught him that Britain was a long way from totalitarianism. "The bigger the machine of government becomes, the more loose ends and forgotten corners there are in it," he wrote just before he left. His own employment was proof of that. If he had lived to learn the truth about his boss he would have been even more astonished by the porousness of the British state. In 1951, Guy Burgess defected to Moscow; he had been a Soviet spy since the 1930s.

Before he knew he would be joining the corporation, Orwell wrote in his April 1941 "London Letter": "I believe that the B.B.C., in spite of the stupidity of its foreign propaganda and the unbearable voices of its announcers, is very truthful." He soon found himself implicated in both of those failings. However you might define a good voice for radio, it's safe to say that Orwell didn't have one. Not a single recording survives, but by all accounts it was thin, flat and, thanks to a Spanish bullet, too weak to be heard above the hubbub of a noisy restaurant. Stephen Spender compared a conversation with Orwell to "going through a London fog." Much of what he wrote for the BBC was assigned to professional announcers. After hearing one of Orwell's own talks, J. B. Clark, the controller of Overseas Services, complained in a memo that his voice might actually repel listeners and embarrass the BBC, "for being so ignorant of the essential needs of the microphone and of the audience as to put on so wholly unsuitable a voice." Nor did Orwell have any love for the medium. He considered radio, as it existed in the 1940s, "inherently totalitarian."

Nonetheless, Orwell did have a fantastic *brain* for radio. Asked by Bokhari to "put on your thinking-cap," he produced a torrent of ideas which he developed with colleagues over pints of beer at the pubs near Portland Place, or with Spanish Civil War veterans over Rioja and paella at the Barcelona restaurant in Soho, forever haloed by a reeking cloud of Nosegay black shag tobacco smoke, before writing them up "in desperate haste."

With great energy, efficiency and good humour, Orwell created for the Indian Section an unprecedented "university of the air." Knowing that his listenership of educated Indians would switch off overbearing British propaganda, and that a more implicit celebration of democracy was required, Orwell experimented with formats that made him rethink his hostility towards the wireless. "Few people are able to imagine the radio being used for the dissemination of anything except tripe," he wrote in "Poetry and the Microphone." But "one ought not to confuse the capabilities of an instrument with the use it is actually put to."

Orwell invited T. S. Eliot, Dylan Thomas and E. M. Forster to give readings; initiated an experimental short story with five authors, including Forster and Inez Holden; adapted stories by Wells, Ignazio Silone, Anatole France and Hans Christian Andersen; wrote essays on Shakespeare, Wilde, Shaw and Jack London; and hosted a poetry magazine show, *Voice,* featuring guests such as Spender, Stevie Smith and Herbert Read. Some of the formats he pioneered would become radio mainstays, but he was candid about their limited utility. His introduction for *Voice*'s launch episode was less an invitation than an apology: "I suppose during every second that we sit here at least one human being will be dying a violent death." Still, on with the show. Enjoy Wordsworth.

Two of his radio ideas anticipated *Nineteen Eighty-Four*'s futurology: one series called "Glimpses of the Future" and another, "A. D. 2000," in which scientists prognosticated about India at the dawn of the next century. A third celebrated the kind of text that Orwell would soon be writing: "Books That Have Changed the World."

On March 14, 1942, Orwell resumed his war diary for the first time in seven months, once again juxtaposing his thoughts on the progress of the conflict with mundane grumbles about the price of tobacco and the scarcity of razor blades—a particular bugbear of Winston Smith's. The next day, he heard his first air-raid siren since the end of the Blitz. He pretended not to notice, but inside he was terrified.

Pleasures were small and precious: "Crocuses now full out. One seems to catch glimpses of them dimly through a haze of war news."

Another recurring theme was his frustration with the BBC: "Its atmosphere is something half way between a girls' school and a lunatic asylum, and all we are doing at present is useless, or slightly worse than useless." Put *that* on a statue. Then, in June: "The thing that strikes one in the BBC . . . is not so much the moral squalor and the ultimate futility of what we are doing, as the feeling of frustration, the impossibility of getting *anything* done, even any successful piece of scoundrelism." Nonetheless, if he had felt that he was no more than a hypocritical hack achieving nothing, then he would have quit considerably earlier. He could confide his doubts in his private diary but if an outsider said something similar, then he would sharply defend his position. According to Lettice Cooper, Orwell's former editor at *Time and Tide* and one of Eileen's closest friends, "He was never quite sure if by being in the BBC he was losing his integrity. I think he felt it was a matter of defending the bad against the worst."

One critic was the anarchist George Woodcock, not yet Orwell's friend, who struck a low blow during a *Partisan Review* debate about pacifism: "And now Comrade Orwell returns to his old imperialist allegiances and works at the BBC conducting British propaganda to fox the Indian masses!" Orwell testily replied that he had no illusions but believed that he had "kept our propaganda slightly less disgusting than it might otherwise have been." Only after daily exposure to the other varieties, he said, can one "realize what muck & filth is normally flowing through the air." His colleague Desmond Hawkins thought that what really shaped the role of propaganda in *Nineteen Eighty-Four* wasn't the BBC but the Nazi broadcasts that its employees were required to study: "We were listening to 'Germany Calling,' every kind of distortion of truth and 'doublethink.' So we were seeing how the new mass media could be used, and bear in mind that for Orwell, as for me, we were born into a world where there was no radio." David Astor, the aristocratic *Observer* editor who was introduced to Orwell by Cyril Connolly, remembered Orwell toying with the idea of re-editing fragments of Churchill's speeches to make it sound as if he were declaring peace, just to show how easy it was to manipulate recordings. "I think he thought that you could use propaganda machines to invent anything and to make people make speeches they hadn't ever made," said Astor.

Orwell was much more tetchy when Alex Comfort, the physician and pacifist who would find fame in the 1970s as the author of *The Joy of Sex,* published a long, pseudonymous poem in *Tribune* which attacked writers who joined the war effort. Orwell shot back with a poem which made plain his defensive ambivalence about his role at the BBC.

> It doesn't need the eye of a detective
> To look down Portland Place and spot the whores,
> But there are men (I grant, not the most heeded)
> With twice your gifts and courage three times yours
> Who do that dirty work because it's needed;
> Not blindly, but for reasons they can balance,
> They wear their seats out and lay waste their talents.

This public defiance masked a great deal of private anguish about the effect of the war on the standard of discourse. "Nowadays," he wrote in his diary, "whatever is said or done, one looks instantly for hidden motives and assumes that words mean anything except what they appear to mean . . . When I talk to anyone or read the writings of anyone who has any axe to grind, I feel that intellectual honesty and balanced judgement have simply disappeared from the face of the earth . . . All power is in the hands of paranoiacs."

It was a dull, damp summer. Orwell's mother, Ida, and sister Avril moved to London, taking jobs at Selfridge's and a sheet-metal factory respectively, until Ida's death the following March. Eileen transferred to the Ministry of Food, compiling thrifty recipes for the BBC Home Service. The couple moved from Langford Court to a large, draughty flat in Mortimer Crescent, Maida Vale. "If George and I didn't smoke so much," Eileen told a friend, "we'd be able to afford a better flat."

The literary criticism that Orwell produced for the Indian Service leaned, due to time constraints and a certain monomania, towards books that he already knew back to front, and which had some relevance to totalitarianism. *Macbeth,* for example, was now "the typical figure of the terror-haunted tyrant, hated and feared by everyone, surrounded by spies, murderers and sycophants, and living in constant dread of treachery and rebellion . . . a sort of primitive medieval version of the modern Fascist dictator."

Another subject was *Gulliver's Travels,* a childhood favourite which constituted "probably the most devastating attack on human society that's ever been written." Orwell thought that Jonathan Swift's 1726 series of satirical utopias was remarkably relevant to the modern age. In a subsequent essay he described Part III as "an extraordinarily clear prevision of the spy-haunted Police-State, with its endless heresy-hunts and treason trials." The writing engine in the Academy of Lagado leads straight to Julia's job as a machine operator in the fiction department of the Ministry of Truth.

Orwell's most eccentric piece for the BBC was an imagined dialogue with the ghost of Swift, in which Orwell played the cautious optimist to Swift's savage misanthrope. His version of Swift was unsurprised by Hitler, Stalin or the Blitz because progress is a con and science merely produces more efficient killing machines. Perhaps Orwell was using Swift to personify his own grimmest impulses, so that he could mount a case against them. However pessimistic he became, he didn't believe that humans were grubby, worthless, self-defeating creatures. "He couldn't see what the simplest person sees," Orwell concluded after his supernatural telephone line to Swift broke down, "that life is worth living and human beings, even if they are dirty and ridiculous, are mostly decent. But after all, if he could have seen that I suppose he couldn't have written *Gulliver's Travels.*" As Arthur Koestler put it, "Orwell never completely lost faith in the knobby-faced yahoos with their bad teeth."

Only when Swift tried to imagine an ideal society in Part IV of *Gulliver's Travels* did his imagination fail him, Orwell thought, by producing the spotlessly noble and thus "remarkably dreary" Houyhnhnms. As we know, Orwell found positive utopias intolerably tedious. In his 1942 review of Herbert Samuel's *An Unknown Land,* he could not resist another dig at Wells: "A certain smugness and a tendency to self-praise are common failings in the inhabitants of Utopias, as a study of Mr. H. G. Wells' work would show."

Orwell also gave a talk about Jack London—one of half a dozen times he wrote about the American author. After Swift and Wells, no book compelled Orwell's attention as much as London's 1908 novel *The Iron Heel,* "a very remarkable prophecy of the rise of Fascism" which found a new European readership during the 1930s. Displaying his usual tendency to disparage the books which most fascinated him, Orwell called it "a very poor book" in many respects, but one he couldn't forget.

London, wrote Orwell, was "a Socialist with the instincts of a buccaneer and the education of a nineteenth-century materialist." Although he joined the Socialist Labor Party of America in 1896, London was a passionate racist and imperialist, guided more by Herbert Spencer's "survival of the fittest" than by Marx. He once shocked a party meeting by yelling, "I am first of all a white man and only then a socialist!" Before his political conversion, the author of *The Call of the Wild* and *White Fang* saw himself as "one of Nietzsche's blond-beasts, lustfully roving and conquering by sheer superiority and strength." He repurposed that instinct, but he never lost it. In the autumn of 1905, London staged a lecture tour about the inevitability of socialism, during which an audience of wealthy New Yorkers reacted hotly to lines such as "You have mismanaged the world and it shall be taken from you!" Their outrage, the failed Bolshevik revolution in Russia, and a reading of Wells's *When the Sleeper Wakes* drove him to craft a nightmare about the brutal suppression of socialism in America.

Subsequent admirers of *The Iron Heel* included US Socialist Party leader Eugene Debs, British Labour politician Aneurin Bevan and Trotsky but, like Orwell, none claimed that the novel was great literature. Reading it inspires, to misquote Philip Larkin, first boredom, then fear. The boring part describes Ernest Everhard, a virile socialist superman who is clearly based on the author, right down to direct quotes from his lectures. Narrated by Everhard's lover Avis, the gushing accounts of "his gladiator body and his eagle spirit" therefore amount to an act of self-love on London's part. The author's biographer Earle Labor described it as "*1984* as it might have been penned by Elizabeth Barrett Browning."

But if the first half is a lecture, then the second is a bloodbath. When Everhard and his socialist faction win election to Congress, the capitalist Oligarchy retaliates by breaking or buying off the labour unions, subduing the media and political opposition, crushing the middle class, conscripting militias, and using agents provocateurs to stage riots and terrorist outrages that justify the suspension of democracy. As Trotsky wrote in 1937, "In reading it one does not believe his own eyes: it is precisely the picture of fascism, of its economy, of its governmental technique, its political psychology!" He admired London's determination "to shake those who are lulled by routine, to force them to open their eyes and to see what is and what approaches." The novel ends abruptly with the off-stage execution of Everhard and the triumph of the Oligarchy, now called the Iron Heel. Orwell thought that London's account of the Oligarchy's ruthlessness and quasi-religious belief in its own righteousness was "one of the best statements of . . . the outlook that a ruling class must have if it's to survive that has ever been written." In brief: "Power. Not God, not Mammon, but Power."

Orwell found it impossible to say where London's political journey would have led if he hadn't died in 1916, at the age of forty. He could conceivably have turned into a communist, a Trotskyist, an anarchist or a Nazi. "Intellectually he knew . . . that Socialism ought to mean the meek inheriting the earth, but that was not what his temperament demanded." At least, wrote Orwell, he would not have made the mistake of not taking Hitler seriously. Because of his "streak of brutality" and "understanding of the primitive," London was "a better prophet than many better-informed and more logical thinkers," such as Wells. Such insight into violence and power was only possible for a man who retained some connection to the blond-beast. "You might say," Orwell wrote, "that he could understand Fascism because he had a Fascist strain himself." Perhaps Orwell could not have imagined the Ministry of Love unless he, too, had a streak of brutality.

The Iron Heel may have informed Nineteen Eighty-Four's hierarchy of oligarchs and proles and its defining image of a boot stamping on a human face forever. Orwell first deployed "the vision of a boot crashing down on a face" in The Lion and the Unicorn and uses boots as a synecdoche for state violence almost twenty times in Nineteen Eighty-Four. London's greatest gift to Orwell, however, may have been structural. Gulliver's Travels and Looking Backward each have a preface from a fictitious editor, so as to make them read like memoirs rather than novels, but London went further. He framed Avis's account as "The Everhard Manuscript," a document introduced and footnoted by Anthony Meredith, a historian who lives in a socialist utopia in the twenty-seventh century and considers the text "a warning to those rash political theorists of to-day who speak with certitude of social progresses." The novel's footnotes are largely a device for shoehorning political context into the narrative, but they also explain that the Iron Heel was finally overthrown after three centuries and replaced by the Brotherhood of Man. That knowledge gives the book's cheerless conclusion a hopeful coda. The end is not really the end.

This brings us to what I'll call the Appendix Theory.

The last words of *Nineteen Eighty-Four* are not "THE END." The novel's actual last word is "2050," which concludes the appendix, "The Principles of Newspeak." The appendix has two striking characteristics: it is written in twentieth-century English, known as Oldspeak, and it is written *in the past tense*. It therefore raises some pressing questions: Who wrote it, when, and for whom?

There are two possible explanations for this. One is that it's a glaring blunder by an author who otherwise seemed to be in full command of his material and could have easily added an analysis of Newspeak to Goldstein's book. Another explanation, the Appendix Theory, is that the story of Winston Smith is a text within the world of the novel, with an unidentified author, hence the solitary footnote, in the first chapter, which directs readers to the appendix.

Logically, this means that all the facts have been accurately remembered, that the English language was not eliminated by 2050 and, therefore, that Ingsoc did not endure "for ever." Winston must have been wrong to think that "The diary would be reduced to ashes and himself to vapour," because the author of the appendix knows the whole story. Encoded in the appendix's dispassionate, essayistic account of Newspeak is a happy ending of sorts—a crack in the monumental despair. Winston can't foresee change "in our own life-time" but he can imagine "leaving a few records behind, so that the next generation can carry on where we leave off." In the introduction to their 2013 stage version, the first adaptation to incorporate the appendix, Robert Icke and Duncan Macmillan wrote that it "daringly opens up the novel's form and reflects its central questions back to the reader. Can you trust evidence? How do you ever know what's really true? And when and where are you, the reader, right now?"

Prominent advocates of the Appendix Theory include Margaret Atwood and Thomas Pynchon. "Orwell is much more optimistic than people give him credit for," Atwood said in 1986. In a later interview, she added that many dystopian novels "have a framing device, like once upon a time all these horrible things happened, but now we're looking back at them from the future." Atwood's "Historical Notes" appendix to *The Handmaid's Tale* is the same kind of device, looking back at an intolerable tyranny from the safe harbour of 2195. "Optimism is relative," Atwood said. "Glimmers are good. Happily ever after we don't believe anymore, but we can live with glimmers."

So that's the Appendix Theory.

One of the last things Orwell wrote for the Indian Service was a dramatisation of H. G. Wells's 1896 short story "A Slip Under the Microscope," a bleak little number about class prejudice, unforgiving bureaucracy and cruel fate, stemming from the writer's experiences at the Normal School of Science.

After the fiery dinner party at Langford Court, William Empson told Inez Holden that he thought Wells was angry because Orwell had been rude; Holden countered that it was because Wells thought Orwell had been wrong. And Orwell *was* wrong, or at least reductive, when he caricatured the older man as a complacent hasbeen with no idea what democracy was up against. In fact, Wells was a depressed, sporadically suicidal old man. His utopian visions had really been warnings as much as prophecies: humanity could either follow the path of progress (as prescribed by Wells) or slide back into the pit. It appeared to have chosen the pit. "We are, as a people, a collection of unteachable dullards at war with an infectious lunatic & his victims," Wells wrote to George Bernard Shaw in 1941.

It's hardly surprising, then, that Wells exploded whenever he felt that somebody had misrepresented his life's work. A reputation is a precious, fragile thing and must be defended. His entire career, he believed, represented "the clearest insistence on the insecurity of progress and the possibility of human degeneration and extinction ... I think the odds are against man but it is still worth fighting against them." How, he thought, could someone as clever as Orwell have missed that crucial point? By the end of the decade, Orwell would discover for himself how it feels to see your fundamental world view misunderstood.

Read my early works, you shit.

By the time "A Slip Under the Microscope" was broadcast in October 1943, Orwell had already tendered his resignation from the BBC. "By some time in 1944 I might be near-human again and able to write something serious," he wrote to Rayner Heppenstall, an old friend who was now working for another branch of the BBC. "At present I am just an orange that's been trodden on by a very dirty boot." Eileen was delighted by his decision to quit. "I should think a municipal dustman's work more dignified and better for your future as a writer," she later told him.

In his resignation letter, Orwell stressed that he had been treated well and allowed a great deal of freedom: "On no occasion have I been compelled to say on the air anything that I would not have said as a private individual." That was a polite exaggeration—he had recently been reprimanded for slipping a criticism of Stalin into a news broadcast—but his main reason for quitting was the nagging conviction that his work was a waste of both his time and the public's money. There were only 121,000 radio sets in India, a country with a population of three hundred million, and those who did tune in weren't in the habit of writing in to give feedback. When the BBC commissioned a listener survey, Orwell's approval rating was a lowly 16 per cent. Only after the war would he learn that his work had any fans in India at all. He never saw the glowing internal report written by Rushbrook Williams, the director of Indian Services, who lauded his talent, work ethic and integrity: "He is transparently honest, incapable of subterfuge, and in early days he would have been canonised—or burnt at the stake! Either fate he would have sustained with stoical courage." On the day he left, Orwell's colleagues threw him a surprise party; had he been forewarned, they suspected, he wouldn't have showed up.

Orwell had, at least, witnessed the propaganda machine in action, via his own work and Eileen's, and it had left him obsessed with the mass production of lies. Just as being an imperialist taught him to hate imperialism, fraternising with tramps and miners gave him a visceral sense of economic injustice, and fighting in Spain solidified his opposition to both fascism and communism, working as a propagandist, even a relatively benign one, gave him the moral authority to critique propaganda in the strongest terms. In a long essay called "Looking Back on the Spanish War," written in 1942, Orwell understood better what he had seen unfolding in Spain: "for the first time, I saw newspaper reports which did not bear any relation to the facts, not even the relationship which is implied by an ordinary lie . . . I saw, in fact, history being written not in terms of what happened but of what ought to have happened according to various 'party lines.'"

This was new, he thought. In the past, people were guilty of deliberate deceit or unconscious bias, but at least they believed in the existence of facts and the distinction between true and false. Totalitarian regimes, however, lied on such a grand scale that they made Orwell feel that "the very concept of objective truth is fading out of the world." What was just an inkling in 1937 had been honed into a conviction that would underpin the Ministry of Truth and the true source of Ingsoc's power: it "controls not only the future but *the past*. If the Leader says of such and such an event, 'It never happened'—well, it never happened. If he says that two and two are five—well, two and two are five. This prospect frightens me much more than bombs—and after our experiences of the last few years that is not a frivolous statement."

Here, undeniably, are the moral and intellectual foundations of *Nineteen Eighty-Four*. Totalitarianism's war on reality was more dangerous than the secret police, the constant surveillance or the boot in the face, because in "that shifting phantasmagoric world in which black may be white tomorrow and yesterday's weather can be changed by decree" there is no solid ground from which to mount a rebellion—no corner of the mind that has not been infected and warped by the state. It is power that removes the possibility of challenging power. That's why it is not enough for O'Brien to force Winston to say that two plus two equals five. He has only truly won when Winston *believes* that two plus two equals five.

During Orwell's time at the BBC, the tide of the war had turned. When he turned up for the first day of "Liars' School" in August

1941, Germany dominated Europe and was advancing on Moscow; Japan was sweeping through Southeast Asia; the USA had not yet entered the war. By November 1943, however, Hitler's forces had been expelled from North Africa and most of the USSR, Italy had surrendered to the Allies, and Emperor Hirohito was describing Japan's situation as "truly grave." Churchill, Roosevelt and Stalin were days away from meeting in Tehran to discuss post-war "spheres of influence"—a summit that Orwell described as a very early inspiration for *Nineteen Eighty-Four.* It was just a matter of time before Germany and Japan folded. Orwell's mind turned to the future of totalitarianism, now that fascism had been routed but Stalinism was flushed with prestige.

At some point he sketched out the blueprint for *Nineteen Eighty-Four,* then called *The Last Man in Europe.* (A trace of the original title survives in O'Brien's taunting words: "If you are a man, Winston, you are the last man. Your kind is extinct; we are the inheritors.") Orwell's notebook is undated, and its contents clearly copied from one or more rough drafts, but scholars tend to place the outline towards the end of 1943 or the very start of 1944. Some key components of the novel don't appear in the outline, but the basic material is there, including Ingsoc, Newspeak and doublethink, and the effect he planned to create: "The nightmare feeling caused by the disappearance of objective truth." That phrase again. If nothing else, his spell at the BBC had given these consuming ideas time to evolve into sophisticated concepts.

"Looking Back on the Spanish War" was published in *New Road* in June 1943, minus the crucial sections about propaganda and the abuse of history. The full version would not be published until 1953, which was a great shame, because these sections didn't just explain the ideas behind *Nineteen Eighty-Four;* they mounted a pre-emptive defence of the book against anyone who would accuse it of hysterical melodrama. "Is it perhaps childish or morbid to terrify oneself with visions of a totalitarian future?" Orwell asked. "Before writing off the totalitarian world as a nightmare that can't come true, just remember that in 1925 the world of today would have seemed a nightmare that couldn't come true."

CHAPTER 6

The Heretic

Orwell and Zamyatin

> I know that I have a highly inconvenient habit of speaking
> what I consider to be the truth rather than saying what may
> be expedient at the moment.
>
> —Yevgeny Zamyatin, letter to Stalin, 1929

In January 1944, a Russian-born professor of literature named Gleb Struve alerted Orwell to the existence of Yevgeny Zamyatin's anti-utopian novel *We*, written in 1920–1921. "I am interested in that kind of book," Orwell replied, "and even keep making notes for one myself that may get written sooner or later."

Orwell located a copy of the 1929 French translation, *Nous Autres*, that summer, and eventually wrote about it in *Tribune* in January 1946 under the title "Freedom and Happiness." Orwell judged that "it is not a book of the first order, but it is certainly an unusual one," and suggested that *Brave New World* "must be partly derived from it." In a subsequent letter to Fredric Warburg, he upgraded that to "partly plagiarised." This was not an outrageous claim—Kurt Vonnegut later said something similar—but Huxley consistently denied having read it and Zamyatin believed him, saying that the resemblance "proves that these ideas are in the stormy air we breathe."

Karma came for Orwell in the form of several critics who accused *him* of plagiarising *We*. The first was the historian Isaac Deutscher, who accused the author of borrowing "the idea of *1984*, the plot, the chief characters, the symbols, and the whole climate of his story" from *We*. There are three problems with this claim. One: Deutscher wildly overstated the similarities between the novels. Two: as we have seen, Orwell had already written his outline months before he read *We*. Three: Orwell made repeated efforts to get Zamyatin's novel republished in English and encouraged his readers more than once to "look out for this book"—surely not the kind of thing that plagiarists usually do.

Originality is a vexing concept in genre fiction. We don't accuse everyone who writes about a brilliant, eccentric detective of ransacking Arthur Conan Doyle. Utopian fiction is a genre, too, with a set of recurring tropes and themes. Edward Bellamy influenced William Morris; both men influenced H. G. Wells; Wells influenced Huxley, Orwell and Zamyatin; and all of these writers introduced some major new idea, technique or tone. As Morris said, each one is "the expression of the temperament of its author." Nonetheless, it's impossible to read Zamyatin's bizarre and visionary novel without being strongly reminded of stories that were written afterwards, Orwell's included.

Zamyatin called *We* "my most jesting and most serious work." The novel he started writing in Petrograd in 1920, at the age of thirty-six, is set hundreds of years in the future, in the ultra-rational despotism of the One State, a hyperbolic expression of the author's belief that urban life "robs people of individuality, makes them the same, machinelike." Zamyatin hones and develops ideas from Wells and Dostoevsky into a sturdy template for numerous tales of individualism versus homogeneity. In the shape of the Benefactor, Zamyatin gives us the mysterious, nameless dictator who poses as a protector. He gives us uniformed "ciphers" with numbers instead of names, and a state which represents "the victory of the many over the one." He abolishes privacy by installing his ciphers in glass houses, constantly monitored by the secret police ("the Guardians"), except during the state-mandated "sex hour," which, in a world without love, is organised via a ticketing system. He provides them with synthetic food, a controlled climate and formulaic, machine-made music (Zamyatin's musicometers anticipate Orwell's versificators), and lashes them to a daily ritual, the Table of Hours, which spoofs the efficiency doctrine of the management consultant Frederick Winslow Taylor. He constructs a rectilinear city of glass, modelled on the geometry of Petrograd, and, beyond the Green Wall, an untamed wilderness to represent humanity's atavistic impulses. Zamyatin also establishes the archetype of a timid cog in the machine who is prodded into rebellion by a bewitching female heretic.

For all its importance, *We* is not more widely read because it is not easily read. Following Zamyatin's compacted, impressionistic prose feels rather like studying a painting by his contemporaries Malevich and El Lissitzky—all colours and shapes. Flocking birds, for example, are "sharp, black, piercing, falling triangles"; laughter is "festive rockets of red, blue, gold"; anatomy is described as geometry. Zamyatin wanted language fit for an accelerating world. "When you are moving fast," he wrote in 1923, "the canonised, the customary eludes the eye; hence, the unusual, often startling, symbolism and vocabulary. The image is sharp, synthetic, with a single salient feature—the one feature you will glimpse from a speeding car." He also wanted to articulate the mindset of his narrator, D-530. Writers such as Bellamy and Wells used a contemporary protagonist as a reader proxy, but Zamyatin, plunging straight into the future, needed a new language to animate his new world. He later compared his writing to cinema: "I never *explained*; I always *showed* and *suggested*."

D-530 is a mathematician working on the Integral, a spacecraft intended to extend the One State to new worlds, and writing a diary that will explain the system to readers who he believes will resemble his barbaric ancestors. His smug, condescending account of "mathematically infallible happiness" parodies the evangelical tone of utopian tour guides like Bellamy's Dr. Leete: "It is amusing to me—and at the same time very laborious to explain all this." Zamyatin enjoyed Jerome K. Jerome's "The New Utopia" and there's comedy in D-530's earnestly proud explanations, like the title of a famous One State tragedy: *He Who Was Late for Work*.* But he ends up documenting instead an unravelling mind, as the perfect equation of his life is disrupted by the unknown X and the impossible $\sqrt{-1}$. As he mentally malfunctions, "like a machine being driven to excessive rotations," his writing is infected with flawed memories, elisions, paradoxes, doubts and dreams: the "ancient sickness" which he has

---

* The British humorist was hugely popular in Russia. According to historian Brian Moynahan, "Every station bookstall from Moscow to Harbin had a copy of Jerome K. Jerome's *Three Men in a Boat*."

contracted from the erotically liberated revolutionary I-330. His story runs away from him.

Orwell thought that *We* had "a rather weak and episodic plot which is too complex to summarize." Put simply, it involves a band of revolutionaries called the Mephi, who try to hijack the Integral, blow up the Green Wall, and bring down the One State, all with the ambivalent involvement of D-530. The Benefactor fights back with the Great Operation, a lobotomy-like process which removes the imagination and renders citizens "machine-equal. The path to one-hundred-per-cent happiness is clear." So much for the perfect society; perfect brains are required. The book ends with I-330 being tortured to death while a smiling, pacified D-530 insists that the One State will win: "Because reason should win."

Zamyatin's own conflict with the state didn't end well either. For this remarkable man, whose principles always overrode his instinct for self-preservation, *We* was primarily the novel that shattered his life. That's why Orwell described it as "one of the literary curiosities of this book-burning age."

"Perhaps the most interesting and most serious stories," Zamyatin once wrote, "have not been written by me, but have happened to me."

Yevgeny Zamyatin was hell-bent on making life difficult for himself. Born in the provincial town of Lebedyan on February 1, 1884, he was a bookish, solitary child. "Gogol was a friend," he wrote, as if he needed no others. When he graduated from school in Voronezh in 1902, he received a gold medal for his academic achievements, and a warning. The school's inspector showed him a pamphlet by a Voronezh graduate who had been arrested for revolutionary activity three years earlier: "He also finished with a gold medal and what does he write? Of course, he ended up in prison. My advice to you is: Don't write. Don't follow this path." Relating this anecdote, Zamyatin drily added: "His admonition had no effect."

That, at least, is how Zamyatin told it, in one of three autobiographical sketches that he wrote for Russian publications during the 1920s. Whether or not the conversation unfolded exactly like that is irrelevant. This is the story he wanted to tell: the man who swam against the tide whatever the cost. Struve called him "an eternal rebel against the established order of things."

Zamyatin went on to study naval engineering at the St. Petersburg Polytechnic Institute and found a city roiled by radical meetings and demonstrations. "In those years, being a Bolshevik meant following the line of greatest resistance," he wrote, "and I was a Bolshevik at that time." Over the next decade, he was arrested three times by the tsar's police. During one period of forced exile from the city, he began writing fiction. "If I have any place in Russian literature, I owe it entirely to the Saint Petersburg Department of Secret Police," he later joked.

During the First World War, Zamyatin was both a known dissident and a valuable citizen with skills that Russia could not afford to lose. In March 1916, he was dispatched to Britain to design and build ice-breakers for the Russian navy. He fitted in quite well. A trim, handsome, stylish man who liked to wear tweeds and smoke a pipe, he had the emotional reserve, his friends thought, of an Englishman. There he wrote *The Islanders*, a knifing satire of middle-class conformity. He returned to Petrograd a few weeks before the October Revolution.* For Zamyatin, who was no longer a Bolshevik, it felt as if a bomb had dropped in February and spun in circles for eight months before actually detonating. "When the smoke of this tremendous explosion had cleared at last," he wrote, "everything turned out to be upside down—history, literature, men, reputations."

Zamyatin had a dialectical view of history. "Yesterday, the thesis; today, the antithesis; and tomorrow, the synthesis," he wrote in his 1919 essay "Tomorrow." He thought Russia's political synthesis, which ensured both social justice and the freedom of the individual, was yet to come. To this he added the idea, from the German physicist Julius Robert von Mayer, of a cosmic struggle between Revolution, the life-force, and Entropy, which tends towards stasis and death. Dogmatism, to Zamyatin, was political Entropy. "Eternal dissatisfaction is the only pledge of eternal movement forward, eternal creation," he declared. "The world is kept alive only by heretics: the heretic Christ, the heretic Copernicus, the heretic Tolstoy."

---

* St. Petersburg became Petrograd in 1914 and Leningrad in 1924, returning to its original name in 1991.

Zamyatin fell in with a group of writers, led by the critic Razumnik Ivanov-Razumnik, who called themselves the Scythians, after the tribe of nomads who had patrolled the Russian steppes two thousand years earlier. But they soon parted company because Zamyatin thought that to say that the October Revolution was the final answer, to turn Bolshevism into a new religion, was fundamentally un-Scythian. The true Scythian, he insisted, was a perpetual rebel who "works *only* for the distant future, never for the near future, and never for the present." His words were both thrilling and exhausting. Amid a long, bloody civil war to safeguard the revolution, most people did not want to live and die for the distant future. Zamyatin practically guaranteed that the new Bolshevik secret police, the Cheka, would dislike him as much as their tsarist predecessors. The magazines who dared to publish his combative articles and satirical short stories were shut down. In February 1919, Zamyatin was arrested, but he talked his way out of jail and found a sympathetic sponsor in the form of Maxim Gorky.

Zamyatin had met Gorky when he returned to Petrograd during the chaos of September 1917, so he always associated him with the sound of gunfire. With his tobacco-yellowed moustache and rattling cough, the forty-nine-year-old Gorky was the titan of Russian literature, lionised for his 1902 social realist landmark *The Lower Depths*, and for his early support for the Bolsheviks, which had led to imprisonment and exile. He fell out with his old friend Lenin in 1917 but mended bridges the following year and used his clout to support writers whose situation was far more precarious.

During the civil war, when Russians were struggling to afford bread and fuel, let alone books, only propaganda-minded writers could make a living. Gorky's remedy was to become, in Zamyatin's words, "a kind of unofficial minister of culture, organizer of public works for the derailed, starving intelligentsia." A one-man bridge between the artists and the bureaucrats, Gorky founded organisations including the House of the Arts, a palace converted into a writers' hostel, and World Literature, a publishing house which translated classic works with new introductions by Russian writers. He was flooded with entreaties from the families of men arrested by the Cheka and often travelled to the Kremlin to petition Lenin personally for their release.

In 1920, Zamyatin cofounded the All-Russian Union of Writers

(VSP), running the office in Petrograd. "The writer who cannot become nimble must trudge to an office with a briefcase if he wants to stay alive," he wrote. The nimble were the ideologically flexible writers who followed the party line. "You really do have to be an acrobat," said Aleksey Tolstoy, an aristocrat who smoothly reinvented himself as an agile sycophant. To Zamyatin, this was artistic suicide: "True literature can exist when it is created, not by diligent and trustworthy officials, but by madmen, hermits, heretics, dreamers, rebels and sceptics." He was a popular man—"amenable, quick-witted, hard-working, easygoing," said one colleague—and an inspiration to the school of experimental young writers known as the Serapion Brothers. He was also a *poputchik,* or "fellow-traveller," Trotsky's term for an intellectual who supported the goals of the revolution but was not a Communist Party member. Fellow-travellers weren't loved, but they were tolerated—for now.

As a member of World Literature's editorial planning board, Zamyatin edited and introduced several volumes by H. G. Wells, whose "mechanical, chemical fairy tales" for the age of aeroplanes and asphalt he adored. When Wells visited Petrograd in 1920, Zamyatin gave a speech at the banquet in his honour. In his 1922 essay "H. G. Wells," Zamyatin understood, as Orwell did not, that Wells's grand schemes were merely a shaky bridge suspended over an abyss of chaos and violence. "Most of his social fantasies bear the − sign, not the + sign," Zamyatin wrote. "His sociofantastic novels are almost solely instruments for exposing the defects of the existing social order, rather than building a picture of a future paradise." Wells therefore used "the murky colours of Goya," not (apart from *Men Like Gods*) "the sugary, pinkish colours of a utopia."

The essay also revealed an encyclopedic knowledge of utopias and science fiction, from Bacon and Swift to recent, Wells-influenced work from the likes of Czechoslovakia's Karel Čapek (whose dystopian play *R.U.R.*, admired by Orwell, gave us the word *robot*), Poland's Jerzy Żuławski and Russia's own Aleksey Tolstoy. Zamyatin made the briefest possible reference to a book that his readers wouldn't have known because it had not yet been (and never would be) approved by the Soviet censors: "*We*, by the author of this essay."

—

It's difficult to say whether Orwell took ideas straight from Zamyatin or was simply thinking along similar lines. His description of D-530 as "a poor conventional creature, a sort of Utopian Billy Brown of London Town" could apply to Winston Smith, but also to Flory, Comstock and Bowling. And if the Thought Police resemble the Guardians, then isn't that because both are extreme versions of Russia's secret police? At a time when Stalin was nicknamed "Uncle Joe," did it take the Benefactor to inspire Big Brother? But the "strange and irritating" I-330, who smokes, drinks, enjoys sex, and arranges clandestine rendezvous, *does* feel like a forerunner of Julia. S-4711, the mysterious hunchback who seems to gaze into D-530's mind, plays an O'Brien-like role. And D-530's final surrender strikes the same note as Winston's love of Big Brother. Remember that Orwell wrote his outline before he read *We*, but Julia, O'Brien, Big Brother and the Thought Police all came later.

Even if Orwell took parts of his fictional chassis from Zamyatin, though, his philosophical engine was completely different. When the Benefactor says that people have always "wanted someone, anyone, to tell them once and for all what happiness is—and then to attach them to this happiness with a chain," he sounds like Mustapha Mond in *Brave New World* and the Grand Inquisitor in Dostoevsky's *The Brothers Karamazov*, who famously argued that the loss of freedom is a price people will pay for happiness. Orwell rejected this idea. When Winston imagines that O'Brien will justify the Party's iron rule with the Inquisitor's argument that "the choice for mankind lay between freedom and happiness," he is punished for his stupidity. The citizens of Oceania are neither free nor happy. Equality and scientific progress, so crucial to *We*, have no place in Orwell's static, hierarchical dictatorship; organised deceit, so fundamental to *Nineteen Eighty-Four*, did not preoccupy Zamyatin.

From another Dostoevsky novel, *Notes from Underground*, Zamyatin took the equation two times two equals four to represent the scientific state's eternal truth in a sonnet called "Happiness." Dostoevsky's narrator insists on the freedom to say otherwise: "After twice two is four, of course there'll be nothing left, not only to do but even to discover." Again, Orwell said the opposite. In the face of mysticism and calculated insanity, "Freedom is the freedom to say that two plus two make four. If that is granted, all else follows." For Zamyatin and Dostoevsky, the simplest of sums was a cage; for Orwell, it was an anchor. The two world views just don't align. It's revealing that Orwell zeroed in on a brief, dissonant note of atavistic cruelty: the Machine of the Benefactor, which reduces enemies of the state to a puddle of liquid in a public "Celebration of Justice." Orwell detected in this ritual a little of what intrigued him about Jack London: "It is this intuitive grasp of the irrational side of totalitarianism—human sacrifice, cruelty as an end in itself, the worship of a leader who has divine attributes—that makes Zamyatin's book superior to Huxley's."

Orwell told Warburg that *We* "seems to me to form an interesting link in the chain of Utopia books." Let's pause for a moment to follow that chain.

There are critics who insist that Ayn Rand could have written her 1938 novella *Anthem* without ever having read *We*, and good luck to them. Perhaps it's a coincidence that she came up with the secret diarist Equality 7-2521, the gleaming, uniform City, the rigid timetable, the state hymns, the compulsory happiness, the hard, angular love interest, the escape to the Uncharted Forest, and the tension between *I* and *we*: "the monster which hung as a black cloud over the earth and hid the sun from man." Perhaps it's simply bad luck that *Anthem* feels like a crude cover version of a strange and beautiful song.

Rand fled Russia in 1926, at the age of twenty, and took with her to America a burning, lifelong hatred of communism. She wrote *Anthem* in three weeks in the summer of 1937, claiming that she had first imagined "a world of the future where they don't have the word 'I'" while at school in Russia. Snubbed in the US, the novella was published first in Britain, where Malcolm Muggeridge in *The Daily Telegraph* called it "a grisly forecast of the future . . . a cri de coeur after a surfeit of doctrinaire intolerance."

In a letter to her publisher, Rand wrote, "It is so very personally mine, it is in a way, my manifesto, my profession of faith. The essence of my entire philosophy." Her militant anti-communism meant that her oppressive, collectivist society couldn't be as technologically advanced as Zamyatin's; it had to be a primitive, inept paper tyranny, easily outwitted by Equality 7-2521. Escaping to the Uncharted Forest, he renames himself Prometheus and delivers the "anthem" of the title: a bombastic rant about his own exceptionalism and his plan to build an even bigger city than the one he has left behind. This is *We* rewritten as a capitalist creation myth, with paradise as a building site. "To be free, a man must be free of his brothers," he concludes. "That is freedom. This and nothing else." The book's working title was *Ego*.

Rand proceeded to sell millions of novels, found a school of political thought called Objectivism, and shape the ideology of more politicians than any other twentieth-century novelist, so it's likely that more people took plot points from her book than from *We*. In George Lucas's 1971 debut feature *THX 1138*, an engineer with an alphanumeric name escapes from a spotlessly regimented subterranean society ("Work hard, increase production, prevent accidents and be happy") and emerges alone beneath an unfamiliar sun. Lucas's desire to represent "the way I see LA right now; maybe a slight exaggeration" produced a satirical twist on Rand's ineffectual state: robot police officers abandon their mission to apprehend THX because they've gone over budget. "It's the idea that we are all living in cages and the doors are wide open and all we have to do is walk out," Lucas explained.

There's no ambiguity about where the Canadian rock band Rush got the idea for their 1976 concept album *2112*, which they released on Anthem Records and dedicated to "the genius of Ayn Rand." Lyricist Neil Peart called it an attack on "any collectivist mentality." In the elephantine title track, a citizen of the despotic Solar Federation discovers an ancient guitar, and thus the lost art of rock 'n' roll. That idea resurfaced in the dystopian kitsch of Ben Elton and Queen's 2002 hit musical *We Will Rock You:* a band of rock 'n' roll rebels, the Bohemians, take up instruments against the Globalsoft Corporation, which anaesthetises the population of Earth (aka iPlanet) with a homogenous commercial culture which includes computer-generated music much like the pablum manufactured by Zamyatin's Music Factory. Globalsoft's Achilles heel, it transpires, is the music of Queen.

Capitalism is also, somewhat ironically for a film based on a toy brand, satirised in *The Lego Movie*. The opening sequence, in which the inhabitants of the automated society of Bricksburg start a typical day, is a version of Zamyatin's Table of Hours ("Each morning, with six-wheeled precision, at the exact same hour, at the exact same minute, we, the millions, rise as one. At the exact same hour, we uni-millionly start work and uni-millionly stop work"), but here the routine includes a trip to a Starbucks-style coffee chain. Bricksburg's answer to "The Hymn of the One State" is the fanatically upbeat "Everything Is Awesome." Like *We*, the movie deploys an obedient technician who stumbles into rebellion (Emmet Brickowski), a female revolutionary (Wyldstyle), a dictator (President Business) and the construction of a super-weapon (the Kragle) in a story which promotes individual imagination over the ersatz happiness of conformity—Revolution over Entropy—via the use of plastic bricks.

This winding path from Lenin to Lego illustrates that anti-utopian narratives have the flexibility and portability of myths. It is not always clear who read what and when, and the changes usually outweigh the resemblances. Take *THX 1138*, for example. Lucas seems to have taken his narrative arc from Zamyatin or Rand, his mind-controlling drugs from Huxley, and his telescreens and mysterious godlike ruler from Orwell, not to mention ideas from *Metropolis, Things to Come* and Jean-Luc Godard's sci-fi noir *Alphaville*, but sieved this broth of influences through the culture of 1970s America, and his own considerable visual imagination, to produce a dystopia with its own distinctive flavour. And of course Zamyatin himself was reworking existing material. His blue-uniformed ciphers, ubiquitous Guardians, and violent rebellion in a city of glass all had precedents in Wells, notably *The Sleeper Awakes* and "A Story of the Days to Come." Another twist: while declining to acknowledge *We*, Rand suggested that Orwell had plagiarised *her*. When she revised *Anthem* for its US hardback debut in 1953, she downplayed the horrors of the collectivist state lest she "give readers the impression that *Anthem* is merely another sordid story on the order of Orwell's *1984* (which, incidentally, was written many years after *Anthem* had been published in England)."

So, rather than thinking of dystopian ideas as the work of individual geniuses, one might compare them to folk songs, forever mutating as they pass between individuals, and between political contexts. "Look at all these things that people built," Emmet tells President Business in *The Lego Movie*. "You might see a mess . . . What

I see are people, inspired by each other, and by you. People taking what you made and making something new out of it."

Much to Ayn Rand's annoyance, it's a collective effort.

Let's return to Zamyatin at his desk in Petrograd in 1920. What was he trying to say? In "Freedom and Happiness," Orwell suggested that Zamyatin, writing before Stalin's ascent, must have been satirising the Machine rather than Bolshevism. Gleb Struve, however, insisted that the writer was speculating on the totalitarian potential of Bolshevik Russia, which was already a single-party dictatorship with an energetic secret police and formidable propaganda operation: "It is important just because it is even more *prophetic* than topical." In a 1932 interview, Zamyatin indicated that they were both correct: "This novel is a warning against the twofold danger which threatens humanity: the hypertrophic power of the machines and the hypertrophic power of the State."

The paranoia and persecution that Orwell associated with Stalin had already taken hold in Russia by the time Zamyatin wrote *We*. In his 1922 play *The Fires of Saint Dominic*, Zamyatin used the Spanish Inquisition to satirise the Red Terror, giving one of his inquisitors a speech with an Orwellian flavour: "if the Church told me that I had only one eye, I would agree even with that, I would believe even that, because, although I well know that I have two eyes, I know even better that the Church cannot make a mistake." According to the Russian exile Marc Slonim, "Zamyatin simply could not call what he saw around him a revolution: doctrine encrusting the lava of rebellion, the bloodthirsty executions, the stupid regimentation, the creation of ideocracy in lieu of autocracy."

Certainly for the Bolshevik censors, the message of *We* was unacceptable. It would not be published in Zamyatin's homeland until 1988, half a century after his death. The novel's provocative title mocked the principle summed up by the proletarian poet Alexander Ilyich Bezymensky: "The collective 'We' has driven out the personal 'I.' " Worse, Zamyatin questioned the revolution. In one daring passage, I-330 explains why another revolution is always possible by asking D-530, as a mathematician, to tell her the final number.

"But, I-330—that is ridiculous. The number of numbers is infinite; which final one do you want?"

"Well, which final revolution do you want then? There isn't a final one. Revolutions are infinite."

This is Zamyatin the galloping Scythian, with his endless "What next?" He quoted this exchange as the epigraph for "On Literature, Revolution, Entropy, and Other Matters," a dazzling 1923 essay in which he applied his theory of infinite revolutions to mathematics, physics, art and politics. This was a wonderfully potent idea and one that was anathema to the guardians of the Bolshevik revolution. Even Gorky denounced *We* as "hopelessly bad, a completely sterile thing. Its anger is cold and dry; it is the anger of an old maid."

For the rest of the 1920s, Zamyatin lived with a sword of Damocles dangling over his head. The many hardline critics who considered him a bourgeois counter-revolutionary, guilty of "ridiculing and humiliating the people of October," were eager to cut the thread. In 1922, Zamyatin was one of scores of intellectuals arrested for undesirable activities and found himself in a cell on the same corridor of the same jail where he had been imprisoned in 1905. He was disappointed when his friends intervened to save him from being deported, so much so that he then officially *requested* deportation, without success. He knew what was coming. For the next few years, he fulfilled his official duties as a translator, editor and lecturer. He also dabbled fruitlessly in writing scenarios for the motion picture industry, started an epic novel that he would never finish, and wrote a play, *Attila*, that was barred from theatres. His letters were censored, his articles rejected by literary journals. He had the smell of heresy about him.

The horizons of Russian literature were narrowing fast. After Lenin died in 1924 and Stalin, not Trotsky, took his place, fellow-travellers were regarded with increasing suspicion. Gorky spent most of the decade abroad, unable to cushion the blows. In 1925, a group of hardliners led by the Marxist critic Leopold Averbakh formed the Russian Association of Proletarian Writers (RAPP), whose third-rate scribes thrived by denouncing the politically unreliable and grinding out propagandistic dross like Minimus the pig in *Animal Farm*. As Orwell wrote, "certain themes cannot be celebrated in words and tyranny is one of them. No one ever wrote a good book in praise of the Inquisition." This was the mentality that Zamyatin had already mocked in his 1921 essay "Paradise": "They all merge into a single monophonic grayness . . . And, indeed, how else? After all, rejecting banality means standing out from the orderly ranks, violating the law of universal equality. Originality is unquestionably criminal." In the summer of 1928, he and Boris Pilnyak, the novelist who ran the Moscow branch of the VSP, were among several writers dispatched to collective farms to write inspiring fiction about the need to accelerate grain collection. The muse did not strike.

In December 1928, the Central Committee announced what amounted to a Five Year Plan for literature. Only the writer who celebrated "socialist construction" qualified as a true Soviet writer, and that writer certainly wasn't Zamyatin. "Everything was levelled, equalised," he wrote. "Everything vanished in the smoke of the literary carnage." Gorky privately joked: "In the old days, Russian writers only had the policeman and the archbishop to fear; today's Communist official is both at once. He is always wanting to lay his filthy paws on your soul." Averbakh, a calculating demagogue whose brother-in-law was the future NKVD chief Genrikh Yagoda, was determined to demolish the fellow-travellers of the VSP by bringing down its leading lights. In 1929, which Hannah Arendt called "the first year of clear-cut totalitarian dictatorship in Russia," he saw his opportunity.

We had been published in English, Czech and French, but Zamyatin declined all requests from abroad to publish an edition in the original Russian. Without his permission, however, a group of liberal émigrés in Prague published Russian-language extracts in the magazine *Volya Rossii* (*The Will of Russia*) in 1927. Zamyatin asked the editors to desist; they ignored him. Nobody in Russia seemed to care until August 1929, when this unofficial publication was discovered (or handily rediscovered) by RAPP. Pilnyak was similarly vulnerable because his novel *Mahogany* had been published by émigrés in Berlin. RAPP accused both authors of collaboration and *The Literary Gazette* printed pages of telegrams attacking them as treacherous bourgeois counter-revolutionaries.

The Moscow branch of VSP immediately crumpled under pressure, ousting Pilnyak and censuring Zamyatin, who drily noted that if they wanted to attack *We*, then they should have done it six years earlier, when he read from it at one of their literary evenings. On September 22, the Leningrad VSP held a special general meeting to investigate the publication of *We*. The hall was so packed that many non-members, intrigued by the Zamyatin affair, were turned away. Read out in his absence, Zamyatin's explanation of his non-involvement in the *Volya Rossii* incident persuaded many writers, most of whom had liked and admired him for years, but it was far easier, in that fearful climate, to denounce him anyway. The Russian revolutionary and anti-Stalinist Victor Serge wrote contemptuously that they "voted whatever was required against their two comrades, only to go and ask their pardon in private." Although the VSP exonerated Zamyatin of active collaboration, it condemned his failure to repudiate "the ideas which were expressed in the novel and which were recognised as anti-Soviet by our public opinion." So *Volya Rossii* was just a pretext; *We* itself was his crime. Zamyatin resigned from the VSP in disgust, just before the entire body was purged, renamed and effectively destroyed. In his resignation letter, he reiterated the particulars of the case in Orwell-like terms: "Facts are stubborn, they are more stubborn than resolutions. Every fact can be confirmed by documents or people. I want to make these facts known to my readers."

Driven to the brink of suicide, Pilnyak recanted his alleged sins so fulsomely and humiliated himself so thoroughly that he became one of the wealthiest writers in 1930s Russia. Zamyatin, however, held fast. "Zamyatin's crime was that he kept his intellectual independence and moral integrity," wrote the anti-Stalinist American journalist Max Eastman in *Artists in Uniform*. "He refused as an artist to take orders from a political bureaucracy."

He paid a heavy price for it. Zamyatin's existing books were withdrawn from publication and pulled from library shelves, and his new work rejected. The *Soviet Literary Encyclopedia* called *We* "a mean libel on the Socialist future." One RAPP critic catalogued his sins: "A complete and unmitigated disbelief in the Revolution, a thorough and persistent scepticism, a departure from reality, an extreme individualism, a clearly hostile attitude to the Marxist-Leninist world view, the justification of any 'heresy,' of any protest in the name of protest, [and] a hostile attitude to the factors of class war."

In June 1931, further demoralised by chronic colitis, Zamyatin gave Gorky a letter to hand to Stalin, requesting permission to leave Russia. Given his delicate position, his letter was remarkably defiant. He said that he would return to Russia only when "it becomes possible in our country to serve great ideas in literature without cringing before little men." Ultimately, he wrote, his blacklisting was a "death sentence": if he could not write in Russia, then he could not live in Russia.

Stalin was a capricious man and sometimes spared people, especially artists, for reasons that only he understood. Zamyatin's request was granted. In November, he left his homeland forever.

Zamyatin hoped to move to the US to write movies for Cecil B. DeMille, but he never made it. Instead, he settled in Paris, where he and his wife lived a pinched and lonely life. He avoided the city's numerous White Russian émigrés and declined to become a celebrity ex-communist. As he had told Stalin, "I know that, while I have been proclaimed a right-winger here because of my habit of writing according to my conscience rather than according to command, I shall sooner or later probably be declared a Bolshevik for the same reason abroad." He worked with little success on short stories, novels, plays, essays and movie scenarios. After a plan to film *We* fell through, the only scenario that made it to the screen was, aptly enough, an award-winning French adaptation of Gorky's *The Lower Depths* for Jean Renoir in 1936.

Gorky never saw it. He died on June 18, 1936, a disappointment to many.* When Wells had reconnected with him in Moscow two years earlier, he had been dismayed: "I did not like to find Gorky against liberty. It wounded me." But Zamyatin, in a powerfully fond obituary, insisted that the old man had thrown a protective force field around many vulnerable writers, including himself: "Dozens of people are indebted to him for their lives and their freedom."

Back home, Zamyatin's friends and foes fell like dominoes. His old Scythian comrade Ivanov-Razumnik spent several years in Moscow

---

* It was widely rumoured that Gorky was poisoned on Stalin's orders in preparation for the show trial that commenced the Great Terror in August.

jails. RAPP was shut down in 1932. "Nothing remained to mark their reign," wrote Eugene Lyons in *Assignment in Utopia*, "except a litter of pronunciamentos and the ashes of artists whom they had hounded to suicide and broken on the rack of persecution." Zamyatin's tormentor Leopold Averbakh was arrested and executed in 1937, followed by his brother-in-law, Yagoda. Pilnyak, who once told Victor Serge, "There isn't a single thinking adult in this country who has not thought that he might get shot," was accused of being a Japanese spy and killed in 1938. In Stalin's Russia, there was always somebody more nimble than you. The new literary doctrine, "Soviet realism," was essentially a form of utopian fiction. Its purpose, observed the American journalist Louis Fischer, was "to treat the present as though it did not exist and the future as if it had already arrived."

Orwell appears to have known very little about Zamyatin's life. Had he known more, had he read *We* a decade earlier, he might have visited the Russian when he passed through Paris on the way to Spain. A conversation might have accelerated his understanding of Russia and his interest in anti-utopias. But perhaps it would already have been too late. Zamyatin was seriously ill with angina pectoris. Shortly after dawn on March 10, 1937—when the light, as he wrote in *We*, was "ringing and fizzy"—his heart gave out. He was fifty-three. A small group of friends buried him in the rain. In Russia, his passing made barely a ripple.

Zamyatin gave the citizens of his One State a choice between painful, chaotic freedom and the mindless happiness of total obedience. For him, as for Orwell, that was never really a choice. He was as stubborn as a fact.

CHAPTER 7

Inconvenient Facts

Orwell 1944–1945

As soon as fear, hatred, jealousy and power worship are
involved, the sense of reality becomes unhinged.

—George Orwell, "Notes on Nationalism," 1945

O rwell never enjoyed writing a book as much as he enjoyed
writing *Animal Farm* during the foul and foggy winter of
1943–1944. Each night in bed at 10a Mortimer Crescent,
he would read the day's work to Eileen and invite feedback. The
next morning, she would quote the best bits to her colleagues at the
Ministry of Food when they went for coffee at Selfridge's. She said,
with justified pride, that it was the best thing he had ever written. It
flew like an arrow, poison-tipped. The real struggle, Orwell knew,
was still to come. "I am writing a little squib which might amuse you
when it comes out," he told Gleb Struve, "but it is so not O.K. politically that I don't feel certain in advance that anyone will publish it.
Perhaps that gives you a hint of its subject."

Animal Farm was made possible by Orwell's much more agreeable
work schedule. In short order, he left the BBC, resigned from the
Home Guard, and joined *Tribune* on Monday November 29, 1943,
working three days a week as literary editor and author of the column
"As I Please." Founded in 1937 by the Labour MPs Stafford Cripps
and George Strauss, *Tribune* had initially backed Stalin, but under
the editorship of Aneurin "Nye" Bevan, who took over in 1942, it had
become the organ of the non-communist Labour left, in the unusual
position of criticising both Stalin and Churchill. Orwell called it
the only weekly paper that made "a genuine effort . . . to combine

a radical Socialist policy with a respect for freedom of speech and a civilised attitude towards literature and the arts." Bevan, the formidably intelligent and pugnacious son of a Welsh coal miner, was the only politician Orwell truly liked and admired, and the respect was mutual.

Orwell was far too soft to make a good literary editor. He paid struggling writers for articles he had no space to print, and perhaps didn't even consider worth printing, because he knew what a difference the fee would make to their pinched finances. He defended his drawer stuffed with expensively unpublished manuscripts by saying that's what happens when you turn a freelance writer into an editor: "It is too like taking a convict out of his cell and making him governor of the prison."

Orwell did, however, excel as a columnist. After years of smuggling his obsessions into reviews or radio programmes, he was finally able to publish whatever was on his mind, from racism, propaganda and freedom of speech to make-up, birdwatching and the price of clocks. The most sombre topics rubbed up against brainteasers, jokes and nuggets of trivia. Orwell had opinions about everything under the sun and they were all worth reading even if you disagreed with them, which many *Tribune* readers did, loudly and often. Michael Foot, the future Labour MP who sat on the *Tribune* board, called "As I Please" "the only column ever written in Fleet Street by a man who came into the office deliberately every week with the idea of offending as many readers as possible."

"As I Please" was Orwell unfiltered, transmitting his thoughts to the page with a confident, chatty fluidity. He would rehearse his ideas in conversation. Friends such as Tosco Fyvel, his former Searchlight Books colleague, would recognise on the page some of the same phrases that they had heard a few days before. Some of them reappeared in *Nineteen Eighty-Four,* making "As I Please" a kind of workshop for the novel. In one column, he described the radio as if it were a telescreen: "a sort of totalitarian world of its own, braying propaganda night and day to people who can listen to nothing else." In another, he recalled meeting a young pacifist painter, on the first night of the Blitz, who insisted that he could weather German occupation with his integrity intact. "The fallacy is to believe that under a dictatorial government you can be free *inside* . . . Out in the street the loudspeakers bellow, the flags flutter from the rooftops, the police with their tommy-guns prowl to and fro, the face of the Leader, four feet wide, glares from every hoarding; but up in the attic the secret enemies of the regime can record their thoughts in perfect freedom." It was a fallacy that he was to directly refute in *Nineteen Eighty-Four*, in which the room above Charrington's shop is a sanctum that turns out to be a trap. "It is intolerable to us that an erroneous thought should exist anywhere in the world," says O'Brien, "however secret and powerless it may be."

The new authority and clarity that Orwell's prose achieved from 1943 onwards was also evident in his book reviews and essays. His quarrelsome mind was attracted to writers he thought were worth arguing with: H. G. Wells, Henry Miller, and now James Burnham.

Quiet and urbane in person but unyielding on the page, Burnham was a professor of philosophy who had been one of America's leading Trotskyists until the Nazi-Soviet Pact and a bitter public row with Trotsky precipitated the complete collapse of his tottering faith in Marxism. Burnham's methodical brain demanded an overarching system to explain the world, so he was forced to build a replacement. Despite being turned down by a dozen publishers and savaged by critics, Burnham's 1941 jeremiad *The Managerial Revolution: What Is Happening in the World* became a surprise best seller, described by *Fortune* as "by all odds the most debated book published so far this year." It was based on two assumptions: capitalist democracy could not survive the war, and socialism could not replace it. Instead, the future was a huge, centralised state run by a class of "managers": technicians, bureaucrats, executives, and so on. Burnham's thesis was not entirely original—Orwell compared it to Hilaire Belloc's "very prescient" 1912 polemic *The Servile State*—but it struck a chord.

Burnham wrote as if everyone else's analysis was clouded by emotion and only he could clearly see reality. "The theory of the managerial revolution is not merely predicting what may happen in a hypothetical future," he wrote in his pedantic, somewhat exasperated prose. "The theory is, to begin with, an interpretation of what *already* has happened and is now happening." Anyone who believed

otherwise was "living in a world of fantastic dreams, not on the earth."
H. G. Wells personally warned Burnham against making overconfi-
dent prophecies (and he, after all, was an expert), but Burnham wasn't
the kind of man to take advice.

By the time Orwell first wrote about Burnham, in January 1944,
The Managerial Revolution's most important short-term prediction—
Germany would first conquer Britain and then crush Russia—had
been blown to bits. Orwell thought that Burnham had blundered
because he overrated the durability of totalitarianism while under-
rating the strength of democracy due to his "contempt for the
common man": if Hitler had been obliged to heed public opinion,
for example, he would never have invaded Russia. Orwell accused
Burnham of "trying to spread the idea that totalitarianism is *unavoidable,* and that we must therefore do nothing to oppose it." Burnham
fired off a haughty complaint to *Tribune,* foreshadowing the defence
that Orwell would later make of *Nineteen Eighty-Four:* "Nor have I
ever stated that 'totalitarianism is *unavoidable.*' I have stated, and I
do believe, that totalitarianism is, in all major nations, *probable.* Does
Mr. Orwell understand the difference between these two judgements?"
But he was being disingenuous, and Orwell had the quotes to prove
it. "We could all be true prophets if we were allowed to alter our
prophecies after the event," Orwell tartly replied. Big Brother can
order his old speeches to be altered "in such a way as to make him
predict the thing that had actually happened," but Burnham couldn't
erase the evidence of his bad calls.

Orwell remained a thorn in Burnham's side for the next three
years, leading the American to complain that the "Orwell business
has become something of an international plague as far as I'm concerned," but he would not have bothered writing thousands of words
about Burnham's ideas, in *Tribune, Polemic, The New Leader* and the
Manchester Evening News, if he hadn't found them fascinating. It was
just hard to unpick the praise from the insults. According to Orwell,
The Machiavellians: Defenders of Freedom was a "piece of shallow naughtiness"; the *Partisan Review* essay "Lenin's Heir" betrayed "a sort of
fascinated admiration for Stalin"; and Burnham was repeatedly led
astray by power worship. "Burnham sees the trend and assumes that
it is irresistible," Orwell wrote in his 1946 essay "Second Thoughts on

James Burnham," "rather as a rabbit fascinated by a boa constrictor might assume that a boa constrictor is the strongest thing in the world."

Yet Burnham's ideas seized Orwell's imagination even as his intellect rejected them, which is why he related *The Managerial Revolution* to the fictional nightmares of *We*, *The Sleeper Awakes*, *The Iron Heel* and *Brave New World*. Burnham's vision of a tripolar world ("three great super-States ... which divide the world between them, make ceaseless war upon one another, and keep the working class in permanent subjection," in Orwell's précis) is a clear blueprint for Oceania, Eurasia and Eastasia. Orwell may have thought that Burnham's "huge, invincible, everlasting slave empire" was a chimera, as was the claim that politics was nothing more than the struggle for power, but surely this is Oceania. The "primal traitor" Goldstein may have been modelled on Trotsky (born Lev Bronstein), but his "Chapter III: War Is Peace" owes more to Burnham than it does to Trotsky's *The Revolution Betrayed*. Orwell thought that, among revolutionaries, "the longing for a just society has always been fatally mixed up with the intention to secure power for themselves." But in the "what-if?" world of *Nineteen Eighty-Four*, the longing for a just society has been eliminated: "One does not establish a dictatorship in order to safeguard a revolution; one makes the revolution in order to establish the dictatorship." Orwell did not agree with Burnham, but he ensured that O'Brien did. In places, the writer ("No theory, no promises, no morality, no amount of good will, no religion will restrain power") and the character ("We are interested solely in power. Not wealth or luxury or long life or happiness: only power, pure power") are almost interchangeable.

Orwell made a crucial connection between Burnham's super-state hypothesis and his own long-standing obsession with organised lying. What better environment in which to rewrite reality than a sealed state whose only relationship with its neighbours is combat? In *Nineteen Eighty-Four*, "each is in effect a separate universe within which almost any perversion of thought can be safely practised." In May 1944, a *Tribune* reader called Noel Willmett wrote to Orwell to ask him if he thought totalitarianism could take hold in Britain. Under the influence of Burnham, Orwell's thoughtful response was *Nineteen Eighty-Four* in embryo: "If the sort of world that I am afraid of arrives, a world of two or three great superstates which are unable to conquer one another, two and two could become five if the fuhrer wished it . . . though, of course, the process is reversible." Hence the importance of describing the worst-case scenario: "If one simply proclaims that all is for the best and doesn't point to the sinister symptoms, one is merely helping to bring totalitarianism nearer." This is not all that far from Burnham's angry letter to *Tribune:* "only through absolute clarity about the probability of totalitarianism, and about the direction of its advance . . . will we be able, precisely, to have a chance to overcome or avoid it."

In 1944, there was a bull market in dire warnings. "Only if we recognize the danger in time can we hope to avert it," wrote the Austrian economist Friedrich Hayek in *The Road to Serfdom,* another unexpected sensation which was to become a sacred text for free-market conservatives. Hayek's diagnosis of totalitarianism was sometimes uncannily close to Orwell's own, but Orwell certainly didn't agree with Hayek's claim that the Labour Party's version of central planning was "the source of the mortal danger to everything we most value."* Orwell reviewed *The Road to Serfdom* alongside *The Mirror of the Past, Lest It Reflect the Future* by the pro-communist Labour MP Konni Zilliacus: "Each writer is convinced that the other's policy leads directly to slavery, and the alarming thing is that they may both be right." The dangers of collectivism had been amply demonstrated but Hayek's free-market fundamentalism, he decided, would mean "a tyranny probably worse, because more irresponsible, than that of the State." Worse? From the author of *Animal Farm,* that was really saying something.

Contractually obliged to give Victor Gollancz first refusal on his novels, Orwell warned that *Animal Farm* was "completely unacceptable politically from your point of view (it is anti-Stalin)." Gollancz asked to read it anyway before conceding the point. Stubbornly using

* Take this Orwell-like passage: "The word truth itself ceases to have its old meaning. It describes no longer something to be found, with the individual conscience as the sole guide; it becomes something to be laid down by authority, something which has to be believed in the interest of the unity of the organised effort, and which may have to be altered as the necessities of this organised effort require it."

the author's birth name, the publisher told Orwell's agent Leonard Moore: "I am highly critical of many aspects of internal and external Soviet policy; but I could not possibly publish (as Blair anticipated) a general attack of this nature." The firm of Nicholson & Watson also considered it bad taste to attack an ally. The publisher Jonathan Cape loved the book but felt compelled to run it past a friend who worked for the Ministry of Information in case its skewering of Stalin might damage the war effort. The official decided it certainly would and Cape performed a weaselly U-turn. He hadn't realised, you see, that *Animal Farm* was specifically about Russia. And did they really have to be pigs? "I think the choice of pigs as the ruling caste will no doubt give offence to many people, and particularly to anyone who is a bit touchy, as undoubtedly the Russians are." Orwell found the rejection laughable. He told Inez Holden, "Imagine old Joe (who doesn't know one word of any European language), sitting in the Kremlin reading *Animal Farm* and saying 'I don't like this.'"

The next recipient of the somewhat bedraggled manuscript was T. S. Eliot at Faber & Faber. Eliot favourably compared it to *Gulliver's Travels,* but he and Geoffrey Faber did not consider "that this is the right point of view from which to criticize the political situation at the present time." George Woodcock brought it to his anarchist colleagues at the Freedom Press but they hadn't forgiven Orwell for his earlier attacks on pacifism. In the US, it was rejected by a dozen publishers, including Angus Cameron, the pro-communist editor-in-chief of Little, Brown. Amid the multifarious political objections, Dial Press's logic was refreshingly simple: they said there was no market for animal stories.

By now fairly demoralised, Orwell considered publishing *Animal Farm* himself as a two-shilling pamphlet via the Whitman Press, an anarchist cottage industry run by his friend the poet Paul Potts. He even wrote a powerful preface, "The Freedom of the Press," about the stealthy power of unofficial censorship: "Unpopular ideas can be silenced, and inconvenient facts kept dark, without the need for any official ban." But the preface would be mothballed until 1972, because Fredric Warburg, who had previously rescued *Homage to Catalonia,* stepped in with a £100 advance, provided he could find enough paper to print it on. Overriding objections from his wife and some colleagues, Warburg's bold decision convinced Orwell to stick with the publisher going forward because "I knew that anyone who would risk this book would risk anything."

In his memoir, Warburg wondered melodramatically what would have happened if he hadn't taken the plunge. "Perhaps even Orwell's morale might have cracked, had *Animal Farm* failed. And then . . . ? *Then there might never have been a novel called 1984.*"

Animal Farm's publication was delayed for several reasons, one of which was an air raid that destroyed Warburg's premises that summer. In June, the Luftwaffe began pummelling London with winged V-1 rockets, known as "doodlebugs," in retaliation for the RAF's raids on Germany. H. G. Wells called them "robot bombs." Inez Holden overheard a scared woman claiming that the rockets were the ghosts of Luftwaffe pilots killed in the Battle of Britain. A V-1 struck the Orwells' flat while they were out, forcing them to move into Holden's empty house in Marylebone, before settling into their final London home at 27b Canonbury Square, Islington. Orwell retrieved dozens of books and the "blitzed" manuscript of *Animal Farm* from the rubble.

He had recently become a father. Orwell believed he was sterile (on what basis is unclear) and turned to Eileen's sister-in-law Gwen O'Shaughnessy, who ran a medical practice in Newcastle, to arrange an adoption. Starting a family had been more of a priority for Orwell than for Eileen but they both became doting parents to three-week-old Richard Horatio Blair, named after Orwell's late father. As soon as the war was over, they planned to move to the countryside. "I hate London," Orwell told the crime writer Julian Symons. "I really would like to get out of it, but of course you can't leave while people are being bombed to bits all around you."

With the war entering its terminal stage, Orwell's mind was turning to the "after-war," but first he had to come clean about his errors: his latest "London Letter" was a masochistically thorough confession of his incompetence as a prophet. Quoting a dozen faulty predictions, he explained how he had been "grossly wrong" about the survival of the Nazi-Soviet Pact, the fall of Churchill, and the likelihood of the war driving Britain towards either fascism or socialism. He had come to realise that he hadn't worked hard enough to identify and overcome his biases, and vowed to redouble his efforts. "It seems to me very important to realize that we have been wrong, and say so. Most people nowadays, when their predictions are falsified, just impudently claim that they have been justified, and squeeze the facts accordingly . . . I believe that it is possible to be more objective than most of us are, but that it involves a *moral* effort. One cannot get away from one's own subjective feelings, but at least one can know what they are and make allowance for them."

London in late 1944 was a glum, crotchety, threadbare city, battered by Hitler's desperate final assault. The new V-2 ballistic missiles—much like the "rocket bombs" that pummel Airstrip One— were enough to make Londoners nostalgic for the evil whine of the doodlebugs: at least those provided some warning. "Every time one goes off I hear gloomy references to 'next time,'" Orwell wrote in "As I Please." "But if you ask who will be fighting whom when this universally expected war breaks out, you get no clear answer. It is just war in the abstract—the notion that human beings could ever behave sanely having apparently faded out of many people's memories."

He was struck by a 1943 Mass Observation report which found that 46 per cent of Londoners definitely expected a Third World War and another 19 per cent thought one was possible. Most of them expected it to take place within the next twenty-five years.

In September 1944, Orwell wrote a brilliant essay for *Tribune* about his friend Arthur Koestler. If James Burnham supplied Orwell with the geopolitical superstructure for *Nineteen Eighty-Four,* then Koestler provided him the mental landscape with his 1940 masterpiece *Darkness at Noon.* The novel was set in a prison, and Koestler certainly knew his way around a cell.

Born in Budapest in 1905, Koestler was a restless adventurer who was first jailed in February 1937, while reporting on the Spanish Civil War for the *News Chronicle.* Unbeknown to his employers, he had been a member of the German Communist Party for six years, working for the Comintern propagandist Willi Münzenberg's network of front organisations. The fascists held Koestler in solitary confinement in Seville for ninety-four days, during which he lived under the constant threat of execution. This proximity to death triggered a spiritual epiphany which fractured his faith in communism. Freed as the result of an international campaign, Koestler resigned from the Communist Party the following year at a meeting in Paris, where he quoted Thomas Mann: "A harmful truth is better than a useful lie."* He later compared himself to an alcoholic emerging from a "Lost Week-end in Utopia." To articulate his disillusionment, he began writing *Darkness at Noon* (originally called *The Vicious Circle*), basing the prison scenes on his experiences in Seville, and those of his friend Eva Striker, who had been imprisoned in Moscow on the fictitious charge of plotting to assassinate Stalin. But there were more cells to come.

Living in Paris when war broke out, Koestler was designated an undesirable alien and placed in Le Vernet internment camp. He was freed for just long enough to finish the novel and send the manuscript to London, before being apprehended yet again when the Wehrmacht invaded France. He escaped to England in November 1940, where he was promptly jailed as an illegal alien *again:* on the day that *Darkness at Noon* was published, Koestler was in solitary confinement in Pentonville Prison. In 1931, Orwell had deliberately got himself arrested for drunkenness in order to see a police cell for himself but he was quickly released and the only memory that proved useful while he was writing *Nineteen Eighty-Four* was the stench of a broken toilet. Koestler's authentic descriptions of incarceration were therefore invaluable source material for the scenes in the Ministry of Love. So, too, were his insights into the mental prison of totalitarianism.

"Who will ever forget the first moment he read *Darkness at Noon?*" wrote Michael Foot. "For socialists especially, the experience was indelible. I can recall reading it right through one night, horror-struck, over-powered, enthralled." Koestler offered a possible solution to the central riddle of the Moscow show trials: why did so many Communist Party members sign confessions of crimes against the state, and thus their death warrants? Either they were all guilty as charged (impossible), or they were broken by torture (inadequate), or, as Koestler argued, their years of unbending loyalty had dissolved their belief in objective truth: if the Party required them to be guilty, then guilty they must be. As Parsons wails in *Nineteen Eighty-Four,* "Of

---

* Contrast this with his party loyalist in *Darkness at Noon:* "Truth is what is useful to humanity, falsehood what is harmful."

course I'm guilty! You don't think the Party would arrest an innocent man, do you?" In Oceania, there are no laws, only crimes, and no distinction between thought and deed. Hence Winston can confess to fabricated charges of espionage, embezzlement, sabotage, murder, sexual perversion and so on, while believing on some level that he is indeed guilty. "All the confessions that are uttered here are true," says O'Brien. "We make them true." So, too, in Soviet Russia. Under Stalin, Orwell wrote in his 1941 review of *Darkness at Noon,* "one is imprisoned not for what one *does* but for what one *is,* or, more exactly, for what one is suspected of being."

Koestler's protagonist Rubashov is a senior Soviet official arrested during a purge that forces him to reckon with the times that he diligently dispatched innocent party members to their deaths. He has been transformed overnight from victimiser to victim at the whim of No. 1, the enigmatic, infallible Stalin surrogate whose face adorns every wall. It was not enough for Stalin to have his enemies eliminated; he needed confession and repentance to destroy them morally and thus confirm his victory over reality. "The horror which No. 1 emanated above all consisted in the possibility that he was in the right," writes Koestler, "and that all those whom he killed had to admit, even with the bullet in the back of their necks, that he conceivably might be in the right." The Soviet official Gyorgy Pyatakov, executed in 1937, said that the true Bolshevik "would be ready to believe that black was white, and white was black, if the Party required it . . . there was no particle left inside him which was not at one with the Party, did not belong to it."

Rubashov is held in a prison where the lights burn day and night and is interrogated relentlessly in a process known in Russia as "the conveyor." He is questioned first by his former friend Ivanov, then by the younger, more fanatical apparatchik Gletkin. Orwell called the latter "an almost perfect specimen of the human gramophone," uninhibited by memories of the old world. "The Gletkins," writes Koestler, "had nothing to erase; they need not deny their past, because they had none." In *Nineteen Eighty-Four,* too, the most fanatical citizens are the young: "It was almost normal for people under thirty to be frightened of their own children." Parsons's daughter, who reports her father to the Thought Police, was probably based on Pavlik Morozov, the thirteen-year-old communist who was allegedly murdered by his family in 1932 for betraying his father to the secret police and subsequently canonised as a "boy hero" in Soviet propaganda. In Airstrip One, where they sing, "Under the spreading chestnut tree / I sold you and you sold me," betrayal is promoted as a virtue. The family is nothing compared with the state.

Yevgeny Zamyatin's old friend Razumnik Ivanov-Razumnik met around a thousand prisoners during his years in Moscow jails and knew only twelve who refused to confess. Unlike most of them, Rubashov is not physically tortured; his dismantling is purely psychological. Nagged by toothache, tobacco deprivation and a bad conscience, he gradually loses every moral and intellectual basis for resistance. By the logic of the party he has loyally served, there is no *I*, only the collective *we*, which is the Party, which represents History, which can never be wrong. "How could the immortal, collective brain be mistaken?" asks Winston Smith. "By what external standard could you check its judgements?" And if mistakes are impossible, then the Party must constantly delete contradictory evidence, leaving only pale rectangular spaces on the walls and gaps in the library shelves to limn the void. "Rubashov remarked jokingly to Arlova that the only thing left to be done was to publish a new and revised edition of the back numbers of all newspapers." Orwell turned Rubashov's joke into Winston Smith's job.

Of course Rubashov eventually confesses. Of course he dies. And yet he is not fully defeated. The Party's ultimate aim is to colonise the brain and eliminate what Orwell dubbed *thoughtcrime*. "We persecuted the seeds of evil not only in men's deeds, but in their thoughts," Rubashov writes. "We admitted no private sphere, not even inside a man's skull." But he goes to his death with a head full of heretical thoughts about the corruption of the revolution and the mystical "oceanic sense" that transcends it all. Koestler was kinder than Orwell. He granted Stalin's victims the possibility that, despite their public disintegration, they did not make that final private surrender. O'Brien seems to be describing this very scene in *Nineteen Eighty-Four:* "Even the victim of the Russian purges could carry rebellion locked up in his skull as he walked down the passage waiting for the bullet." Not so in Oceania: "We make the brain perfect before we blow it out."

In his *Tribune* essay, Orwell typically counterbalanced his praise for *Darkness at Noon* with rough treatment of Koestler's latest book,

Arrival and Departure, a "shallow" novel about a refugee from fascism. He felt that Koestler combined the blackest cynicism about short-term progress with a "quasi-mystical belief" in a far-off Utopia, because he was too hedonistic (a terrible character flaw in Orwell's eyes) to accept life as the painful, messy, compromised experience it is. "Perhaps some degree of suffering is ineradicable from human life," Orwell offered, "perhaps the choice before man is always a choice of evils, perhaps even the aim of Socialism is not to make the world perfect but to make it better. All revolutions are failures, but they are not all the same failure."

Orwell and his contemporaries were a robust, pugnacious bunch. Correlating Orwell's correspondence with the names of writers that he reviewed, or who reviewed him, you might expect them to have formed a cosy circuit of mutual log-rolling. In fact, they prided themselves on their critical integrity and pulled few punches. If Orwell had been cold-shouldered by everybody he had criticised in print, then his literary social circle would have shrunk to the size of a farthing.

Still, his rough honesty could lead to some awkward moments. In 1945, Koestler and his partner Mamaine Paget invited Orwell to spend Christmas with them in Wales. The day before Orwell's arrival, Koestler read a recent issue of *Tribune* and was dismayed to see his friend describe his new science-fiction play *Twilight Bar* as "an unworthy squib." So when Koestler collected Orwell from Llandudno station, he was furious.

"That was a bloody awful review you wrote, wasn't it?"

"Yes," Orwell flatly replied. "And it's a bloody awful play, isn't it?"

Only on the drive back to Llandudno a week later did Orwell quietly concede that yes, perhaps he had been a little too harsh. Yet the issue had not spoiled the holiday. Perhaps, knowing what Orwell had been through that year, Koestler was disinclined to press the point.

In February 1945, Orwell finally got his chance to be a war correspondent. *The Observer* and the *Manchester Evening News* dispatched him to liberated Paris while Eileen and Richard went to stay with Gwen O'Shaughnessy in Stockton-on-Tees, County Durham.

In Thurston Clarke's *Thirteen O'Clock,* a 1984 conspiracy thriller about an MP's wife who discovers Orwell's lost diaries, Orwell spends his time in Europe on the trail of the US colonel who betrayed his Spanish comrades to the NKVD. The truth is less dramatic but far from dull. When Captain Eric Blair checked in to the Hotel Scribe in Paris on February 15, he found as many writers in the French capital as there had been in Spain. He befriended the philosopher A. J. Ayer; dined with P. G. Wodehouse; crossed paths with Malcolm Muggeridge, who was working for MI6; reconnected with his Spanish commander Jose Rovira; introduced himself to André Malraux, now an adviser to Charles de Gaulle; and allegedly bumped into Hemingway.* Orwell also arranged to meet Albert Camus at Les Deux Magots, but Camus was ill with tuberculosis that day, thwarting what could have been a remarkable meeting between two natural rebels who put principles before political expediency and turned political writing into an art. Orwell later sent Camus a copy of the French translation of *Animal Farm.*

In late March, Orwell accompanied Allied forces on their march into Cologne. "After years of war it is an intensely strange feeling to be at last standing on German soil," he wrote in his only dispatch before he fell ill and was admitted to hospital. While there, he missed the urgent letters Eileen was sending to the Hotel Scribe—her last. Eileen was due an emergency hysterectomy in Newcastle on March 29 to remove several rapidly growing tumours from her uterus. In her letters, she was heartbreakingly self-effacing about the cost of the operation ("I really don't think I'm worth the money") and briskly unsentimental about the possibility of dying on the operating table, but adamant about the future she wanted. She told Orwell that he needed to drop journalism, concentrate on novels, and move to the country as soon as possible. "I don't think you understand what a nightmare the London life is to me . . . All these years I have felt as though I were in a mild kind of concentration camp." On his return to Paris, Orwell read the letters and telegraphed Eileen, but too late.

---

* The two accounts of this meeting don't tally at all. According to Hemingway, a paranoid Orwell asked to borrow a gun. The story that the poet and anarchist Paul Potts claimed to have heard from Orwell involved a raucous drinking session but no firearms. Orwell himself never wrote about it. Memory is doubly unreliable when the desire to tell a good story gets in the way.

The next day a telegram from *The Observer* regretfully informed him that his wife of nine years was dead at the age of thirty-nine. She had suffered cardiac arrest under anaesthesia.

Orwell hitched a lift on a military aircraft to London, materialising at Inez Holden's door in a desperate state, and travelled on to Stockton-on-Tees for the funeral. The marrow-deep reserve that he had inherited from his father confused some friends into thinking that he was stoic about his loss, but his feelings leaked out in his letters, in which he was less concerned with his own grief than with the unfairness of Eileen's stolen future. "It was a most horrible thing to happen because she had five really miserable years of bad health and overwork, and things were just beginning to get better," he wrote to Anthony Powell. He felt enormously guilty that he had been sexually unfaithful, selfish, oblivious to the seriousness of her illness, and absent when she needed him most. The shock, and the ensuing loneliness, haunted him for the next four years. "I don't think he looked after her much, but I think he loved her," said Eileen's friend and colleague Lettice Cooper. "I think he didn't know how to look after anybody, not even himself."

As usual, Orwell buried himself in work. A few days after the funeral he was back in Europe. In Paris when Germany surrendered, he witnessed celebrants jamming the streets for two whole days as they chanted "*Avec nous!*" and sang "La Marseillaise." He then visited Stuttgart, Nuremberg and Austria to see for himself the immediate aftermath of a collapsed dictatorship. The devastation moved him to horror and pity: "To walk through the ruined cities of Germany is to feel an actual doubt about the continuity of civilization."

It was easy for a man who had never experienced Nazi occupation to say, but when Orwell saw defeated SS officers being beaten and humiliated in a POW camp, he felt strongly that "the whole idea of revenge and punishment is a childish daydream." He worried that war crimes trials and the partition of Germany would only make Europe harder to heal, satisfying nothing but the public's bloodlust. If war criminals were herded into Wembley Stadium to be eaten by lions or trampled by elephants, he thought, there would be a packed house. That image had occurred to him in January when he visited an exhibition in London called "Horrors of the Concentration Camp" and left feeling that it was a kind of pornography. In Airstrip One,

St. Martin's-in-the-Fields Church has become an atrocity exhibition and the public hanging of war criminals is a big day out for all
the family. After the war, he found the return of such executions at
Nuremberg and Kharkov "barbarous" and decried the way the British
public, like Winston Smith, "participate at second hand by watching
the news films." This marked "another turn on the downward spiral
that we have been following ever since 1933."

Another problem occupying Orwell's mind in 1945 was prejudice.
Antisemitism is only implied in *Nineteen Eighty-Four*, via the character of Emmanuel Goldstein, and racism doesn't figure at all. In
fact, Goldstein's book insists that there is no racial discrimination
in Oceania because the Party is united by ideology, not blood. Yet
Orwell considered making racism a feature of Ingsoc. His original
outline includes antisemitism and "anti-Jew propaganda." In early
drafts, the drowning refugees that Winston sees in a newsreel are
targeted because they are Jewish and there is a gruesome account of
a televised lynching in the American portion of Oceania.
    So it would be wrong to conclude that Orwell didn't think ethnic
prejudice mattered. As far back as *The Road to Wigan Pier*, he called
racial prejudice "entirely spurious" in all its forms. In "As I Please,"
he decried racist slurs and the mistreatment of black soldiers in
London, and attacked the way African-Americans were disenfran-
chised, "pushed out of skilled jobs, segregated and insulted in the
Army, assaulted by white policemen and discriminated against by
white magistrates." In "Antisemitism in Britain," his 1945 essay for
Contemporary Jewish Record, he wrote, "Something, some psychological
vitamin, is lacking in modern civilization, and as a result we are all
more or less subject to this lunacy of believing that whole races or
nations are mysteriously good or mysteriously evil."
    Orwell called this lunacy *nationalism,* a word which encompassed
every form of partisanship from fascism to Zionism. He certainly
did not believe they were all as bad as each other, but they all
demonstrated the same mental habits. Patriotism, he thought, was
largely subconscious and benign: a feeling rather than an ideology.
Nationalism, he explained in "Notes on Nationalism," written while
he was in Europe, "is power hunger tempered by self-deception.

Every nationalist is capable of the most flagrant dishonesty, but he is also—since he is conscious of serving something bigger than himself—unshakably certain of being right." Orwell listed dozens of examples of people believing emotionally satisfying lies, dismissing inexpedient truths, applying outrageous double standards, and rewriting events. These are the psychological ingredients for doublethink, or "reality control," defined in *Nineteen Eighty-Four* as "the power of holding two contradictory beliefs in one's mind simultaneously and accepting both of them . . . To tell deliberate lies while genuinely believing in them, to forget any fact that has become inconvenient, and then, when it becomes necessary again, to draw it back from oblivion for just so long as it is needed, to deny the existence of objective reality and all the while to take account of the reality which one denies."

Nationalism was Orwell's unifying theory of political psychology: a skeleton key that unlocked all manner of biases, fallacies and pernicious mental phenomena. The patterns of thought that he would push to extremes in *Nineteen Eighty-Four* sprang up everywhere, like deadly weeds. The only herbicide was to make the "moral effort" to admit one's biases and to subject oneself to relentless self-examination. Orwell argued that antisemitism, for example, should be investigated "by people who know that they are not immune to that kind of emotion." That included himself. During the 1930s, notably in *Down and Out in Paris and London,* he had made a few casually hostile remarks about Jews, typical of his generation and class, and only made an effort to examine his prejudice during the war, although he neglected also to reconsider his knee-jerk homophobia and thoughtless dismissal of feminism. He noticed that the general consensus that antisemitism was unacceptable did not, as one might hope, force people to examine their own prejudices but to redraw the definition in a way that excluded them, while reaching for examples of bad behaviour by Jews. "It is obvious that these accusations merely rationalize some deep-rooted prejudice," he wrote. "To attempt to counter them with facts and statistics is useless, and may sometimes be worse than useless." In fact, one of the features of antisemitism was "an ability to believe stories that could not possibly be true."

Orwell visualised racial prejudice as a nerve that might go unnoticed until it was prodded. Ideologies such as Nazism activated that nerve for their own ends, but a dictatorship could only function if the mass of people went along with it, whether through malice, apathy or fear. Orwell's belief in self-criticism on both a personal and a national level meant acknowledging that totalitarianism was not a disease unique to Germany and Russia but one with the potential to seize any society on Earth. Everybody is wired to believe themselves righteous and to defend their positions with whatever degree of hypocrisy and self-deception is required. In Airstrip One, it doesn't matter whether Big Brother really exists, or whether the Thought Police are watching at any given time, once the virus has taken hold, because the most powerful lies are the ones people tell themselves. In a 1944 column about pamphlets, Orwell noticed that across the political spectrum, "Nobody is searching for the truth, everybody is putting forward a 'case' with complete disregard for fairness and accuracy, and the most plainly obvious facts can be ignored by those who don't want to see them . . . To admit that an opponent might be both honest and intelligent is felt to be intolerable."

Reading "Notes in Nationalism" now, you can apply to its catalogue of cognitive biases labels that did not exist at the time: *confirmation bias, filter bubbles, backfire effect, groupthink.** Orwell was less interested in the personalities of Hitler and Stalin, about whom he wrote surprisingly little, than in the reasons why so many ordinary people followed them. One was the decay of consensus reality. He described how newspaper readers, faced with genuine confusion and outright dishonesty, surrendered the idea that the truth was attainable *at all:* "The general uncertainty as to what is really happening makes it easier to cling to lunatic beliefs."

On June 4, 1945, Winston Churchill's first radio broadcast of the general election campaign amounted to a piece of dystopian fiction about a one-party police state. "There can be no doubt that socialism is inseparably interwoven with totalitarianism and the abject worship of the state," he railed. "No socialist government conducting the

---

* *Groupthink*, a term coined by the psychologist Irving Janis in 1971 to describe "a deterioration in mental efficiency, reality testing and moral judgements as result of group pressures," was an explicit homage to Newspeak.

entire life and industry of the country could afford to allow free, sharp or violently worded expressions of public discontent. They would have to fall back on some form of Gestapo, no doubt very humanely directed in the first instance."

The Labour leader Clement Attlee correctly identified Churchill's broadcast as a "second hand version" of *The Road to Serfdom*. The public, meanwhile, found this hysterical prognosis hard to square with the shy, steady, incorruptibly honest man who had spent five years shoulder to shoulder with Churchill in the wartime coalition government. Attlee may, as Orwell noted, have borne a cranial resemblance to Lenin but, with his dry, dull voice and modest demeanour, he was nobody's idea of a power-hungry strongman. The British public was not necessarily craving socialism—in a 1943 poll, only 3 per cent of the people who wanted "great changes" after the war mentioned it—but it was interested in the fairer society Labour was offering in its manifesto, *Let Us Now Face the Future*.

Covering the election for *The Observer* after his return from Paris, Orwell's plan was to report the views of the man on the street, but the man on the street wouldn't play ball. In the pubs and on the buses, the election barely registered. "In the face of terrifying dangers and golden political opportunities, people just keep on keeping on, in a sort of twilight sleep," he grumbled. Poorly informed by frustrated campaigners and inadequate opinion polls, Orwell predicted that Churchill's party would still win a slim majority on July 5. Instead, Labour won 393 out of 640 seats, with an unprecedented 12 per cent swing. "I was wrong on several points," Orwell admitted in his postmortem for *Partisan Review*, but "everybody else, so far as I know, was also wrong." That included the victors. The morning after the results came in, the US embassy in London cabled Washington to say "no one was more surprised than were the leaders of the Labour Party." At the end of "that queer, dramatic, dreamlike day," *The New Yorker*'s London correspondent Mollie Panter-Downes covered the celebration at Westminster's Central Hall, where Labour members sang "Jerusalem" and party chairman Harold Laski mischievously introduced himself as "the temporary head of the socialist Gestapo."

Orwell can be forgiven for failing as an election pundit. A greater disappointment was his muted enthusiasm for a government that went on to do more to make democratic socialism a reality than any

Labour administration before or since. Attlee's brand of socialism was patriotic, pragmatic, both anti-imperialist and anti-Stalinist, grounded in "the fundamental decencies of life," and informed, in his youth, by the friendly utopianism of William Morris and Edward Bellamy. Attlee's insistence that socialism must be reconfigured "in accordance with the native genius of the people of that country" echoed *The Lion and the Unicorn,* and Labour's agenda overlapped considerably with that essay's six-point programme.

Orwell, however, was close to the Labour left and shared its dim view of Attlee's statesmanship. Bevan, now minister of health, had recently said that Attlee "brings to the fierce struggle of politics the tepid enthusiasm of a lazy summer afternoon at a cricket match." *Tribune,* nodding to H. G. Wells, dubbed him "the invisible man." Orwell himself had once compared the Labour leader to "a recently dead fish, before it has had time to stiffen," so he was being relatively kind when he now called Attlee "colourless" and lacking "the magnetism that a statesman needs nowadays."* But even as he worried about the government's capacity to solve immense problems at home and abroad, he thought that the party's surprise landslide was welcome proof that the British people had not lost their heads. "As a sign of the vitality of democracy," Orwell wrote in the American magazine *Commentary,* "of the power of the English-speaking peoples to get along without fuehrers, the outcome of this election is a thing to be rejoiced at, even if the men it has brought to power should utterly fail." The election posters of Churchill's face, he noticed, were reassuringly small compared to those of Stalin or de Gaulle.

While he was still in Europe, Orwell made a last-minute request to Secker & Warburg to change one word of *Animal Farm,* in a description of the autocratic Napoleon, to reflect the fact that Stalin had not fled Moscow when the Germans advanced. "I just thought the alteration would be fair to J.S.," he wrote. "J.S." may have been a murderous tyrant, but that was no reason to call him a coward. "To

* Attlee nonetheless became an Orwell fan. After Churchill's death in 1965, he wrote, "Some of the generals out in the field thought he was like Big Brother in Orwell's book, looking down on them from the wall the whole time."

me this single sentence throws as much light on Orwell's character as any I know," said Warburg.

Orwell claimed two years later that the impulse behind the book dated back to his time in Spain, which left him convinced that "the destruction of the Soviet myth is essential if we wanted a revival of the Socialist movement." And vice versa. Having seen revolutionary idealism destroyed in Barcelona, he thought it essential to create a workable alternative to Stalinism. He thought the task would require a book that could be universally understood in any language.

Notwithstanding some artistic licence with the chronology, *Animal Farm* is a scrupulous allegory of Russian history from the revolution to the Tehran conference. Each animal represents an individual—Napoleon is Stalin, Snowball is Trotsky, Mr. Frederick is Hitler, and so on—or a common type. Yet at the same time, and despite its abundant wit, the story can bring to tears a reader who knows nothing of Russia. "It is a sad fable," wrote Graham Greene, "and it is an indication of Mr. Orwell's fine talent that it is really sad—not a mere echo of human failings at one remove." When Boxer, the hard-working, gullible horse, is sent to the knacker's yard, it is Boxer that the reader mourns, not a clever symbol of the Russian proletariat.

Orwell called *Animal Farm* "a sort of fairy story, really a fable with a political meaning." He loved fairy tales, adapting *The Emperor's New Clothes* and *Little Red Riding Hood* for radio, and pondering a version of *Cinderella*, which he considered "the tops." His farmyard tragedy is something a child can feel keenly: hopes dashed, goodness betrayed, lies unpunished. One such child was the nine-year-old Margaret Atwood. "To say that I was horrified by this book would be an under-statement," she remembered. "The fate of the farm animals was so grim, the pigs were so mean and mendacious and treacherous, the sheep were so stupid. Children have a keen sense of injustice, and this was the thing that upset me the most: the pigs were so *unjust*."

Animal Farm can be read as a thematic prequel to *Nineteen Eighty-Four:* first the revolution betrayed, than tyranny triumphant. Although there are passing references to a revolution and civil war in Oceania, following a limited nuclear war, there is no clear description of how Ingsoc seized and cemented power, but *Animal Farm* strongly suggests how it played out, with Snowball as a younger version of the "sinister enchanter" Goldstein, transformed by paranoia into "some kind of invisible influence, pervading the air about them and menacing them with all kinds of dangers." In fact, an early draft of *Nineteen Eighty-Four* winked at *Animal Farm* by having O'Brien compare the unlikelihood of a prole uprising with the "theoretical possibility that the animals might one day revolt against mankind and conquer the earth."

The two books also share an obsession with the erosion and corruption of memory. The word *remember* appears 110 times in *Nineteen Eighty-Four, memory* forty-seven, and *forget* or *forgotten* forty-six. Whereas in Oceania the manipulation of the past is an elaborate industrial process, in *Animal Farm* it is described with an eerie ambiguity, as if it were a magic spell: "They all remembered, or thought they remembered . . ." Only the reader can see clearly how the animals' memories are gradually erased.

Firstly, by the falsification of evidence. The seven commandments of the revolution are gradually amended and ultimately reduced to one famous oxymoron: "ALL ANIMALS ARE EQUAL BUT SOME ANIMALS ARE MORE EQUAL THAN OTHERS." When the other animals protest, Napoleon's lieutenant Squealer asks, "Are you certain that this is not something you have dreamed, comrades? Have you any record of this resolution? Is it written down anywhere?" Of course it is not, and therefore they must be mistaken. And if Squealer has statistics "proving" that life is better now, then it must be better. Winston Smith remembers that aeroplanes existed in his childhood, so the Party could not have invented them, "But you could prove nothing. There was never any evidence."

Secondly, by the infallibility of the leader. When Boxer swears that Snowball was a war hero, and not a traitor all along, Squealer cites Napoleon as the ultimate authority. "Ah, that is different!" Boxer relents. "If Comrade Napoleon says it, it must be right." The propagandist poet Minimus glorifies him as a figure of godlike (or Big Brother–like) omniscience: "Thou watchest over all / Comrade Napoleon."

Thirdly, by language. Only the pigs, the "brainworkers," can write, so only they control the narrative. When they contract the vocabulary ("Four legs good, two legs bad" is proto-Newspeak), they narrow the range of thought. Other ideas are drowned out by the bleated slogans of the sheep, or rendered beyond articulation. Clover knows that this is not what the animals fought and laboured for, "though she lacked the words to express it." In Newspeak, similarly, dissent cannot be voiced because "the necessary words were not available."

Ultimately, by time. The old revolutionaries leave or die, while new animals are born or bought: a generation of four-legged Gletkins with nothing to forget. Winston Smith reflects that within twenty years, "the huge and simple question, 'Was life better before the Revolution than it is now?' would have ceased once and for all to be answerable." The war on memory would be complete.

In June 1945, Orwell told Warburg that he had written twelve pages of his next novel and hired a housekeeper to help look after Richard. Susan Watson adored her new employer, and he appreciated the way her vivacity brought light into a home that was dusty with grief. He also enjoyed her chocolate cake. "Once it went sad in the middle," she remembered, "but he liked them sad, you see. He liked things that went wrong a little."

He certainly did. On a fundamental level, Orwell believed himself to be a failure, at home with defeat. Warburg noticed that he "never liked being associated with anything that was too powerful or successful." Many of Orwell's friends, however, believed that he was destined for greatness. In September 1941, Inez Holden had attended the PEN world congress lunch along with Arthur Koestler, Cyril Connolly and Stevie Smith, and Koestler had wagered five bottles of burgundy that Orwell would have a bestseller within five years.

Koestler won the bet with a year to spare. Published on August 17, *Animal Farm: A Fairy Story* quickly sold all the copies that Secker & Warburg had the paper to print: almost twenty thousand. Orwell was proud to at last be able to pick up the tab after a lunch with Warburg. He was pleasantly shocked, given his struggle to find a publisher, by the chorus of praise from critics, inevitably excepting *The Daily Worker* and *The New Statesman*. Foreign translations brought further acclaim, even if the only words he could make out in some reviews were *Swift* and *Gulliver*. "I have been surprised by the unfriendly reactions it *didn't* get," he told *Partisan Review* founder Philip Rahv. Orwell's only cause for complaint was that some bookshops had mistakenly racked it in the children's section, so he took it upon himself to relocate copies to their rightful position.

Animal Farm was also a hit with people he had never sought to impress. Churchill's son Randolph borrowed a copy; the Queen was said to have read it; Lord Beaverbrook, the belligerently right-wing newspaper baron whom Orwell had memorably described as "looking more like a monkey on a stick than you would think possible for anyone who was not doing it on purpose," invited him to lunch. Soon, Orwell was forced to remind admirers that he was in fact a socialist. When the Duchess of Atholl invited him to speak at a meeting of the right-leaning League for European Freedom, he explained that he could not respect an organisation which championed freedom in Europe but not in India. "I belong to the Left and must work inside it," he wrote back, "much as I hate Russian totalitarianism and its poisonous influence on this country."

Orwell had told A. J. Ayer in Paris that he was worried about gratifying his political enemies. William Empson expressed similar concerns in a friendly letter: "the danger of this kind of perfection is that it means very different things to different readers . . . I thought it worth warning you . . . that you must expect to be 'misunderstood' on a large scale about this book; it is a form that inherently means more than the author means, when it is handled sufficiently well." The author of *Seven Types of Ambiguity* was absolutely right, and twice over: everything he said about *Animal Farm* would be doubly applicable to *Nineteen Eighty-Four*.

Plaudits from the right raised eyebrows on the left, mostly due to uncertainty about what Orwell was saying about revolution.* Some of former *Partisan Review* editor Dwight Macdonald's friends in New York thought the message was "to hell with it and hail the status quo." Orwell's old foe Kingsley Martin accused him of "reaching the exhaustion of idealism and approaching the bathos of cynicism" and perceived the author in Benjamin, the dour old donkey to whom life is always "hunger, hardship and disappointment" whoever's in charge. But Benjamin sounds much more like a pessimistic conservative than

---

* Ayn Rand somehow contrived to misread it as "the mushiest and most maudlin preachment of Communism . . . I have seen in a long time."

Orwell, who made clear in his essay on Koestler that one can reject the possibility of paradise on Earth without giving up on the idea that life can be improved.

It's notable that there is no Lenin surrogate in *Animal Farm*. By folding Lenin's finest qualities into the visionary boar old Major and his basest into Napoleon, Orwell left his assessment ambiguous although he wrote shortly after the book's publication that "all the seeds of evil were there from the start and . . . things would not have been substantially different if Lenin or Trotsky had remained in control." Yet to read *Animal Farm* as simply anti-revolutionary is to think that Orwell preferred Mr. Jones. Major's rhetoric is genuinely inspiring, and the animals' post-revolutionary ecstasy is justified. "The most encouraging fact about revolutionary activity is that, although it always fails, it always continues," Orwell wrote in 1948. "The vision of a world of free and equal human beings, living together in a state of brotherhood . . . never materialises, but the belief in it never seems to die out."

For Orwell, the story's point of no return comes when the other animals allow the pigs to monopolise the milk and apples, an episode which represents the crushing of the 1921 Kronstadt rebellion, the last stand of democratic socialism in Russia. "If people think I am defending the status quo," he told Macdonald, "that is, I think, because they have grown pessimistic and assume that there is no alternative except dictatorship or laissez-faire capitalism." *Animal Farm* would not be half as sad without the knowledge that things could have been different.

Animal Farm was launched, narrowly, into a post-war world. Orwell had written to David Astor from Paris in April, volunteering to travel to Burma in November to document the final stages of the war with Japan for *The Observer*, but the end came sooner than he expected. On August 14, three days before the publication of *Animal Farm*, Orwell was on Fleet Street when the news broke that Japan was about to surrender. Office workers shredded paper and rained confetti on people celebrating in the street below. Orwell's reaction was perversely irritable: "In England you can't get paper to print books on, but apparently there is always plenty of it for this kind of thing."

The jubilation was short-lived. Rationing, acute housing shortages, and the sudden cessation of lend-lease money from the US fostered a widespread sense of anticlimax and gloom. A Mass Observation survey in June found that only one in seven Londoners was "happy or elated" by the war's end, with 40 per cent worried or depressed. "The mood of the country seems to me less revolutionary, less Utopian, even less hopeful, than it was in 1940 or 1942," Orwell wrote in his latest "London Letter." He was embarrassed to take Ignazio Silone, visiting from Italy, for lunch in such a bedraggled city until Silone pointed out that it was a considerable improvement on Rome.

In *The New Yorker,* Mollie Panter-Downes wrote that Britons were coming to terms with the reality of an "enormous economic blitz": "Almost the only thing that they seem perfectly sure about now is that peace is going to be nearly as hard to survive as the war." The taste of victory was also soured by the implications of the two atomic bombs that the US had dropped on Hiroshima and Nagasaki. "In England, as elsewhere," wrote Panter-Downes, "the shadow of atomic energy, that enormous potential Frankenstein monster, fell darkly across the victory flags and bunting and chillingly across most hearts."

Orwell thought that this shocking development made C. S. Lewis's new novel *That Hideous Strength,* about an evil cabal of scientists conspiring to enslave the world, "all too topical," and made H. G. Wells's final book, the apocalyptically dejected *Mind at the End of Its Tether,* more credible than it would otherwise have been. "This is not a moment at which one can simply disregard the statement that humanity is doomed," Orwell wrote in his review. "It quite well may be doomed."

In a prescient *Tribune* piece called "You and the Atom Bomb," Orwell suggested that this was the weapon that might prove Burnham right after all, by locking the US and the USSR (once it developed its own bomb) into a long, paranoid stalemate. He could now picture "the kind of world-view, the kind of beliefs, and the social structure that would probably prevail in a State which was at once *unconquerable* and in a permanent state of 'cold war' with its neighbours." The minor nuclear exchange in the background of *Nineteen Eighty-Four* is much less convincing than Orwell's suggestion, two years later, "that the fear inspired by the atomic bomb and other weapons yet to come will be so great that everyone will refrain from using them." Having invented the phrase "cold war," he also anticipated the doctrine of mutual assured destruction.

Amid the post-war malaise, Orwell's friends thought he looked even more gaunt and run down than usual. He desperately needed a change. For five years he had dreamed of squirreling himself away on a Hebridean island. The well-connected David Astor recommended Jura in the Inner Hebrides, where he owned a large estate. Robin Fletcher, the laird of Jura, and his wife, Margaret, held a remote farmhouse, Barnhill, that needed a tenant to save it from ruin. Orwell had put in motion plans to move there while Eileen was still alive. That September, he made the long journey north alone and spent his first two weeks in the house where he would write *Nineteen Eighty-Four*.

CHAPTER 8

Every Book Is a Failure

Orwell 1946–1948

To mark the paper was the decisive act.

—George Orwell, *Nineteen Eighty-Four*

Orwell once said that *Nineteen Eighty-Four* "wouldn't have been so gloomy if I had not been so ill." The evidence suggests otherwise. In the final days of 1945, *Tribune* readers were confronted with a dispiriting article called "Old George's Almanac." The title was designed to put a semi-comic spin on Orwell's predictions for 1946, which included economic disaster, resurgent fascism, "civil wars, bomb outrages, public executions, famines, epidemics and religious revivals." Happy new year! "It may be objected that my forecasts are unduly gloomy," he concluded. "But are they? I fancy it will turn out that I have been over-optimistic rather than the contrary." Walking away from a lunch with Orwell around this time, the poet and critic Herbert Read, no Pollyanna himself, exclaimed, "My God, Orwell *is* a gloomy bird!"

The anecdote gives the impression that Orwell was the doomiest man in London, but he held no monopoly on pessimism. In his introduction to the 1946 edition of *Brave New World,* Aldous Huxley predicted a worldwide epidemic of totalitarianism, lulling populations into servitude with drugs, sexual promiscuity and genetic engineering. He decided that his novel's six hundred-year countdown to dystopia had been far too rosy: "To-day it seems quite possible that the horror may be upon us within a single century. That is, if we refrain from blowing ourselves to smithereens in the interval."

That same year, Albert Camus wrote: "Our twentieth century is the century of fear."

This is to say that Orwell was magnifying a widespread sense of bomb-haunted unease rather than projecting onto the world some freakish private torment. As he wrote in a 1946 "London Letter," "No thoughtful person whom I know has any hopeful picture of the future." For all that, he remained excellent company. One lunch companion, Michael Meyer, called him "the best informed and most illuminating talker about politics whom I have ever met. His conversation was like his writing, unaffected, lucid, witty and humane." Another writer, Christopher Sykes, remembered that whenever they met, "we talked of melancholy subjects—and he made my day."

There was a manic quality to Orwell's activity after the war. Perhaps this was his last hurrah as a full-time journalist and Londoner, or perhaps he was filling his days to the brim so as to leave no space for grief. He worked like a Stakhanovite and socialised like never before: high tea at Canonbury Square with old friends like Fyvel and Potts, and lunches in Fleet Street with literary acquaintances like Malcolm Muggeridge, Julian Symons and Anthony Powell—the first cohort of friends to know him only as George and never Eric. Although he lionised the common man, he spent most of his time with uncommon men. Muggeridge remembered a lively lunch with Orwell, Symons and another writer: "We were all anti-Communist, but for different reasons, and it was interesting how we disagreed about our agreement."

Despite his aversion to groups and committees, Orwell agreed to become vice-chair of George Woodcock's Freedom Defence Committee, whose politically diverse supporters, including E. M. Forster, T. S. Eliot, Bertrand Russell and Victor Gollancz, campaigned for an amnesty for anyone convicted under draconian wartime legislation, whether they be anarchists, communists or fascists. One *Tribune* reader accused Orwell of "an irresistible attraction towards unpopular causes for their unpopularity's sake," but he had maintained for years that behaviour is right or wrong regardless of who's doing it. If you suppress the rights of your political enemies, he thought, then you can be sure that one day they will suppress yours. He was therefore proud to say that during the war he had defended the rights of both Oswald Mosley (once he was no longer dangerous) and *The Daily Worker*, despite his intense dislike for both. As he told Woodcock: "no one should be persecuted for expressing his opinions, however anti-social, & no political organisation suppressed, unless it can be shown that there is *a substantial threat to the stability of the state*."*

Orwell also tried to fill the emotional hole left by Eileen's death with a series of desperately inept marriage proposals to younger women: Celia Paget, twin sister of Koestler's partner Mamaine and cousin of Inez Holden; Sonia Brownell, Cyril Connolly's famously desirable *Horizon* protégé; and Anne Popham, the art historian who lived downstairs. "It is only that I feel so desperately alone sometimes," he told Popham when he apologised for putting her on the spot. "I have hundreds of friends, but no woman who takes an interest in me and can encourage me." If this seems to lack romance, then it's hearts and flowers compared to the gloomily pragmatic marriage proposal in his next letter: "What I am really asking is whether you would like to be the widow of a literary man." Needless to say, Popham was not swept off her feet.

So, back to work. Orwell was averaging two or three pieces a week, for more than half a dozen publications. It took coughing up blood from an undiagnosed tubercular haemorrhage to make him take a week off in February. Most of his letters contained some complaint about his workload ("smothered under journalism") and a vow to drop everything to concentrate on his book. "It will probably be an awful job to start, but I think with six clear months I could break the back of it," he told Popham.

Reading everything that Orwell wrote between October 1945 and May 1946, two thoughts recur. One is that his style had matured to such a degree that very little of his work betrays signs of strain or haste. The other is that almost everything, in retrospect, seems in some way pertinent to *Nineteen Eighty-Four*, right down to specific phrases and images; he had no qualms about using a good line twice.

---

* He was less strict about unofficial sanctions. When Ezra Pound was vilified for his viciously anti-Semitic, pro-fascist wartime radio broadcasts, Orwell did not leap to his defence: "Antisemitism . . . is simply not the doctrine of a grown-up person. People who go in for that kind of thing must take the consequences."

The book had taken up permanent residence in his head. "At various dinners and high teas and lunches and quick drinks in saloon bars, I heard expounded almost every idea expressed in *Nineteen Eighty-Four*," George Woodcock remembered, "though I had no inkling of the plot until the book appeared."

Orwell couldn't help unpacking the sinister implications of any new development. He worried that the much-needed housing estates springing up across the country would become "labour-saving colonies where [people] will lose much of their privacy," and described holiday camps such as Butlin's as if they were police states, offering the kind of enforced communal recreation and regimented exercises that plague Winston in Airstrip One. "One is never alone," complained the man who saw privacy and solitude as fundamental human rights. In "The Prevention of Literature," a brilliant distillation of his thoughts on art, politics, and totalitarianism's fundamental need for lies, he used Disney animation to illustrate the "conveyor-belt process" by which masscult entertainment might be mechanically produced in the future. The example may have been unfair to animators, but it led him to the fiction department in the Ministry of Truth.

Conversely, his elegant little articles about the perfect cup of tea, the ideal pub and the meditative appeal of mating toads expressed values that were worth snatching from the jaws of politics: "The atom bombs are piling up in the factories, the police are prowling through the cities, the lies are streaming from the loudspeakers, but the earth is still going around the sun, and neither the dictators nor the bureaucrats, deeply as they disapprove of the process, are able to prevent it." His description of an archetypal junk shop in a column for the *Evening Standard* reads like a blueprint for Mr. Charrington's shop, including the coral paperweight that Winston Smith cherishes, like an ink pen, Shakespeare's name or the song "Oranges and Lemons," as definitive proof of life before Ingsoc.

All the strands were coming together. "In Front of Your Nose" saw Orwell mapping out the process of doublethink, or political "schizophrenia": "the power of holding simultaneously two beliefs which cancel each other out. Closely allied to it is the power of ignoring facts which are obvious and unalterable, and which will have to be faced sooner or later." Even when people were proved wrong, he noticed, they were liable to twist the facts, or bury their earlier opinions, to suggest that they were right all along. "To see what is in front of one's nose is a constant struggle." Orwell was studying the ways in which people already lie to themselves, without needing a totalitarian state to force them. Tyranny needs accomplices.

Woodcock observed that another of Orwell's preoccupations was "the way in which the concern for freedom and truth had grown weak in public consciousness." In "Freedom of the Park," Orwell drew *Tribune* readers' attention to the arrest for obstruction of five people selling pacifist newspapers outside Hyde Park—a minor incident but an ominous reminder of something that citizens of mature democracies tend to forget: "The point is that the relative freedom which we enjoy depends on public opinion. The law is no protection." The argument that people would only enjoy freedom of speech, or any other liberty, if they cared enough to demand it lies behind the proles in *Nineteen Eighty-Four,* who have immense power but fail to use it.

If the right to speech was paramount, then the quality of that speech also mattered. Orwell's *Horizon* essay "Politics and the English Language" has been deployed to teach generations of pupils how to write clearly. To be honest, the essay is rather a muddle, jumbling together powerful examples of the "swindles and perversions" of bad prose with an eccentric miscellany of pet peeves. Even the relationship between the degradation of politics and the corruption of language is not as simple as he makes out: you can lie in words of one syllable (War Is Peace) and illuminate a great truth with a cliché. But what is often missed is Orwell's humility. He admits that his "rules"—really aspirations—aren't binding and anyway, he contravenes some of them in this very essay. Still, few would disagree that "orthodoxy, of whatever colour, seems to demand a lifeless, imitative style," or that thinking hard about the words you use will sharpen your thoughts. Only by clearing away the verbal flotsam can you clearly understand not just what you think but how you think. The aim is to write in such a way that you cannot lie to yourself without being fully aware that you are doing so.

"Why I Write," commissioned by the short-lived literary quarterly *Gangrel,* helpfully crystallised Orwell's priorities as he prepared to start *Nineteen Eighty-Four.* He argues that four major motives jostle for supremacy in every author's mind—ego, aesthetic enthusiasm, historical impulse and political purpose—and decides that his best work since 1936 has been galvanised by the fourth of these. He writes because "there is some lie that I want to expose, some fact to which I want to draw attention, and my initial concern is to get a hearing." Without some mission to focus his pen, his writing becomes lifeless humbug, and his next novel, he promises, has a mission. "It is bound to be a failure, every book is a failure, but I know with some clarity what kind of book I want to write."

The last journalism Orwell filed before his self-imposed hiatus revealed a hunger for change. Two beautiful pieces about paying close attention to nature contrasted with one darkly hilarious riff on the grinding routine of book-reviewing. In his last "London Letter" he noted that, despite the arrival of spring, London was "as shabby and dirty as ever." It was time to go.

Orwell's journey to Jura was delayed by the unexpected death from kidney disease of his older sister Marjorie on May 3. In a little over three years, he had lost his mother, his wife and a sibling. Accompanied by his younger sister Avril, Orwell finally arrived on the island towards the end of the month.

Jura is where the myth of *Nineteen Eighty-Four* takes hold: the compelling image of a sad, sick man who incarcerated himself on a godforsaken rock in a shivering sea and, in a state of agonising despair about his future and the world's, wrote the book that killed him. Among other things, that cliché does a disservice to Jura, which has a temperate (though damp) climate and a raw, startling beauty. Situated at the north end of an island with fewer than three hundred inhabitants, Barnhill was certainly remote: seven miles of rough road from the nearest village, Ardlussa, and another twenty from the main settlement of Craighouse. The rough-and-ready four-bedroom farmhouse had no telephone or postal service. Supplies of water and fuel were unreliable. The closest hospital was in Glasgow—a taxi, two boats, a bus and a train ride away—which made Jura a reckless choice for a sick man. Nonetheless, Orwell loved it, especially after Susan Watson arrived with Richard. For such an ascetic personality, the adversity was surely part of the appeal. Jura offered the life that Eileen had demanded in her final letters: fresh air, family and fiction.

Orwell had no desire to become a hermit, and he extended invitations to many of his friends. Among those who made the long journey were the Indian writer Mulk Raj Anand, whom he knew from the BBC, and Inez Holden, fresh from covering the Nuremberg trials. He formed a friendship with his landlord Robin Fletcher, who told him about his experiences in a Japanese concentration camp. Paul Potts, the poet who had been a regular companion in the pubs of Islington, stayed for a few months, before leaving in a huff after Watson accidentally used his latest manuscript for kindling. Another difficult guest was Watson's boyfriend, a young ex-soldier and communist called David Holbrook, who found Orwell to be a "miserable, hostile old bugger . . . It was disturbing to see this man shrinking away from humanity and pouring out this bitter hopelessness."

That's not at all the impression you get from Orwell's letters and diaries, in which he relished his new son-of-the-soil routine: planting fruit and vegetables, shooting rabbits, raising geese, and fishing for mackerel, pollock and lobster. He even kept a pig at one point, although it confirmed his low opinion in *Animal Farm:* "They are most annoying, destructive animals, and hard to keep out of anywhere because they are so strong and cunning." He told friends that his remote location and nutritional independence would be useful in the event of nuclear war, because Jura was "not worth a bomb." He did not appear to be joking.

As for the novel he had been dying to crack on with, well, freed from the treadmill of journalism, Orwell found that he didn't want to write much at all. Chronic procrastinators will enjoy the series of letters in which Orwell cheerfully explains why he hasn't started yet and shunts the completion date back to the end of 1947 at the earliest. Not until the end of September, in a letter to *Polemic* editor Humphrey Slater, did he reveal that he had finally put pen to paper: "I have at last started my novel about the future, but I've only done about 50 pages and God knows when it will be finished. However it's something that it is started." When he was feeling well and the weather was clement, he worked in the sitting room; otherwise he typed in his study-cum-bedroom in a fog of cigarette smoke and paraffin fumes. Probably the first people to read any of *Nineteen Eighty-Four* were Watson and Holbrook, who sneaked into his room to read a few pages. "It just seemed depressingly lacking in hope, as he was in everything," was Holbrook's jaundiced assessment. Most likely, those first pages included the first draft of Goldstein's book. Some readers may find it indigestibly long, but it explains the reasons Orwell wrote the novel in the first place. Ideas, not plot, were his way in.

The only article that Orwell managed to complete on Jura that summer suggested that he was working through issues arising from the novel. The title of "Politics vs Literature: An Examination of *Gulliver's Travels*" came from the dissonance between Orwell's fundamental disagreement with Swift—misanthrope, reactionary, "one of those people who are driven into a sort of perverse Toryism by the follies of the progressive part of the movement"—and the pleasure he derived from *Gulliver. Critical Essays,* published in early 1947, was obsessed with that idea. The fact that Kipling was a crude imperialist, Yeats a proto-fascist, and Dalí a maniac, Orwell maintained, did not diminish the quality of their work. But nor were those facts irrelevant: "One ought to be able to hold in one's head simultaneously the two facts that Dalí is a good draughtsman and a disgusting human being. The one does not invalidate or, in a sense, affect the other." When political or moral values clash with literary judgement, he later wrote, it is tempting to say: "This book is on my side, and therefore I must discover merits in it." Conversely, the merits of a book that is *not* on your side must be played down. Orwell went out of his way to do the opposite. His duty as a critic was to state both his moral and aesthetic judgement with unapologetic candour, and not to confuse the two.

Orwell concluded that Swift appeals to that dark corner of human nature that really does suspect that humanity is mired in corruption, folly and filth, and is thrilled by exposure to the worst, as long as it's only temporary. What Swift described was far from the whole truth but it was not a lie. This is what was on Orwell's mind that first summer on Jura: the satirical technique of "picking out a single hidden truth and then magnifying it and distorting it." Yes, that could work.

H. G. Wells died alone at home on August 13, 1946, a few weeks short of his eightieth birthday. In his playful "My Auto-Obituary" a few years earlier, he had imagined himself roughed up by fascists in

1948 and imprisoned by "the brief Communist dictatorship of 1952" before dying in 1963, but yet again history had other ideas.

The next day the *Manchester Evening News* ran an obituary that Orwell had filed nine months earlier. Though a disappointingly businesslike retread of his previous judgements (i.e., Wells's decades of banging the drum for a world state had clouded the brilliance of his early novels), it revealed a tenderness and respect that was undented by his unfortunate relationship with Wells: "He was so big a figure, he has played so great a part in forming our picture of the world, that in agreeing or disagreeing with his ideas we are apt to forget his purely literary achievement."

In his comically short preface to the 1941 edition of *The War in the Air,* Wells had proposed his own epitaph: "I told you so. You *damned* fools."

As Orwell returned to London for the winter, the money-god finally smiled on him from across the Atlantic. "In the United States there is more money, more paper and more spare time," he later wrote in a survey of American literature, and that was good news for the US edition of *Animal Farm.* The first print run was 50,000—more than ten times the size of Warburg's—and the Book-of-the-Month Club, which made it a September 1946 selection, printed a total of 540,000. One of the club's committee members anonymously called it "The *Uncle Tom's Cabin* of our time": a mixed compliment for Orwell, who nominated Stowe's novel as the quintessential "good bad book" that is at once moving and ludicrous. Edmund Wilson in *The New Yorker* approvingly compared it to Voltaire and Swift, although George Soule at *The New Republic* thought Orwell was out of his depth: "the satire deals not with something the author has experienced, but rather with stereotyped ideas about a country which he probably does not know very well . . . He should try again, and this time on something nearer home." The American public disagreed; *Animal Farm* spent eight weeks on *The New York Times'* best seller list.

Used to earning so little that he didn't even bother opening letters from the Inland Revenue, the financially illiterate Orwell now had to worry about income tax for the first time in his life. In 1947 he established his own company, George Orwell Productions, Ltd., on the advice of his accountants, Harrison, Son, Hill & Co. ("No one is patriotic about taxes," he once wrote.) The windfall caused such a tax headache that he called it "fairy gold"—fairy gold for a fairy tale—but he still had enough money to make generous donations to the Freedom Defence Committee and help several writers in less fortunate positions. Prestige in America brought offers of work from publications like *The New Yorker,* interest from Walt Disney in making a movie of *Animal Farm,* and even a short profile in *Vogue.* "Fairly much a leftist, George Orwell is a defender of freedom," wrote Allene Talmey, "even though most of the time he violently disagrees with the people beside whom he is fighting." Not a bad capsule description.

Orwell's life was thus transformed by a country he had never visited (by the time the opportunity arose in 1948, he was too ill to travel) and regarded with condescension and suspicion. In his writing, he consistently portrayed the USA as a spirited but crude and unruly teenager, liable to break things. In *Keep the Aspidistra Flying,* Comstock says, "The Americans always go one better on any kinds of beastliness, whether it is ice-cream soda, racketeering, or theosophy," and Orwell showed few signs of moderating that opinion over the following decade.

America was Orwell's biggest blind spot. Cyril Connolly thought he was "anti-American, except for the Trotskyites of *Partisan Review.*" Although he could write sensitively about British popular culture—seaside postcards, boys' comics, murder mysteries, music hall—Orwell had no interest in jazz, blues, Broadway or Tin Pan Alley, maintained a puritanical disgust for pulp fiction and American comic books, and had a low opinion of Hollywood. He paid scarce attention to the achievements of Roosevelt's New Deal. As for the country's impact on the English language, "It ought to be realised that on the whole American is a bad influence and has already had a debasing effect."

Although he loved Mark Twain, and had even pitched a biography of the author in 1934, Orwell rarely engaged with living American writers, with the exception of Henry Miller and Richard Wright, whose *Native Son* he called "a truly remarkable book, which ought to be read by anyone who wants to understand the nature of colour-hatred." While having no illusions about slavery or the slaughter of Native Americans, he felt that the nineteenth-century America of Whitman and Twain represented, in the imagination at least, a world of democracy, opportunity, adventure and innocence, made possible by ample untapped resources, that was a long time gone. "The world of the American novelist is a chaos, moral as well as physical," he wrote in 1940. "No one has a trace of public spirit, or at bottom, any standard except success, usually masquerading as 'self expression' . . . There is no emotional depth. Everything is permitted, and therefore nothing matters." He could only make such ridiculous generalisations because he knew so few Americans. Meeting some didn't seem to help. A 1943 "As I Please" was so hostile towards US troops stationed in Britain ("It is difficult to go anywhere in London without having the feeling that Britain is now Occupied Territory") that several readers complained. "This anglophile was rather shocked to find that George Orwell is still no closer to knowing the Americans than before," wrote one.

Most American reviewers of *Nineteen Eighty-Four* would fail to see their own country's reflection in Oceania, despite the use of dollars and the name of the national anthem, "Oceania, 'Tis for Thee." The posters and slogans of Airstrip One (i.e., Occupied Territory) owe a great deal to American advertising, as, in reality, did totalitarian propaganda. "The Nazis, without admitting it, learned as much from American gangster organisations as their propaganda, admittedly, learned from American business publicity," wrote Hannah Arendt.

After the war, however, Orwell seemed to move towards an intellectual détente with the US, just as most of the British left was becoming more hostile. "It is clear that on the matters that most affect Britain today," claimed *The New Statesman,* "the United States is nearly as hostile to the aspirations of Socialist Britain as to the Soviet Union." Swimming against the tide as usual, Orwell bemoaned *Tribune*'s growing antagonism ("To be anti-American nowadays is to shout with the mob"), and accused the socialist historian Douglas Goldring of "Americophobia." He considered it hypocritical to demonise the country on which Britain's economic recovery depended, and thought that the cold war enforced a binary decision. "I don't, God knows, want a war to break out," he wrote to Victor Gollancz, "but if one were compelled to choose between Russia and America—and I suppose that is the choice one might have to make—I would always choose America."

Towards the end of "The Principles of Newspeak," the passage of Oldspeak chosen to illustrate the most elegant language and the most noble ideals that the pre-totalitarian age had to offer is the preamble to the Declaration of Independence.

The winter of 1946–1947 was an onslaught. Starting in January, Britain was terrorised by heavy snow and Siberian temperatures. Coal supplies iced over in the pits or languished in depots because so many roads and railways were snowed in, leading to fuel rationing and shuttered factories. Food rations dipped below wartime levels, as vegetables froze in the ground and thousands of chickens died of cold, and bread was restricted for the first time ever. Unemployment exploded from 400,000 people to 1.7 million in just four weeks. Fuel and paper shortages forced publishers, including *Tribune,* to halt the presses. Television broadcasts were suspended. During February, the worst month, electricity supplies were halted for five hours a day. The government, too, was frostbitten. The *Financial Times* called the fuel crisis the domestic equivalent of the events that brought down Chamberlain in 1940. "Everybody in England was shivering," observed the expatriate British novelist Christopher Isherwood, visiting from his home in Hollywood. Some of his friends in London told him that it was worse than the war.

Orwell later traced his final period of ill-health back to that winter's assault on his lungs. Apart from a brief New Year's return to Barnhill to plant trees and bulbs, he spent November to April in London, which was actually colder and more fuel-deprived than Jura. You get a flavour of his last "unendurable" winter in broken-backed, bombed-out London in the opening chapters of *Nineteen Eighty-Four:* the power cuts, the economy drives, the patchwork buildings, the blunt razor blades, the bad food, the clothing coupons, the cairns of rubble, the grit in the air. Orwell had to climb six flights of stairs to get to 27b Canonbury Square; Winston coughs his way up seven in Victory Mansions. The prole district, "to the north and east of what had once been Saint Pancras Station," is Islington.

Orwell resumed "As I Please" (his typically eclectic first column covered fashion magazines, jury service, bread rationing and road safety) and wrote two of his last great essays, "How the Poor Die" and "Lear, Tolstoy and the Fool." He also attended to his literary career, which was finally up and running. He consulted with Warburg on plans to reprint the best of his earlier books in a uniform edition, and convinced Gollancz to relinquish his contractual right to publish *Nineteen Eighty-Four*. *Animal Farm* was doing brisk business in translation—in Japan, an astonishing forty-eight publishers competed for it—and made its radio debut on the BBC's new Third Programme, with a script by Orwell edited by his old flatmate Rayner Heppenstall. "I had the feeling that they had spoilt it," he told Mamaine Paget, "but one nearly always does with anything one writes for the air."

In March 1947, Orwell checked in on James Burnham, whose journey to the right was continuing apace. In *The Struggle for Power,* the three managerial super-states had predictably dwindled to two, representing communism and democracy. While the new Truman Doctrine established a policy of containing Soviet communism, Burnham believed that the Third World War had already begun and that America should be prepared to make a preventive strike before the Russians could develop their own atom bomb—a suggestion which led one congressman to compare the book to *Mein Kampf.* "He is too fond of apocalyptic visions, too ready to believe that the muddled processes of history will happen suddenly and logically," Orwell wrote. Voraciously well-read about Russia (in a 1947 letter to Dwight Macdonald he recommended almost twenty books), he thought that Burnham's call to suppress communist parties in the West was also based on a hyperbolic fantasy: "a huge secret army of fanatical warriors, completely devoid of fear or scruples and having no thought except to live and die for the Workers' Fatherland."

As a democratic socialist, Orwell felt like "a doctor treating an all but hopeless case." The "mental disease" that gripped the world in the 1930s had not yet been diagnosed, let alone cured. Like Attlee, who talked of combining "individual freedom with a planned economy, democracy with social justice," Orwell was looking for a third way, dominated by neither America nor Russia. He hoped for a socialist United States of Europe: "If one could somewhere present the spectacle of economic security without concentration camps, the pretext for the Russian dictatorship would disappear and

Communism would lose much of its appeal." But the obstacles were immense. The future was "very dark."

In hindsight, Orwell *was* too pessimistic. Within a few years he would have seen that the British economy could recover, thanks in part to the Marshall Plan, even while dismantling the Empire, and that France and Germany could come together to lay the foundations of a united Western Europe, if not the federation of socialist republics he had in mind. But the extreme desolation of *Nineteen Eighty-Four* was as much a strategy as an expression of his own fears. Reviewing *In Darkest Germany*, Victor Gollancz's book of post-war reportage, he worried that accounts of suffering were no longer moving the British public: "As time goes on and the horrors pile up, the mind seems to secrete a sort of self-protecting ignorance which needs a harder and harder shock to pierce it, just as the body will become immunised to a drug and require bigger and bigger doses." To generate that irresistible shock, he thought, "a new literary technique will have to be evolved."

Orwell, Avril and Richard arrived back on Jura on April 11, just as the snow was melting and spring was nudging through. The garden at Barnhill was buttery with daffodils. By the end of May, he had written about a third of his novel, even if it was "a ghastly mess." "I don't like talking about books before they are written," he wrote to Warburg, "but I will tell you now that this is a novel about the future—that is, it is in a sense a fantasy, but in the form of a naturalistic novel. That is what makes it a difficult job—of course as a book of anticipations it would be comparatively simple to write." Over the next few months, he mailed everything except the last chapter and the appendix to Miranda Christen, a friend of Anthony Powell who was renting his Canonbury Square flat and volunteered to type up a clean manuscript. Having spent the war in Java under Japanese occupation, Christen was "rivetted from the start. There were analogies with my recent past." The Japanese invaders who rebranded occupied countries as the Greater East Asia Co-Prosperity Sphere "would have taken to the Ministry of Truth like a duck to water."

Barnhill was busy that broiling summer. Richard Rees, Orwell's literary executor, came to Jura to paint and stayed for several weeks. Inez Holden returned for a long spell. Bill Dunn, an injured ex-soldier new to the island, helped to run Barnhill and developed a relationship with Avril that led, after Orwell's death, to marriage and the adoption of Richard. Marjorie's widower Humphrey Dakin came with his grown-up children for a holiday that almost ended in tragedy. Orwell's motor boat, containing Henry and Jane Dakin and Richard, was sucked into the notorious whirlpool in the Gulf of Corryvreckan, one of Britain's most dangerous stretches of water, and the party made a narrow escape. It was the closest Orwell had come to death since Spain, but Henry noted that he showed not a flicker of panic: "He almost seemed to enjoy it."

Was this nonchalance a sign of courage, recklessness or fatalism? Had he grown too used to the possibility of an early death? His health worsened in the autumn, kiboshing an optimistic plan to report on life in the American South, and an *Observer* commission to spend three months in Kenya and South Africa. He wasn't going anywhere. He'd been ill all year and losing weight, he told Fyvel, but "like a fool" decided to press on with his novel instead of seeing a doctor who, he suspected, would force him to down tools. He finished the first draft of *Nineteen Eighty-Four* in bed on November 7. Shortly before Christmas, he succumbed to medical advice, travelling to Hairmyres hospital in East Kilbride, near Glasgow, to seek treatment. He would not be able to return to Jura, or his novel, for another seven months. At that point, he later admitted to Celia Paget, "I really felt as though I were finished."

Orwell dreamed of death. The nightmares continued for the rest of his life, especially when his lungs felt constricted and he woke gasping for breath, fearing that he would never be well again. In his dreams he was walking by the sea, or between grand, towering buildings, but always in sunshine and always, he wrote in his hospital notebook, "with a peculiar feeling of happiness." Orwell didn't fear death itself, only the pain that would precede death. He thought it better to die "violently and not too old," he wrote in "How the Poor Die." The alternative would necessarily be "slow, smelly and painful."

The problem with seeing *Nineteen Eighty-Four* as the anguished last testament of a dying man is that Orwell never really believed he was dying, or at least no more than usual. He had suffered from lung problems since childhood and had been ill, on and off, for so long that he had no reason to think that this time would be the last. At Hairmyres, he was diagnosed with chronic fibrotic tuberculosis in the upper part of both lungs, particularly the left. According to James Williamson, one of his doctors, Orwell had "probably forgotten, almost, what it was like to feel completely well," but he could still live for a long time.

Winston Smith similarly dreams of deep water and sunlit ruins and he doesn't fear death either. What he cannot bear, what will destroy him, is the pain, "because the body swells up until it fills the universe." Only thirty-nine but already feeling like an old man, Winston embodies Orwell's horror at his own physical decay. In hospital, Orwell tallied the symptoms of disintegration: tight chest, painful back, weak knees, aching gums, greying hair, watering eyes, and a chill that wouldn't go away. Thanks to David Astor's connections, Orwell was able to acquire some streptomycin, the new anti-TB wonder drug from the US, but a severe and unexpected allergic reaction eventually forced the doctors to suspend treatment. He shed clumps of skin, hair and nails. He erupted in rashes, ulcers and blisters. At night the blood from blisters in his throat would bubble up and congeal on his lips so that he would need to wash it away before he could open his mouth. "I suppose with all these drugs," he wrote to Julian Symons, "it's rather a case of sinking the ship to get rid of the rats."

The crucial difference between Orwell and Winston is that Winston knows, from the moment he first writes in his diary, that he is doomed. But Orwell never gave any indication that he thought he wouldn't recover. Right up until his final days, he did not lose faith in the future.

What Orwell really hated about his illness was its effect on his brain. He could think, talk and read normally, but whenever he tried to translate his thoughts to paper, his language was stale, his arguments inchoate. He wondered if there was some medical explanation for this: perhaps there was enough blood to the brain to produce dull, obvious writing but not enough to inspire anything worthwhile? For someone who was not fully himself unless he was writing, it was agony.

He somehow managed to finish one article of real substance. "Writers and Leviathan" cracked the conundrum that had defeated him in "Inside the Whale": how can a writer engage with politics without compromising his integrity on the page? Eight years earlier, Orwell had advocated a kind of intellectual quarantine. Now he insisted that it was "impossible and undesirable" to hide inside the whale and that one *should* be politically active as a citizen as long as one's writing remains uncontaminated by dishonesty and self-censorship. It was his final argument for the prophylactic power of rigorous self-awareness: in an age when everything one read or wrote was coloured by politics, contradictory thoughts inevitably arose, and it was essential to confront the dissonance openly rather than "to push the question, unanswered, into a corner of one's mind." The outline in his notebook captures it in twenty-nine words: "Conclusion: must engage in politics. Must keep issues separate. Must not engage in party politics as a *writer*. Recognition of own prejudices only way of keeping them in check."

By May, Orwell was well enough to get his typewriter back and resume work in earnest. As well as making notes to revise the novel, he wrote short critical pieces on Wilde, Attlee and Graham Greene, and a decent essay on George Gissing, the close friend of H. G. Wells who, like Orwell, died of lung disease at the age of forty-six. In his notes for the essay, Orwell wrote: "Gissing's novels are among the things that make one feel the world has improved (emphasize gloom)." You would not think that Orwell ever needed to remind himself to emphasise gloom. His debt to Gissing—"a chronicler of vulgarity, squalor and failure"—can be felt in the grubbier passages of description in *Nineteen Eighty-Four*.

Orwell also managed to finish "Such, Such Were the Joys," his lacerating memoir of his schooldays at St. Cyprian's. He'd started pondering (and possibly writing) it ten years earlier, and had sent Warburg a first draft in 1947, but it took him this long to complete it. It was so savagely libellous that it couldn't be published until after his death, and even then, the school appeared pseudonymously as Crossgates.* Orwell portrayed St. Cyprian's/Crossgates as "a world of force and fraud and secrecy" which tormented children with "irrational terrors and lunatic misunderstandings."

There's no doubt that Orwell genuinely hated the school, but old schoolmates found "Such, Such Were the Joys" overblown and unfair. It feels as if *Nineteen Eighty-Four* leaked into Orwell's memories and twisted an averagely unpleasant prep school into a totalitarian nightmare of cruelty and injustice. O'Brien is repeatedly compared to a schoolmaster, and in a deleted line from Orwell's rough draft, Parsons in the Ministry of Love looks "exactly like a fat, overgrown schoolboy awaiting a caning." Conversely, when Orwell describes being caned for wetting his bed, he sounds like Parsons, arrested for shouting out a heresy in his sleep: "It was possible, therefore, to commit a sin without knowing that you committed it, without wanting to commit it, and without being able to avoid it."

So the possibility of the novel infecting the memory makes sense; the reverse leads to some appalling armchair psychology. Anthony West (the son of H. G. Wells and Rebecca West) wrote an influential article in *The New Yorker* after Orwell's death which argued, "Whether he knew it or not, what he did in *1984* was to send everybody in England to an enormous Crossgates to be as miserable as he had been." This is far too tidy. Orwell was by no means the only writer to describe boarding school as a miniature tyranny. The convent-educated Sonia Brownell, for example, branded Catholic priests "totalitarians" who want to "control, utterly, every thought and feeling." Orwell would not have been much of a writer if his final novel had been merely a vengeful satire of his prep school.

Orwell was discharged from Hairmyres on July 28. Avril thought he could have made a full recovery if he had moved to a sanatorium, but the siren song of the novel was too powerful. He returned to Jura and rewrote it line by line between August and November, in the company of Rees, Avril and Bill. His neighbours were glad to see

---

* The essay only appeared in the US. Mrs. Wilkes, who ran St. Cyprian's with her husband, continued to block UK publication up until her death in 1967.

him back home, getting the garden back into shape. "What surprised me mostly was the first time I read *1984*," remembered one lobster fisherman. "I couldn't think that it was the same man that was doing this writing was the Eric Blair that I knew. I just couldn't place them together at all."

As far as Orwell was concerned, "a book doesn't exist until it is finished." He would neither share his drafts with friends nor discuss the contents in anything but the vaguest terms. In case he died in hospital, he instructed Rees to destroy the rough draft of what was still called *The Last Man in Europe*. It would either be finished or it would be shoved down the memory hole and reduced to ashes.

Given Orwell's fear of anyone seeing his work in progress, it's remarkable that early versions of *Nineteen Eighty-Four* survived at all. Pages from four drafts, amounting to 44 per cent of the novel, ended up in the hands of Daniel G. Siegel, a collector from Massachusetts, who agreed to publish a facsimile in 1984. Even this collage of fragments gives a decent impression of Orwell's process and priorities. He was a ruthless self-editor, rewriting paragraphs several times over, on pages almost unreadably dense with amendments, to eliminate flabby phrasing and reinforce key ideas. The novel's famously disorienting first line, for example, originally read: "It was a cold, blowy day in early April, and a million radios were striking thirteen." This was the sixth of his books to open with the time of day.

The detailed notes Orwell made at Hairmyres laid out his priorities: clarify the role of the proles, the falsification of history and the suppression of sex in Oceania, and write the final chapter. Little was lost. The visit to O'Brien's apartment was abbreviated, minimising the role of his sinister manservant Martin, and a subsequent encounter with Julia was dropped. Orwell drastically reduced allusions to real-world geography, references to race (including the lynching scene), and ironies that felt excessive. There is bone-dry humour in the novel, in the planned "spontaneous demonstrations" and compulsory "voluntary subscriptions," but Orwell presumably considered the "Christian Pacifists" who call for twenty thousand Eurasian prisoners to be buried alive too heavy-handed. None of these amendments fundamentally altered the book's narrative or agenda. To the contrary, the early drafts reveal just how consistent and focused Orwell was during those three years.

Orwell's recovery faded with the summer. His health spiralled down so dramatically that by October he was sure he needed to go to a sanatorium, but still he kept working instead. He even managed to find time to write short pieces on Jean-Paul Sartre and T. S. Eliot, and a substantial article which made clear what his novel was *not* about.

In hindsight, Orwell might have regretted the name he chose for his totalitarian regime. As the ugly Newspeak contraction implied, Ingsoc was no more socialist than National Socialism. In a book where the Ministries of Truth, Love, Peace and Plenty are dedicated to the opposite values, it would be bizarre to interpret it literally, as English socialism. The Labour Party no longer exists and Goldstein's book spells out the lie embedded in Ingsoc's name: "Thus, the Party rejects and vilifies every principle for which the Socialist movement originally stood, and it chooses to do this in the name of Socialism." Still, many American fans, as we shall see, were to assume that he was satirising the Attlee government. The way he used the physical furniture of post-war London to give Airstrip One a lived authenticity compounded this false impression. Even Warburg, before realising his error, initially interpreted the book as "a deliberate and sadistic attack on Socialism and socialist parties generally." In his publisher's report, he suggested it would delight Churchill and the right-wing press and be "worth a cool million votes to the Conservative Party." And he knew Orwell personally. Why wouldn't readers who knew nothing of the man and his beliefs make the same mistake?

To American eyes, Britain under Labour may well have appeared nightmarish. *The New York Times*'s London correspondent Anthony Bower described its citizens as "slightly underfed, very tired, rationed, restricted, and struggling desperately for economic recovery." An opinion poll in the spring of 1948 found that 42 per cent of Britons had considered emigrating. Orwell, however, remained a supporter of the Labour government until the end, albeit a demanding one. Annoyed by Labour's failure to immediately do away with the House of Lords, the honours system and private education—the three great symbols of class privilege—and bored by more bureaucratic reforms, he had previously offered to write a piece for Tosco Fyvel at *Tribune*, complaining that Bevan had become distracted by house-building and the National Health Service, thus dismissing what would become two of the government's greatest achievements. Fortunately, Fyvel turned it down.

"The Labour Government After Three Years," written for *Commentary* in 1948, painted a picture of a government struggling to solve tremendous problems, not a dictatorship-in-waiting. "So far, in spite of the cries of agony from the Beaverbrook press, the government has encroached very little upon individual liberty," Orwell emphasised. "It has barely used its powers, and has not indulged in anything that could reasonably be called political persecution." He did wonder if Labour might eventually take an authoritarian turn if, after several years, the economy was still on its knees, but he didn't detect any totalitarian leanings in Attlee's government of practical men. If anything, he thought them too cautious, especially when it came to messaging. Austerity and Polish immigration, he wrote, had "caused more resentment than they need have done if the underlying facts had been properly explained." Orwell was appalled by the public's hostility towards Polish and Jewish refugees and argued that "it is doubtful whether we can solve our problems without encouraging immigration from Europe."* But he still hoped for the best, regarding a successful democratic socialist government the best possible antidote to Stalinism.

Orwell's final substantial essay was "Reflections on Gandhi," a complex assessment of the man who had been assassinated earlier that year, just a few months into the life of the independent India that he had done so much to bring about. Orwell greatly admired Gandhi's courage, openness and intellectual honesty but recoiled from his abstinence and religiosity. A life without sex, meat, alcohol and tobacco seemed to Orwell vaguely inhuman. Who would want to be a saint? "The essence of being human is that one does not seek perfection," he wrote, "that one *is* sometimes willing to commit sins for the sake of loyalty, that one does not push asceticism to the point where it makes friendly intercourse impossible, and that

* While Orwell was living in Islington, he and Paul Potts had spotted a notice in a newsagent's window reading, "Rooms to let all nationalities welcome." Orwell turned to Potts and said, "That's a real poem, for you."

one is prepared in the end to be defeated and broken up by life, which is the inevitable price of fastening one's love upon other human individuals." It was certainly the essence of being Orwell.

Did Orwell wreck his health beyond repair for want of a typist? Fredric Warburg thought so. When Orwell finished the final draft in November, he asked his publisher to find him someone who could come to Barnhill to retype the manuscript, which was such a mess of scribbles that he thought nobody could make sense of it unless he was right there with them. But Christen had returned to the Far East, no typist who was willing to travel to Jura could be found in a hurry, and Orwell was impatient. He typed it himself at the punishing rate of around four thousand words a day, seven days a week, propped up in bed for as long as he could bear in between bouts of fever and bloody coughing fits. In the first week of December, he typed the final words, came downstairs, shared the last bottle of wine in the house with Avril and Bill, then went back to bed, demolished by his efforts.

On January 2, 1949, Orwell left Barnhill for the last time to make the long journey to the Cotswold Sanatorium in Cranham, Gloucestershire. It pained him to leave somewhere so full of life. As he glumly told Astor, "Everything is flourishing here except me."

CHAPTER 9

The Clocks Strike Thirteen

Orwell 1949–1950

> My new book is a Utopia in the form of a novel. I ballsed
> it up rather, partly owing to being so ill while I was writing
> it, but I think some of the ideas in it might interest you.
> We haven't definitively fixed the title, but I think it will be
> called "Nineteen Eighty-four."
>
> —George Orwell, letter to Julian Symons, February 4, 1949

So, why 1984?

There's a very popular theory—so popular that many people don't realise that it is just a theory—that Orwell's title was simply a satirical inversion of 1948, but there is no evidence for this whatsoever. This idea, first suggested by Orwell's US publisher, seems far too cute for such a serious book, not to mention restricting: a one-dimensional joke. Scholars have raised other possibilities. Eileen wrote a poem for her old school's centenary called "End of the Century: 1984." G. K. Chesterton's 1904 political satire *The Napoleon of Notting Hill,* which mocks the art of prophecy, opens in 1984. The year is also a significant date in *The Iron Heel.* But all of these connections are exposed as no more than coincidences by the early drafts of the novel that Orwell was still calling *The Last Man in Europe.* First he wrote 1980, then 1982, and only later 1984. The most fateful date in literature was a late amendment.

The important thing is that it's the not-so-near future. Dystopian novels tended to be set either at least a century hence or just around the corner. Close enough to 1949 to be palpable yet far away enough to be credible, Orwell's chosen date had the same purpose as his

London location—to say that it *could* happen here, and soon. Thirty-nine when the novel opens, Winston knows that he was born in either 1944 or 1945, making him a close contemporary of Richard Blair, so perhaps Orwell was imagining the world in which his son would enter middle age. A lot can happen in thirty-five years. Thirty-five years before the novel's publication was the glorious summer of 1914. Archduke Franz Ferdinand was still alive, Orwell was about to turn eleven, and death camps and atom bombs were science fiction.

One of the novel's dark jokes is that it may not even *be* 1984. When Winston comes to write his diary, he realises he isn't sure, because "it was never possible nowadays to pin down any date within a year or two." So the very first line he writes may be untrue. Orwell is telling the reader early on that this is a book in which you can trust nobody and nothing, not even the calendar.

During the months leading up to publication Orwell talked down the novel. In letters to friends, he called it a "beastly book," "an awful book really," and "a good idea ruined." He wrote to Warburg: "I am not pleased with the book but I am not absolutely dissatisfied . . . I think it is a good idea but the execution would have been better if I had not written it under the influence of TB." Worried about his inability to earn money (he wryly referred to tuberculosis as "an expensive hobby"), he anticipated that it would bring in around £500: "it isn't a book I would gamble on for a big sale."*

How seriously should we take Orwell's claim that he "ballsed it up"? He always undersold his novels, owing to a tangle of modesty, expectation management and genuine self-doubt: *Burmese Days* "made me spew"; *A Clergyman's Daughter* "was a good idea, but I am afraid I have made a muck of it"; *Coming Up for Air* was "a mess." The man who maintained that every book, like every revolution, is a failure also wrote that "any life when viewed from the inside is simply a series of defeats." In his hospital notebook, he looked back on twenty-one years of wasted time and unfulfilled promise. Even when he was busy, which he usually was, he fretted that his energy

---

* By way of comparison, various editions of *Animal Farm* had earned him £12,000 by the time of his death, equivalent to £400,000 today.

and talent were running out, "that I was idling, that I was behind with the current job, & that my total output was miserably small." For Orwell, the writer's life was a neurotic treadmill. In reality, nobody considered Orwell a failure except for the voice in his head, without which perhaps he wouldn't have achieved what he did.

As he was laid up in bed after an exhausting three-year struggle to write the book, it's not surprising that he thought *Nineteen Eighty-Four* could have been better. But apart from some confusion about the time frame of Winston's arrest, Secker & Warburg's Roger Senhouse identified no significant errors at the proof stage. Orwell's only acknowledged regret concerned the Room 101 scene, telling Julian Symons that he was right to accuse it of "schoolboyish sensational-ism." Indeed, that scene has the lurid flavour of M. R. James and Edgar Allan Poe, writers he had loved as a schoolboy. The novel may not be perfect, but it has no flaws serious enough to be attributed to sickness or haste. Its pessimism is energetic and intense, not weary.

Warburg was knocked flat by the manuscript. His reader's report, designed to guide his team in marketing the book, was full of shocked praise: "This is amongst the most terrifying books I have ever read . . . Orwell has no hope, or at least he allows his reader no hope, no tiny flickering candlelight of hope. Here is a study in pessimism unrelieved, except perhaps by the thought that, if a man can conceive '1984,' he can also will to avoid it." The novel's first reader was also its first misreader, because Warburg made two faulty assumptions that would be echoed by many subsequent readers. One, as we've seen, was to conclude that Orwell had given up on socialism. The second was to determine that the novel's desolate conclusion stemmed directly from Orwell's illness: "I cannot but think that this book could have been written only by a man who himself, however temporarily, had lost hope." Still, Warburg's enthusiasm was undiluted and his publicist colleague David Farrer concurred: "Orwell has done what Wells never did, created a fantasy world which yet is horribly real so that you *mind* what happens to the characters which inhabit it." He was sure it had best-seller potential, and that if they couldn't sell at least fifteen thousand copies, then they "ought to be shot."

Secker & Warburg moved fast. Even before Orwell left Jura, he was able to reject Senhouse's proposed blurb, which made the novel sound "as though it were a thriller mixed up with a love story," instead of a serious attempt "to indicate by parodying them the intellectual implications of totalitarianism." Of course, it was all of those things at once—and more. It's fortunate that the manuscript didn't require rewriting, because Orwell was incapable of such work. It was all he could do to examine the proofs that arrived during February and March, and draw up lists of friends and contemporaries who should receive advance copies, including Aldous Huxley and Henry Miller. He suggested to Warburg that Bertrand Russell might be willing to write a blurb, which indeed he was. It's unlikely he would have approved had he known that his American publishers Harcourt, Brace had sought a back-cover endorsement from J. Edgar Hoover, the red-baiting director of the FBI: "We hope you might be interested in helping to call this book to the attention of the American public—and thus, perhaps, helping to halt totalitarianism." Always a creature of paranoia, Hoover declined the request and instead opened a file on Orwell.

Orwell resisted any attempt to have the book "mucked about." He flatly refused to let the US Book-of-the-Month-Club publish an edition minus the appendix and Goldstein's book, even at the risk of losing, Warburg estimated, around £40,000 in sales. Anyone who thought these essayistic sections were disposable because they didn't advance the story didn't grasp Orwell's purpose at all. Even before *Nineteen Eighty-Four* was out, people seemed determined to misunderstand it.

Cranham, a private sanatorium high up in the Cotswold hills, was a considerably more privileged environment than Hairmyres. In Orwell's chalet, the greatest aural nuisance was not the constant burble of the radio but the fatuous braying of upper-class patients in neighbouring chalets: "No wonder everyone hates us so." His greatest sadness was missing Richard; terrified of infecting his son, he kept the boy away for long stretches. Orwell was beginning, reluctantly, to accept that this hospitalisation was different—he would not be patched up in time for another summer on Jura. Still, he hoped to stay alive for another five to ten years and asked Warburg to arrange a second opinion that would tell him honestly how much time he

Edward Bellamy, author of
Looking Backward 2000–1887

H. G. Wells meets Orson Welles at a radio station
in San Antonio, Texas, October 28, 1940.

Yevgeny Zamyatin,
author of *We*

Arthur Koestler, author of
Darkness at Noon and
Orwell's friend

Aldous Huxley, author of *Brave New World*

Orwell's first wife, Eileen Blair (née O'Shaughnessy), photographed in 1938

The POUM militia at the Lenin barracks in Barcelona, early 1937

Recording the second episode of the poetry programme *Voice* for the BBC's Eastern Service, September 8, 1942. Clockwise from left: George Woodcock, Mulk Raj Anand, George Orwell, William Empson, Edmund Blunden and Herbert Read

If liberty
means anything at all
it means the right to tell people
what they do not want
to hear

The statue of Orwell that stands outside the BBC's
Broadcasting House in Portland Place, London

The BBC in 1932

Orwell at home, 27b Canonbury Square, London, October or November 1945

Barnhill, the farmhouse on Jura where Orwell wrote *Nineteen Eighty-Four*

Fredric Warburg, Orwell's
British publisher

Orwell's second wife, Sonia Blair
(née Brownell), at the premiere of the
Animal Farm movie, December 1954

The Secker & Warburg
first edition, 1949

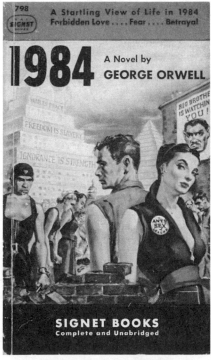

In 2018 the Signet Classics edition sold
270,000 copies in the United States.

Donald Pleasence as Syme and Peter Cushing as Winston in
the BBC adaptation, broadcast December 12, 1954

Eddie Albert as Winston in the CBS
Studio One version, broadcast
September 21, 1953

Poster for the 1956 movie version

avid Bowie with
s band during the
iamond Dogs tour,
os Angeles, 1974

The "1984"
commercial for the
Apple Macintosh,
conceived by Chiat/
Day and directed
by Ridley Scott

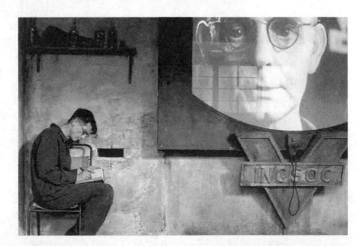

hn Hurt as
inston (left) in
e 1984 movie
rsion, directed by
ichael Radford

Jonathan Pryce as Sam Lowry in *Brazil*, directed by Terry Gilliam

Hugo Weaving as V in the 2005 movie *V for Vendetta*, directed by James McTeigue

Planned Parenthood supporters dress as characters from *The Handmaid's Tale* by Margaret Atwood to protest the Republican Party's healthcare bill in Washington, DC, June 2017.

had left: "Don't think I am making up my mind to peg out. On the contrary, I have the strongest reasons for wanting to stay alive."

Warburg's friend Dr. Andrew Morland, a Harley Street specialist, told Orwell that if he wanted to survive, he would have to avoid work for at least a year. That was painful news for this most industrious of writers, leaving him nothing to do but read, solve crossword puzzles and write letters which crackled with the wit, gossip and analysis that had nowhere else to go. His career as a freelance journalist ended with short reviews of Churchill's autobiography and a biography of Dickens. The latter piece mentioned the theory that the author's final reading tour "exhausted Dickens disastrously" and, therefore, that he "in effect committed suicide" by working too hard. Could Orwell ever write about Dickens without describing himself?

Orwell looked to the future. He drew up a new will. He pondered spending winters somewhere nice by the sea, maybe Brighton, and summers on Jura. When he was able to return to work in 1950, he planned to finish a new collection called *Essays and Sketches*, including an essay about Evelyn Waugh ("about as good a novelist as one can be ... while holding untenable opinions") and another about Joseph Conrad, particularly his political novels *The Secret Agent* and *Under Western Eyes*. He thought that Conrad, another writer-adventurer fascinated by the psychology of nationalism, power and idealism gone awry, had "a sort of grown-upness and political understanding which would have been almost impossible to a native English writer at that time." Like G. K. Chesterton's *The Man Who Was Thursday*, *The Secret Agent* was animated by the wave of anarchist bomb plots and assassinations that swept Europe at the turn of the century, and traces of both novels can be detected in the parts of *Nineteen Eighty-Four* in which Winston is recruited and double-crossed by O'Brien: that tense, secret world of codes, pledges and swapped briefcases. In Orwell's first draft, Winston and Julia actually fantasise about becoming terrorists: "They would get hold of five kilograms of dynamite & a detonator, make their way in among a crowd of Inner Party members & blow everyone to pieces, themselves included."

Orwell also had two novels in mind in 1949, both a long way from Oceania. One was to be set in 1945; the other in the 1920s: "a novel of character rather than ideas, with Burma as background," according to

Warburg. Only one short extract, "A Smoking-Room Story," survives. Lively and playful, it suggests, like his reading diary, that he had finally got totalitarianism out of his system, and that *Nineteen Eighty-Four* was meant to conclude one phase of his work, not his entire career.

While Orwell lay in bed, the post-war order took shape. In April, a dozen Western nations formed NATO. In August, Russia successfully detonated its first atom bomb in the Kazakh steppe. In October, Mao Zedong established the People's Republic of China.

Oceania, Eurasia, Eastasia.

Orwell was rarely short of companionship at Cranham. As well as the usual suspects—Warburg, Muggeridge, Powell, Fyvel, Potts, Holden, Connolly—he was visited by Evelyn Waugh and his untenable opinions, the socialist historian R. H. Tawney, and a rather taxing interviewer from the *Evening Standard,* Charles Curran, who wore him out by arguing about politics and complaining about his "frightful cigarettes." His most frequent and exciting well-wisher was twenty-nine-year-old Sonia Brownell, who re-entered his life in May. She was famously good company.

Sonia would end up living with *Nineteen Eighty-Four* for thirty-one years. A complicated woman, she owes her one-dimensional reputation as a gold-digger, snob and unworthy steward of Orwell's estate to the numerous biographers, producers and screenwriters whose efforts she obstructed and who therefore had no incentive to be kind. Her neurotic obsession with protecting her late husband's legacy doomed her to a life of enemies.

Like Orwell, Sonia was born in India, where her father was a merchant, and raised in England. She attended a Catholic boarding school, which she loathed perhaps even more passionately than he hated St. Cyprian's. One admirer thought her revolt against her upbringing was "an inexhaustible rocket fuel." After she left school, an otherwise glorious nine months at a college in Switzerland was shattered by a boating accident in which a Swiss friend died. Pushing him away before, in his desperation, he dragged her down left her with a traumatic sense of guilt.

Sonia then threw herself into the bustle and thrum of bohemian London, becoming friend, muse, and, in some cases, lover to the Euston Road School of painters. Stephen Spender remembered "the Venus of Euston Road" this way: "With a round Renoir face, limpid eyes, cupid mouth, fair hair, a bit pale perhaps, she had a look of someone always struggling to go beyond herself—to escape from her social class, the convent where she was educated, into some pagan aesthete world of artists and literary geniuses who would save her." Men were infatuated by her dazzling, dancing laugh, and the sadness it couldn't conceal. Though fiercely intelligent, with a sharp and flashing wit, she doubted her own talent while being magnetised to the brilliance of others, especially older men. "My own father had died when I was six months old, my stepfather had gone mad, and there had never been anyone who 'looked after me' in my life," she later wrote.

When Cyril Connolly and the art collector Peter Watson launched *Horizon* in April 1940, Sonia soon became an indispensable part of the team, which is how she first crossed paths with Orwell. Bracingly frank and efficient, with little patience for humbug, she knew how to get things done. She spent most of the war at the Ministry of War Transport and returned to *Horizon* in 1945 an even more formidable character. She got to know Orwell better around this time, during his days of desperate loneliness, and slept with him at least once: an act of charity on her part. They met again in London during the winter of 1946–1947 and she gave him a bottle of brandy to take back to Jura with him. His subsequent letter inviting her to visit the island (she never made it) was coolly pragmatic but for a single note of affection: "meanwhile take care of yourself & be happy."

Sonia did try to be happy. She was spending time in Paris in the intoxicating, maddening company of the existentialists Sartre, de Beauvoir, Camus and the enormously charming, enormously married Maurice Merleau-Ponty. Like Sartre, Merleau-Ponty was a Marxist; he unsuccessfully pitched Sonia an essay for *Horizon,* attacking Orwell's "so-called humanism." (Orwell, for his part, regarded Sartre as "a bag of wind.") Sonia and Merleau-Ponty embarked on a long, turbulent affair, which left her devastated when he broke it off in late 1948. So when they reconnected, Sonia and Orwell were both bruised, vulnerable people who recognised each other's deep reservoirs of sadness. As Julia says to Winston, "I'm good at spotting people who don't belong."

The title of Hilary Spurling's sympathetic biography, *The Girl from the Fiction Department*, supports the popular theory that Sonia was the model for Julia: "her youth and prettiness, her toughness, above all her radiant vitality," Spurling writes. Both women were also brisk, direct and extremely practical. But is that enough to connect the two? Orwell was also close to Inez Holden and Celia Paget, and he saw more of them while writing *Nineteen Eighty-Four* than he did of Sonia. Sonia and the dark-haired Julia didn't look alike, and they certainly didn't think alike.

Outwardly, Julia is a model citizen who cranks out cheap fiction and pornography for the proles, participates noisily in the Anti-Sex League and the Two Minutes Hate, and conveys a puritanical "atmosphere of hockey-fields and cold baths and community hikes"—so convincingly that Winston initially assumes she is a spy for the Thought Police and fantasises about smashing her skull with a cobblestone. In private, she's more hustler than heretic, devoting her considerable cunning to securing black market treats and seducing members of the Party. Ingenious but not intellectual (she doesn't like to read), she's "only a rebel from the waist downwards." She is above all a realist with a genius for survival who has worked out how to play the game without ever questioning the rules. This line from an early draft makes the difference clear: "It was characteristic of the two of them that whereas it was Winston who dreamed of overthrowing the Party by violent insurrection, it was Julia who knew how to buy coffee on the Black Market."

Philosophically, Julia represents a third way to live under Ingsoc. O'Brien claims there is no such thing as objective truth; Winston insists there is; Julia maintains that *it doesn't matter*. Because she can't remember the past and doesn't care about the future, she lives entirely in the present, which is what the Party wants. In fact, she is so incurious about the society she inhabits that she falls asleep while Winston is reading Goldstein's book out loud. In some ways, she is cleverer than Winston, intuiting that Goldstein and the revolutionary Brotherhood are probably fictions concocted by the Party, but it is a cynical, even nihilistic, intelligence. She has said things she doesn't believe so many times that she doesn't really believe in anything that she can't touch. When Winston forces her to remember that Oceania was once at war with Eurasia, she can't understand why it matters: "'Who cares?' she said impatiently. 'It's always one bloody war after another, and one knows the news is all lies anyway.'"

Totalitarian states depended on the Julias. Not long after the war, during an argument with Orwell in the pages of *Polemic*, the communist writer Randall Swingler cited the findings of US troops who had interviewed former Nazi supporters in occupied Germany: "The Nazis explained to their people that since all truth was relative, it was impossible to know or understand anything . . . it absolved the ordinary man from the effort to understand and at the same time gave him a consciousness of disillusioned honesty."

Hannah Arendt confirmed this impression in *The Origins of Totalitarianism:* "The ideal subject of totalitarian rule is not the convinced Nazi or the convinced Communist, but people for whom the distinction between fact and fiction (i.e., the reality of experience) and the distinction between true and false (i.e., the standards of thought) no longer exist." Arendt concluded that Germans were already primed to feel this way by the chaotic uncertainty that preceded Hitler:

> In an ever-changing, incomprehensible world, the masses had reached the point where they would, at the same time, believe everything and nothing, think that everything was possible and that nothing was true . . . Mass propaganda discovered that its audience was ready at all times to believe the worst, no matter how absurd, and did not particularly object to being deceived because it held every statement to be a lie anyhow.

Now there's a Party slogan as good as anything Orwell came up with: *Everything is possible and nothing is true.*

It's remarkable how much of the outline Orwell wrote in 1943 or 1944 survived in the final manuscript. Ingsoc, Newspeak, "dual standard of thought," the three super-states, the oxymoronic Party slogans, falsification of history, the Two Minutes Hate, the three traitors, the proles: they're all there in his notebook. Key plot elements, too. "The writer" (Winston) has a significant conversation with "X" (possibly O'Brien) and a brief affair with "Y" (Julia). The second part of the book was always intended to include arrest, torture, confession and, like all his novels, "the final consciousness of failure."

Orwell did, however, make some crucial additions. One was the two-way telescreen. Like most of the population, Orwell didn't own a television set. By June 1948, there were only fifty thousand TV licences in a country of fifty million people (although that number was increasing exponentially), and there was very little to watch.* For some people, the fear that the new device would watch them back was real. When the Postmaster General Sir Kingsley Wood had announced the arrival of television in 1935 he felt obliged to add, "I would like to reassure any nervous listeners, that, wonderful as television may be, it cannot, fortunately, be used in this way." But it was logical to assume that the technology would one day catch up with the political desire for a surveillance state. The Nazi official Robert Ley once boasted, "The only person who is still a private individual in Germany is somebody who is asleep." In Airstrip One, between the telescreen, the Thought Police, the informants, the helicopters, the hidden microphones and the eerie intensity of Big Brother's eyes, citizens feel that they are being watched "asleep or awake" and act accordingly.

The "infallible and all-powerful" Big Brother was another late innovation. Oceania's ubiquitous, intangible ruler is a hybrid of Koestler's No. 1, Zamyatin's Benefactor, Hitler and, most of all, "Uncle Joe" Stalin, about whom André Gide wrote, "His portrait is seen everywhere, his name is on everyone's lips and praise of him occurs in every public speech. Is all this the result of worship, love or fear? Who can say?" Stalin was often called "the insoluble mystery," "the Enigma" or "the Communist Sphinx," obscured from the masses by his inner circle. The less like a real, and therefore imperfect, human being he appeared, the more powerful he became. "The chief qualification of a mass leader," wrote Arendt, "has become unending

* Coincidentally, the controller of the BBC Television Service from 1947 to 1950 was the novelist Norman Collins, who had edited Orwell's work when he worked at Gollancz (he suggested that Orwell had "some kind of mental instability") and crossed paths with him again in the Overseas Talks Department. The British media was a very small world.

infallibility; he can never admit an error . . . Mass leaders in power have one concern which overrules all utilitarian considerations: to make their predictions come true."

Nobody knows where in Oceania Big Brother lives, nor indeed *if* he lives. "Does he exist in the same way as I exist?" Winston asks O'Brien. "You do not exist," O'Brien replies, avoiding the question by upending it. *Nineteen Eighty-Four* is full of such questions. Was Big Brother ever a real person? Was Goldstein? Who wrote "the book"? Does the Brotherhood really exist? Are the rockets that rain on Airstrip One actually being fired from Oceania itself? Is the old woman in the Ministry of Love Winston's mother? Is Julia a member of the Thought Police after all? What year is it? How much time is passing? It is no surprise that the novel has a following among the paranoid, because it describes an unstable world in which conspiracy theories are entirely valid. As O'Brien tells Winston, avoiding a question about the Brotherhood, "As long as you live it will be an unsolved riddle in your mind." Most of what Winston knows about how the world operates comes from Goldstein's book, which may be a hoax authored by the Party, and what O'Brien tells him during his interrogation, which may be untrue, including the claim that Goldstein's book is a hoax authored by the Party. There is so little that is definitively true.

This constant ambiguity is what makes *Nineteen Eighty-Four* a sophisticated work of fiction rather than an essay with a plot bolted on. Orwell's reputation as a paragon of clarity, with his windowpane prose and love of hard facts, obscures his artistry, tempting people to read the book literally even as the text itself tells them not to. Pitted with dreams, hallucinations, shaky memories, falsified information, and references to mental illness, the novel is a deeply unstable narrative. This was present in Orwell's original outline: "Fantasmagoric effect, rectification, shifting of dates, etc., doubts of own sanity." With its absence of control and incomprehensible menace, it is both a true nightmare and a fair approximation of life in a totalitarian state. "Everything melted into mist," Winston thinks, or "faded away into a shadow-world."

There is only one thing Winston knows for sure. *Nineteen Eighty-Four* may not be a prophecy, but it contains one: a prevision of defeat and death. All of Orwell's protagonists fail, but only Winston *knows* he will fail. Seven years earlier, O'Brien told him in a dream that they would meet "in the place where there is no darkness," which turns out to mean the relentless electric glare of the Ministry of Love. "Winston did not know what it meant, only that in some way or another it would come true." This foreknowledge haunts him constantly. The moment he starts his diary, he knows the Thought Police will find him eventually. There are several references to "predestined horror," "impending death" and "the working-out of a process that had started years ago." He experiences premonitions of Room 101 and even some of the exact arguments that O'Brien will make. In Winston's head the boundaries between memory and prophecy, between past, present and future, wobble and blur. "The end was contained in the beginning."

So the novel's famous twist, when Charrington and O'Brien reveal their true natures, isn't really a twist at all. It's what was always going to happen, one way or another. Orwell writes several times that Winston's actions "made no difference." The whole novel is a chronicle of a death foretold—worse than death: vaporisation, unpersonhood—although it ends just before Winston receives the inevitable bullet. Whether Winston's determination to press forward displays immense courage or numb fatalism is left open, but he knows and accepts the consequences of his actions. "In this game that we're playing, we can't win," he tells Julia, setting up a quintessential Orwell sentence: "Some kinds of failure are better than other kinds, that's all."

O'Brien tells Winston in the Ministry of Love, "Don't deceive yourself. You did know it—you have always known it." But how does O'Brien know that Winston knows? Who *is* O'Brien? Orwell reveals that he is bulky yet graceful, ugly yet charming, with an air of formidable intelligence, subtle irony and mysterious invincibility. As an instrument of state power, he is infinitely more engaging and empathetic than Koestler's cold-blooded Gletkin, and therefore more dangerous. "He was the tormentor, he was the protector, he was the inquisitor, he was the friend."

Inquisitor points towards Catholicism, as does O'Brien's name and his twisted versions of the catechism and Holy Communion. At O'Brien's apartment, Winston feels "a wave of admiration, almost worship" towards this "priest of power." Orwell had a complicated relationship with religion, as an atheist who nonetheless believed that totalitarianism could only have evolved in a spiritual void and felt an emotional attachment to Protestantism. In Airstrip One, a former church is a place to have forbidden sex or exhibit propaganda, or it's just a name in that strange old song "Oranges and Lemons." But he was a consistent critic of Catholicism, often comparing it to fascism and communism as a prime example of oppressive dogma. The Confiteor's conflation of thought, word and deed could even be seen as the logical basis for the concept of thoughtcrime.

Perhaps O'Brien also has godlike powers. We know that he has read Winston's diary—hence his weaponisation of $2 + 2 = 5$—but he also uses phrases, like "lifted clean out of the stream of history" and "we are the dead," that Winston never wrote down. He seems to know Winston's every thought, and to speak to him in dreams. The first time Winston sees him, he feels "as though their two minds had opened and the thoughts were flowing from one into the other through their eyes." Later, he has the impression that he is "writing the diary for O'Brien; *to* O'Brien." O'Brien is both the only person he instantly and wholly trusts, and the last person he *should* trust. He is both real and a part of Winston: his shadow self. "There was no idea that he had ever had, or could have, that O'Brien had not long ago known, examined and rejected. His mind *contained* Winston's mind."

Once Winston is inside the Ministry of Love, it is impossible to take the novel literally. Even if you believe that O'Brien is an actual telepath (Ingsoc scientists are said to be working on "how to discover, against his will, what another human being is thinking"), why would he start surveilling an insignificant Outer Party worker seven years before he rebels? And even then, Winston's revolt consists of nothing more than a few muddled diary entries (which mostly serve to illustrate a mind deformed by propaganda) and some al fresco sex. He only bothers to read one and a half chapters of Goldstein's book and sets it down midway through the very sentence that promises to explain the Party's true motive. Some revolutionary he is.

So Winston is not truly "the last man"; he's just the latest symbolic victim to be broken down and rebuilt. "This drama that I have played out with you during seven years will be played out over and over again, generation after generation, always in subtler forms," O'Brien says. There were Winstons before and there will be Winstons to come. Like Stalin's regime during the Great Terror, the Party doesn't fear heretics; it *needs* them, because its power is renewed by crushing them. Malcolm Muggeridge called this the "continuous performance" of power: "A government based on terrorism requires constantly to demonstrate its might and resolution."

Orwell criticised Stalinists for saying that the ends justified the means, but in Oceania the means justify themselves. The point is to break eggs without proceeding to make an omelette. The perfect citizen is boring, a closed case; the challenge is to tear a free mind to pieces. Only that way can there be "victory after victory" in the bowels of the Ministry of Love: victory over the past, over the individual, over reality itself. As Orwell wrote in "The Prevention of Literature," totalitarianism "in the long run probably demands a disbelief in the very existence of objective truth."

Now we come to Orwell's greatest satirical feat: the logical endgame of totalitarianism's war on the real. When O'Brien claims that he could rise from the floor like a soap bubble, or snuff out the stars like candles, or prove that the sun travels round the earth, he's not a madman; he's a philosopher. In the face of O'Brien's limitless subjectivity, Winston's protestations that there are things that are true and things that are false are sandcastles at high tide. "We control matter because we control the mind," O'Brien says, taking gaslighting to its ultimate extreme. "Reality is inside the skull." Before he can get Winston to say that two plus two is five, he has to abolish the sense that four and five have any independent reality. It's five because O'Brien says it's five. If he said it was $\sqrt{-1}$, it would be $\sqrt{-1}$.

"How many fingers am I holding up, Winston?"
"I don't know. I don't know. You will kill me if you do that again. Four, five, six—in all honesty I don't know."
"Better," said O'Brien.

In other words, everything is possible and nothing is true.

A satire without laughter is still a satire, and the whole point is to go too far. O'Brien is not a man; he's a thought experiment—a modest proposal. Broadly speaking, the first two-thirds of the novel explain through exaggeration what had already happened in Europe, while the last third suggests what could happen if every conceivable limit were removed. Stephen Spender called it "a kind of arithmetic [sic] progression of horror." O'Brien is the answer to the question

"What's the worst that can happen?" He's Hitler and Stalin stripped of their self-justifying rhetoric. He's the boot in the face. "The object of persecution is persecution. The object of torture is torture. The object of power is power."

Orwell's motive for making such an extreme scenario at least imaginable was not despair, but not exactly hope either. "The moral to be drawn from this dangerous nightmare situation is a simple one," he explained in a press statement after the book came out. "*Don't let it happen. It depends on you.*"

Nineteen Eighty-Four was published by Secker & Warburg on June 8, 1949. In Blackpool, the Labour Party held its annual conference. In Paris, foreign ministers were deadlocked over the future of Germany. In Washington, President Truman reaffirmed US support for South Korea. That morning's edition of the London *Times* carried a front-page report of a press conference by General Jan Smuts, the former prime minister of South Africa and a prominent supporter of the United Nations: "Mankind was living in a spiritual twilight, and none knew whether dawn or dusk would follow."

Orwell certainly delivered the shock treatment he had talked about in his review of Gollancz's *In Darkest Germany*. *The New York Times Book Review* reported that the critical reaction to *Nineteen Eighty-Four* was overwhelmingly positive, "with cries of terror rising above the applause," and compared the "state of nerves" to the uproar over Orson Welles's *The War of the Worlds*. The book was variously compared to an earthquake, a bundle of dynamite, and the label on a bottle of poison. "I read it with such cold shivers I haven't had since as a child I read Swift about the Yahoos," John Dos Passos wrote to Orwell, confessing that he'd had nightmares about the telescreen. Several booksellers told Warburg that they were unable to sleep after reading their advance copies. For E. M. Forster, it was "too terrible a novel to be read straight through."

Praise reached Cranham from Arthur Koestler in Paris ("a glorious book"), Aldous Huxley in California ("profoundly important"), Margaret Storm Jameson in Pittsburgh ("the novel which should stand for our age"), and Lawrence Durrell in Belgrade ("Reading it in a Communist country is really an experience because one can see it all around one"). Within just a few weeks, it had been mentioned in Parliament by Conservative MP Hugh Fraser, who saw in Eastern Europe "the type of state which Mr. Orwell has just described in his book *1984*." Not every early reader was impressed. Jacintha Buddicom, who had only recently learned that the famous writer George Orwell and her childhood friend Eric Blair were one and the same, was so horrified that she broke off contact. "I thought *Nineteen Eighty-Four* was a frightful, miserable, defeatist book," she remembered, "and I couldn't think why he'd written it, so I didn't write to him at all."

The most astute critics were those who understood Orwell's message that the germs of totalitarianism existed in Us as well as Them. In Goldstein's book, the supposedly irreconcilable ideologies of the three super-states are "barely distinguishable" and the social structures not at all. "Behind Stalin lurks Big Brother," Forster wrote, "which seems appropriate, but Big Brother also lurks behind Churchill, Truman, Gandhi, and any leader whom propaganda utilizes or invents." Golo Mann of the *Frankfurter Rundschau* summed up Orwell's theme as "the totalitarian danger that lies within ourselves." Daniel Bell, in his philosophical *New Leader* review, observed, "Orwell, actually, is not writing a tract on politics but a treatise on human nature."

Yet not every critic grasped this essential fact. It was a book that pressed down hard on readers' political nerves and revealed their biases. Conservative reviewers thought it was an emphatic denunciation of not just the Soviet Union but *all* forms of socialism, including Attlee's. Henry Luce's fiercely anti-communist *Life* treated it to an eight-page spread with cartoons by Abner Dean, and wrote: "his book reinforces a growing suspicion that some of the British Labourites revel in austerity and would love to preserve it." Lord Beaverbrook's *Evening Standard* mischievously suggested that it should be "required reading" for delegates en route to the Labour Party conference in Brighton.

Communist critics also read it as a straightforward slur on socialism. Samuel Sillen, the editor of *Masses and Mainstream,* wrote a hysterical denunciation of Orwell's "sickness," motivated largely by his disgust that the book was doing so well. *Nineteen Eighty-Four,* he wrote, was not just "cynical rot" but free-market propaganda on a par with Hayek. *Pravda* called it a "filthy book" written "on the orders and instigation of Wall Street." The novelist and communist Arthur Calder-Marshall's savage attack on Orwell's work and character in *Reynold's News* prompted the Labour MP Woodrow Wyatt to agree that Orwell's "blank hopelessness" did not align with "the aims and beliefs of the Labour Party."

Orwell laughed off Calder-Marshall's review ("if I was going to smear somebody I would do it better than that"), but he was dismayed by the conservative caricature of himself as a disillusioned ex-leftist waving the flag for untrammelled capitalism. Presumably this is what he meant, in a letter to Rees, by "some very shame-making publicity." When Warburg visited him at Cranham on June 15, Orwell dictated an emphatic statement explaining the novel's argument that totalitarianism could arise anywhere and that rival super-states "will pretend to be much more in opposition than in fact they are."

He drew up a second statement the next day after Francis A. Henson, an official from the United Automobile Workers in Detroit, wrote to seek clarification that *Nineteen Eighty-Four* was a suitable book to recommend to union members. Orwell responded that it was "NOT intended as an attack on socialism, or on the British Labour Party (of which I am a supporter)" but a warning that "totalitarianism, *if not fought against,* could triumph anywhere." The qualification was essential. "I do not believe that the kind of society which I described necessarily *will* arrive, but I believe (allowing of course for the fact that the book is satire) that something resembling it *could* arrive." To his irritation, the union slipped up while typing up his handwritten letter and replaced *could* with *will,* so when *Life* rang to ask permission to reprint it, he had to insist that the error wasn't repeated. Even his clarification needed a clarification.

Orwell said so little about *Nineteen Eighty-Four* before he died that these two statements are priceless evidence of his intentions, but at the time, thought Warburg, they "didn't do two pennorth of good." The truth is that ambiguity about Orwell's politics boosted his sales. Within six months the book had sold over a quarter of a million copies in the UK and US and writers were eager to adapt it for other media. Orwell corresponded with the Oscar-winning screenwriter and playwright Sidney Sheldon about a possible stage version (never completed) that would give it an anti-fascist slant. Orwell's former colleague Martin Esslin adapted it for the BBC, while Milton

Wayne wrote a thoughtful version for the NBC University Theater, with David Niven as Winston Smith and a scholarly intermission from the novelist James Hilton: "Having read Mr. Orwell's *Nineteen Eighty-Four,* you may not feel you'd like to meet any of its characters but you *do* feel you'd like to meet Mr. Orwell, if only for an argument."

The rush to adapt *Nineteen Eighty-Four* may have stemmed from an assumption that this was a book for the current moment, not one for the ages. In *The New York Times Book Review,* Mark Schorer suggested that its "kinetic" brilliance "may mean that its greatness is only immediate, its power for us alone, now, in this generation, this decade, this year, that it is doomed to be the pawn of time."

Then again, maybe not.

After his visit to Cranham on June 15, Warburg wrote a sobering report on Orwell's "shocking" condition. If he had not recovered by the same time next year, Warburg thought, then he never would, yet Orwell's optimism was infectious.

In July, Orwell proposed to Sonia in his typically self-effacing way. Unlike Celia Paget and Anne Popham, she said yes. Some of his friends found the idea ghoulish. "Orwell was totally unfit to marry anyone," said David Astor. "He was scarcely alive." Muggeridge thought the marriage "slightly macabre and incomprehensible." But Orwell firmly believed that it would give him something to live for. As Winston says of Julia, "Her body seemed to be pouring some of its youth and vigour into his."

Nobody thought that Sonia truly loved him. Some who knew her said that she was a ruthless, selfish woman who married him for the money and prestige because *Horizon* was running on fumes and she would soon lose her job. Others thought it was an act of chivalrous self-sacrifice, motivated by pity and respect. "He said he would get better if I married him," she told Hilary Spurling twenty years later, "so, you see, I had no choice." It is likely that Orwell and Sonia's motives overlapped: he needed her, and she needed to be needed. Many years earlier, while writing about the love life of Thomas Carlyle, Orwell had ruminated on "the astonishing selfishness that exists in the sincerest love."

On September 2, Orwell moved from Cranham to a private room

at University College Hospital in London. Friends doubted he would ever leave. It's very possible that he was already beyond repair when, on October 13, he married Sonia in his hospital room, in front of just half a dozen guests. Astor was reminded of Gandhi: "skin and bone." The wedding lunch took place at the Ritz minus the groom.

Orwell's health and mood were revitalised by marriage—he said he had five more books in mind and couldn't die until he'd written them—but not for long. For the many friends who visited him late in the year, including Symons, Spender, Fyvel and Potts, it was likely that each conversation could be their last with him. He still enjoyed talking about books and politics but increasingly he was drawn back into the past, reminiscing about Eton, Burma, Spain and the Home Guard in a way his friends had never heard before. Dropping in on Christmas Day, Muggeridge saw in Orwell's face no sense of acceptance or peace: "There was a kind of rage in his expression, as though the approach of death made him furious."

Sonia's plan was to deal with Orwell's correspondence and business matters, entertain his friends, and look after him while he wrote, but his condition called for a dramatic change of scene, so the couple made plans to move to a sanatorium at Montana-Vermala in the Swiss Alps. An air ambulance was booked for January 25, 1950, with the painter Lucian Freud, Sonia's close friend, joining them as a kind of nurse. Seven days before the trip, Orwell revised his will, making Sonia his sole heir and (with Rees) the executor of his literary estate. He had no idea how difficult being "the widow of a literary man," as he had put it to Anne Popham, would be.

Orwell asked for his fishing rod to be delivered, with a view to fishing in Alpine lakes. It was propped up in the corner of his room in the early hours of January 21 when a blood vessel in his lung ruptured and he rapidly bled to death.

George Woodcock was attending a party in Vancouver when another guest told him that news of Orwell's death had just been announced on the radio. "A silence fell over the room," Woodcock remembered, "and I realised that this gentle, modest and angry man had already become a figure of world myth."

Orwell had eloquent friends and admirers, whose ringing phrases had an enormous and immediate effect on his posthumous reputation, especially for readers who only knew his final two novels. In *The New Statesman*, the critic and short-story writer V. S. Pritchett crystallised Orwell in a few hundred words: his integrity, his independence, his eccentricity, his rebelliousness, his austerity, his guilt, his "fast, clear, grey prose." He was "the wintry conscience of his generation . . . a kind of saint." In *The Observer*, Koestler claimed that "the greatness and tragedy of Orwell was his total rejection of compromise" and claimed there was "exceptional concordance between the man and his work." Reading the obituaries, Muggeridge observed "how the legend of a human being is created." The fable of the rebel saint who could not tell a lie was born, but so was the fallacy that *Nineteen Eighty-Four* was a deathbed howl. None of the reviews had mentioned Orwell's health, but the fact of his death coloured his final work forever. Sonia thanked Koestler for his obituary because "everyone else—above all Pritchett—wrote such depressing nonsense."

Sonia's grief was so raw and explosive that it convinced even the sceptics. According to Stephen Spender's wife, Natasha, "She had persuaded herself she loved him intellectually, for his writing, but she found she *really* loved him." Stephen agreed: "She blamed herself and thought she had done the wrong thing, and so took over the cause of George Orwell for the rest of her life, and she never really recovered from this."

Muggeridge arranged the funeral at Christ Church on Albany Street in Camden, where the mourners came from every corner of Orwell's peculiarly compartmentalised life—from Eton, Spain, the ILP, the BBC, the Home Guard, *Tribune*, literary London, the European diaspora, the streets of Islington, and the social circles of his two wives. Though an atheist, Orwell was enough of a traditional-ist to want burial in a country churchyard, and David Astor pulled strings for the last time to secure a plot at the Church of All Saints, Sutton Courtenay, in Berkshire. Only he and Sonia were present when Orwell's body was lowered into the ground, to lie beneath a typically matter-of-fact headstone, bearing just his name and dates. The name was still Eric Arthur Blair; he never did get around to changing it.

Orwell's life overlapped with the public life of his final novel by just 227 days.

PART TWO

CHAPTER 10

Black Millennium

Nineteen Eighty-Four *and the Cold War*

If that is what the world is going to be like, we might as
well put our heads in the gas ovens now.

—Viewer complaint to the BBC, December 1954

The evening of Sunday, December 12, 1954, was rough going
for George Orwell, a shipping company employee from south
London. At 8:30 p.m., just after the popular quiz show *What's
My Line?*, more than seven million Britons sat down to watch the
BBC's two-hour adaptation of *Nineteen Eighty-Four.* This was the
largest television audience since the coronation of Queen Elizabeth
II the previous June. Indeed, Prince Philip later let slip that he
and the Queen had watched it and admired "the production and
message." With twenty-two actors, twenty-eight sets and innovative
pre-recorded inserts, *Nineteen Eighty-Four* was Britain's most ambitious and expensive television play to date. It was also, in the words
of *The New York Times,* "the subject of the sharpest controversy in the
annals of British television." Consequently, the only George Orwell
in the telephone directory spent the evening fielding calls from
viewers infuriated by this "horrible play." His wife, Elizabeth, asked
The Daily Mirror to set the record straight: "PLEASE tell people my
husband did NOT write that TV play."

Screenwriter Nigel Kneale and director Rudolph Cartier had previously collaborated on the sci-fi chiller *The Quatermass Experiment.*
Their confident, intelligent take on Orwell, starring Peter Cushing as
Winston Smith, was even harder on the nerves, with its atmosphere
of creeping dread and its horrific climax in the Ministry of Love.

Cartier thought it was the combination of television and telescreen that made it uniquely potent. When the viewer saw Big Brother, he said, "cold eyes stared from the small screen straight at him, casting into the viewer's heart the same chill that the characters in the play experienced whenever they heard his voice coming from *their* watching TV screens."

Hundreds of viewers complained to the BBC and newspapers about the play's unusual amount of violence and sexuality. "It was so awful that I felt like putting a hammer through my TV set," raged one. "Never has anything more vile and repulsive ever been shown on TV," claimed another, "or any other screen." Some newspaper critics agreed, branding it "a nauseating story which held out no hope for the future" and "a picture of a world I never want to see again." *The Daily Express* headlined its coverage "A Million NIGHTMARES."

The plan to broadcast a second performance the following Thursday kept the controversy rolling. The BBC assigned a bodyguard to Cartier after he received a death threat, while Cushing disconnected his telephone to avoid abusive calls. On the current-affairs show *Panorama,* Malcolm Muggeridge debated an alderman from Tunbridge Wells who claimed such broadcasts would inspire a crime wave. When the controversy reached Parliament on Wednesday, one group of Conservative MPs, capitalising on the current moral panic about horror comic books, put forward a motion condemning the BBC's tendency to "pander to sexual and sadistic tastes," while another countered that the play offered valuable insight into totalitarian methods.

The broadcast made both novel and author nationally famous. For most of that year, Secker & Warburg had been selling 150 hardbacks a week. The week after the broadcast, that leaped to one thousand, while the new Penguin paperback edition sold a remarkable eighteen thousand. The story was suddenly so well-known that the comedians of *The Goon Show* recorded a parody called *Nineteen Eighty-Five,* in which Harry Secombe's Winston Seagoon toiled in the Big Brother Corporation, i.e., the BBC. "Listeners!" announced Secombe, mocking the uproar. "You are warned. This programme is *not* to be listened to!" Orwell might have appreciated the jokes about his former workplace's maddening bureaucracy and wretched catering.

Many viewers came away from the BBC play with a distorted impression of Orwell's output, leading one critic to predict that he would "probably acquire an undeserved reputation as the first of a new generation of literary horror-mongers." But as Cartier told the *Express*, "if someone had written a novel in 1910 and called it '1954' and forecast the existence of totalitarian Governments, 'brain-washing,' extermination camps, slave labour, the horrors of atomic and hydrogen bombs, he would probably have been accused of wild exaggeration and morbid, crooked thinking."*

The play reinforced the novel's political importance. The *Express* began serialising an abridged version, while *The Daily Mail* praised its exposure of "the beastliness of Communism." Applause from the right mingled with catcalls from the left, some of which began suspiciously early. A BBC source told the press that telephone calls had started coming in just minutes into the broadcast, indicating that they "probably arose from political prejudice." The letters page of *The Manchester Guardian* turned into a running battle between Orwell fans and British Communist Party hardliner R. Palme Dutt. Dutt claimed that *Nineteen Eighty-Four* was "the lowest essence of commonplace Tory anti-Socialist propaganda by an ex-Etonian former Colonial policeman" and he relished the backlash: "Authority has tried to force Orwell down the throats of the public, and the public has spewed him up." The following week's correspondents unanimously disagreed, with one suggesting that the play's impact was confirmed by "a typical brain-washing letter from Britain's 'Big Brother' himself—Mr. R. Palme Dutt."

This contretemps epitomised the fate of *Nineteen Eighty-Four* during the decade of Korea, Hungary, Mao and McCarthy. In such a febrile context, liberals and socialists struggled to stand up for Orwell's more complex intentions, while the right and the hard left respectively cheered and denounced the novel as cold war propaganda. For the Marxist historian Isaac Deutscher, *Nineteen Eighty-Four* had been turned into "an ideological superweapon," whether Orwell would have liked it or not.

---

* *Brainwashing* had entered the lexicon in 1950, due to the Korean War, and was retrospectively applied to Winston's climactic transformation.

—

The London *Times* described the cultural impact of *Nineteen Eighty-Four* prior to the BBC play as "marginal." That may hold true when measured against seven million viewers, but by any other standard the book was already an emphatic success. The Secker & Warburg hardback sold 50,000 copies in its first two years and the Penguin paperback quickly dwarfed that figure. In the US, where it remained on *The New York Times* best-seller list for twenty weeks, it sold 170,000 in hardback, 190,000 through the Book-of-the-Month Club, 596,000 in a Reader's Digest Condensed Books edition, and 1,210,000 as a New American Library paperback. Not *that* marginal, then.

One of the keys to the novel's popularity was Orwell's genius for snappy neologisms. He wrote in 1942 that "Kipling is the only English writer of our time who has added phrases to the language," but by now he would have been justified in adding himself. Journalists love finding new words to play with, especially ones which simplify complicated phenomena. As Nigel Kneale wrote in *Radio Times,* "Some of the words he coined in the process—'thoughtcrime,' 'doublethink,' 'unperson,' 'facecrime,' 'Newspeak' and others—have passed warningly into the language of the fifties."

According to the Oxford English Dictionary, *Newspeak* first appeared independently of the novel in 1950; *Big Brother* and *doublethink* in 1953; *thoughtcrime* and *unperson* in 1954. *Orwellian* was coined by Mary McCarthy in a 1950 essay about, of all things, fashion magazines.* In 1950, Chancellor of the Exchequer Hugh Gaitskell accused the Conservative opposition of "what the late George Orwell, in his book, which honourable members may or may not have read, entitled *Nineteen Eighty-Four,* called doublespeak." That word does not, in fact, appear in the novel, but it has since entered the vocabulary of politics. Winston Churchill himself decreed *Nineteen Eighty-Four* "a very remarkable book."

Big Brother proved especially popular. During the 1950s, the name was applied in Parliament to targets as diverse as the Conservative government, the Labour left, President Eisenhower, Lord

---

* "[*Flair*] is a leap into the Orwellian future, a magazine without contest or point of view beyond its proclamation of itself."

Beaverbrook, Mao's China, the caliphate of Oman, the House of Lords, the trade union leadership, the Coal Board and the Post Office. Not everybody caught the reference. When, during a 1956 debate about fuel policy, one MP objected to being labelled Big Brother, the speaker of the House of Commons was nonplussed: "I thought it was a term of affection."*

To quote Orwell was to assume, deservingly or not, some of his moral prestige. The writer who didn't merit an entry in *Who's Who* until the year of his death and won only one award (a $1,000 literary prize from *Partisan Review*) quickly became a byword for honesty and decency. Whenever one of his books was republished, reviewers admitted his limitations as a novelist, critic and political thinker but acclaimed him as a *moral* genius who emerged from a dirty time with clean hands. "Orwell was *really* what hundreds of others only pretend to be," claimed Stephen Spender in a special issue of *World Review*. "He was really classless, really a Socialist, really truthful." In his influential introduction to the 1952 US edition of *Homage to Catalonia*, Lionel Trilling established Orwell in the minds of many American readers as a role model in the tradition of Twain, Whitman and Thoreau: "the man who tells the truth."

Specifically, it was felt that he told the truth about totalitarianism. Orwell was not a political scientist. Apart from a few days in communist-controlled Barcelona, he had no first-hand experience of totalitarianism. He was simply a working journalist who read a lot. So it is remarkable that the theory he pieced together from memoirs, biographies, essays, novels and reportage was broadly confirmed by such rigorous studies as Carl J. Friedrich and Zbigniew Brzezinski's *Totalitarian Dictatorship and Autocracy* and Hannah Arendt's *The Origins of Totalitarianism*.

Although Arendt was more knowledgeable about Germany and Orwell more interested in Russia, they came to many of the same conclusions: totalitarianism was the unprecedented intersection of ideology, bureaucracy, technology and terror. Arendt argued that

---

* By far his most quoted (and misquoted) line in Parliament was "All animals are equal but some animals are more equal than others." And some references were more accurate than others. Lord Balfour of Inchrye cited "the book written by the late Mr. George Orwell called *1980*."

totalitarianism aimed to actualise a fantasy, and the gap between myth and reality could only be closed by relentless deceit and unparalleled cruelty.

> It is chiefly for the sake of this supersense, for the sake of complete consistency, that it is necessary for totalitarianism to destroy every trace of what we commonly call human dignity . . . What totalitarian ideologies therefore aim at is not the transformation of the outside world or the revolutionising transmutation of society, but the transformation of human nature itself.

This echoed Orwell's worst fear, which he expressed as far back as 1939: "In the past every tyranny was sooner or later overthrown, or at least resisted, because of 'human nature' . . . But we cannot be at all certain that 'human nature' is constant." The two books had the same US editor, Robert Giroux, and have been intertwined ever since.

Another companion piece was *The God That Failed*, Labour MP Richard Crossman's 1949 anthology of essays of disenchantment by former communists Arthur Koestler, Stephen Spender, Ignazio Silone, Richard Wright, André Gide and Louis Fischer. The book appealed to many of the same readers as *Nineteen Eighty-Four* and featured some similar observations. Spender, who explicitly referenced doublethink in his essay, wrote that communists "distorted the meaning of epithets . . . without the slightest realisation that to misuse words produces confusion. 'Peace' in their language could mean 'War'; 'War'—'Peace'; 'Unity'—'betrayal from within'; 'Fascism'—'Socialism.'" Orwell, however, knew that they realised exactly what they were doing.

Another crucial difference between Orwell and the *God That Failed* group, the difference that gave him exceptional moral authority, was that he had never been fooled. In fact, some admirers refused to accept that he had ever belonged to the left at all. When Orwell wrote that "Dickens is one of those writers who are felt to be worth stealing. He has been stolen by Marxists, by Catholics and, above all, by Conservatives," he was unwittingly foreseeing his own fate. The Tory Catholic Christopher Hollis and the right-wing libertarians at

The Freeman each claimed Orwell for their camp, while Conservative MP Charles Curran (formerly the *Evening Standard* journalist who had aggravated Orwell at Cranham) made the ridiculous claim that the novel's effect on the British public "probably had more to do than any other single factor with the Socialist defeat in the 1951 General Election." One can imagine Orwell's reaction to *that* claim.

On the far left, meanwhile, the Communist Party historian A. L. Morton concluded his history of utopian literature, *The English Utopia,* by accusing Orwell of writing a vicious libel on socialism: "no slander is too gross, no device too filthy: *Nineteen Eighty-Four* is, for this country at least, the last word to date in counter-revolutionary apologetics." Morton followed this condemnation with fulsome praise for Stalin's "realisation of Utopia." On a similarly feverish note, James Walsh in *The Marxist Quarterly* charged Orwell with running "shrieking into the arms of the capitalist publishers with a couple of horror-comics which bring him fame and fortune." Walsh and Morton shared the tone of shrill disgust that Orwell had identified in 1944 as "Marxist English, or Pamphletese," and parodied in *Nineteen Eighty-Four* in the form of the Speakers' Corner zealot who denounces Labour politicians as lackeys and hyenas. He would not have been surprised.

Next to those seething indictments, Isaac Deutscher's 1955 essay "The Mysticism of Cruelty" was an elegant character assassination, putting a gloss of fair-mindedness on a series of very shaky allegations. Deutscher unjustly accused Orwell of plagiarising Zamyatin and Trotsky, rejecting socialism, and, on the basis of meeting him in Germany in 1945, being a paranoiac whose world view was "a Freudian sublimation of persecution mania." Deutscher finally charged Orwell with producing a lurid melodrama that encouraged panic, hate, anger and despair:

> *1984* is in effect not so much a warning as a piercing shriek announcing the advent of the Black Millennium, the Millennium of damnation . . . *1984* has taught millions to look at the conflict between East and West in terms of black and white, and it has shown them a monster bogy and a monster scapegoat for all the ills that plague mankind.

There was indeed a concerted effort to frame *Nineteen Eighty-Four* as a book about Russia alone, most urgently in the fledgling nation of West Germany. In his review, Golo Mann had argued that Germans, "perhaps more than any other nation, can feel the merciless probability of Orwell's utopia." But by 1949, anti-communism had eclipsed denazification as official policy and converged with Germans' emotional craving to forget the recent past. This was embodied by *Der Monat*, a popular new US-funded magazine which valorised Orwell as an anti-Stalinist prophet, serialising both *Animal Farm* and *Nineteen Eighty-Four*. German readers therefore mentally scrubbed Nazism from the novel and looked to the East. Yet it was not as if officials and intellectuals behind the Iron Curtain disagreed. According to Polish writer Czesław Miłosz, "Because it is both difficult to obtain and dangerous to possess, it is only known to certain members of the Inner Party . . . The fact that there are writers in the West who understand the functioning of the unusually constructed machine of which they themselves are a part astounds them." When, in 1958, an East German judge sentenced a teenager to three years in prison for reading and discussing the book, he called Orwell "the most hated writer in the Soviet Union and the socialist states."

During the war, the UK and US governments had marketed Stalin as "Uncle Joe" and "Our Gallant Ally." In 1943, *Life* dedicated an entire issue to Russia, encouraging readers to "make allowances for certain shortcomings, however deplorable," while Warner Brothers whitewashed Stalin in *Mission to Moscow*, a propaganda film that Orwell attacked for its distortion of history. Orwell himself had been obliged to celebrate Russian military prowess in his news broadcasts for the BBC. Now, as the cold war dawned, the West was extremely keen to dismantle that heroic image. *Oceania was at war with Eurasia: Oceania had always been at war with Eurasia.*

In February 1948, UK Foreign Secretary Ernest Bevin formed the Information Research Department, which the historian Frances Stonor Saunders has called "the secret Ministry of Cold War." Although its methods gradually degenerated into dirty tricks during the 1950s, the IRD's initial priority was to counteract Soviet propaganda with reports and articles which the department covertly encouraged friendly intellectuals to launder through their own work. It also circulated in European translations of such anti-Soviet books as *Animal Farm, The God That Failed* and *Darkness at Noon*. Two of the IRD's key advisers were Orwell's friends Malcolm Muggeridge and Arthur Koestler.

When Orwell had spent Christmas 1945 with Koestler, the two men had sat by the open fire designing a political movement to promote human rights and free speech. Via the new United Nations, this "League for the Rights of Man" would encourage dialogue between East and West in the form of travel, radio, books and newspapers. As Orwell wrote in "Notes on Nationalism," "Indifference to objective truth is encouraged by the sealing-off of one part of the world from another." This "psychological disarmament" would, he hoped, puncture that bubble. Their plan fizzled out for various reasons, but for Koestler, the idea lived on.

In 1948, Koestler went on a US lecture tour on behalf of the International Rescue Committee, during which he met almost every American anti-communist who mattered: the ex-Trotskyite hawks James Burnham, Sidney Hook and Max Eastman; liberal intellectuals such as Dwight Macdonald, Mary McCarthy and Lionel Trilling; and the founders of the CIA. As someone who had spent six years in the 1930s working for the Comintern's Willi Münzenberg, Koestler knew the enemy's playbook better than any of them.

Comintern is one of the examples of proto-Newspeak given in the appendix to *Nineteen Eighty-Four:* "a word that can be uttered almost without taking thought." The Comintern's post-war successor as a forum for European communist parties was Cominform. In 1949, it sponsored conferences of artists, scientists and intellectuals in Paris and New York to promote Russia as a force for peace and frame the Americans as imperialist warmongers. In consultation with Koestler, the US intelligence agencies hatched a plan for a cultural counteroffensive: if the Russians had laid claim to *peace,* then the West would have *freedom.* In June 1950, intellectuals from all over the US and Western Europe flocked to Berlin for the inaugural Congress for Cultural Freedom, secretly sponsored by the CIA. The original list of invitees, drawn up months earlier, had included Orwell. After four days of panel discussions, dinners and cocktail parties, the Congress closed with a rally, where Koestler delivered a fourteen-point manifesto based on the ideas he had thrashed out with Orwell in Wales, concluding with a stirring slogan: "Friends, freedom has seized the offensive!"

Backed by the CIA, the Congress for Cultural Freedom became a permanent body with affiliated national committees. Over the next seventeen years, it sponsored numerous conferences, festivals, concerts, art exhibitions, seminars and magazines in more than thirty countries. Its success depended on the informal group that the State Department designated "the Noncommunist Left," on the basis that socialists and liberals could sap communism's prestige much more effectively than a militant like Burnham. "The noncommunist left has brought what measure of hope there is in our political life today," wrote Arthur Schlesinger Jr. in *The Vital Center,* the 1949 book that was effectively a manifesto for the group. Schlesinger proposed a canon of "prophets" including Koestler, Silone, Gide and "George Orwell, with his vigorous good sense, his hatred of cant."*

Most of the writers who befriended, published, edited, corresponded with, or positively reviewed Orwell during the 1940s ended up playing some role in this new *Kulturkampf. Tribune* and *Partisan Review* were kept afloat in the rough seas of the post-war economy by funds from, respectively, the IRD and the CIA. The British Committee for Cultural Freedom was led by Malcolm Muggeridge, Fredric Warburg and Tosco Fyvel—the same three men who met with Sonia after Orwell's funeral to discuss his literary estate. When, in 1953, the Congress for Cultural Freedom and the IRD jointly funded a new magazine called *Encounter,* an Anglo-American answer to *Der Monat,* its publisher was Warburg and its British co-editor was Spender. *Tempo Presente,* the Italian equivalent, was co-edited by Silone, while the editor of the Spanish-language *Cuadernos* was a former POUM member.

---

* It's worth quoting from Schlesinger's introduction, with its powerful echoes of Edward Bellamy in the 1880s and H. G. Wells in the 1900s: "Western man in the middle of the twentieth century is tense, uncertain, adrift. We look upon our epoch as a time of troubles, an age of anxiety. The grounds of our civilisation, of our certitude, are breaking up under our feet, and familiar ideas and institutions vanish as we reach for them, like shadows in the falling dusk." Perhaps every generation feels like this at some point.

Accustomed to being outcasts—Koestler called them "that bunch of homeless Leftists . . . whom the Stalinites call Trotskyites, the Trotskyites call Imperialists, and the Imperialists call bloody Reds"— the members of the Noncommunist Left were now in demand and swimming in government money. Some knew; some didn't; most refused to think about it. When the CIA's covert funding was definitively exposed by *Ramparts* magazine in 1967, some contributors still maintained that they'd suspected nothing. "I was made an unwitting 'accomplice' of the CIA's dirty work," protested Dwight Macdonald. "I was played for a sucker." One could argue that he'd played himself by not asking questions.

Would Orwell, the absent Galahad of the Noncommunist Left, also have been a sucker? Or even an enthusiastic participant? He was no great fan of conferences and committees, but his name might well have appeared on the *Encounter* masthead. The Irish radical Conor Cruise O'Brien, however, thought that Orwell would have revolted against this new anti-communist orthodoxy, just as he had rejected every other dominant clique. For the Congress, O'Brien wrote after the *Ramparts* revelations, "it was rather fortunate that Orwell died when he died. Had he lived, it might not have been so easy to claim him. As it is, it has been possible to claim him as a patron saint, and to exploit his merits, by a sort of parasitic reversibility, in the service of some dubious activities."

Those activities included mucking about with his two great novels.

In December 1951, the husband-and-wife animation team John Halas and Joy Batchelor signed a contract with producer Louis de Rochemont to make a movie version of *Animal Farm*. Halas assured *The New York Times* that the film would "deviate very little from the Orwell" and would "retain the spirit of the book." What the couple didn't know was that de Rochemont's main source of financing, and the driving force behind the film, was the Office of Policy Coordination (OPC), the CIA department dedicated to covert operations.

Orwell did not object in principle to fiction being used for political purposes. As a critic, he had recommended that both *The Great Dictator* and *Take Back Your Freedom* be promoted as anti-Nazi propaganda.

Later, he was quite happy for *Animal Farm* to be used to promote anti-Stalinism. He waived royalties for translations in Eastern Europe, personally paid for the production of a Russian-language version, and wrote a preface for a 1947 Ukrainian edition to be distributed to anti-Stalinist socialists living in displaced persons camps in Germany, although most of the copies were intercepted by the US Army at the request of the Russians. The edition was prompted by the Ukrainian writer Ihor Szewczenko, who had written to tell Orwell that he had read passages to Soviet refugees and found that they were profoundly moved: "the mood of the book seems to correspond with their own actual state of mind."

The notion of government agencies actually rewriting books for the purposes of propaganda, however, was a different matter. Every time Batchelor submitted a new draft of her *Animal Farm* screenplay, the "investors" would demand changes. Perhaps Napoleon and Snowball could have the same facial hair as Stalin and Trotsky? Could she cut back on the farmers so as to focus the blame on the pigs (and to avoid offending the agriculture industry)? Snowball was too sympathetic; why not make him a "fanatic intellectual"? And so on. One memo bemoaned Orwell's "apparent inference [*sic*] that Communism is good in itself but that it was betrayed by Stalin & Co." De Rochemont's right-hand man Lothar Wolff pushed back against some of the sillier suggestions, but the investors were relentless and usually got their way.* Furthermore, budget constraints led to the erasure of several characters and plot points essential to Orwell's allegory.

The OPC's biggest issue with *Animal Farm* was the ending. Famously, the pigs and humans form a tense rapprochement over beer and cards and the other animals can no longer tell the difference between the revolutionaries and the oppressors. According to the cold war calculus, however, any focus on the perfidy of capitalist democracies was unhelpful. In the movie, the farmers are gone and the pigs' decadence spurs the animals into a second revolution. It could be argued that Orwell left that possibility open in the book's final paragraph: for the first time, the animals keenly realise that the

---

* It could have been worse. The movie's first screenwriter suggested inserting a scene in which Napoleon dispatches a pig to Mexico to assassinate Snowball, in the hope that it would appeal to Trotskyite viewers.

revolution has been betrayed, so they might do something about it. But having animals from neighbouring farms join forces to trample Napoleon and his cronies to death made a travesty of Orwell's melancholy ending. By the time Batchelor's thoughtful, Orwell-derived voiceover was replaced with cold war boilerplate, Halas and Batchelor must surely have worked out the identity of the meddling investors.

Yet when the film premiered in New York on December 29, 1954, it turned out that all the painstaking effort to ensure that *Animal Farm* sent exactly the right CIA-approved message was helpless against critics' own biases. There were still reviewers who variously interpreted the movie as anti-fascist, subversively pro-communist, a "bitter satire on the Welfare State," or blandly apolitical. While the FBI's file on Orwell claimed that the movie had "hit the jackpot," the public wasn't interested either way—*Animal Farm* flopped, only later reaching a wide audience when it became standard viewing in schools. David Sylvester in *Encounter* judged it "a failure aesthetically, imaginatively, and intellectually," seemingly unaware that both movie and magazine were backed by the CIA.

Perhaps the movie suffered from unfortunate timing. It was released just a few weeks after the BBC's *Nineteen Eighty-Four* and its attendant controversy—a subject which overshadowed *Animal Farm* in the promotional interviews that Sonia gave to the US press. "Did she approve of their interpretation?" asked *Today's Cinema*. "I must be loyal to the brave BBC," she said. "But not really." In Britain, the studio attempted to piggyback on the TV play's success with the promotional tagline "Pig Brother is watching you."

By that point Peter Rathvon, the former president of RKO Pictures, had obtained the rights to *Nineteen Eighty-Four* and secured $100,000 from the United States Information Agency to help make "the most devastating anti-Communist film of all time." He sought advice on the screenplay from Sol Stein from the American Committee for Cultural Freedom, who attempted to do to this story what the OPC had done to *Animal Farm*. Stein took similar exception to Orwell's downbeat conclusion: "I think we agreed that this presents a situation without hope when, in actuality, there is some hope . . . that human nature cannot be changed by totalitarianism and that both love and nature can survive even the horrendous encroachments of Big Brother." He suggested a grossly sentimental alternative in which Winston flees from the Chestnut Tree Café to the Golden Country, where he rediscovers his unquenchable humanity. Thankfully, Rathvon quashed that idea.

The movie's Oscar-nominated screenwriter, William Templeton, had previously written an acclaimed 1953 adaptation for the CBS anthology series *Studio One,* but the opening credit ("freely adapted from the novel *1984* by George Orwell") warned that more liberties would be taken this time. Those liberties were not, however, propagandistic. Templeton and director Michael Anderson seemed far less interested in politics than in the romance between the two badly miscast (and inexplicably American) leads: the burly gangster movie star Edmond O'Brien as Winston and the glowingly cheerful Jan Sterling as Julia. Just before the couple are arrested by the Thought Police in the novel, Winston says flatly, "We are the dead." In the movie, Julia trills, "It's wonderful to be alive!" The CIA might have appreciated the portentous voiceover ("This, then, is a story of the future. It could be the story of our children if we fail to preserve their heritage of freedom"), but probably not the poster, which depicted Winston and Julia in a passionate clinch while an officer of the Anti-Sex League (who does not appear in the novel) spied on them through a telescreen. "Will Ecstasy Be a Crime . . . in the Terrifying World of the Future? Amazing wonders of tomorrow! Nothing like it ever filmed!"

Anderson shot two different endings. American audiences still saw Winston come to love Big Brother, but British viewers were surprised to see Winston and Julia defiantly crying, "Down with Big Brother!" before being gunned down. It is a mark of *Nineteen Eighty-Four*'s uncommon bleakness that a "happy" ending is one in which its protagonists are shot to death, having achieved nothing. "The change seemed to me to show that they had not understood the book at all," protested Sonia, who was so cross that she refused to attend the premiere. "It was awful." Rathvon had the chutzpah to claim that it was "the type of ending Orwell might have written if he had not known when he wrote the book that he was dying." Like *Animal Farm,* the movie failed to impress critics and audiences in either country when it was released in 1956. Even the US government couldn't make Orwell a box-office smash.

Many of Orwell's friends and fans saw his appropriation by the right as a species of bodysnatching, while his critics maintained that he had brought it on himself. Decades after his death, the debate was reopened by the discovery of Orwell's own secret participation in cold war skulduggery.

On March 29, 1949, Orwell received a visit at Cranham from his friend and former crush, Celia Paget, who told him about her new job at the IRD. According to Paget's report, Orwell "expressed his wholehearted and enthusiastic approval of our aims" and recommended some suitable writers. A week later, he sent a letter volunteering to send Paget "a list of journalists & writers who in my opinion are crypto-Communists, fellow-travellers or inclined that way & should not be trusted as propagandists." Orwell had been keeping a pale blue quarto notebook of names of people in public life who he believed had Soviet sympathies, just as he had once speculated about who might sell out in the event of a Nazi invasion (he always loved making lists). Over the past year or so, the Soviet Union had seized control of Czechoslovakia, bullied Yugoslavia, blockaded Berlin, and persecuted Jewish writers, and Orwell was furious that Stalin still had prominent apologists. Paget replied enthusiastically, and Orwell sent her an abbreviated list of thirty-eight names, culled from his notebook's 135. "It isn't very sensational," he wrote, "and I don't suppose it will tell your friends anything they don't know."

The notebook does not show Orwell at his finest. Many of the entries are petty, gossipy, mean and tenuous, his uncertainty betrayed by the numerous question marks, asterisks and crossings out that darken the pages. If he had handed the notebook to the IRD, it would have been reckless, shabby behaviour. But he kept it private, and took great care in editing and amending the list for Paget. "The whole difficulty is to decide where each person stands, & one has to treat each case individually," he told Richard Rees. It was "very tricky" working out whether someone was a true believer, an opportunist, a half-hearted sympathiser, or merely stupid.

It is legitimate to be disappointed by the very act of sending such a list to a government agency (even a Labour one), but the edited version was at least largely accurate. Orwell was particularly concerned by fellow-travellers within the Parliamentary Labour Party such as Konni Zilliacus and John Platt-Mills—men he had already attacked in print as "publicity agents of the USSR." They were who he had in mind in his statement about the message of *Nineteen Eighty-Four*: "Members of the present British government ... will *never* willingly sell the pass to the enemy ... but the younger generation is suspect and the seeds of totalitarian thought are probably widespread among them." Anyone who reminded him of the people who had pursued him in Spain, or attempted to block his writing for political reasons, raised his hackles. For the crime of criticising Stalin, he complained in 1946, "I have been obliged at times to change my publisher, to stop writing for papers which represented part of my livelihood, to have my books boycotted in other papers, and to be pursued by insulting letters, articles ... and even threats of libel action."

It's important to remember that Orwell was advising Paget on who to avoid for the specific purpose of writing for the IRD. Beyond that, there is no evidence that the list damaged the careers of anybody on it, nor that it was intended to do so. The knowledge that the actor Michael Redgrave went on to play the O'Brien figure in the 1956 movie proves that it wasn't used as a blacklist, as does the fact that the only person Orwell fingered as "some kind of Russian agent," Austrian-born journalist Peter Smollett, wasn't exposed as a Soviet spy until after his death in 1980. Smollett was almost certainly the man who advised Jonathan Cape to drop *Animal Farm* when he was head of Soviet relations at the Ministry of Information.

Orwell's intentions also have to be judged in the light of his support for free speech. He had called any attempt to suppress Western communist parties "calamitous" and rallied members of the Freedom Defence Committee against a government effort to purge the civil service of communists. He told Woodcock that, while governments had the right to combat infiltration, Labour's approach was "vaguely disquieting, & the whole phenomenon seems to me part of the general breakdown of the democratic outlook." Ironically, Orwell himself had been monitored by the British government since he was a journalist in Paris in 1929. One police sergeant, surveilling him at the BBC, reported that he held "advanced communist views," although his superior officer, after reading Orwell's journalism, rightly concluded that "he does not hold with the Communist Party, nor they with him."

Nevertheless, when Orwell's letter to Paget was made public in 1996, his detractors on the left relished the irony of Saint George playing the role of Thought Policeman.* Here was the (very faintly) smoking gun that served to justify decades of animosity. "I always knew he was two-faced," said the Marxist historian Christopher Hill. "There was something fishy about Orwell . . . it confirms my worst suspicions about the man." Journalist Alexander Cockburn couldn't disguise his glee: "The man of conscience turns out to be a whiner, and of course a snitch, an informer to the secret police, *Animal Farm's* resident weasel." More in sorrow than in anger, Orwell's former *Tribune* colleague Michael Foot expressed disappointment, while his nephew, the campaigning journalist Paul Foot, said: "I am a great admirer of Orwell, but we have to accept that he did take a McCarthyite position towards the end of his life."

McCarthyite? No, we don't have to accept that at all.

Nineteen days after Orwell's death, Joseph McCarthy, the forty-one-year-old junior senator from Wisconsin, told an audience of Republican women in Wheeling, West Virginia, that he possessed a list of scores of communists working in the State Department, and thus initiated one of the most shameful episodes of the cold war.

McCarthy was one of those hot-breathed monsters who surface noisily from the depths of the American id from time to time to maul the democratic values that they claim to defend. Bombastic, narcissistic, power-hungry and pathologically dishonest, McCarthy might have been designed in a laboratory with the specific purpose of offending Orwell. "I always disagree when people end by saying that we can only combat Communism, Fascism, or what not if we

---

* The story of the list leaked out slowly. In 1980, Orwell's biographer Bernard Crick revealed the existence of the notebook in a single line, but nobody seemed to pay attention. In 1996, the Public Record Office released Orwell's first letter to Paget. In 1998, the list in his notebook was published. Not until 2003, after Paget's death, did the Foreign Office release Orwell's edited list. This meant that for several years critics and defenders alike were jumping to conclusions.

develop an equal fanaticism," Orwell told Richard Rees. "It appears to me that one defeats the fanatic precisely by not being a fanatic oneself."

As a law student, McCarthy had enjoyed gambling and boxing, and he applied both skills to politics. By the time he began his crusade, Soviet spies such as Alger Hiss had been exposed, the major trade unions had been purged, and party membership was in free fall. The fear of communist infiltration was exponentially greater than the danger, and that created an opening for an expert fear-monger. Within months, McCarthy was a magazine cover star and celebrity speaker who pulled in up to $1,000 a day in donations. The historian Ted Morgan defined McCarthyism as "the use of false information in the irrational pursuit of a fictitious enemy." To use Orwell's word, it was phantasmagoric, and it destroyed innocent lives. In Hollywood, victims of the McCarthyite blacklist included two performers from *Studio One*'s "1984": star Eddie Albert and narrator Don Hollenbeck, who committed suicide a few months after the broadcast. Director Paul Nickell considered his version an implicit critique of McCarthy's methods. Democratic presidential candidate Adlai Stevenson condemned McCarthy's "self-appointed thought police," thus becoming the first major US politician to reference *Nineteen Eighty-Four*.

McCarthyism, described by the senator as "Americanism with its sleeves rolled," was anathema to many members of the Congress for Cultural Freedom. One US propagandist in Rome called McCarthy "the chink in our shining armour, the embodied refutation of everything I'm saying." The American Committee for Cultural Freedom was therefore sliced in two. Liberal members—Dwight Macdonald, Arthur Schlesinger, Mary McCarthy (no relation)—decried the senator's thuggish dishonesty, while the conservative wing—James Burnham, Max Eastman, Irving Kristol—believed that the threat of communist infiltration justified extreme measures. Burnham's *The Web of Subversion: Underground Networks in the US Government* was McCarthyism with its cuffs buttoned; his hawkishness led him to quit the committee, *Partisan Review* and his consultancy job with the Office of Policy Coordination. Orwell was right about him all along: "Burnham thinks always in terms of monsters and cataclysms . . . Everything must happen suddenly and completely, and the choice must be all or nothing, glory or bust."

The McCarthyites were a prime example of what the historian Richard Hofstadter later called "the paranoid style," obsessed with "the existence of a vast, insidious, preternaturally effective international conspiratorial network designed to perpetrate acts of the most fiendish character." Hofstadter observed that anti-communism had rapidly degenerated into a mirror-image orthodoxy, different only in degree. Most of the worst culprits were themselves ex-communists who wielded the authority of apostasy. Refugees from doublethink, traumatised by their old lies and excuses, they turned to what Orwell described as "Transferred Nationalism." Louis Fischer diagnosed the type brilliantly in *The God That Failed:*

> He abandons Communism intellectually, yet he needs an emotional substitute for it. Weak within himself, requiring security, a comforting dogma, and a big battalion, he gravitates to a new pole of infallibility, absolutism and doctrinal certainty . . . When he finds a new totalitarianism, he fights Communism with Communist-like violence and intolerance. He is an anti-Communist "Communist."

Orwell never possessed the quasi-religious faith in communism that for so many turned into its negative image, nor was he motivated by the "group-advancement and cultural monopoly" that Mary McCarthy thought motivated the zealots. Uninterested in accruing power, he never craved membership of the winning tribe. "In five years it may be as dangerous to praise Stalin as it was to attack him," he wrote in 1946. "But I should not regard this as an advance. Nothing is gained by teaching a parrot a new word. What is needed is the right to print what one believes to be true, without having to fear bullying or black mail from any side."

McCarthy's career ended in ignominy because he managed to alienate the White House, the CIA, the State Department, the Army and his fellow congressmen. But McCarthyism, which outlasted him, was the kind of thing that Orwell had described in his statement on the broader relevance of *Nineteen Eighty-Four:* "In the USA the phrase 'Americanism' or 'hundred percent Americanism'"—a phrase dating from the First World War—"is suitable and the qualifying adjective is as totalitarian as anyone could wish."

One of McCarthy's malign innovations was to successfully operate a quasi-totalitarian disregard for the truth by exploiting democracy's weaknesses. Ostensibly, he and the press were bitter enemies. He compared *Time* and *Life* to *The Daily Worker*, singled out a reporter for abuse in front of a jeering crowd, and once ranted about his mistreatment by the press to an audience of bewildered schoolchildren. Yet reporters loved, pursued and ultimately sustained him, because he could always be relied upon for juicy front-page copy. Even though much of what he told them was groundless, McCarthy knew, like no politician before him, how to hack the American press. He would embellish stories over several days to maximise coverage and hold press conferences an hour before reporters' deadlines, leaving them no time to fact-check his statements, not that many even tried.

In 1952, *The New York Times* admitted that it had misled its readers by printing McCarthy's claims without question but abdicated responsibility for the deception: "It is difficult, if not impossible, to ignore charges by Senator McCarthy just because they are usually proved exaggerated or false. The remedy lies with the reader." By gaming the system, McCarthy thus carved out his own unique post-truth zone in which he could say anything. Decades later, *Times* reporter James "Scotty" Reston explained McCarthy's success: "He knew that big lies produced big headlines. He also knew that most newspapers would print almost any outrageous charge a United States senator made in public . . . McCarthy knew how to take advantage of this 'cult of objectivity.'" Almost everybody, he added, "came out of the McCarthy period feeling vaguely guilty."

One of McCarthy's ugliest stunts, in 1953, was to dispatch his fanatical young lieutenants Roy Cohn and David Schine on a tour of the United States Information Agency's libraries in Europe, where they aggravated everyone they met and drew up a list of "red" books to be removed, including titles which had previously fallen foul of Hitler, Stalin and Mao. Some overeager German librarians actually incinerated the blacklisted books, an image so shocking that President Eisenhower broke his silence on McCarthy. "Don't join the book-burners," he told a graduating class at Dartmouth College. "Don't think that you are going to conceal faults by concealing evidence that they ever existed."

The incident chimed with the theme of a forthcoming novel that became, culturally and politically, a kind of American answer to *Nineteen Eighty-Four:* Ray Bradbury's science-fiction novel *Fahrenheit 451.* "Whether or not my ideas on censorship via the fire department will be old hat by this time next week, I dare not predict," Bradbury wrote. "When the wind is right, a faint odour of kerosene is exhaled from Senator McCarthy." Bradbury's satire on mass media includes an alienated employee of a totalitarian regime; the suppression of knowledge and erasure of memory; the constant shadow of war; the "televisor"; and a very Orwellian inversion: in a world of fireproofed buildings, firemen start blazes instead of putting them out, and insist that it's never been any different.

Perhaps these affinities were coincidental. When asked whether he'd been influenced by Orwell, Bradbury instead named *Darkness at Noon* as the "true father, mother, and lunatic brother" of *Fahrenheit 451.* But from now on, a comparison to *Nineteen Eighty-Four* would be the price of entry for anyone publishing dystopian fiction. Between the Korean War and the Cuban missile crisis, the genre included Kurt Vonnegut's *Player Piano: America in the Coming Age of Electronics,* Evelyn Waugh's *Love Among the Ruins: A Romance of the Near Future,* David Karp's *One,* L. P. Hartley's *Facial Justice,* Michael Young's *The Rise of the Meritocracy 1870–2033,* and Ayn Rand's *Anthem* (finally making its US hardback debut) as well as many justly forgotten imitators. "Whereas twenty years ago the average yawn-enforcer would locate its authoritarian society on Venus or in the thirtieth century, it would nowadays, I think, set its sights on Earth within the next hundred years or so," wrote the novelist Kingsley Amis in his survey of science fiction, *New Maps of Hell.* With the notable exceptions of B. F. Skinner's *Walden Two* and Aldous Huxley's 1962 swansong *Island,* writers had lost their appetite for designing utopias.

In the US, where *Anthem* filled an entire issue of *Famous Fantastic Mysteries,* the dystopian genre blurred into science fiction. With its sensationalist, futuristic cover ("A Startling View of Life in 1984. Forbidden Love . . . Fear . . . Betrayal"), the 1950 Signet edition of *Nineteen Eighty-Four* was clearly pitched at fans of Isaac Asimov and

Robert A. Heinlein. But Amis noted that literary snobs refused to accept that Orwell's book belonged in a category they believed was beneath serious consideration. In terms of genre as well as politics, *Nineteen Eighty-Four* resembled the contested territory on the fringes of Oceania: worth fighting over.

In his *Marxist Quarterly* hatchet job, published in January 1956, James Walsh predicted, "*1984* is already on the way out. We need the extra push now to get rid of it altogether." In fact, what was on the way out was Soviet communism's credibility in the West.

In June, newspapers published the leaked text of "On the Cult of Personality and Its Consequences," the February speech in which Soviet leader Nikita Khrushchev had denounced many of Stalin's crimes. Five months later Khrushchev trampled hopes of a cold war thaw by sending in tanks to crush a popular uprising in Hungary. The two events triggered an avalanche of disenchantment, as Communist Party members across the West walked out in their tens of thousands. It has even been claimed that a *samizdat* Hungarian translation of *Nineteen Eighty-Four* was a set text for the 1956 rebels.

This explains the subsequent importance of Orwell's list to his critics on the left. After Hungary, many of them had to accept that they had been wrong about the nature of Soviet communism and that he had been infuriatingly right. The most widely read socialist intellectual of the 1950s was a vindicated anti-communist and, what's more, a dead one, encircled by a halo of moral rectitude. He therefore inspired a kind of resentful admiration. Sometimes the resentment swallowed the admiration. For the Marxist critic Raymond Williams, looking back years later, Orwell was a political roadblock: "if you engaged in any kind of socialist argument, there was an enormously inflated statue of Orwell warning you to go back. Down into the Sixties political editorials would regularly admonish younger radicals to read their Orwell and see where that all led to."

The first phase of the cold war certainly enabled the right to pull off a heist on Orwell in general, and *Nineteen Eighty-Four* in particular, but it was not permanent. History moved on, like sunlight passing through a room, and threw different shadows.

CHAPTER 11

So Damned Scared

Nineteen Eighty-Four *in the 1970s*

It is difficult to imagine a previous period when such an all-pervasive hopelessness was exhibited at all levels of British life.

—Stephen Haseler, *The Death of British Democracy*, 1975

On a bright, cold day in April 1973, David Bowie and his percussionist Geoff MacCormack boarded the Trans-Siberian Railway in Khabarovsk. The aviophobic singer was taking the long way home to London from his Japanese tour. The week-long journey to Moscow was a lark to begin with, but the closer they got to the capital, the thicker the atmosphere of tension and suspicion. In Moscow, Bowie watched a day-long military parade from the window of his hotel on Red Square. "On my trips through Russia I thought, well, this is what fascism must have felt like," he later said. "They marched like them. They saluted like them." As the train to Paris passed through the no-man's land between East and West Berlin, the two men were stunned into silence by the still bombed-out ruins. "The sad reminders of man's failings seemed to drag on forever as the train crawled onward," remembered MacCormack. "Nobody uttered a word."

This heavy trip intensified Bowie's growing sense of paranoia and panic. On the last leg of the journey home, he spoke to Roy Hollingsworth from *Melody Maker* about how it had changed him. "You see Roy," he said, chain-smoking manically. "I've seen life, and I think I know who's controlling this damned world. And after what

I've seen of the state of this world, I've never been so damned scared in my life."

One did not need to have travelled through Brezhnev's Russia to feel fearful in 1970s Britain. IRA bombs were almost as much a feature of life as the rocket bombs in Airstrip One. The economy was gripped by stagflation, an ugly word for an ugly condition which combined inflation with economic stagnation. In October 1973, a miners' strike conspired with an Arab oil embargo to produce the worst fuel shortages since February 1947. With the return of blackouts, petrol rationing, reduced television service, and non-functioning elevators, Britain began to feel like the opening pages of *Nineteen Eighty-Four.* "There is a great sense of crisis everywhere," wrote Labour MP Tony Benn, using the word of the moment. During the festive break, Conservative cabinet member John Davies told his family to enjoy themselves, "because I deeply believed then that it was the last Christmas of its kind we would enjoy."

On New Year's Eve, the country switched to a three-day week for all nonessential businesses in order to conserve fuel. The resulting plunge in productivity cruelly exposed the underlying weakness of the economy, leading the governor of the Bank of England to predict a decade of austerity—ending, therefore, in 1984. Recession, terrorism, industrial unrest, a sense of irreversible national decline: an ocean of troubles which Conservative prime minister Edward Heath appeared utterly incapable of navigating. *The New York Times* observed "a gradual chilling, a fear of dreadful things."

One of those dreadful things, a military putsch like the one recently mounted by General Pinochet in Chile, surfaced in an article by political editor Patrick Cosgrave in the Christmas issue of *The Spectator.* "A country rent apart by warring factions, not one of which retains the support of the public for its veracity or ability, is already ripe for a coup," speculated Cosgrave. Talk in the bars and corridors of Westminster had grown feverish. Could it happen here? Yes, he concluded, it really could. "Nothing is, of course, inevitable. But if the process of disillusion, failure and subversion, conscious or unconscious, which I have described goes on it can have only one result."

Of course, not everybody in Britain felt that democracy was on its deathbed. This economic crisis, unlike most, hit the well-off harder than the working class, so the fretful middle-class politicians, journalists and novelists were not showing the whole picture. Millions of Britons listened to Slade and the Osmonds, went to see *Live and Let Die* and *The Way We Were*, relaxed in front of *Are You Being Served?* and *Porridge*, enjoyed their extra days off, and generally went about their business. But Bowie's antennae were attuned to shriller frequencies. His song "Life on Mars?" had looked for a way forward amid the debris of the 1960s; "Five Years" was a histrionic countdown to Armageddon; the ominous parenthetical in "Aladdin Sane (1913–1938–197?)" pencilled in a Third World War. "I'm an awful pessimist," Bowie confessed to the *New Musical Express*. "That's one of the things against me. I'm pessimistic about new things, new projects, new ideas, as far as society is concerned. I think it's all over, personally. I think the end of the world happened ten years ago. This is it." It was not at all surprising that his mind was turning to writing a rock musical based on *Nineteen Eighty-Four*.

Nor was Bowie the only person in an Orwellian frame of mind. The German magazine *Merkur* declared, *"1974: der Countdown für 1984 hat begonnen."* It certainly *hat begonnen*. To borrow one of Orwell's own phrases, his fateful date exerted the same hypnotic pull on anxious minds as a boa constrictor on a rabbit. "It is a shock to realize that the year is only a decade away," wrote Richard N. Farmer in *The Real World of 1984: A Look at the Foreseeable Future*. "Instead of being way out there in the misty future, many of us will live to see what 1984 is really all about." As the libertarian Jerome Tuccille wrote in *Who's Afraid of 1984?*, "Never before in history has a single year held such ominous connotations for such a broad cross-section of humanity."*

By 1973, sales of *Nineteen Eighty-Four* had passed one million in the UK and at least ten million in the US. It had become all-purpose shorthand for not just a grim future but also an uncertain present. "The term Orwellian is made to apply to anything from a computer

---

* Both books were in fact forcefully anti-Orwellian: quasi-utopian visions of a cleaner, freer, wealthier future. Like Lord Gladwyn's *Halfway to 1984* and Ronald Brech's *Britain 1984: Unilever's Forecast*, both published in the 1960s, they exploited Orwell's date as a handy promotional gimmick.

print-out to the functional coldness of a new airport," wrote the novelist Anthony Burgess, pointing out that neither have much to do with the colourless decay of Airstrip One. In Parliament, *Nineteen Eighty-Four* surfaced in debates on China, Cambodia, civil liberties and privacy. *The Washington Post* called it "the most famous, the most frequently alluded-to book written in the past 25 years."

Summoning Orwell's ghost was the order of the day. The publication of *The Collected Essays, Journalism and Letters of George Orwell* in four volumes in 1968 hugely enriched readers' understanding of his personality and ideas, leading to another round of What Would Orwell Think? Several reviewers wondered what he might have said about such burning issues as Richard Nixon, Harold Wilson, Adolf Eichmann, Vietnam, Israel, the Prague Spring and the Campaign for Nuclear Disarmament; none could answer confidently. Mary McCarthy concluded her essay in *The New York Review of Books* on a stark and callous note: "If he had lived, he might have been happiest on a desert island, and it was a blessing for him probably that he died." Sonia was so offended that she wrote a methodical, six-page retort for *Nova*. Her late husband seemed to disappoint McCarthy, she wrote tartly, "if he does not set down his thoughts on events which happened after his death."

Guessing what Orwell might have thought was a much dicier proposition than saying what *Nineteen Eighty-Four* meant now. For most readers, disinclined to comb through letters and journals, the novel was a world entire. In the years since Stalin's death in 1953, it had broken the bonds of cold war propaganda and become a book that almost any political faction could claim; it was increasingly claimed by the left. Even as the ultra-McCarthyite John Birch Society made 1984 the last four digits of its phone number, the Black Panthers added Orwell to the syllabus of their Oakland Community School. In Saul Bellow's 1970 novel *Mr. Sammler's Planet,* a veteran of the 1930s left is told by an indignant student that Orwell was a "a fink . . . a sick counterrevolutionary. It's good he died when he did," but Philip Roth quoted "Politics and the English Language" in an epigraph for his anti-Nixon satire *Our Gang.* The New Left intellectual Bruce Franklin scoffed, "this trash can't withstand the storms of rising revolution. For instance, how can you assert that revolutionary leaders are just pigs, as Orwell does, in the face of Malcolm X and Ho Chi Minh?"

But the equally left-wing Noam Chomsky maintained that Orwell sided with "the common man" against "repressive powers," so "the idea that his writings should be used for anti-communist ideology would have been horrifying to him. At least I find it horrifying." The real-life radicals at *International Times* magazine were quite happy to accept a gift of Orwell's typewriter from Sonia, while the FBI monitored campus societies named after Orwell in case they were fronts for socialist subversion.

Rock bands assimilated the novel into rallying cries for the counterculture. "Oh, where will you be when your freedom is dead fourteen years from tonight?" asked Spirit on their single "1984," released in the dying weeks of the 1960s. "We don't want no Big Brother scene," cried John Lennon (middle name Winston) on "Only People." Towards the end of "Hey Big Brother," the white soul group Rare Earth warned listeners, "If we don't get our thing together, Big Brother will be watching us." In Stevie Wonder's cool, contemptuous "Big Brother," BB represented the Nixon administration. Orwell's dictator was now another name for The Man.

It feels apt that *Nineteen Eighty-Four* was also one of Lee Harvey Oswald's favourite books. Oswald was both a victim and an agent of paranoia, a condition which flourished in the 1960s and went viral in the '70s. The Soviet mystique had largely evaporated, but so too had the rival myth of America as a citadel of freedom and fair play, eaten away by wars, scandals, cloak-and-dagger interventions, and assassinations at home and abroad. Nourished by Orwell's own fear of being surveilled, *Nineteen Eighty-Four* functioned as an essential paranoid text, in which all the worst fears were justified. Yes, they are lying to you. Yes, they are watching you. Yes, paternal figures of authority will betray your trust in the most terrifying way. The Orwellian mood rhymed most potently with the spirit of the '60s in Patrick McGoohan's remarkable television series *The Prisoner.*

McGoohan was an Irish Catholic with a tough, ironic manner which gave the impression that he knew more than he was letting on, and that he found it bleakly amusing. He would have made an excellent screen O'Brien, though his politics were very different. He attributed his fierce hatred of authority to a Catholic education reminiscent of St. Cyprian's: "it was almost impossible to do anything that wasn't some kind of sin." In 1966, McGoohan used his clout as the star of the cold war spy drama *Danger Man* to negotiate an unprecedented budget, and complete creative control, for an extended allegory about "the way we're being made into ciphers."

In *The Prisoner*, McGoohan plays a secret agent who resigns from the security services, is gassed into unconsciousness, and wakes up in a boutique police state called the Village to find that he no longer has a name; he is only Number Six. Orwell's line about the future belonging to "the holiday camp, the doodle-bug and the secret police" could almost have been a blueprint for the Village's very English totalitarianism, which masks its oppressive violence with a brisk cheerfulness. The Orwellian slogan "Questions Are a Burden to Others, Answers a Prison for Oneself" sounds like advice from a guide to etiquette. To be rebellious—or "unmutual"—is not so much a crime as a faux pas. When people bid goodbye in the Village, where every move is monitored by cameras, they say, "Be seeing you." Between escape attempts, Number Six tries to wake the villagers from their zombie politesse. "You still have a choice!" he hollers. "You can still salvage your right to be individuals! Your rights to truth and free thought! Reject this false world of Number Two!"

While Number One, like Big Brother, remains unseen and unidentified, a succession of Number Twos go to outlandish lengths to find out why Number Six resigned, less for the information than for the satisfaction of breaking him. To this end, he is tortured, tricked, seduced, beaten, electroshocked, brainwashed and gaslighted over and over again. "If you insist on living a dream, you may be taken for mad," one Number Two tells him. The philosophical meat of the show lies in the cryptic dialogues between prisoner and captor, in which questions are constantly dodged, parried or turned on their heads. The back-and-forth in the opening credits ("Who is Number One?" "You are Number Six") has a similar evasive rhythm to Winston and O'Brien talking about Big Brother. One exchange in the second episode indicates that the location of the Village and the allegiance of its rulers are as irrelevant as the differences between Oceania, Eurasia and Eastasia:

> NUMBER TWO: It doesn't matter which side runs the Village.
> NUMBER SIX: It's run by one side or the other.

NUMBER TWO: Oh certainly, but both sides are becoming
identical. What in fact has been created is an international
community—a perfect blueprint for world order. When
the sides facing each other suddenly realize that they're
looking into a mirror, they will see that *this* is the pattern
for the future.

NUMBER SIX: The whole Earth as the Village?

NUMBER TWO: That is my hope.

The sternly moralistic McGoohan was no flower child, but *The Prisoner*'s psychedelic eccentricity, enveloping paranoia and satire of every brand of authority—bureaucracy, religion, education, media, science—chimed with the counterculture. The final episode brought that connection to the surface by putting the anarchic jester Number Forty-Eight on trial as a representative of irreverent youth, heralded by a festive blast of the Beatles' "All You Need Is Love."

In Peter Watkins's *Privilege,* also released in 1967, the fascists and the rock 'n' rollers went hand in hand. To the angry, sceptical Watkins, pop music promised not groovy liberation but submission. Narrated by Watkins and set in the mid-'70s, the mock documentary follows Steven Shorter, a pop star who is exploited by Britain's unity government to "usefully divert the violence of youth" with his phony rebel routine: "keep them happy, off the streets and out of politics." Played by actual pop star Paul Jones with a bewildered blankness which may or may not have been deliberate, Shorter is later relaunched as a born-again advertisement for God and flag, performing folk-rock hymns at the National Stadium, where fans chant "We will conform!" amid red-and-black banners and burning crosses. When Shorter finally revolts, he and his career are effectively plunged down the memory hole, "to ensure that he does not again misuse his position of privilege to disturb the public peace of mind." The film ends with a crisp promise from the narrator: "It is going to be a happy year in Britain, this year in the near future."

Watkins wasn't the only person who looked at a rock concert and saw Nuremberg. In October 1973, an ITV documentary called *The Messengers* compared glam-rock hero Marc Bolan to Adolf Hitler: "Two superstars of their time . . . totally different but both subject to mass adulation." Looking back on Ziggy Stardust, the alien alter ego through which he willed himself to stardom, Bowie was having similar thoughts. "I could have been Hitler in England," he told *Rolling Stone*. "I think I might have been a bloody good Hitler. I'd be an excellent dictator. Very eccentric and quite mad."

In 2013, Bowie included *Nineteen Eighty-Four* on a list of his one hundred favourite books, alongside *Inside the Whale and Other Essays* and *Darkness at Noon*. He had been obsessed with Orwell's novel since growing up in post-war Bromley, in a house less than a mile away from the birthplace of H. G. Wells. "You always felt you were in *1984*," he said. "That's the kind of gloom and immovable society that a lot of us felt we grew up in . . . It was a terribly inhibiting place."

In November 1973, Bowie told the novelist William Burroughs that he was adapting the novel for television and gave his NBC TV special the mischievous title *The 1980 Floor Show*. During the show he debuted a new song called "1984/Dodo," one of twenty he claimed to have composed for the adaptation, although attempts to write an actual script with the American playwright Tony Ingrassia had come to nothing. He was therefore furious when Sonia Orwell refused permission for his rock musical. "For a person who married a Socialist with Communist leanings, she was the biggest upper-class snob I've ever met in my life," he told *Circus* writer Ben Edmonds. " 'Good heavens, put it to *music?*' It really was like that." Doubtless Sonia did hate the idea, but then she had approved almost no adaptations in any medium since the fiasco of the 1956 movie, and she certainly didn't meet Bowie in person, so that anecdote can be taken with a pinch of salt.* It's debatable whether a hypermodern, hedonistic, bisexual rock star would have had better luck with a seventy-year-old Orwell, especially if he had told him he had communist leanings.

Bowie's eighth album, initially titled *We Are the Dead*, was therefore a salvage operation. "To be quite honest with you . . . the whole thing

---

* The exception was 1965, when Nigel Kneale revamped his BBC adaptation of *Nineteen Eighty-Four* for a season of Orwell programmes and a new radio version starred Patrick Troughton as Winston, just before he became a household name as the Doctor in *Doctor Who*. Coincidentally, Troughton had made an uncredited appearance as a telescreen announcer in the 1956 movie.

was originally *19-bloody-84*," he told Edmonds. "It was the musical, and she put the clappers on it by saying no. So I, at the last minute, quickly changed it into a new concept album called *Diamond Dogs*. I didn't ever want to do *Diamond Dogs* as a stage musical; what I wanted was *1984*."

Diamond Dogs was a sick joke from a mind at the end of its tether, writhing with decadence, disease and dread. Bowie called it "a backward look at the sixties and seventies and a very political album. My protest." It was stitched together from the body parts of two abandoned projects—*Nineteen Eighty-Four* and a Ziggy Stardust stage musical—and a vivid but half-baked narrative about a place called Hunger City. In the title track and the spoken-word intro "Future Legend," Hunger City emerges as a very '70s dystopia, where feral urchins squat atop abandoned skyscrapers and prowl the streets on roller skates (due to the fuel crisis) to loot jewels and furs. "I had in my mind this kind of half *Wild Boys*/*1984* world," Bowie explained, adding that the gang members "staggered through from *Clockwork Orange* too."* The brutal youth of Anthony Burgess's 1962 novel and Stanley Kubrick's 1971 movie version were an enduring influence: a lurid flash of colour that Bowie couldn't find in Airstrip One. "That was *our* world, not the bloody hippy thing," he later said. Although Burgess came to see it as "not, in my view, a very good novel," *A Clockwork Orange* offered the most compelling and original near-future society since Orwell's, updating the struggle between freedom and control for the era of Mods and Rockers and telling the story in Nadsat, an Anglo-Russian teen slang. Like Winston, Burgess's violent protagonist Alex is mentally destroyed by the state in order to create an obedient citizen. "It is better to have our streets infested with murderous hoodlums than to deny individual freedom of choice," Burgess explained.

As for Orwell's mark on *Diamond Dogs*, it might be fanciful to trace the image in "Future Legend" of "rats the size of cats" back to the old army song quoted in *Homage to Catalonia* ("Rats as big as cats"), but then again, anything was possible now that Bowie was obsessed

---

* Bowie was referring to the post-apocalyptic gang in William Burroughs's 1971 novel *The Wild Boys: A Book of the Dead*. Ziggy Stardust's appearance merged *The Wild Boys* with *A Clockwork Orange*.

with William Burroughs's cut-up writing technique. Bowie's previous album, *Pin Ups,* consisted of cover versions, and *Diamond Dogs* was, in a way, his irreverent cover, or sampling, of *Nineteen Eighty-Four,* collaging his own preoccupations with fragments of the novel to phantasmagoric effect. Bowie was the first person to treat the book as a trove of fungible ideas and images, famous enough to mess around with.

Some of the fragments are substantial. The gothic hysteria of "We Are the Dead" reimagines Winston and Julia's final moments before their arrest: "Oh dress yourself my urchin one, for I hear them on the stairs." "Dodo," dropped from the album but released later, feels like Winston waking from a dream inside the Ministry of Love as it scatters references to informants, memos, files and "scorching light" around a strikingly precise account of Parsons's betrayal by his daughter. "Big Brother" is an anthem of ecstatic supplication to power: "Someone to claim us, someone to follow . . ." John Lennon and Stevie Wonder predictably hated Big Brother; only Bowie could imagine loving him. Other references are more fleeting. How many listeners to the funk melodrama of "1984" have spotted a reference to the year that Orwell's alleged traitors Jones, Aaronson and Rutherford were arrested ("Looking for the treason that I knew in '65"), or noticed that the reference to a "room to rent" allows "Rock 'n' Roll With Me," ostensibly about Bowie's relationship with his audience, to be also read as a desperate love song about Winston and Julia? And when he sings "I'm looking for a party" in "1984," it isn't necessarily the fun lower-case kind. It was as if Bowie were leaving a breadcrumb trail for fellow Orwell buffs to follow.

The closing track, "Chant of the Ever Circling Skeletal Family," is the Two Minutes Hate rendered as a diabolical dance craze. It ends (or fails to end) with a stuttering metallic loop of *bruh-bruh-bruh-bruh* which threatens to last forever, like a boot stamping on a human face.

According to pianist Mike Garson, the *Diamond Dogs* sessions, in January and February 1974, had "a heavy vibe." So, too, did Britain, gripped by the three-day week and an unusually panicky general election campaign. In his election report, "Battle of Britain, 1974," bemused *New York Times* writer Richard Eder diagnosed the country's crisis as primarily psychological. Times were hard, he wrote, but not hard enough to justify "the warnings from right and left, in the newspapers, on television, that the fabric of British society is about to be ripped up." Visiting from a country wracked by Watergate and recession, Eder wondered how this famously sensible island nation had lost its mind: "It is very difficult to make any assertion about the future in this peculiarly British climate that mingles hysteria, humour, despair and optimism."

The same four conditions contributed to the queasy brew of *Diamond Dogs*. Released on May 24, it was billed as an album that "conceptualizes the vision of a future world with images of urban decadence and collapse." *Collapse*, like *crisis*, was a word on every commentator's lips. Nobody looks for political consistency in a rock album, but there is a fundamental contradiction between Airstrip One and Hunger City. One state has absolute control, the other none at all. Bowie seemed both thrilled and alarmed in equal measure by totalitarianism and post-apocalyptic anarchy, but the fact that the most blissful, stirring song on the album was "Big Brother" was an unsettling clue as to where he was headed.

For the *Diamond Dogs* tour, Bowie gave set designer Mark Ravitz three cues: "Power, Nuremberg and Fritz Lang's *Metropolis*." The singer also made sketches and models for a never-realised Hunger City film, which would open on the lower floors of the "World Assembly building," where the city's mutant dregs would indulge in gambling, pornography and a synthetic foodstuff called "mealcaine." The word was a fair description of Bowie's own diet at the time. Since he started taking cocaine the previous autumn, he had become vampirically pale and thin: a human white line. For an already paranoid man, it was not a wise choice.

Bowie was living in America now. He was done with England, and with rock 'n' roll. His next album, *Young Americans*, explored a new black-influenced sound he called "plastic soul." Its most disturbing song, "Somebody Up There Likes Me," is a slick, insinuating rumination on power narrated by a character who merges the roles of messianic rock star, demagogic politician and advertising pitchman.*

---

* Like Comstock in *Keep the Aspidistra Flying*, Bowie briefly worked for an ad agency, which he called "diabolical." He was fascinated by Vance Packard's study of the industry's psychological manipulations in *The Hidden Persuaders*.

"Really I'm a very one-track person," Bowie explained. "What I've said for years under various guises is that 'Watch out, the West is going to have a Hitler!' I've said it in a thousand different ways."

In interviews, however, he began to drop the "Watch out!" as his long-standing obsessions with power, mass media, Nietzschean supermen, black magic and the Nazi mystique curdled into something grotesque. Hitler, he said admiringly, was a "media artist" who "staged a country." Liberal democracy had grown weak and decadent, and needed a revival of "a very medieval, firm-handed, masculine God awareness where we go out and make the world right again." It would take a temporary fascist dictatorship. "You've got to have an extreme right front come up and sweep everything off its feet and tidy everything up," Bowie said, sounding rather like H. G. Wells at his worst. "Then you can get a new form of liberalism."

Reading these interviews in the light of Bowie's subsequent liberal-left politics, the obvious explanation is that he was a paranoid, cocaine-maddened, sleep-deprived, deeply confused man searching for answers in dangerous places and amusing himself by throwing borderline incoherent provocations at hippyish music journalists. Bowie soon grew out of this phase when he moved to Berlin, where totalitarianism was a past and present reality, not a rock star's babbling daydream. Looking back with a shudder many years later, he said: "my whole life would be transformed into this bizarre nihilistic fantasy world of oncoming doom, mythological characters and imminent totalitarianism. Quite the worst."

It speaks volumes about the fervid climate of the mid-'70s that several members of the British establishment who had never touched a narcotic in their lives were thinking along similar lines. At one point Bowie tried to justify his outlandish comments as "a theatrical observation of what I could see happening in England." True enough, for the first time since the 1940s, powerful people were talking seriously about dictatorship.

Whispers of a coup first bubbled to the surface in December 1973, in Patrick Cosgrave's *Spectator* article. Two months later, while Bowie was immersed in *Diamond Dogs,* the far-right Conservative candidate and former deputy director of MI6 George Kennedy Young raised the stakes by leaking news of his Unison Committee for Action to Chapman Pincher, the security correspondent of *The Daily Express.* Pincher reported that leading businessmen, ex-servicemen and former intelligence operatives had formed "a formidable vigilante group to help protect the nation against a Communist takeover" and quoted Young anonymously: "We are not Fascists. We are democratic Britons who put the nation's interests before those of Russia and its political agents." Young later called Unison "an anti-Chaos organisation."

Young was floating a more extreme version of sentiments that Conservatives were expressing openly during the February general election campaign. The Tory manifesto claimed that Harold Wilson's Labour Party had been infiltrated by hardliners who were "committed to a left-wing programme more dangerous and more extreme than ever before in its history." The right-wing lobby group Aims of Industry took out full-page newspaper ads which, echoing the anti-POUM posters of 1937, tore aside a smiling mask to reveal the face of Stalin. Their bogeymen were left-wing Labour MPs, led by Tony Benn, and union leaders such as Mick McGahey, the openly communist vice-president of the National Union of Mineworkers. The fear cut both ways. Several union leaders, hearing rumours of assassination plots, required armed guards. After all that, the election resulted in a hung Parliament and Wilson, who had served as prime minister from 1964 to 1970, returned to Number 10 Downing Street on March 5 at the helm of a minority government. The famously intelligent and upbeat Wilson was now ailing, paranoid and rudderless, much like his country between the February and October elections.

Some conservatives compared Britain to Weimar Germany, while others talked of Chile before the coup. Pinochet's takeover, and the subsequent "shock treatment" recommended by economist Milton Friedman, had a sinister allure—Chile's Big Brother spoke of "scrubbing our minds clean." Visiting the country in May for *The Daily Telegraph,* Peregrine Worsthorne advised readers to be "more open-minded," because despite the murders, tortures and disappearances, Pinochet's junta wasn't as bad as all that. "All right, a military dictatorship is ugly and repressive," he wrote, clearing his throat. "But if a minority British Socialist Government ever sought, by cunning, duplicity or corruption, terror and foreign arms, to turn this country into a Communist State, I hope and pray our armed forces would intervene to prevent such a calamity as efficiently as the armed forces did in Chile." Friedman went so far as to say that this was "the only outcome that is conceivable."

This was the kind of febrile thinking that led renegade spooks and disgruntled grandees to gather in well-furnished rooms in order to brainstorm treason and discuss the rumour that Harold Wilson himself was a KGB mole, masterminding a communist cell in Downing Street. Fears of a general strike stoked talk of helicopter-borne commandos descending onto the picket lines. In Robin Maugham's wartime pamphlet *The 1946 MS.*, General Pointer justifies his state of emergency to the nation: "Today, because of the strikes throughout his country, neither confidence nor security exist . . . I am certain that you will agree with me that we must therefore, take every step possible to restore security in this country." In July 1974, General Sir Walter Walker, until recently NATO's commander in northern Europe, sounded uncomfortably similar in a letter to *The Daily Telegraph* calling for a dynamic strongman to save Britain from "the Communist Trojan horse in our midst." The response, he claimed, was overwhelmingly positive. Asked if there was public appetite for a British Pinochet, he smoothly replied, "Perhaps the country might choose rule by the gun in preference to anarchy." Oswald Mosley, the ghost of fascism past, materialised on television to endorse a similar binary choice. Lord Chalfont, a former Labour peer fond of quoting Orwell in the House of Lords, summed up these baleful manoeuvres in an article for the *Times* headlined "Could Britain be heading for a military takeover?," berating both "the militants of the neo-Marxist left [and] the bullyboys of the neo-fascist right."

Walker, a virulent bigot and red-baiter, became leader of Civil Assistance, which merged a breakaway faction of Unison with the similarly minded Red Alert. Colonel David Stirling, founder of the SAS, launched yet another organisation of "apprehensive patriots" called GB 75. When Stirling's plans were leaked to *Peace News,* Tony Benn divined their real purpose: "Although I don't for a moment take any of them seriously, there is no doubt that it is intended to create a feeling that anarchy is about to break out, and therefore we need a strong authoritarian Government." Benn, who became industry secretary after the October election, was the lightning rod for efforts to undermine Wilson's government, weathering a relentless campaign of smears, surveillance and death threats.

The storm clouds rolled on into 1975. "What is certain, and felt instinctively by almost everybody, is that things cannot go on in their present way," pronounced a *Times* leader column in May 1975, setting no limit on how bad the situation could get before Britain got a grip on itself: "When you have reached 1938, you have sometimes to wait for 1940." The following January, Lord Chalfont presented a polemical documentary called *It Must Not Happen Here*, in which he stood beside Karl Marx's grave sombrely ticking off the ways in which Britain had already slid towards communism. Watching at home, Benn felt that he was "looking at the faces of the Junta."*

During 1975 and 1976, the theme of doughty patriots thwarting Soviet plots to destroy British democracy was parodied in the sitcom *The Fall and Rise of Reginald Perrin*, attacked in David Edgar's play *Destiny* and celebrated in thrillers like Ted Allbeury's *The Special Collection* and Kenneth Benton's *A Single Monstrous Act*. Both Allbeury and Benton used to work for the intelligence services. There is no better illustration of the paranoia that seized mid-'70s Britain than the fact that some former agents were novelising scenarios that other former agents were simultaneously debating in earnest. The boundaries between fiction and reality became increasingly sketchy. One leaked dossier of MI5 dirty tricks was code-named "Clockwork Orange."

Lord Chalfont later attributed the success of new Tory leader Margaret Thatcher to "all these fears of bureaucracy, of too much government, of the erosion of freedom of the individual, fears of anarchy." Thatcher, he said, "struck a chord which was waiting to be struck." While Unison, Civil Assistance and GB 75 all faded as quickly as they had arrived, the National Association for Freedom (NAFF) was a slick, professional operation with strong ties to Thatcher and the Tory right. One of NAFF's leading figures, the Australian academic and journalist Robert Moss, marked the group's

---

* Benn was especially alarmed to hear himself named as a menace by Woodrow Wyatt, who had travelled an awfully long way in the twenty-seven years since he had scolded Orwell for being insufficiently pro-Labour and was now firmly on the Conservative right.

launch in late 1975 with a hair-raising book called *The Collapse of Democracy*. Faced with either totalitarianism or anarchy, he suggested, Britain might find that the kind of authoritarianism seen in Chile, Spain and Brazil was the least worst option: "you do not pit Hamlet against Lady Macbeth." He described the dreadful alternative in "Letter from London 1985," a hyperventilating foray into dystopian fiction about an economically ravaged Republic of Britain under the heel of the Working People's Government. In Moss's nightmare the police have given way to "factory militias," the House of Lords has been replaced by the Trade Union Congress, and Buckingham Palace is now the Ministry of Equality. Members of the banned Conservative Party live like guerrillas, listening to Radio Free Britain while trying to outwit the surveillance state. "It is a cold world we have entered in the name of equality and peace," Moss concludes solemnly, "and I doubt whether there is any return from it, at least in our lifetimes."

All prophecies are fiction until they come true. If the utopian novel began as an effort to sweeten political arguments with characters and plots, then it's unsurprising that serious polemicists would add some Orwellian spice to their jeremiads. In *The Death of British Democracy*, Stephen Haseler, a self-described "cold war liberal" from the Labour right, sketched two equally dire near-future scenarios: either ungovernable chaos, poverty and violence, or a union-led dictatorship with "all the gobbledegook of thought involved in the Orwellian nightmare of *1984*." The essay collection *1985: An Escape from Orwell's 1984: A Conservative Path to Freedom* raised the spectre of Labour turning Britain into "a national-socialist member of the Warsaw Pact." Only the resonance of the date mattered to the contributors: Orwell's name was mentioned only once in its 146 pages of hard-right brainstorming, and he was quoted not at all.

It was getting hard to tell the forecasts from the fiction. The spectre of a trade union dictatorship went prime time with Wilfred Greatorex's anti-socialist TV thriller *1990*, which pitted Edward Woodward's action-hero journalist against the KGB-like Public Control Department in a shabby totalitarian Britain brought about by national bankruptcy. "It's much more frightening than *1984*," Woodward informed *Radio Times*, "because it's closer to us than Orwell's book was to his own generation. It's really just around the corner." Socialist playwright Howard Brenton's *The Churchill Play* took place in an internment camp established by a fascistic government of national unity in 1984. In Brenton's Orwellian words: "It is a satire which says, 'Don't let the future be like this ...'"

The new comic book *2000 AD* also based its future shocks on the wildest fears of the era. Conceived by writer John Wagner and artist Carlos Ezquerra, the world of *Judge Dredd* resembled a mongrel of *Diamond Dogs, Dirty Harry, The Sleeper Awakes* and a berserk parody of General Walker's authoritarian fantasies. The survivors of nuclear war live in seething mega-cities policed by militaristic lawmen with a cavalier disregard for due process. The anti-hero Dredd is a brutal quasi-fascist whose look Ezquerra modelled on his memories of Spain under General Franco.* The BBC television series *Blake's 7* knitted the cruellest innovations from Orwell, Huxley and Wells into a kind of *Star Trek* for the chronically pessimistic. Patrick McGoohan was filled with apprehension, too. In a 1977 television interview, he said: "I think progress is the biggest enemy on Earth, apart from oneself . . . I think we're gonna take good care of this planet shortly." An audience member asked if the public would rise up and set things right. "No," said McGoohan, "because we're run by the Pentagon, we're run by Madison Avenue, we're run by television, and as long as we accept those things and don't revolt we'll have to go along with the stream to the eventual avalanche."

As the novelist Martin Amis observed in 1978, "no one creates utopias anymore: even the utopias of the past now look like dystopias." Amis, whose formerly socialist father Kingsley was now venting his fears in gloomy right-wing science fiction, was writing this in a review of Anthony Burgess's very peculiar *1985*. Burgess was an avid scholar of Orwell and his precursors, and was the first major writer to popularise the word *dystopia*. He even claimed, some years later, to have spent time drinking with Orwell in post-war London, though this was probably a fantasy. The first half of *1985* is an idiosyncratic critique

---

* In 2016, *2000 AD* published its 1,984th issue. The cover portrayed a giant poster of Dredd reading, "The Justice Department Is Watching You" and the tagline "Orwell That Ends Well . . . ?"

of *Nineteen Eighty-Four*, driven by Burgess's conviction that the novel was fundamentally a black comedy about post-war Britain. Having dismissed Orwell's "improbable tyranny," Burgess then proceeds to fall flat on his face with a satirical novella whose furious working title was *Don't Let Them Get Away with It*. Critic Clive James mockingly suggested *Look Forward in Mild Irritation*. His "Tucland" has the same basic premise as Robert Moss's Republic of Britain—economic ruination and drab egalitarianism brought about by over-mighty trade unions—but Burgess stuffs it with prime-time pornography, knife-wielding street gangs, the brutish lingo of Worker's English, and wealthy, fundamentalist Arabs. The new names of the Arab-owned hotels—the Al-Hiltons and Al-Idayinns—sum up the novella's unhappy blend of leaden satire and neurotic conservatism. Every explicit nod to Orwell is an act of literary self-harm.

Among the book's innumerable problems was Burgess's inability to predict 1978, let alone 1985. Martin Amis guessed that it had been conceived in 1976, when "everything seemed ready for the terminal lurch," but the fever had already broken by the time it came out. Britain remained fragile and fractious, with Margaret Thatcher warning that the Labour government would somehow usher in both "the nightmare world of *A Clockwork Orange*" and "the Big Brother state," but its acute existential crisis was subsiding. The private armies had stood down. The violent far-right National Front, which had briefly become Britain's fourth largest party, was in retreat. It had not happened here.

As for Burgess's contention that Orwell's "prophecy" was proving false, it was beside the point. "Novels don't care whether they come true or not," wrote Amis, "and Orwell has withstood the test of time in quite another sense." *Nineteen Eighty-Four* had become a vessel into which anyone could pour their own version of the future. Whereas the '60s generation invoked it in a spirit of defiant unity, the punks embraced the book's sense of dread. "Look, you know what happened to Winston," snapped the Jam. "Now it's 1984 / Knock-knock at your front door," sneered the Dead Kennedys. The B-side of the Clash's debut single, "1977," climaxed with Joe Strummer shooting into the future, screaming the dates of years to come. He stopped abruptly, like a body plunging through a gallows: "In 1984!"

CHAPTER 12

Orwellmania

Nineteen Eighty-Four *in 1984*

> Orwell was floating around in the ether. I hadn't read *1984,*
> but we all know what it is.
>
> —Terry Gilliam

A few minutes before midnight on New Year's Eve 1983, a small number of viewers in Twin Falls, Idaho, became the first members of the public to see what would become the most celebrated television commercial of the decade.

This is what they saw. Legions of grey ciphers march like robots into an auditorium to hear a face on a colossal screen rant about the "Information Purification Directives" which will rid society of "contradictory truths." Charging through their ranks, ineptly pursued by riot police, comes a young athlete with a picture of a computer on her vest, bearing a sledgehammer. She is the only woman in the room; the only source of colour and vitality. As the speech approaches its climax, she spins her hammer and flings it at the screen. The dictator's face explodes, flooding the room with white light and shockwaves. The ciphers gawp in shock, like sleepers waking. "On January 24th, Apple Computer will introduce Macintosh," the narrator intones. "And you'll see why 1984 won't be like *1984.*"

Several months earlier, Apple's mercurial co-founder Steve Jobs had asked ad agency Chiat/Day for a "thunderclap" idea to launch his make-or-break product. Creative director Lee Clow, art director Brent Thomas and copywriter Steve Hayden proposed an Orwellian concept that they'd been toying with for a few months. Jobs, who still saw himself as a countercultural insurgent, loved it. Chiat/Day hired

Ridley Scott, the director of *Blade Runner*, to film the commercial at London's Shepperton Studios with an unprecedented budget. Scott cast discus-thrower Anya Major as the hammer-wielding heroine and David Graham, a character actor who had voiced Daleks in *Doctor Who*, as the ersatz Big Brother whose speech Hayden wrote by "kick[ing] around phrases from Mussolini to Mao."

The low-key New Year's Eve screening was booked solely to categorise the ad as a 1983 production and thus qualify it for awards season. The real showcase was to be the broadcast of the Super Bowl three weeks later, routinely the biggest US television event of the year. There was just one problem: the ad that had delighted Apple's annual sales conference horrified the board of directors, who asked Jobs to kill it. "They said it would be irresponsible to spend all that money on an ad that didn't show the Mac," said Clow. Chiat/Day only kept it alive by dragging their heels and pretending they couldn't sell off the top-dollar Super Bowl slot. It was a shrewd act of passive resistance. On January 22, midway through the game between the Washington Redskins and the Los Angeles Raiders, ninety-six million Americans saw "1984." One admiring rival adman called it the first Super Bowl spot ever to get "people in bar rooms talking about a commercial instead of the game." The ad immediately became a news story, generating priceless free publicity. According to *Advertising Age*, "No commercial in recent memory has created such widespread industry and public interest so quickly."

The commercial was a brilliant example of anti-corporate corporate marketing, twisting Orwell's warning into an upbeat fable for the information age. Major's hammer-throwing rebel represented both Apple and the Apple user: the plucky underdog who takes power back from The Man. At the Mac launch on January 24, Jobs made a speech portraying industry leader IBM as a wicked Goliath trying to crush its only serious challenger: "Will Big Blue dominate the entire computer industry? The entire information age? Was George Orwell right?" Chiat/Day, however, didn't care about IBM. Their target was the negative image of computers as instruments of intrusion and control, put across by movies like Ridley Scott's own *Blade Runner*. The best way to combat malign technology, implied the ad, was with benign technology. If Winston Smith only had a hammer.

The "1984" commercial also demonstrated that the iconography of dystopia was now so well-established that it could be distilled into a sixty-second spot: the passive uniformed drones, the militarised police, the television screens, the generic totalitarian rhetoric, the lone rebel, the looming face. Viewers immediately knew where they were. The scenario of mechanised unanimity ("We are one people, with one will, one resolve, one cause") is in fact more Zamyatin than Orwell, and Scott's key visual reference was the H. G. Wells movie *Things to Come*. Chiat/Day account director Paul Conhune bluntly called the commercial "a B-grade interpretation of Orwell's book" designed to "seize the notoriety Orwell created for this year." For all its virtuosity, it didn't take a maverick visionary to make that connection.

"THERE IS ONLY ONE YEAR LEFT!" screamed the Orwell-themed window display of a Greenwich Village bookstore in January 1983. A few streets away, more than seventy international luminaries, including conceptual artist Jenny Holzer and architect Rem Koolhaas, participated in an exhibition called *1984: A Preview*, "casting its appraising eye on the Orwellian prophecies." In the press, journalists of all political persuasions polished their crystal balls and sharpened their swords. In a special issue of *The Village Voice* ("LET'S FACE IT"), Geoffrey Stokes wrote that the novel had "almost as much impact on the eve of 1984 as it did when it was published in 1949." One year was apparently not enough for the German novelist Günter Grass, who branded the 1980s "Orwell's decade."

By December, Orwellmania was pandemic. "If you don't have an opinion about Orwell's portrait of the ultimate totalitarian state, you had better get one," advised *The San Francisco Chronicle*. Bernard Crick, Orwell's biographer and tireless advocate, warned of a "black plague" of Orwelliana that would approach the scale of *Star Wars*. The estate's literary executor, Mark Hamilton, was certainly earning his keep. He told *The Guardian* that he had turned down applications for T-shirts, calendars, board games, a stage musical, and anything else that might "cheapen" Orwell's reputation. When the reporter informed him of bootleg T-shirts reading "1984: Doublethink About It," Hamilton sighed. "We can't control everything."

During 1983 and 1984, *Nineteen Eighty-Four* sold almost four million copies in sixty-two languages. In January of what Penguin dubbed "the Year of the Book," it became the first book ever to top the *New York Times* mass-market fiction best-seller list years after its initial publication. The celebrations were manifold: a new US edition with an afterword by Walter Cronkite; another annotated by Crick; the publication of a facsimile of the extant manuscript; cover stories in *Time, Encounter, Radio Times* and *Der Spiegel;* a movie; two television dramas; a stage adaptation by Czech dissident Pavel Kohout; a Madame Tussaud's waxwork of the writer typing under the visored eye of an armed policeman; and an endless stream of documentaries and conferences. Journalists walked in Orwell's size-twelve footsteps through Paris, London and Wigan. The *Thoughtcrimes* series at London's Barbican Theatre featured political work by Samuel Beckett, Václav Havel and Harold Pinter, whose new play *One for the Road* was a meditation on language, violence and power.

Most of the commemorations were predictable, but who would have anticipated that Steve Martin and Jeff Goldblum would appear in a comedy sketch in which the disco mecca Studio 54 became "the Ministry of Nightlife"? Or that Oceania's slogans would be deployed to advertise carpets? "WAR IS PEACE," began a press ad for retailer Einstein Moomjy. "FREEDOM IS SLAVERY. IGNORANCE IS STRENGTH. And our crisp new Sisal-like look in wool broadloom is $19.84 a sq.yd. At $19.84 it's well worth watching, Big Brother." The craving for a connection, any connection at all, to Saint George got a little desperate. *TV Guide* figured that Orwell's empathy with the working man would surely have endeared him to the sitcom *Cheers*. "Big Brother meets the band with the Big Balls," raved *Musician* in a review of Van Halen's unrelated album *1984*. The magazine of the British Tourist Authority outdid them all with the audaciously dishonest headline "The Orwell/Animal Farms/1984." The story concerned livestock husbandry near the River Orwell.

It's hardly surprising that Orwell fatigue set in while the year was still young. "Can we be allowed to forget George Orwell for a minute or two?" sighed James Cameron in *The Guardian* on January 3. *The Spectator*'s Paul Johnson complained that the excesses of the Orwell industry had become "a kind of Orwellian nightmare in themselves." Liberal Party MP Alex Carlile mocked colleagues who used "the already hackneyed analogies with the attempts of George Orwell to predict what might happen in 1984." Even Snoopy flopped on top of his kennel in a Charles M. Schulz strip, exhausted by "thinking about all the George Orwell jokes we're going to have to listen to in 1984." Orwell had graduated from literary hero to ubiquitous celebrity, while *Nineteen Eighty-Four* had mutated from a novel into a meme.

Inevitably, much of the Orwelliana focused on *Nineteen Eighty-Four*'s alleged status as prophecy. Writers in *The Futurist* queued up to whack it like a piñata: "As a forecaster of the actual world of 1984, Orwell is so wrong as to be drummed out of the company of forecasters—or even to be made into an 'unperson'!" crowed the editor.* Isaac Asimov insisted that Orwell would be "proved wrong" about computers and space travel, neither of which happen to feature in the book. An ad for Olivetti Computers had a similarly nonsensical take: "According to Orwell, in 1984 man and computer would have become enemies. But his pessimistic outlook was wrong." In fact, Orwell wasn't even trying to foresee technological progress in functioning democracies. But you'd need to have read the book to know that.

One person who didn't was the pioneering video artist Nam June Paik. On New Year's Day 1984, he orchestrated an international satellite-linked multimedia television show to celebrate the power of the medium to foster communication. Contributors included Philip Glass, John Cage, Peter Gabriel, Laurie Anderson, Merce Cunningham, Allen Ginsberg, Joseph Beuys and Salvador Dalí (whom Orwell once described as "a dirty little scoundrel"). Its sarcastic title was *Good Morning, Mr. Orwell.* "Big Brother's screaming but we don't care," sang Oingo Boingo in "Wake Up (It's 1984)." " 'Cause he's got nothing to say / Think of the future, think of the prophecy / Think of the children of today." Paik told *The New York Times:* "I never read Orwell's book—it's boring. But he was the first media communications prophet." Paik seems to have assumed that *Nineteen Eighty-Four* was a novel about television.

One newspaper asked Orwell's son, Richard Blair (now thirty-nine,

---

* The magazine seemed to be trying to memory-hole a 1978 article by David Goodman, which identified 137 separate predictions in the novel and concluded that more than one hundred had already come true.

like Winston Smith), what his father might have made of Orwellmania. "I believe," he said, "that he would have been very dismayed by the way that people have interpreted *Nineteen Eighty-Four*."

How can a novel be "wrong"?

Orwell didn't say much about *Nineteen Eighty-Four,* but what he did say, very firmly, was that it was not a prophecy. A satire, a parody and a warning, yes, but not that. As he spelled out in his 1949 statement to Francis A. Henson, "I do not believe that the kind of society which I described necessarily *will* arrive, but I believe . . . that something resembling it *could* arrive." Clearly, it had not. The West had been debased and distorted in many ways by the machinations of the cold war, but it had not become an equivalent despotism. By definition, a country in which you are free to read *Nineteen Eighty-Four* is not the country described in *Nineteen Eighty-Four.* Absent that development, the launch of the Apple Mac was neither here nor there. If you were selling a product in 1984, whether it was a personal computer or neoliberal economics, then it was obligatory to say that Orwell, the avatar of pessimism, was wrong, but that wasn't an argument; it was a catchphrase. When *The San Francisco Chronicle* asked Ursula K. Le Guin (who had received more than forty invitations to speak at Orwell-related events) to assess Orwell's clairvoyance, she demurred: "I am not in the prediction business." Science fiction, she said, uses metaphors for the "here and now," so how can it be right or wrong about the future?*

It's worth pausing to note what an extraordinary achievement it is for a book to define a planet's journey around the sun. The year 2000 was always going to be a major event, but 1984 only became a banner year because one man decided, late in the day, to change the title of his novel. If Orwell had stuck with *The Last Man in Europe,* none of this would have happened. As George Steiner wrote in a good, tough *New Yorker* essay, "*never* has any single man or stroke of the pen struck a year out of the calendar of hope . . . Will "Nineteen Eighty-Four"

---

* Le Guin's 1974 novel *The Dispossessed,* like Marge Piercy's *Woman on the Edge of Time,* revived utopian science fiction with the countercultural politics of the 1970s, thus bypassing Orwell's influence completely.

fade from immediacy and mass awareness after 1984? This is, I think, a very difficult question."

On April 4, 1984, the date of Winston Smith's first diary entry, the London *Times* carried news of the British miners' strike, then just a month old. Protesters were evicted from the women's peace camp at the Greenham Common airbase. A Silicon Valley engineer went on trial for conspiring to sell missile research data to Polish agents. A short news item covered a screening of the 1954 and 1956 versions of *Nineteen Eighty-Four* at London's National Film Theatre, beneath a picture of a glum-looking John Hurt on the set of the latest adaptation.

Sonia Orwell had died of a brain tumour on December 1, 1980, exhausted by a bitter legal battle to regain control of George Orwell Productions, the company established by Orwell's accountants in 1947, and by thirty years of living in her late husband's overwhelming shadow. She was sixty-two. "I've fucked up my life," she told a friend towards the end.

A few weeks before her death, Sonia met a Chicago attorney and aspiring film-maker named Marvin Rosenblum, who had saturated himself in Orwell's work in order to charm her into selling him the film and television rights to the novel. After several conversations, during which he "spouted Orwell like a fountain," Rosenblum succeeded. Over the next three years, he found no shortage of interest in remaking *Nineteen Eighty-Four* for 1984 but he couldn't nail down a director and producer who would abide by the contract's prohibition against "the *Star Wars* or *2001: A Space Odyssey* genre of science-fiction." Not until October 1983 did he reach an agreement with British director Michael Radford and producer Simon Perry, fresh from the success of their World War Two drama *Another Time, Another Place.* "We had to guarantee that the movie would come out by the end of 1984, so we had to get started right away," the seventy-two-year-old Radford told me in London's Chelsea Arts Club in the summer of 2018.

The film-makers moved fast. By Christmas 1983, Radford had written the screenplay and Perry had secured $6 million from Richard Branson's fledgling venture Virgin Films. The two men agreed that

Winston Smith could only be played by John Hurt, the consumptive British actor who always looked as if he had a bad cough and a worse conscience. "He was the perfect Winston Smith," said Radford. "This hungry-looking, haunted character. He was very athletic, actually, but he could contort himself." Fortunately, Hurt was a fan who had wanted to play Winston ever since he read the novel as a student in the 1950s. "The great thing about Orwell," said Hurt, "is that he backs up what you yourself instinctively feel." Former child actress Suzanna Hamilton was Julia, while an open casting call for potential Big Brothers in *The Guardian* led Radford to Bob Flag, a club comedian with "very penetrating eyes." Casting O'Brien was not so easy: Sean Connery was busy, Marlon Brando was too expensive, and Paul Scofield broke his leg. It wasn't until weeks into the shoot that Radford lured Richard Burton out of retirement in Haiti for what was to be his final performance before his death in August. According to the director, Burton wore the only boiler suit ever to be tailored in Savile Row. "He was an extraordinary actor," Radford said. "The only thing I did with him was keep taking him down, softer and softer." Burton began to find O'Brien's insane logic unnervingly seductive. "You know, this really is frightening," he told Hurt, "because I'm seriously beginning to believe that what I'm saying is correct."

When Radford first read the book as a teenager, he knew "exactly what it looked like. There's a lot to work with." Orwell's book contains several unforgettable set-pieces, and his use of news broadcasts and posters for the purposes of storytelling and world-building is still part of the standard toolkit for films about near-future societies. "The telescreens were the big shock for me," said the director, who used back projection to create the illusion of gargantuan screens. "They dominated everything, as television does. But it was great to be able to say two things at the same time." Immersing himself in the history of propaganda, Radford designed his own salute, flag, logo and anthem, and based one of the broadcasts in the film on a genuine wartime reel scripted by the poet Dylan Thomas for the Ministry of Information. "I used to say to people that this is a parallel universe: a 1984 envisaged in 1948," Radford said, explaining his use of archaic technology and retro fashion. To create the film's chilly, desaturated look, cinematographer Roger Deakins used an innovative process. Usually, silver nitrate is bleached from film reels to make the colours pop, but Deakins left it in. "The important thing for me was to create a world that people believed in," said Radford.*

News of the film reignited David Bowie's interest in *Nineteen Eighty-Four*. He met with Radford and Branson to discuss writing the soundtrack, but Bowie kept talking about "organic music" and nobody else knew what that meant. It certainly didn't sound like the potential hits Branson wanted, so he got cold feet and turned instead to his own Virgin Records pop duo Eurythmics—a contentious hiring that Radford only learned about when singer Annie Lennox rang from a studio in the Bahamas to ask him why he wasn't there. Radford and Branson's heated row over whether to use the Eurythmics' ill-fitting synth-pop ("Sex-sex-s-s-sex-s-sex-sexcrime") or Dominic Muldowney's score spilled onto the news pages and provided excellent publicity for a film that wasn't an easy sell.

"The thoughts in the film industry were that it wasn't going to be successful because it didn't have a happy ending," remembered Radford. "And also it wasn't really a book—it was essentially a gigantic essay. They said, 'Your audience is going to be over thirty-five and will know who Orwell is. It's going to be small.' But it was huge and it was fifteen- to twenty-year-olds. Why?" He laughed. "Because it was so completely about despair. Young people love despair."

Perry said at the time, "We were lumbered with an indescribable duty to get it right, for all time." Radford's film looks and feels much like the reader imagines *Nineteen Eighty-Four* should look and feel. This fidelity means that, Eurythmics aside, the film hasn't dated. But at the same time as Radford was making it, other artists were integrating Orwellian concepts into brand-new dystopian visions that plugged straight into the mood of the 1980s: *V for Vendetta, The Handmaid's Tale, Brazil*.

It would not be accurate to say that director Terry Gilliam was inspired by *Nineteen Eighty-Four* while he was making *Brazil*, because he hadn't read it yet. He was inspired instead by the *idea* of *Nineteen*

---

* While visiting the set, Marvin Rosenblum received phone calls asking whether Apple's "1984" was a clip from the film, leading him to threaten Chiat/Day with legal action, but that ship had sailed.

Eighty-Four, as it had permeated the culture: "general knowledge that was in the atmosphere, the stuff you get from college and talking about *1984.*"

When Gilliam started developing the idea in the late 1970s, one working title was *The Ministry.* Another was *1984½:* a dual homage to Orwell and Fellini to convey the film's dance of fear and fantasy. "*Brazil* came specifically from the time, from the approaching of 1984," he later told Salman Rushdie. "It was looming ... Unfortunately, that bastard Michael Radford did a version of *1984* ... so I was blown." You can get a sense of the film's unique tone from the fact that Gilliam also considered *The Ministry of Torture* and *How I Learned to Live with the System—So Far* before settling on *Brazil,* after the song that winds through it. They sound like titles for three totally different films.

Clearly, Gilliam had picked up some important ideas from Orwell second-hand. The passive bureaucrat Sam Lowry (Jonathan Pryce) and flinty truck-driver Jill Layton (Kim Greist) are roughly in the mould of Winston and Julia. There is a Ministry of Information which uses "Information Retrieval" as a euphemism for torture. And the name of the official form 27B-6 is a playful reference to Orwell's final London address, 27b Canonbury Square. Gilliam's target, however, was not totalitarianism. There are no fanatics in *Brazil,* no dictator, only the managerial pencil-pushers and card-punchers who keep the machinery of the state turning. The seed was sown when Gilliam read a document from the seventeenth-century witch trials which listed the prices the accused had to pay for their own torture and execution. The absurd cruelty of turning state violence into a business inspired a satire on remorseless, self-justifying bureaucracy—the plot is set in motion by a clerical error at the Ministry.

Gilliam's satire is epitomised by the terrorist outrages which replace Orwell's rocket bombs as a means to keep the populace on a permanent war footing. The director frustrated interviewers by saying that even he didn't know if the terrorists were real or agents of the state. "The Ministry needs terrorists whether they actually exist or not," explains Sam's boss Mr. Helpmann in an early draft of the screenplay written by Gilliam and Charles Alverson. "If they didn't exist, the Ministry will create them ... once the system started operating it proved to be totally self-generating ... fuelled by an abundant internal supply of paranoia and ambition." Oceania, too, requires a steady supply of criminals, guilty or not, because "purges and vaporisations were a necessary part of the mechanics of government," but Gilliam reworks that notion into a crazed joke.

The opening title card locates *Brazil* "somewhere in the twentieth century." Like *1984,* it blurs the present and the future with the 1940s, by way of wartime propaganda posters, art deco design, pneumatic tubes and clunky technology. In fact, both movies employed the same location scouts. "We used a lot of the same locations," Radford remembered. "We'd keep finding traces of *Brazil* but I had no real idea what he was doing at the time." The two films were like estranged twins: Suzanna Hamilton auditioned for the part of Jill, while Jamie Lee Curtis was considered for both Jill and Julia.

Gilliam's quasi-homage to Orwell became a mixed blessing once the film was finished. Frank Price, the president of Universal Pictures, had been a story editor on the 1953 *Studio One* version of *Nineteen Eighty-Four* and considered *Brazil* nothing more than a bad rip-off. Film critic Judith Crist dubbed it "*1985,*" while *The New Yorker*'s Pauline Kael described it as "a stoned, slapstick *1984.*" Of course, a stoned, slapstick *Nineteen Eighty-Four* isn't *Nineteen Eighty-Four* at all. Gilliam's lifelong habit of kicking against the pricks, which included a famously acrimonious battle with Universal over the final cut of *Brazil,* inoculated him against pessimism. The ending may have been too downbeat for Universal, but by Orwell's standards, the fact that Sam dies before he capitulates is pretty idealistic. Gilliam told Salman Rushdie that Sam becomes a hero when he stops being a cog: "To me, the heart of *Brazil* is responsibility, is involvement—you can't just let the world go on doing what it's doing without getting involved." That is also the heart of *V for Vendetta.*

Orwell had a glancing familiarity with superhero comic books. In 1945, he received a package of comics published by DC and Timely (the precursor to Marvel), which introduced him to the likes of Superman, Batman and the Human Torch. He was not a fan. "Quite obviously they tend to stimulate fantasies of power," he wrote, "and in the last resort their subject matter boils down to magic and sadism. You can hardly look at a page without seeing somebody flying through the air . . . or somebody socking somebody else on the jaw, or an under-clad young woman fighting for her honour—and her ravisher is just as likely to be a steel robot or a fifty-foot dinosaur as a human being. The whole thing is just a riot of nonsensical sensationalism."*

Orwell might never have changed his mind, but by the 1980s, as *Judge Dredd* demonstrated, comic books had become a potent vehicle for left-wing satire. Writer Alan Moore first came up with the idea of a freakish terrorist battling a totalitarian state in the roiling year of 1976. Six years later, he and the equally pessimistic artist David Lloyd launched *V for Vendetta* in the British anthology comic book *Warrior* and set it fifteen years in the future. Assuming (wrongly) that Margaret Thatcher's unpopular government would lose the next general election, Moore imagined Labour adopting a policy of unilateral disarmament that spares Britain from a nuclear war that devastates most of the world. But the havoc the war wreaks on the climate and food supplies makes Britain easy prey for a new fascist movement, Norsefire, which seizes power in 1992 and dispatches political enemies and undesirable minorities to concentration camps. One of those enemies, transformed by a scientific experiment in the series' only major concession to superhero norms, escapes and becomes the anarchist terrorist V. Lloyd, who conceived V's Guy Fawkes mask, called it a comic for "people who don't switch off the news."

Moore's long list of influences, published in *Warrior,* included the dystopian trinity of Orwell, Huxley and Bradbury alongside *Judge Dredd, The Prisoner,* David Bowie and New Wave science fiction. Lloyd's illustrations of a grey, debilitated London have an Orwellian flavour, as do the regime's slogans, "Strength Through Purity, Purity Through Faith" and—more unnerving now than it was then—"Make Britain Great Again." As in Airstrip One, the heritage of literature and music has been eradicated; only in V's Shadow Gallery can the voices of the past, from Shakespeare to Motown, still be heard. Moore's obviously deep knowledge of the genre produces at least one very good joke. Norsefire Television's hit drama serial follows the racist adventures of Aryan action man Storm Saxon in the

---

* That year *Time* ran an article called "Are Comics Fascist?," in which Jesuit professor Walter J. Ong called Superman "a super state type of hero with definite interest in the ideologies of herdist politics."

"nightmarish future England" of 2501. So this is what the rulers of a dystopia consider dystopian.

V for Vendetta was left in limbo when *Warrior* closed in 1985. By the time Moore and Lloyd revived and completed it for DC in 1988, after nine years of Thatcher, they were able to scrutinise their earlier predictions. Moore decided that he had been too optimistic in thinking that "it would take something as melodramatic as a near-miss nuclear conflict to nudge England towards fascism." He now thought that it wouldn't be that difficult at all.

Margaret Atwood started writing *The Handmaid's Tale* in West Berlin in the spring of 1984. Like Orwell when he began *Nineteen Eighty-Four,* she was in her early forties and she knew exactly what she wanted to say. The novel originated with a file of newspaper cuttings she had begun collecting while living in England, covering such topics as the religious right, prisons in Iran, falling birth rates, Nazi sexual politics, polygamy and credit cards. She let these diverse observations ferment, like compost, until a story grew out of them. Her travels in East Germany and Czechoslovakia, where she experienced "the wariness, the feeling of being spied on, the silences, the changes of subject, the oblique ways in which people might convey information," nourished the novel, too, as did her adolescent obsession with dystopias and World War Two. She remembered identifying with Winston because he was "silently at odds with the ideas and the manner of life proposed for him. (This may be one of the reasons *1984* is best read when you are an adolescent: most adolescents feel like that.)" The novel persuaded her that it really could happen to her, even in Canada in the early 1950s. She denied that *The Handmaid's Tale* was science fiction, preferring to call it "speculative fiction of the George Orwell variety."

The novel is narrated by Offred (i.e., she belongs to Fred), a "handmaid" whose only role in Gilead, a fascistic theocracy brought to power by a chronic fertility crisis and a savage coup, is to bear children for the sterile ruling class.* The architects of Gilead are utopian

---

* The word *prole,* Orwell noted while writing about *The Iron Heel,* comes from the Latin *proletarii:* those whose sole value to the state is producing offspring.

fanatics who truly believe they are building a better, happier world. "There is more than one kind of freedom," the matronly apparatchik Aunt Lydia tells the handmaids. "Freedom to and freedom from. In the days of anarchy, it was freedom to. Now you are being given freedom from. Don't underrate it." In Newspeak, the word *free* only means freedom from; the concept of freedom to has ceased to exist.

Atwood's appendix, "Historical Notes on *The Handmaid's Tale*," combines a homage to "The Principles of Newspeak" with an arch parody of academia: the title that the twenty-second-century scholars give to Offred's story is a Chaucerian joke. But this is only the last and most obvious of the traces left by *Nineteen Eighty-Four*. There is a secret diary—narrated to tape rather than written, because the written word is taboo for the women of Gilead—with no guarantee of a reader. There are public hangings, informants, forbidden books (which is to say all books) and the erasure of history. There are "Unwomen" and all-seeing policemen called "Eyes." There is a ritual of controlled violence called a "Salvaging," which is like the Two Minutes Hate with blood on its hands. Then again, such ideas came from the real world as much as from Orwell. Atwood had a rule: "I would not include anything that human beings had not already done in some other place or time." The appendix mentions Iran, Russia and Romania; Atwood also took monstrous innovations from the Nazis, American slave-owners, South American juntas and Salem witch-hunters. Gilead's genius, like Oceania's, is synthesis.

It comes back to the question of influence. So much of *The Handmaid's Tale* is Atwood's own, from the mordant humour and ringing prose to the engagement with issues of gender, sexuality, race and religious extremism that barely registered with Orwell. He was well aware that totalitarianism weaponised motherhood and sexual puritanism: *sexcrime* is any activity except "normal intercourse between man and wife, for the sole purpose of begetting children, and without physical pleasure on the part of the woman," which makes Winston and Julia's coupling "a political act." But his interest in women's interior lives, to his detriment as a writer and a person, was minimal.

What makes Atwood's Gilead feel truly Orwellian is the climate of paralysing unreality. Offred assumes that the news of distant battles between Gilead and rival religious factions may be faked and that the Mayday resistance movement might, like Orwell's Brotherhood, not exist. Even her own memories are treacherous—when she tries to picture the faces of her missing husband and daughter, they shrivel like burning photographs. She calls herself "a refugee from the past." The next generation of women will be happier, more obedient, "Because they will have no memories of any other way." Like Winston Smith, Offred is no radical; she's just looking for things to hold on to, before they turn to mist. At least Winston gets to keep his name, though England does not: another name for Airstrip One might be Ofoceania.

The first fully realised near-future dystopia to focus on the oppression of women, *The Handmaid's Tale* sold over one million copies in its first two years. A film, based on a screenplay by Harold Pinter, followed in 1990. Atwood has since regularly been asked if the book was a prediction. Her answer could apply equally to *Nineteen Eighty-Four*: "Let's say it's an antiprediction: If this future can be described in detail, maybe it won't happen."

Orwell would have turned eighty-one in 1984. All of his friends who granted interviews, addressed conferences or published memoirs in and around that year were north of seventy.* Even the younger admirers who had first clashed over his legacy in the early 1950s were in their sixties. Their opinions were thus freighted with decades of baggage, and the pressing sense that whoever won this latest battle for Orwell's imagined blessing would win the war. They were fighting for the validity of their own memories, and the choices they had made, even as some acknowledged the folly of claiming him for any political position. "I understood him up to a point," V. S. Pritchett told *Time*. "It was hard to define him because just when you had fixed on a view, he would contradict it."

The solution—still popular to this day—was to hold to the light the quotations that supported the writer's argument and shove the unhelpful ones down the memory hole. But in their heads, these

---

* The survivors included Stephen Spender, Tosco Fyvel, Malcolm Muggeridge, Anthony Powell, Julian Symons, Jacintha Buddicom, George Woodcock, David Astor and Paul Potts. Richard Rees, Inez Holden and Jack Common were long gone. Fredric Warburg, Arthur Koestler and Avril Dunn had passed relatively recently.

writers were simply insisting on the truth. They identified so intensely with Orwell's moral integrity and independence of mind that to see him "stolen" by their opponents was to suffer an emotional wound. While a few remnants of 1930s communism were eager to see the back of him (seventy-four-year-old journalist Alaric Jacob called *Nineteen Eighty-Four* "one of the most disgusting books ever written") almost all other commentators wanted Saint George on their side and accused each other, with apparently sincere outrage, of gross dishonesty.

Orwell made it clear that he was a democratic socialist who opposed conservatives as well as communists, so the most inflammatory reputation grab was a 1983 *Harper's* cover story called "If Orwell Were Alive Today," by the leading American neoconservative Norman Podhoretz. "Normally, to speculate on what a dead man might have said about events he never lived to see is a frivolous enterprise," he acknowledged, before gamely pressing on to insist that an octogenarian Orwell would have said that Norman Podhoretz was right. Given that the neocon think tank Committee for the Free World had already christened its publishing arm the Orwell Press, any other conclusion would have been inconvenient. The pugnacious British socialist Christopher Hitchens retaliated with his own arsenal of quotations to "prove" that Orwell would still be a democratic socialist who took a dim view of "the sort of well-heeled power worshiper who passes for an intellectual these days." The tug-of-war continued for months and was, of course, unwinnable. *National Review,* the conservative journal cofounded by James Burnham, applauded Orwell, but so did the left-wing novelist E. L. Doctorow and the civil libertarians behind *The 1984 Calendar: An American History.* Democrats and Republicans alike cited *Nineteen Eighty-Four* in fundraising letters during the 1984 presidential election campaign.

Another battlefront opened up in the pages of the British press, where *Tribune* published a series of essays about its most famous alumnus. *Nineteen Eighty-Four* was plainly anti-socialist, insisted conservatives Peregrine Worsthorne and Alfred Sherman. No, it wasn't, countered Bernard Crick and Tony Benn. On New Year's Eve, the leaders of Britain's three main political parties all mentioned the book in their New Year messages. Margaret Thatcher declared that 1984 would be "a year of hope and a year of liberty," and therefore "George Orwell was wrong," even as Labour's Neil Kinnock published an essay in the London *Times* which defended the novel from the "tomb-robbers" of the right. *The Sun*, precisely the kind of tabloid newspaper that Orwell loathed, retorted that in fact Kinnock's own party was Ingsoc in embryo: if Labour had won the 1983 general election under the "Marxist" Michael Foot, Orwell's erstwhile *Tribune* colleague, "we would have been taken so far down the path to the Corporate State, there could have been no turning back." But—phew!—Britain had been spared this Orwellian nightmare by Margaret Thatcher. *The Sun*'s "20 Things You Never Knew About George Orwell" contrived not to mention the word *socialism* once.

The Spectator's Paul Johnson observed that this "ideological overkill" could only result in a tic: "since everyone, Left, Right and Centre, can and does hijack the wretched man for every conceivable political purpose, the net result is almost exactly nil." Still, nobody considered the possibility that the ranks of those attempting to appropriate Orwell would include Russian propagandists.

In an obviously coordinated effort, three prominent Soviet journals published articles claiming that Orwell was really satirising the West, whether he knew it or not. *Novoye Vremya* presented *Nineteen Eighty-Four* as "a grim warning to bourgeois-democratic society, which, as he pointed out, is rooted in anti-humanism, all-devouring militarism and denial of human rights." *Literaturnaya Gazeta* explained that Ronald Reagan was Big Brother, the telescreens were the National Security Agency, and Airstrip One was manifest in the siting of American nuclear weapons at Britain's Greenham Common. *Izvestiya* said that history had turned Oceania into "a fully realistic picture of contemporary Capitalism-Imperialism."

These writers could have claimed that the novel took place on Mars for all that most of their readers knew, because only the party elite could legally access a copy, just as only the Inner Party can lay hands on Goldstein's book. On the black market, it cost two-thirds of the average monthly salary. In a spectacular example of Soviet doublethink, this revisionism coincided with the trial of Latvian translator Gunārs Astra, who was sentenced to seven years in the gulag for "anti-Soviet agitation and propaganda"—crimes which included circulating a *samizdat* copy of *Nineteen Eighty-Four*.

It was easy for Margaret Thatcher or Steve Jobs to say that *Nineteen Eighty-Four* was a bad guess, but for some readers, it was a startlingly detailed anatomy of a system they knew intimately. "No one has ever lived in Lilliput, etc.," wrote Conor Cruise O'Brien, "but hundreds of millions of people live today under political conditions quite closely comparable to the essentials of Orwell's picture." That included Iran, China and North Korea, but the book had particular cachet in the Soviet bloc. During his travels in Eastern Europe, the journalist Timothy Garton Ash regularly met underground Orwell fans who asked, "How did he know?" Well, he knew because he paid attention. He observed communist behaviour in Spain, he listened to exiles, he read every book he could. And his efforts were appreciated. In *Utopia in Power,* Mikhail Heller and Aleksandr Nekrich described Orwell as "probably the single Western author who understood the nature of the Soviet world."

The arrival of 1984 therefore unleashed a flood of memories. The Lithuanian émigré Tomas Venclova, who read a clandestine copy of *Nineteen Eighty-Four* in the early 1960s and related the story to his friends as if it were a folk tale, said that it had changed his life: "He was the first person to explain to me that a normal person cannot live in that society." In his introduction to a new Czech *samizdat* edition (read aloud by Pinter at *Thoughtcrimes*), Milan Šimečka recalled a similar epiphany: "When I read the story of Winston Smith, I received a shock because I realised all of a sudden that this was my own story I was reading . . . Wherever I go, whatever I hear on our radio and television, I am reminded of the London of *1984.*" So while some left-wing critics in the West accused Orwell of misanthropy and defeatism, many people who woke up to totalitarianism every day found the book inspirational, because they felt understood: they were used to being watched, but not *seen.* Šimečka compared his reading experience to Winston's reaction to Goldstein's book: "The best books, he perceived, are those that tell you what you know already." Hungary's György Dalos published a bitterly witty sequel called *1985,* in which the revolutionaries of the "London spring" overthrow Ingsoc before being suppressed, just like their real-world predecessors in Hungary and Czechoslovakia.

Nineteen Eighty-Four became such a cliché among the Iron Curtain intelligentsia that Milan Kundera grew to hate it. Kundera's famous line "The struggle of man against power is the struggle of memory against forgetting" may sound like something from Orwell, but he thought that the novel encouraged his Czech friends to see their life as "an undifferentiated block of horrors." Even life under Soviet rule was not *quite* as bad as Oceania, he insisted. Hadn't they still enjoyed, despite everything, art, jokes, friendship, love? All the stubborn pleasures of life that can't be reduced to politics? "In their talk of forty horrible years," he complained, "they were all *Orwellising* their recollection of their own lives."

By the time Kundera published those words, in 1993, Eurasia had fallen.

It's often forgotten that Orwell did not agree with O'Brien on the subject of totalitarianism's invincibility, and maintained in his journalism that the system contained the seeds of its own downfall. The Russian dissident Andrei Amalrik agreed. In 1970, he published a much-discussed essay called "Will the Soviet Union Survive Until 1984?" (He originally chose 1980 as the date of collapse, but a friend convinced him to adopt the Orwellian deadline instead.) For the sin of writing it, Amalrik served five years in the gulag and later died in exile. Come 1984, one of his friends was taunted in prison by KGB officers: "Amalrik is long dead, but we are still very much present." In hindsight, Amalrik wasn't wrong about the USSR's fatal weaknesses, just premature. By 1984, argued the veteran Yugoslavian socialist Milovan Djilas, totalitarianism had effectively disintegrated, leaving nothing more than "a ritualistic code." The language of that code was known as *Novoyaz:* Newspeak.* Power without belief did not, as O'Brien believes, mean perfection. It meant decay. Without ideology and terror, the Soviet regime was no longer totalitarian; without totalitarianism, it could not endure.

In 1987, Mikhail Gorbachev's reformist government asked the seasoned sociologist Yuri Levada to mastermind an unprecedented

---

* In her 1989 book *Newspeak: The Language of Soviet Communism*, Françoise Thom's analysis aligned with Orwell's: "it must show that power is at once arbitrary and limitless and it must also incarnate the violence of power. Newspeak does so in two ways: by flying in the face of all evidence and by not bothering to conceal its own contradictions."

study of Russian public opinion. Levada took the opportunity to explore his own theories about the kind of human being that had been created by decades of isolation, paternalism and conformity: Homo Sovieticus. To describe the contradictory thoughts required of the average Russian, obliged to believe in progress and equality while experiencing neither, Levada turned to Orwell and double-think. Answers to his questionnaire confirmed his hypothesis that most Soviet citizens were only pretending to believe in communism: everybody knew the steps so well that they kept dancing even when they could no longer hear the music. Thirty years later, the Russian-American journalist Masha Gessen summarised Levada's findings about Homo Sovieticus in *The Future Is History:* "His inner world consisted of antinomies, his objective was survival, and his strategy was constant negotiation—the endless circulation of games and doublethink." In Orwell's terms, Homo Sovieticus was Julia: "She took it for granted that everyone, or nearly everyone, secretly hated the Party and would break the rules if he thought it safe to do so."

Gorbachev's chief architect of *glasnost* and *perestroika* was Aleksandr Nikolaevich Yakovlev. One of Yakovlev's projects was the lifting of censorship and the publication, for the first time, of books such as *Nineteen Eighty-Four* and *We.* In July 1991, he described Russia in terms that new readers of those books would have recognised: "Our society is deeply ill. Our souls are permanently empty. We have grown to presume everyone guilty at all times, thus creating hundreds of thousands of guards watching over our morality, conscience, purity of world view, compliance with the wishes of authorities. We have turned truth into a crime."

Five months later, the Union of Soviet Socialist Republics officially ceased to exist.

The fall of communism might have been expected to render *Nineteen Eighty-Four* a period piece like *Darkness at Noon* or Aleksandr Solzhenitsyn's *The Gulag Archipelago,* but discussion of the book had already pivoted to the subject of the machine. It should be emphasised that Orwell was far less interested in science than Wells, Zamyatin or Huxley were. Although the telescreen is mentioned in the novel no fewer than 119 times, its operation is thinly sketched and it is less effective as a means of control than the old-fashioned tools of policemen and informants, or the almost supernatural power of Big Brother's eyes. The science of Oceania does not even fill two pages of Goldstein's book. As the Polish neoconservative Leopold Labedz wrote in *Encounter* in 1984: "For Orwell the problem was the technology of power rather than the power of technology . . . Big Brother is not a Dalek." But this was the impotent cry of an old cold warrior. When a teacher in New York assigned the novel to forty-nine adult students in 1982, only one read it as anti-communist; the rest were reminded of the FBI, CIA, Watergate, television and computers. The book was now resonating at different frequencies.

The Orwell issue of *The Village Voice* included a short story by Bob Brewin called "Worldlink 2029," in which "obriens" work for a global computer network that is somewhere between an advanced telescreen and a primitive internet. "The worst kind of Big Brother," wrote Brewin, was "a machine with no soul run by men who had come close to turning into machines themselves." As early as 1949, *Tribune* had tied its review of *Nineteen Eighty-Four* to a news item about the ominous implications of a new mechanical "brain" developed at Manchester University. Now the fictional popularity of the all-powerful computer—Fate in *V for Vendetta,* Skynet in *The Terminator*—reflected public concerns about databases, satellites and surveillance cameras. It was exactly this mounting anxiety that made Chiat/Day want to "smash the old canard that the computer will enslave us" and herald a new era of Apple-driven techno-utopianism. It was also why Walter Cronkite wrote in a *New York Times* op-ed to promote his CBS special *1984 Revisited:* "If Big Brother could just get all the major private and government data banks in America linked, he might be 80 percent of the way home." *The New York Times* television critic broadly agreed with Cronkite's diagnosis but thought that he had missed something important: "the complaisance, the eagerness even, with which we embrace the new technologies."

This was an apprehension that flew in the face of Apple's "1984." What if loss of freedom didn't require a Big Brother or an Ingsoc? What if we did it to ourselves?

CHAPTER 13

Oceania 2.0

Nineteen Eighty-Four in the Twenty-First Century

The stubbornness of reality is relative. Reality needs us to protect it.

—Hannah Arendt, 1951

I n 1984, during a panel discussion on *Nineteen Eighty-Four,* the American media critic Neil Postman argued that television had radically transformed culture, politics and human behaviour in America in a way that more closely resembled *Brave New World* than Orwell's book. He developed this theory into a potent polemic called *Amusing Ourselves to Death:* "Orwell feared that what we hate will ruin us. Huxley feared that what we love will ruin us. This book is about the possibility that Huxley, not Orwell, was right." This striking line appears in the final chapter: "In the Huxleyan prophecy, Big Brother does not watch us, by his choice. We watch him, by ours." Postman did not expect to be taken literally.

Big Brother, the reality television show that debuted in the Netherlands in 1999, flowed from the realisation that while people still claimed to be concerned about surveillance, a significant number would happily volunteer for it. In 1996, a Pennsylvania college student called Jennifer Ringley installed a webcam in her dorm room and "lifecasted" her every move via her enormously popular JenniCam website. Three years later, the eccentric internet entrepreneur Josh Harris went several steps further by staging an art-project-cum-social experiment called *Quiet: We Live in Public.* He invited more than one hundred volunteers to live in a six-storey Manhattan warehouse, equipped with all the food, intoxicants and entertainment they could require, and told them that they were free to do as they pleased, on the understanding that it was all recorded by an arsenal of webcams. Harris produced a living metaphor for what the internet would become: a place where people enthusiastically bartered privacy for pleasure, convenience and attention. "I loved living in a world with no secrets and no sense of time," said one volunteer, "where we were little children, being taken care of." Both Harris's and Ringley's projects were quickly branded "Orwellian."

If *Quiet* was the avant-garde expression of a powerful idea, then *Big Brother* was the primetime version: a social experiment that frequently devolved into a voyeuristic freakshow. Its Dutch creator, John de Mol Jr., was coy about the source of the series title, but when the format arrived in the US in 2000, the name of the production company rather gave the game away: Orwell Productions, Inc. Lawyer William F. Coulson filed a lawsuit on behalf of Marvin Rosenblum and the Orwell estate, accusing the US programme-makers of "dilution and cheapening of the distinctive quality of this mark." Coulson was referring to the value of the screen rights but the show did something similar to Orwell's ideas. In *Big Brother,* housemates live under twenty-four-hour surveillance ("asleep or awake, working or eating, indoors or out of doors, in the bath or in bed," to quote the novel) and are summoned to the Diary Room (known in some territories as the Confession Room) on behalf of a non-existent Big Brother. In most versions of the show, books and writing implements are forbidden. "Orwell understood the difference between 'what the public is interested in' and 'the public interest,'" wrote Orwell's outraged biographer Bernard Crick. "That is why he wrote that book whose warning has been treated with cynical contempt and is itself treated as 'prolefeed.'" Around the same time, the BBC's *Room 101* rebuilt Orwell's torture chamber as a cute repository for celebrities' pet hates.

Not all references to *Nineteen Eighty-Four* during the 1990s were lightweight. Room 101 was the main character's address in *The Matrix,* a 1999 film steeped in questions of freedom, society and the nature of reality, while quotes from the novel still packed a punch in "Testify" by Rage Against the Machine and "Faster" by the Manic Street Preachers. Nevertheless, it felt as if the book might ultimately be trivialised, ironised and, like Winston Smith, squeezed empty. This

could only have happened in the decade of end-of-history complacency, when intelligent people could suggest with conviction that
Orwell's warning had worked. "The world of *Nineteen Eighty-Four*
ended in 1989," wrote Timothy Garton Ash in May 2001. Orwell
remained an essential guide to the obfuscations and deceptions of
political language, Garton Ash allowed, but his unholy trinity—
imperialism, fascism and communism—had fallen: "Forty years after
his own painful and early death, Orwell had won."

Four months later, two passenger jets were flown into the World
Trade Center.

In 2003, George Orwell's centenary, with its inevitable biographies,
reissues, conferences and documentaries, took place in a world
divided by the US-led invasion of Iraq. Perhaps that's why, in a
listener poll for BBC Radio 4, *Nineteen Eighty-Four* was voted the
quintessential English book, ahead of friendlier shortlisted works by
Zadie Smith, Jeremy Paxman, Bill Bryson and Jonathan Coe. "*Nineteen Eighty-Four* is about power out of control," commented Bernard
Crick. "Maybe people are feeling a sense of horror about two 'Big
Brothers' who cannot be controlled, or perhaps three. We must throw
in Saddam alongside Bush and Blair."

Critics of the war scrambled for *Nineteen Eighty-Four*. Paul Foot
in *The Guardian* decried the "doublethink" of "Oceania (the US and
Britain)." Radiohead's album *Hail to the Thief* opened with a fierce,
panicky song called "2 + 2 = 5," provoked by the "Orwellian euphemisms" that frontman Thom Yorke heard on the news. The Bush
administration's post-9/11 policies loomed large in the documentaries *Orwell Rolls in His Grave* and *Orwell Against the Tide*, while Michael
Moore's polemic *Fahrenheit 9/11* closed with a paraphrased passage
from Goldstein's book: "The war is waged by the ruling group against
its own subjects and its object is not the victory over either Eurasia or
Eastasia but to keep the very structure of society intact." The idea of
an interminable "war on terror" certainly brought to mind Oceania,
where every restriction is justified because "there is a war on." Life
mirrored art to an alarming degree when a senior aide to President
Bush (later identified as Karl Rove, though he has denied it) told *The
New York Times* that the administration had nothing to fear from "the

reality-based community . . . who believe that solutions emerge from your judicious study of discernible reality. That's not the way the world really works anymore. We're an empire now, and when we act, we create our own reality." Reading those words, you could almost hear O'Brien's voice. As a popular slogan put it, *Nineteen Eighty-Four* was not meant to be a how-to manual.

At the same time, hawks such as Norman Podhoretz and Christopher Hitchens, united by the war against "Islamofascism" twenty years after crossing swords in *Harper's,* deployed Orwell's words to shame their opponents on the left. This tactic went beyond the Iraq war; conservatives routinely threw the term "Thought Police" at anyone who advocated "politically correct" language. The obsession with imagining what Orwell might have said about current events was breeding resentment and fatigue. The political scientist Scott Lucas, the author of two harsh, revisionist books about the writer, distinguished Orwell the man from "Orwell" the symbol: " 'Orwell' has been used as a stick to beat those whose opinions are perceived as troublesome or in any way threatening." Daphne Patai, one of the most respected authorities on dystopian literature, shared Lucas's impatience to be rid of "Saint George" and see Orwell as a complex, contradictory figure rather than a moral exemplar. "Shakespeare doesn't have the moral authority to give us an opinion on the invasion of Iraq," she said in 2003. "No one would have dreamed of such a thing, but Orwell does get cited for that."

For many creators of new dystopian fiction, meanwhile *Nineteen Eighty-Four* remained the tallest building in the city of nightmares; one didn't have to enter it, but one couldn't entirely ignore it. In *1Q84,* Haruki Murakami tweaked Orwell's title (nine and Q are homophones in Japanese); set the action in 1984, beginning in April; and made noisy reference to Orwell in the context of parallel universes and religious cults. The protagonist of Gary Shteyngart's *Super Sad True Love Story,* a satire on corporate excess and intellectual decline, is a worn-out, thirty-nine-year-old diarist in love with a cynical younger woman. James McTeigue, director of the 2005 *V for Vendetta* movie, paid tribute by casting John Hurt as dictator Adam Sutler (the name could have been subtler), who berates his underlings from a giant screen, thus turning Michael Radford's Winston Smith into a thuggish Big Brother. Politically sophomoric and visually inert, the movie nonetheless resonated widely when cheap plastic versions of V's Guy Fawkes mask became a global emblem of protest. "*V* was designed to warn against a grim possibility—like a kind of *1984* in comics," said David Lloyd, the artist responsible for the design. "And as George Orwell's message was one that reached out to a wide readership because it spoke of universal matters of importance to us all, it's no surprise that ours did as well."*

The most resonant twenty-first-century dystopias, however, were notable for their distance from Orwell. Works as diverse as Kazuo Ishiguro's novel *Never Let Me Go*, Suzanne Collins's Young Adult series *The Hunger Games*, Mike Judge's savage comedy *Idiocracy* and the Pixar movie *Wall-E* satirised decadent capitalism rather than totalitarianism.[†] Philip Roth denied that *The Plot Against America*, his novel about an alternate timeline where the aviator Charles Lindbergh defeats President Roosevelt in the 1940 election and institutes fascism in America, had much in common with *Nineteen Eighty-Four*: "Orwell imagined a huge change in the future with horrendous consequences for everyone; I tried to imagine a small change in the past with horrendous consequences for a relative few." The most striking dystopia of the 2000s was *Children of Men*, Alfonso Cuarón's alchemical film adaptation of P. D. James's 1992 novel. The movie's near-future England is mean, tawdry and violent but incapable of totalitarianism. Despite surveillance cameras and concentration camps, the prevailing mood is of chaos rather than control, and the furniture of capitalism remains in place, albeit faded and threadbare, because in a world where no babies have been born for eighteen years, there is literally no future. Cuaron's landscape of exhausted possibilities felt more relevant to the new century's anxieties, especially after the 2008 financial crisis, than Orwell's all-powerful tyranny.

So, too, did British screenwriter Charlie Brooker's anthology TV series *Black Mirror*, which became the definitive dystopia of the 2010s because it expressed up-to-the-minute anxieties about our

* *V for Vendetta* writer Alan Moore revisited *Nineteen Eighty-Four* in his 2007 graphic novel *The League of Extraordinary Gentlemen: Black Dossier*, which opens in London after the fall of Ingsoc.
† Like Woody Allen's 1973 comedy *Sleeper* before it, *Idiocracy* kept alive the tradition of *Looking Backward* and *The Sleeper Awakes*, with an ordinary man waking up after a five-hundred-year slumber.

insufficiently examined reliance on technology. Each episode takes a current tendency—reality TV, social media, virtual reality, politics as showbusiness—to Swiftian extremes. "Any time there's a new invention, people say, 'Oh, that's a bit *Black Mirror*,'" said Brooker in 2016. They were missing the point. The theme of *Black Mirror*, as Huxley said of *Brave New World*, is "not the advancement of science as such; it is the advancement of science as it affects human individuals." Neil Postman's line about Huxley's book—"what we love will ruin us"—could serve as a motto for Brooker's dystopias of complicity. In HBO's *Black Mirror*–ised 2018 version of *Fahrenheit 451*, the book-burning tyranny is the result of an alliance between government and tech companies. "The Ministry didn't do this to us," says one character. "We did it to ourselves. We demanded a world like this."

There is truth in that. The currency of the twenty-first-century tech industry is data. All but the cagiest internet users routinely tell companies such as Facebook and Google what they like, who they know, where they go, and much more. The writer Rebecca Solnit calls Google "Big Hipster Brother." She wrote about another of those companies, Apple, on the thirtieth anniversary of its most famous commercial: "Maybe Apple's '1984' ad is the beginning of Silicon Valley's fantasy of itself as the solution, not the problem—a dissident rebel, not the rising new Establishment." Citing government surveillance, hacking, revenge porn and iPhone addiction, Solnit argued that the "Orwell was wrong" triumphalism of the 1980s had been at best premature, if not dishonest. Shaped by powerful corporations with a commercial and philosophical disdain for privacy, online culture "wasn't a rupture with the past but an expansion of what was worst about that past . . . 2014 has turned out quite a bit like *1984*."

Dave Eggers explored such misgivings in his 2013 novel *The Circle*. The story of a young woman called Mae Holland's initiation into the monolithic tech company of the title is an agile satire of Silicon Valley utopianism with sly nods to its predecessors. The famous triad of slogans from *Nineteen Eighty-Four* is rewritten for the social-media age: "SECRETS ARE LIES / SHARING IS CARING / PRIVACY IS THEFT." The earthy refusenik driven to his death by a voyeuristic mob recalls John the Savage at the end of *Brave New World*. The Circle's ultimate goal of "transparency"—living one's entire life in public, in "a new and glorious openness, a world of perpetual light"—makes Zamyatin's glass houses and Orwell's telescreens look primitive. The bulk of the novel is simply an exaggeration of current trends. Only in its very last chapter does it become a true dystopia in which *ownlife* has been abolished without any need for force: Mae proves her love for Big Brother by effectively turning her life into a *Big Brother* house. "What happens to us if we must be 'on' all the time?" asked Margaret Atwood in her review. "Then we're in the twenty-four-hour glare of the supervised prison. To live entirely in public is a form of solitary confinement." *The Circle* offers a new incarnation of the place where there is no darkness.

Eggers's timing was fortuitous. On June 5, 2013, a few months before he published *The Circle, The Guardian* and *The Washington Post* revealed the existence of a massive NSA electronic surveillance programme, using documents leaked by computer engineer Edward Snowden. Snowden later said that Orwell "warned us of the danger of this kind of information" but Oceania's surveillance apparatus was "nothing compared to what we have available today." As President Obama defended the NSA from Big Brother comparisons, Senator Bernie Sanders called it "very Orwellian," and *The New Yorker* asked, "So, Are We Living in 1984?," sales of *Nineteen Eighty-Four* shot up by several thousand per cent on Amazon, itself a data-hungry tech giant.*

George Orwell did not predict the internet (although E. M. Forster arguably did), and had only a rudimentary understanding of technology, yet he had been lurking in the wings of such conversations since the 1980s. Optimists like Nam June Paik, the creator of *Good Morning, Mr. Orwell*, saw the internet as the unstoppable force that would render tyranny impossible: "So George Orwell was wrong after all, when he wrote *1984*." Peter Huber irreverently rewrote *Nineteen Eighty-Four* in *Orwell's Revenge: The 1984 Palimpsest* to argue that Orwell was "completely, irredeemably, outrageously wrong" about the telescreen because networked communication, such as the nascent World Wide Web, would bring about a world in which "the proles do the watching, and the Party is whipped into submission."

---

* In another coincidence, BBC Radio 4 had recently broadcast a season of Orwell adaptations. Christopher Eccleston starred in *Nineteen Eighty-Four*, making him the fourth actor (alongside Peter Cushing, Patrick Troughton and John Hurt) to have played both Winston Smith and the Doctor.

Conversely, Thomas Pynchon wrote in his foreword to the 2003 edition of *Nineteen Eighty-Four* that the internet was "a development that promises social control on a scale those quaint old twentieth-century tyrants with their goofy mustaches could only dream about." The Snowden revelations moved the needle towards Pynchon's analysis. Optimism about the potential of the internet to hold power to account in the perpetual light of unlimited information was beginning to look foolish.

Nineteen Eighty-Four and *Brave New World* used to be seen as mutually exclusive dystopias. In 1984, however, while Neil Postman was writing *Amusing Ourselves to Death*, Aldous Huxley's biographer Sybille Bedford came to a different conclusion, describing the choice as a false binary: "We have entered the age of mixed tyrannies." By this she meant that the modern power-seeker would assemble whatever combination of coercion, seduction and distraction proved most effective.

Effectiveness is one of the watchwords of Vladimir Putin's mixed tyranny, or "managed democracy." Since first becoming Russia's president in 2000, buoyed by a craving for strength and stability after the nerve-grinding upheavals of the post-communist '90s, the former KGB officer has gradually brought back such features of the old regime as leader-worship, martial parades, mass arrests, show trials, political prisoners, territorial aggression, the one-party state, censorship, Newspeak and endemic paranoia. In 2012, Putin declared his dream of building a Russian-led replacement for the European Union, "from Lisbon to Vladivostok," unbound by such bothersome concepts as human rights and free and fair elections. Inspired by the fascist thinker Aleksandr Dugin, he called it Eurasia. In 2014, Stalin's posthumous approval rating in Russia reached a new peak of 52 per cent, proving beyond doubt that Homo Sovieticus had outlived the Soviet Union.

Putin's justification is, of course, different from Stalin's—nationalism and cultural conservatism rather than Marxist ideology—and his execution less brutish, retaining the pretence of freedom of speech and political opposition. The aim of his brand of authoritarianism is not total control but *effective* control. In his last substantial interview before his death in 2005, the great reformer Aleksandr Nikolaevich Yakovlev called Russia's weakness for strong leaders a "disease" and bemoaned its backsliding towards a centralised state at the expense of a healthy society. "If the state so wishes, the society will be civil, or semicivil, or nothing but a herd," he said. "Look to Orwell for a good description of this." Yes, but look to Huxley, too.

When the journalist and film-maker Peter Pomerantsev began working for Russian state television in 2006, he noticed how it synthesised "show business and propaganda, ratings with authoritarianism." Putin's media mastermind at the time was Vladislav Surkov, a former theatre director and PR manager with a soft, bland face and a steel-trap mind who defined "the very language and categories the country thinks and feels in." Surkov was a pioneer of post-truth politics, generating a destabilising fog of lies, hoaxes and contradictions to which the natural response was a nihilistic cynicism about the very status of hard facts. The title of Pomerantsev's book about Putin and Surkov's Russia paraphrased Arendt's memorable formulation about totalitarianism and truth: *Nothing Is True and Everything Is Possible.* The Russia expert Luke Harding calls it "Versionland."

This is a new kind of Orwellianism. Orwell's generation experienced the consequences of Big Lies so absurd that they could only be sustained by the extreme control of totalitarianism. Twenty-first-century authoritarians, however, don't need to go that far. "They don't require belief in a full-blown ideology, and thus they don't require violence or terror police," wrote the historian Anne Applebaum in a 2018 essay for *The Atlantic.* "They don't force people to believe that black is white, war is peace, and state farms have achieved 1,000 percent of their planned production." Instead, they rely on "Medium-Sized Lies": "all of them encourage their followers to engage, at least part of the time, with an alternative reality."

The internet enabled this mentality to spread far beyond Russia's borders, as the world's leading producer of disinformation exported its alternative reality to democracies that had no idea how vulnerable they were.

—

When President Trump's adviser Kellyanne Conway first used the phrase "alternative facts" on January 22, 2017, *Nineteen Eighty-Four* came roaring back onto the best-seller lists. *The Hollywood Reporter* called the novel, which was then attached to director Paul Greengrass, "the hottest literary property in town." Scores of cinemas across the US announced that they would be screening Michael Radford's *1984* on April 4, because "the clock is already striking thirteen." And theatre producers Sonia Friedman and Scott Rudin asked British playwrights Robert Icke and Duncan Macmillan to transfer their hit Headlong production *1984* to Broadway as soon as possible. "It went from zero to a hundred in the space of five days," Icke told me when I spoke to him and Macmillan at London's Almeida Theatre the following year. "They said, 'We think it's important this play is on Broadway now.'"

As one character asks at the start of the play: "how do you begin to talk about one of the most significant things that has ever been put on paper?" A totalitarian regime like Ingsoc is itself a kind of theatre, with a script, assigned roles, sets, props, and cues for applause. But when, in 2011, Icke and Macmillan started thinking about bringing *Nineteen Eighty-Four* to the stage, they wanted to avoid the obvious. "I remember saying we don't want a guy with blue overalls walking along with a big poster, because it's so familiar that it doesn't speak anymore," Icke said. "To make you engage with the book properly requires a certain amount of distance and confusion: do you know this as well as you think?" They read *Nineteen Eighty-Four* over and over again, looking for a "back-door key" that no previous adaptors had found. That key was the Appendix Theory, which turns the rest of the book into a historical document that has been studied and edited by persons unknown. Once entered by that route, the novel becomes an unnerving maze of riddles, paradoxes and mysteries. "If you're reading it properly, it comes for all of us in different ways," Macmillan said. "Everything is both true and false at the same time. It's doublethink as a structural device."

Whereas Michael Radford's movie clarifies Orwell's text, maintaining a distinction between what is real and what is not, the play plunges into its ambiguity. Icke and Macmillan's touchstones included David Lynch, *The Shining, Eternal Sunshine of the Spotless Mind,* and Tony Soprano's coma dreams in *The Sopranos:* works which explore the netherworld between reality, fantasy and memory. The actors were then required to exercise their own form of doublethink by playing the characters in such a way as to allow for multiple theories about what was real and who to trust. The play ends with a reader in the post-appendix future asking one final question: "How do we know the Party fell? Wouldn't it be in their interest to just structure the world in such a way that we believed that they were no longer . . ."

"We didn't want to solve the puzzle for people," said Macmillan. "We wanted to try and present the complexity of it. It was so interesting reading the reviews and hearing people coming out every night arguing about what they'd just seen." He laughed. "We looked at Twitter during the Broadway run and everyone thinks everyone else doesn't understand it."

Icke suspected that their experimental take on the book would be "a party nobody will want to come to apart from us," but when *1984* opened at the Nottingham Playhouse in September 2013, three months after the Snowden revelations, it was a hit. In collaboration with the Cultural Institute at King's College London, Headlong designed an app, Digital Double, whose terms and conditions licensed theatres to cull images from ticket-holders' social media accounts and project them in the theatre foyer. The idea was that users would be horrified by the misuse of data that they had unwittingly given away and think twice about their online behaviour. To the designers' surprise, audience members were delighted by the attention. Its three subsequent West End runs each inhabited a different political context: the third opened in June 2016, during the Brexit referendum campaign and just before the murder of Labour MP Jo Cox by a far-right terrorist. During the run at New York's Hudson Theatre, which began on May 18, 2017, the directors noticed that the audience's reaction each night was affected by whatever Donald Trump had done that day. The night after Trump tweeted the nonsense word *covfefe*, there was such a desire for humour that one actor was distraught: "I've been in comedies that have had less laughter than this." On another night, the news was so bad and the mood so intense that people passed out. At a third performance, when O'Brien asked, "What year is it?," a woman shouted: "It's 2017 and this is fucked up!" Although Icke and Macmillan added the passage from the Declaration of Independence in Orwell's appendix to the Broadway production, they resisted pressure to make the play more topical and actually removed a couple of lines that now felt too on-the-nose. Icke subsequently wondered if the transfer was *too* timely: "The city at that moment felt ashamed and sad as well as angry. They weren't ready to confront this." Scott Rudin's other Broadway production at the time was the pure escapism of *Hello, Dolly!* Julia, suggested Icke, would have chosen *Hello, Dolly!*

During the Broadway run, an uncannily prescient quotation from *Nineteen Eighty-Four* went viral: "The people are not going to revolt. They will not look up from their screens long enough to notice what's really happening." Except that the line wasn't from the book at all: it was written for the play. Icke and Macmillan appreciated the irony of inadvertently rewriting history.

"I think dad would've been amused by Donald Trump in an ironic sort of way," said Richard Blair in 2017. "He may have thought, 'There goes the sort of man I wrote about all those years ago.'"

It must be said that Donald Trump is no Big Brother. Nor, despite his revival of such toxic phrases as "America First" and "enemy of the people," is he simply a throwback to the 1930s. He has the cruelty and power hunger of a dictator but not the discipline, intellect or ideology. A more apt comparison would be Buzz Windrip, the oafish populist from Sinclair Lewis's *It Can't Happen Here,* or, in the real world, Joseph McCarthy, a demagogue who displayed comparable levels of narcissism, dishonesty, resentment and crude ambition, and a similarly uncanny ability to make journalists dance to his tune even as they loathed him.*

Still, there are precedents in Orwell's writing. During Trump's campaign against Hillary Clinton, it was hard to watch the candidate whipping supporters into a cry of "Lock her up!" without being reminded of the Two Minutes Hate and Orwell's description of the Party mindset: "a continuous frenzy of hatred of foreign enemies and internal traitors, triumph over victories, and self-abasement

---

* McCarthy's protégé Roy Cohn became Trump's mentor in the 1970s, as if passing on a virus.

before the power and wisdom of the Party." Trump's slogan "Make America Great Again" calls to mind Orwell's reference to "hundred percent Americanism." The president meets most of the criteria of Orwell's 1944 definition of fascism: "something cruel, unscrupulous, arrogant, obscurantist, anti-liberal and anti-working-class . . . almost any English person would accept 'bully' as a synonym for 'Fascist.'"

Orwell contended that such men can only rise to the top when the status quo has failed to satisfy citizens' need for justice, security and self-worth, but Trump's victory required one more crucial ingredient. He did not seize power through a revolution or coup. He was not potentiated by a recession or a terrorist atrocity, let alone a nuclear war or a fertility crisis. His route to the White House passed through America's own Versionland.

When some listeners to Orson Welles's *The War of the Worlds* believed the radio play without checking other sources, they were motivated by excessive faith in the authority of the media. The modern spreaders of disinformation, however, are driven by too little. As the science-fiction writer Marta Randall argued in 1983, the collapse of trust in establishment narratives brought about by scandals such as Watergate and the Pentagon Papers could result in a country where citizens "may quit relying on 'authoritative' news stories entirely," far beyond the point of healthy scepticism.

During the two decades preceding the 2016 election, groups such as climate change deniers, anti-vaxxers, creationists, birthers, 9/11 truthers and conspiracy theorists of every variety all demonstrated a fierce disregard for factual evidence that contradicted their beliefs, often reinforced by right-wing media outlets such as Fox News and talk radio, and by online echo chambers. This increasingly popular mindset was a toxic cocktail of cynicism and credulity. People who were proudly sceptical of CNN or *The New York Times* were perfectly happy to take unsourced Facebook posts and quack science at face value; those who doubted the BBC eagerly rubber-stamped the state propaganda of Putin or Syria's Bashar al-Assad.

Perhaps the most damning scene in *Nineteen Eighty-Four* is the Two Minutes Hate. On the screen, Goldstein is speaking the truth, "crying hysterically that the revolution had been betrayed," for anyone who cares to listen and believe, but nobody except Winston does that. The Party wouldn't broadcast him uncensored unless it *knew* that he would be ignored, and if you don't believe that Goldstein really exists, then the cynicism is even more obscene. Similarly, the effectiveness of the fake news that Winston manufactures at the Ministry of Truth depends on its readers' ignorance, laziness and prejudice as much as it does on state power.

The consequences of so many Americans' abdication from reality have been disastrous. During the 2016 election campaign, the Internet Research Agency, a Russian troll farm, flooded social media with fake news stories designed to generate confusion, cynicism and division. One of the agency's popular memes read: "The People Believe What the Media Tells Them They Believe: George Orwell." The quotation was fabricated. Orwell never used the phrase *the media*, which did not enter common usage until after his death, and he would never have made such a simplistic claim. The irony of Russian propagandists putting words into Orwell's mouth in order to hijack his prestige as a truth-teller to erode faith in journalism is breathtaking.

Some of the social media accounts that disseminated these stories and memes were themselves bogus—fake names, fake photographs, fake biographies—but many were not, because the architects of *dezinformatsiya* found that they were pushing at an open door. After a post-mortem into the epidemic of hoax news on Reddit's message-boards, the company's CEO, Steve Huffman, wrote: "I believe the biggest risk we face as Americans is our own ability to discern reality from nonsense. I wish there was a solution as simple as banning all propaganda, but it's not that easy." Former president Barack Obama made a similar point: "One of the biggest challenges we have to our democracy is the degree to which we don't share a common baseline of facts. What the Russians exploited . . . is we are operating in completely different information universes." America's epistemological crisis was Trump's golden opportunity. He could only win the 2016 election because a significant number of Americans were effectively living in a parallel reality.

Social media made this process all too easy as it became the primary news source for millions of Americans while lacking the editorial oversight of traditional media. Responding to criticism in 2017, Facebook's chief of security, Alex Stamos, pointed out that using the blunt instrument of machine learning to eliminate fake news could turn the platform into "the Ministry of Truth with ML systems," but by failing to act in time, Facebook was already allowing bad actors such as the Internet Research Agency to spread disinformation unchecked. The problem is likely to get worse. The growth of "deepfake" image synthesis, which combines computer graphics and artificial intelligence to manufacture images whose artificiality can only be identified by expert analysis, has the potential to create a paranoid labyrinth in which, according to the viewer's bias, fake images will pass as real while real ones are dismissed as fake. With image synthesis, Winston's fictional Comrade Ogilvy could be made to walk and talk while the crucial photograph of Jones, Aaronson and Rutherford could be shrugged off as a hoax. There is no technological remedy; the bug resides in human nature.

It is truly Orwellian that the phrase "fake news" has been turned on its head by Trump and his fellow authoritarians to describe real news that is not to their liking, while flagrant lies become "alternative facts." In March 2019, *The Washington Post* calculated that Trump had made 9,014 false claims during his first 773 days in office; the average had risen from just under six a day during his first year to twenty-two a day in 2019. Trump creates his own reality and measures his power by the number of people who subscribe to it: the cruder the lie, the more power its success demonstrates. Trump's lawyer Rudy Giuliani accidentally provided a crude motto for Versionland USA when he snapped at an interviewer, "Truth isn't truth!" *Reality is inside the skull.* Like Trump and Conway in previous years, Giuliani received the barbed tribute of a Doublespeak Award from the National Council of Teachers of English.

Old dystopian nightmares resurfaced in Trump's America with renewed force. Thanks to Hulu's television adaptation of *The Handmaid's Tale,* Atwood's novel sold another three and a half million copies, inspired a new wave of feminist dystopias, and made the handmaids' uniform of red cloaks and white hoods almost as popular with protesters as V's mask. One woman protesting Trump's inauguration held a placard reading: MAKE MARGARET ATWOOD FICTION AGAIN! Atwood announced that she would be publishing a second novel about Gilead, *The Testaments,* in 2019; unlike Orwell, she has lived to write her own sequel. Trumpism formed the backcloth to Hulu's *The Handmaid's Tale,* as well as HBO's *Fahrenheit 451,* and *Electric Dreams,* a Channel 4/Amazon Video anthology series based on Philip K. Dick's science-fiction short stories. Writer-director Dee Rees revealed that her radical adaptation of "The Hanging Stranger," now a biting commentary on political paranoia, flowed directly from the 2016 campaign. "Many dangerous ideas," she wrote, "were declared, nurtured, and allowed to propagate . . . This is not really happening, they said. What you are seeing is not what you are really seeing, they said. What you are hearing is not really what is meant, they said."

During a speech in July 2018, Trump himself said: "What you're seeing and what you're reading is not what's happening." Another line from *Nineteen Eighty-Four* went viral—a real one this time: "The party told you to reject the evidence of your eyes and ears. It was their final, most essential command."

One might feel wistful for those days twenty years ago when Big Brother was a joke and Orwell had "won." An era plagued by far-right populism, authoritarian nationalism, rampant disinformation and waning faith in liberal democracy is not one in which the message of *Nineteen Eighty-Four* can be easily dismissed.

Orwell was both too pessimistic and not pessimistic enough. On the one hand, the West did not succumb to totalitarianism; consumerism, not endless war, became the engine of the global economy. But he did not appreciate the tenacity of racism and religious extremism. Nor did he foresee that the common man and woman would embrace doublethink as enthusiastically as the intellectuals and, without the need for terror or torture, would choose to believe that two plus two was whatever they wanted it to be.

Nineteen Eighty-Four is about many things, and its readers' concerns dictate which one is paramount at any point in history. During the cold war, it was a book about totalitarianism. In the 1980s, it became a warning about invasive technology. Today, it is most of all a defence of truth. At the end of Trump's first week in office, *The New Yorker*'s Adam Gopnik apologised for previously thinking that Orwell's warning was too crude for the modern world: "one is reminded of what Orwell got right about this kind of brute authoritarianism—and that was essentially that it rests on lies told so often, and so repeatedly, that fighting the lie becomes not simply more dangerous but more

exhausting than repeating it . . . People aren't meant to believe it;
they're meant to be intimidated by it. The lie is not a claim about
specific facts; the lunacy is a deliberate challenge to the whole larger
idea of sanity." And so we come back to where we began, with Orwell
in Spain. "Looking Back on the Spanish War" has probably been
quoted more in the last four years than in the previous sixty-three,
from newspaper op-eds to *Spider-Man: Far From Home*:

> I am willing to believe that history is for the most part inac-
> curate and biased, but what is peculiar to our own age is the
> abandonment of the idea that history *could* be truthfully writ-
> ten. In the past people deliberately lied, or they unconsciously
> coloured what they wrote, or they struggled after the truth, well
> knowing that they must make many mistakes; but in each case
> they believed that "the facts" existed and were more or less
> discoverable . . . It is just this common basis of agreement, with
> its implication that human beings are all one species of animal,
> that totalitarianism destroys . . . The implied objective of this
> line of thought is a nightmare world in which the Leader, or
> some ruling clique, controls not only the future but *the past.*

Orwell's fear that "the very concept of objective truth is fading out
of the world" is the dark heart of *Nineteen Eighty-Four.* It gripped
him long before he came up with Big Brother, Oceania, Newspeak
or the telescreen, and it's more important than any of them. In its
original 1949 review, *Life* correctly identified the essence of Orwell's
message: "If men continue to believe in such facts as can be tested
and to reverence the spirit of truth in seeking greater knowledge,
they can never be fully enslaved." Seventy years later, that feels like
a very large *if.*

Afterword

You know how *Nineteen Eighty-Four* ends. Shattered by Room 101, Winston Smith sits at a table in the Chestnut Tree Café, anesthetised with Victory Gin, and numbly traces an equation in the dust. But what exactly is it? In the first edition, and every edition since 1987, he writes: "2 + 2 = 5." But for almost forty years the Penguin paperback omitted the five: "2 + 2 = ."

Nobody has yet uncovered evidence that explains the omission. One theory is that it was just a printing error, albeit a suspiciously meaningful one. Another is that a renegade compositor, unable to contemplate total defeat, removed it. A third possibility is that Orwell himself made the alteration shortly before his death. None are fully convincing. Whatever the reason, the chink in the text lets in a ray of hope for Winston, and thus radically changes Orwell's message. In Michael Radford's movie, John Hurt writes, "2 + 2" and then stops. "I think you need that moment," said Radford. "Maybe he'll get out of this. I would have been very upset to put 2 + 2 = 5. It's too dark. It doesn't speak to the human spirit anymore."

Like the Appendix Theory, the case of the missing five reveals a powerful desire to believe that Winston's story isn't as dismal as it seems and that Orwell was holding out a scintilla of hope for attentive readers: the "spirit of Man" endures after all. Personally, I don't think the book is devoid of hope. Inspired by each other's company, a coward and a cynic become heroic to the point of risking everything, and Winston is ultimately destroyed only because an immensely powerful man makes it his full-time job to destroy him. Remember, too, that O'Brien's crowing about the immortality of Ingsoc and the impossibility of resistance is not to be taken at face value. But I think that the force of Orwell's warning depends on the reader *feeling* that, for Winston and Julia in 1984, it is already too late, so as to be reminded that, in the real world, there is still time.

Since day one, hostile critics of *Nineteen Eighty-Four* have accused Orwell of giving up on humanity: the future will be dreadful, and you can't do anything about it. But nothing in Orwell's life and work supports a diagnosis of despair. On the contrary, aside from the brief wobble of "Inside the Whale," he consistently used his "power of facing unpleasant facts" to inspire greater awareness, including self-awareness, so as to root out the lies and fallacies that plague political life and threaten freedom. He would not have gone to such ruinous lengths to write *Nineteen Eighty-Four* if he only wanted to inform his readers that they were doomed. He wanted to galvanise, not paralyse, as Philip Rahv of *Partisan Review* emphasised in his 1949 review: "To read this novel simply as a flat prediction of what is to come is to misread it. It is not a writ of fatalism to bind our wills . . . His intention is, rather, to prod the Western world into a more conscious and militant resistance to the totalitarian virus to which it is now exposed." In other words: the future *might* be dreadful *unless* you do something about it.

The seventieth anniversary of *Nineteen Eighty-Four* falls at a dark time for liberal democracy, no doubt. Yet around the world, millions of people in the "reality-based community" continue to push back against the Medium-Sized Lie, to reaffirm that facts matter, to fight for the preservation of honesty and integrity, and to insist on the freedom to say that two and two make four. For them, the book still has much to offer. Because Orwell was more interested in psychology than in systems, *Nineteen Eighty-Four* is a durable compendium of everything he ever learned about human nature as it relates to politics—every cognitive bias, unexamined prejudice, moral compromise, trick of language and mechanism of power that enables injustice to gain the upper hand—and remains an unbeatable guide to what to watch out for. Orwell was writing for his own time but also, like Winston, "for the future, for the unborn." As he wrote in his preface to *Animal Farm,* liberal values "are not indestructible, and they have to be kept alive partly by conscious effort."

Nineteen Eighty-Four was Orwell's final, essential contribution to that collective effort. In the statement he dictated to Fredric Warburg from his bed in Cranham sanatorium during his final months, he explained the fundamental reason why he wrote it: not to bind our wills but to strengthen them. "The moral to be drawn from this dangerous nightmare situation is a simple one. *Don't let it happen. It depends on you.*"

ACKNOWLEDGEMENTS

"Writing a book is a horrible, exhausting struggle, like a long bout of some painful illness," George Orwell claimed in "Why I Write." At the risk of disappointing him, I have to say that writing this book was one of the most rewarding and enjoyable experiences of my life. That was largely due to the feeling that I was not alone.

My agents Antony Topping and Zoë Pagnamenta believed in me and my idea when I was at a low ebb. Without their hard work, encouragement and advice, this book would not exist. My editors, Gerald Howard at Doubleday and Ravi Mirchandani at Picador, understood from the start exactly what I was trying to do; their wise counsel and good humour enabled me to do it. I am also grateful to their colleagues, notably Alisa Ahmed, Imogen Morrell and Kate Rizzo at Greene & Heaton; Jillian Briglia, Keith Goldsmith, Nora Grubb and Emma Joss at Doubleday; and Ansa Khan Khattak and Paul Martinovic at Picador. Thanks to David Pearson and Michael Windsor for their striking jacket designs, Linda Huang for the paperback cover design, Amy Stackhouse for her rigorous copyediting, and Alexandra Dao for my first proper author photograph in too many years.

Dan Jolin, Lucy Jolin, John Mullen, Alexis Petridis, Padraig Reidy and Jude Rogers all read early drafts of various chapters (every single one in Lucy's case) and gave me invaluable feedback. I discussed the idea with Dan before I'd written a word of the proposal and he helped me turn something sprawling and incoherent into a focused project. Countless friends encouraged me during the writing of this book, giving me the vital conviction that it would be something that people wanted to read. Every thoughtful question or enthusiastic Facebook comment helped. Particular thanks to Joshua Blackburn, Matt Blackden, Jude Clarke, Sarah Ditum, Sarah Donaldson, Tom Doyle, Ian Dunt, Paul Hewson, Caitlin Moran, Brídín Murphy Mitchell, Richard Niland, Hugo Rifkind, my mother, Tola, and my sister, Tammy.

I'm enormously grateful to Robert Icke, Duncan Macmillan and Michael Radford for taking the time to sit down with me to discuss their adaptations of *Nineteen Eighty-Four* and their personal theories about the book. Emma Pritchard at the Almeida Theatre and Alice Phipps at United Agents facilitated those interviews. Helen Lewis kindly introduced me to Robert. Tony Zanetta, Chris O'Leary and Paul Trynka answered my questions about David Bowie's relationship with *Nineteen Eighty-Four*. Susie Boyt generously offered to show me unpublished letters that Orwell had written to her father-in-law, David Astor. Michaelangelo Matos shared Orwell-related research from his forthcoming book about music in the year 1984, which I can't wait to read. Ewan Pearson sent me an elusive piece of source material. John Niven wisely advised me to ditch the working title, and it only took me a year to follow his advice. I hope he likes the new one.

As a freelance journalist, I relied on my editors to give me time off from my regular commitments and to hold the door open for when I was ready to return. I'm very grateful to Ted Kessler, Niall Doherty and Chris Catchpole at *Q;* Bill Prince at *GQ;* Helen Lewis at *The New Statesman;* Nick de Semlyen at *Empire;* Rob Fearn, Laura Snapes and all my editors at *The Guardian;* and Andrew Harrison and my colleagues on the Remainiacs podcast. Thanks also to Remainiacs listeners for putting up with an unreasonable number of Orwell references. What can I say? The man got into my head.

So, too, did some of the people who have written about Orwell. I've never met any of them but I enjoyed spending time in their company, in a manner of speaking, especially Robert Colls, Peter Davison, Jeffrey Meyers, John Rodden, William Steinhoff, D. J. Taylor and the late Bernard Crick. I am indebted to their scholarship. I am also grateful to the staff of the Orwell Archive at University College London and of the British Library, where the vast majority of this book was researched and written. After the National Health Service,

I consider the BL to be Britain's most cherishable public institution. Writing a book whose central theme is the importance of objective truth sharpened my appreciation of all the journalists, scholars and fact-checkers who endeavour to get the facts straight in an era when lies, hoaxes, rumours and errors proliferate. Their ranks include the editors and contributors of Wikipedia and Snopes, tireless online communities which renew my faith in people's determination to see things as they are.

Nobody has done more to ensure that this book was not a horrible, exhausting struggle than Lucy Aitken, who has been with me every step of the way, from the first inkling to the final edit. In addition to reading drafts of several chapters, and bringing her deep knowledge of the advertising industry to the section about Apple's "1984" commercial, she offered endless encouragement, curiosity and love. It is to her, and our daughters Eleanor and Rosa, that this book is dedicated. May we all live to see better times.

A PRÉCIS OF
NINETEEN EIGHTY-FOUR

PART ONE

CHAPTER 1

It is a bright cold day in April and the clocks are striking thirteen. Winston Smith, thirty-nine, goes home to his apartment in Victory Mansions, London, Airstrip One, Oceania, to begin a secret diary. This is a dangerous endeavour in a one-party state where the Thought Police, spy helicopters and two-way telescreens create a culture of constant surveillance. The ubiquitous posters of Oceania's mysterious leader read: "BIG BROTHER IS WATCHING YOU." Winston manufactures propaganda in the Records Department of the Ministry of Truth, a towering white building emblazoned with the slogans of the Party: "WAR IS PEACE / FREEDOM IS SLAVERY / IGNORANCE IS STRENGTH." The Ministries of Love, Peace and Plenty have similarly ironic names. Winston has been inspired to start the diary by that morning's Two Minutes Hate, a ritual directed at Emmanuel Goldstein, the alleged traitor, author of a book of heresies, and leader of the underground resistance movement known as the Brotherhood. During the ritual, Winston fixated on two people who felt significant: a charismatic official from Ingsoc's Inner Party called O'Brien and a dark-haired young woman who works for the fiction department and may be a spy for the Thought Police. The memory spurs him to write "DOWN WITH BIG BROTHER." From that moment, Winston knows he is doomed.

CHAPTER 2

The wife of Winston's neighbour and Records Department colleague Parsons asks him to help her unblock her kitchen sink. The Parsons' children are Spies, encouraged by the Party to report anyone, even their own parents, whom they suspect of *thoughtcrime*. While working on the sink, Winston remembers a dream seven years earlier in which O'Brien promised to meet him in the place where there is no darkness. Back in his apartment, he dedicates his diary to the future and the past.

CHAPTER 3

Winston dreams of his mother and sister, who disappeared during the 1950s, and feels immense guilt, though he can't say why. The dream shifts to the dark-haired girl, removing her clothes in a rural paradise he calls the Golden Country. While performing compulsory physical exercises in front of the telescreen, Winston's mind wanders to the way the Party rewrites history: "Who controls the past controls the future: who controls the present controls the past." It cannot be publicly admitted, for instance, that Oceania was once at war with Eastasia and not Eurasia. This is an example of *doublethink,* the mental habit of believing two contradictory things at the same time, as the Party demands. Winston cannot trust his own memories.

CHAPTER 4

Winston goes back to work at the Ministry of Truth, where he amends back copies of the *Times* to reflect the latest party line, incinerating previous versions in the *memory hole.* He studies his colleagues: a small, nervous man called Tillotson and an absent-minded poet called Ampleforth. He rewrites a recent speech by Big Brother to eliminate Withers, a war hero who has since been purged and rendered an *unperson,* and replace him with Comrade Ogilvy, who is his own invention. When he is finished, Ogilvy exists and Withers does not.

CHAPTER 5

Winston has lunch in the canteen with the servile drudge Parsons and the philologist Syme, who rhapsodises about the advance of Newspeak: a condensed vocabulary designed to restrict thought. Winston sees the dark-haired girl again and still suspects her of being a Party spy.

CHAPTER 6

Winston recalls his brief, unhappy marriage to the Party loyalist Katharine a decade earlier, and a visit to a prostitute three years ago. The memories make him consider the suppression of sexual desire in Oceania.

CHAPTER 7

Winston ponders the status of the proles and the destruction of history. He remembers seeing the alleged traitors Jones, Aaronson and Rutherford in the Chestnut Tree Café and, years later, finding a photograph that proved their innocence, though he immediately destroyed it. He vows to cling onto his own sanity and belief in objective truth, exemplified by the equation $2 + 2 = 4$.

CHAPTER 8

Defying the prohibition against individualism, or *ownlife*, Winston ventures into the prole district, where he unsuccessfully questions a confused old man about life before Ingsoc. He visits the junkshop where he bought his diary and purchases a coral paperweight. The owner, Mr. Charrington, tells him about an old song called "Oranges and Lemons." On the way home, Winston sees the dark-haired girl again. He thinks about his inevitable torture and death.

PART TWO

CHAPTER 1

The dark-haired girl passes Winston a note saying "I love you." They agree to meet in Victory Square during a display of Eurasian prisoners, where they arrange a rendezvous in the countryside west of London.

CHAPTER 2

Winston meets the dark-haired girl in fields which are almost identical to the Golden Country of his dreams. Introducing herself as Julia, she reveals that she, too, hates the Party. They make love among the bluebells.

CHAPTER 3

May. As Winston and Julia's secret affair develops, he learns more about her private, apolitical rebellion against the Party. "We are the dead," he tells her.

CHAPTER 4

Winston rents the room above Charrington's shop as a love nest. From the window he hears a prole woman singing a song manufactured by the Music Department. It is improbably potent.

CHAPTER 5

June. Syme disappears. Preparations for Hate Week accelerate. Winston and Julia compare world views.

CHAPTER 6

O'Brien invites Winston to visit his home and collect a copy of the latest Newspeak dictionary.

CHAPTER 7

In a dream Winston remembers betraying his mother and sister over a piece of chocolate on the day they disappeared. The dream reminds him that the proles, unlike Party members, have stayed human. Winston and Julia vow that they will never betray each other.

CHAPTER 8

Winston and Julia visit O'Brien's apartment and ask to join Goldstein's Brotherhood. Attended by his manservant Martin, O'Brien makes them pledge to make enormous sacrifices and commit terrible crimes in the name of the Brotherhood. He arranges for Winston to receive a copy of Goldstein's book, which explains the true nature of Ingsoc. The two men swap lines from "Oranges and Lemons."

CHAPTER 9

August. Just as Hate Week reaches its climax, it is declared that Oceania is in fact at war with Eastasia: Oceania has always been at war with Eastasia. At the rally, Winston receives Goldstein's book, *The Theory and Practice of Oligarchical Collectivism.* In bed with Julia, he reads the best part of two chapters, which explain the reason for continual war, the similarity between the three super-states, the structure of the Party and the operation of doublethink. He stops reading at a crucial point because Julia has fallen asleep.

CHAPTER 10

Winston awakes with the conviction that the future belongs to the proles. His optimism is destroyed when a metallic voice from a concealed telescreen announces that he and Julia are under arrest. Mr. Charrington reveals himself to be a member of the Thought Police. The paperweight shatters.

PART THREE

CHAPTER 1

Winston wakes up in a windowless white cell in the Ministry of Love. His cellmates include Parsons (who has been reported by his own daughter), Ampleforth and an old woman who might be his mother. Some of the prisoners are taken to a place called Room 101. O'Brien arrives and reveals that he has been working for the Party all along.

CHAPTER 2

Winston is tortured for weeks and confesses to numerous imaginary crimes. One day he is strapped to a bed and interrogated by O'Brien, receiving an electric shock every time he gives the wrong answer. O'Brien tells him that he is insane and must be cured before he is killed.

CHAPTER 3

The interrogation continues. O'Brien claims that he and fellow members of the Inner Party co-authored the book credited to Goldstein. He explains that the motive of the Party is pure power, which must be demonstrated by constant terror and control over reality. When Winston protests that the spirit of humanity will prevail, O'Brien forces him to look in the mirror and confront his physical ruination. He is broken, as he predicted, except in one respect: he has not betrayed Julia, although O'Brien claims that she has betrayed him.

CHAPTER 4

Weeks or months have passed. Winston feels much better now that he has succumbed to doublethink and the wisdom of the Party. But he still loves Julia and he still, to his surprise, hates Big Brother. O'Brien tells him he must go to Room 101.

CHAPTER 5

Room 101 contains the worst, most unendurable thing in the world. For Winston, that is a rat. Threatened with hungry rats tearing at his face, he betrays Julia. He is utterly defeated.

CHAPTER 6

Winston is drunk and alone in the Chestnut Tree Café, waiting for the news. Oceania is at war with Eurasia: Oceania has always been at war with Eurasia. He recalls meeting Julia in the park, similarly crushed. They felt nothing for each other. He remembers his mother and sister for the last time. News of military victory in Africa fills him with joy, as does the thought of his execution. He loves Big Brother.

APPENDIX: THE PRINCIPLES OF NEWSPEAK

A scholarly explanation of Newspeak, looking back at the events of 1984. The date and author of the appendix are not supplied.

NOTES

EPIGRAPH

ix   "It's a sad commentary on our age"—Margaret Atwood, "Writing Utopia," *Curious Pursuits: Occasional Writing 1970–2005* (Virago, 2005), p. 89.

ix   "There was truth and there was untruth"—George Orwell, *The Complete Works of George Orwell IX: Nineteen Eighty-Four* (Secker & Warburg, 1997), p. 226. All twenty books in the *Complete Works* series are edited by Peter Davison, assisted by Ian Angus and Sheila Davison.

INTRODUCTION

xiii   "largest audience to ever"—White House press conference, January 21, 2017.

xiii   "alternative facts"—*Meet the Press*, NBC, January 22, 2017.

xiii   "an apocalyptical codex"—Anthony Burgess, *1985* (Arrow, 1980), p. 51.

xiv   "for a novel that is not designed"—Fredric Warburg, *All Authors Are Equal: The Publishing Life of Fredric Warburg 1936–1971* (Hutchinson & Co., 1973), p. 115.

xvi   "Orwell was successful"—Richard Rorty, *Contingency, Irony, and Solidarity* (Cambridge University Press, 1989), p. 170.

xvi   "free intelligence"—"Charles Dickens," March 11, 1940, *The Complete Works of George Orwell XII: A Patriot After All 1940–1941* (Secker & Warburg, 2000), 597, p. 56.

xvii   "something shone through"—*Arena: George Orwell* (BBC, 1983–84).

xvii   "forced into becoming a pamphleteer"—Orwell, "Why I Write," *Gangrel*, no. 4, Summer 1946, *The Complete Works of George Orwell XVII: I Belong to the Left 1945* (Secker & Warburg, 2001), 3007, p. 319.

xvii   "It matters not what you think"—Christopher Hitchens, *Why Orwell Matters* (Basic Books, 2002), p. 211.

xvii   "old maids bicycling"—John Major, speech to Conservative Group for Europe, April 22, 1993.

xviii   "political thought disguised as a novel"—Milan Kundera, *Testaments Betrayed*, trans. Linda Asher (Faber & Faber, 1995), p. 224.

xviii   Bookshop shelves began filling up—see David Runciman, *How Democracy Ends*

(Profile, 2018); Madeleine Albright, *Fascism: A Warning* (William Collins, 2018); Timothy Snyder, *The Road to Unfreedom: Russia, Europe, America* (Bodley Head, 2018); Michiko Kakutani, *The Death of Truth* (William Collins, 2018).

xix "a nonfiction bookend"—Hannah Arendt, *The Origins of Totalitarianism* (Penguin, 2017).

xix "I was asleep before"—*The Handmaid's Tale* (Hulu, 2017).

xix "If you pretend"—Orwell, *The Complete Works of George Orwell V: The Road to Wigan Pier* (Secker & Warburg, 1997), p. 199.

xix "For me it's like a Greek myth"—Author interview with Michael Radford, London, August 9, 2018.

xix "It's a mirror"—Robert Icke and Duncan Macmillan, *1984* (Oberon Books, 2013), p. 21.

xix "Every time I read it"—Backlisted podcast, August 20, 2018.

PART ONE

CHAPTER 1: HISTORY STOPPED

3 "We are living in a world"—Orwell, *CW V*, p. 158.

3 "I'm going to Spain"—Bernard Crick, *George Orwell: A Life* (Penguin, 1982), p. 312.

4 "History stopped in 1936"—Orwell, "Looking Back on the Spanish War," *The Complete Works of George Orwell XIII: All Propaganda Is Lies 1941–1942* (Secker & Warburg, 2001), 1421, p. 503.

4 "Until I was about thirty" and "simply as a gruff-voiced elderly man"—Orwell, "Such, Such Were the Joys," *The Complete Works of George Orwell XIX: It Is What I Think 1947–1948* (Secker & Warburg, 2002), 3409, p. 379.

4 "lower-upper-middle-class"—Orwell, *CW V*, p. 113.

4 "odious little snob" and "Your snobbishness"—Ibid., p. 128.

5 "Failure, failure, failure"—"Such, Such Were the Joys," *CW XIX*, 3409, p. 382.

5 "I was educated at Eton"—Orwell letter to Stanley J. Kunitz and Howard Haycraft, April 17, 1940, *The Complete Works of George Orwell XI: Facing Unpleasant Facts 1937–1939* (Secker & Warburg, 2000), 613, p. 147.

5 "a boy with a permanent chip"—John Wilkes, quoted in Steven Wadhams, *Remembering Orwell* (Penguin, 1984), p. 11.

5 "he was more sardonic"—Christopher Eastwood, quoted in Wadhams, p. 17.

5 "In order to hate imperialism"—Orwell, *CW V*, p. 134.

5 "sentimental nonsense"—Ibid., p. 137.

5 "an immense weight of guilt"—Ibid., p. 138.

6 "How can you write about the poor"—Jack Branthwaite, quoted in Wadhams, p. 84.

6 "in the process of rearranging himself"—Crick, p. 221.

6 "no interest in Socialism"—Orwell, *CW V*, p. 139.

6 "It is a sort of world-within-a-world"—Ibid., p. 144.

6 "as a kind of penance"—Richard Rees, *George Orwell: Fugitive from the Camp of Victory* (Secker & Warburg, 1961), p. 29.

6 "shabby-genteel"—Orwell, *CW V*, p. 115.

6 "not thirty yet"—Orwell, *The Complete Works of George Orwell IV: Keep the Aspidistra Flying* (Secker & Warburg, 1997), p. 4.

7 "She knew well enough"—Orwell, *CW V*, p. 15.

7 "facecrime"—Orwell, *CW IX*, p. 65.

7 "a boot stamping"—Ibid., p. 280.

7 "I am afraid I have made"—Orwell letter to Jack Common, October 5, 1936, *The Complete Works of George Orwell X: A Kind of Compulsion 1903–36* (Secker & Warburg, 2000), 327, p. 507.

7 "hate, fear and despise"—Orwell, *CW V*, p. 127.

7 "drives away the very people"—Ibid., p. 159.

8 "aeroplanes, tractors"—Ibid., p. 201.

8 "left-wingers of all complexions"—Ibid., p. 205.

8 "admirable propaganda"—H. J. Laski, *Left News*, March 1937, reprinted in Jeffrey Meyers (ed.), *George Orwell: The Critical Heritage* (Routledge & Kegan Paul, 1975), p. 104.

8 "The truth is"—Victor Gollancz, preface to Left Book Club edition of *The Road to Wigan Pier*, *CW V*, p. 221.

8 "gut socialist"—Wadhams, p. 95.

8 "nothing else can save us"—Orwell, *CW V*, p. 204.

9 "smells of crankishness"—Ibid., p. 201.

9 "began to realize"—Rees, p. 146.

9 "The Spanish Civil War"—Antony Beevor, *The Battle for Spain: The Spanish Civil War 1936–1939* (Weidenfeld & Nicolson, 2006), p. 267.

10 "common decency," "a plague of initials" and "I was not only uninterested"— Orwell, *The Complete Works of George Orwell VI: Homage to Catalonia* (Secker & Warburg, 1997), p. 188.

11 "a world where lost and lonely people"—Jason Gurney, quoted in Beevor, p. 178.

11 Up to 35,000 men—see Beevor, p. 177.

11 "It was in part an anarchist's war"—Richard Crossman (ed.), *The God That Failed: Six Studies in Communism* (Hamish Hamilton, 1950), p. 245.

11 "it seemed certain"—Malcolm Muggeridge, *The Thirties: 1930–1940 in Great Britain* (Hamish Hamilton, 1940), p. 249.

11 "Though he was a wonderful chap"—*Paris Review*, no. 28, Summer-Fall 1962.

11 "It was overwhelming"—Franz Borkenau, *The Spanish Cockpit* (Faber & Faber, 1937), p. 69.

11 "It is as if the masses"—Cyril Connolly, *The Condemned Playground: Essays: 1927–1944* (Routledge, 1945), p. 186.

12 "I have come to Spain"—Crick, p. 317.

12 "a bad copy of 1914–18"—Orwell, "My Country Right or Left," *Folios of New Writing*, no. 2, Autumn 1940, *CW XII*, 694, p. 271.

12 "firewood, food, tobacco"—Orwell, *CW VI*, p. 22.

12 "Nothing ever happened"—Ibid., p. 47, and *CW IV*, p. 41.

12 "This is not a war"—Ibid., p. 32.

12 "breathed the air of equality"—Ibid., p. 83.

12 "not less but more"—Ibid., p. 186.

13 "She caught George's dreams"—T. R. Fyvel, *George Orwell: A Personal Memoir* (Weidenfeld & Nicolson, 1982), p. 136.

13 "Come on, you bastards!"—D. J. Taylor, *Orwell: The Life* (Vintage, 2004), p. 214.

13 "visibly a fellow creature"—"Looking Back on the Spanish War," *CW XIII*, 1421, p. 501.

13 so alarmed by a rat—see Bob Edwards's account in Coppard and Crick, p. 147.

13 "If there is one thing"—Orwell, *CW VI*, p. 59.

13 "The political side of the war"—Ibid., p. 200.

14 "She was the first person"—Rees, p. 147.

14 "It is an atmosphere"—Borkenau, p. 241.

14 "liked by nobody"—Ibid., p. 182.

14 "A Trotskyist"—Ibid., p. 240.

14 "It goes without saying"—Beevor, p. 226.

14 "an unmistakable and horrible feeling"—Orwell, *CW VI*, p. 97.

14 "a furtive, gutted look"—John Dos Passos, *The Theme Is Freedom* (Dodd, Mead & Company, 1956), p. 141.

14 "to be talking to an honest man"—Ibid., p. 145.

15 "The match that fired"—Orwell, *CW VI*, p. 225.

15 "It was the first time"—Ibid., p. 121.

15 "Tear the mask"—Ibid., p. 126.

15 "To hear what was said"—Orwell, *The Complete Works of George Orwell II: Burmese Days* (Secker & Warburg, 1997), p. 140.

15 "The only broadcasting service"—Taylor, p. 205.

16 "One of the dreariest effects"—Orwell, *CW VI*, p. 208.

16 "I hope I shall get the chance"—Orwell letter to Victor Gollancz, May 9, 1937, in *CW XI*, 368, p. 23.

16 "almost a mental disease"—Beevor, p. 271.

16 "This was simply"—Crossman (ed.), p. 253.

16 "I gradually acquired"—Ibid., p. 254.

17 "They couldn't hit a bull"—Wadhams, p. 90.

17 "a violent resentment"—Orwell, *CW VI*, p. 139.

17 "Get out"—Taylor, p. 230.

17 "the best of the bunch"—Orwell, *CW VI*, p. 39.

17 "his face was no more"—Robert Conquest, *The Great Terror: A Reassessment* (Pimlico, 2008), p. 410.

18 "nightmare atmosphere"—Orwell, *CW VI*, p. 151.

18 "however little you were actually conspiring"—Ibid., p. 148.

18 "pronounced Trotskyists"—David Caute, *Politics and the Novel During the Cold War* (Transaction, 2010), p. 47.

18 "It was a queer business"—Orwell letter to Rayner Heppenstall, July 31, 1937, *CW XI*, 381, p. 53.

18 "It was about the only time"—Wadhams, p. 96.

18 "He said he used to take"—Ibid., p. 93.

18 "Almost every journalist"—Quoted in Paul Preston, *We Saw Spain Die* (Constable, 2008), p. 15.

18 "The Spanish War and other events"—Orwell, "Why I Write," *CW XVIII*, 3007, p. 319.

19 "There has been a quite deliberate conspiracy"—Orwell, "Spilling the Spanish Beans," *New English Weekly*, July 29 and September 2, 1937, *CW XI*, 378, p. 46.

19 "there can be no argument"—Orwell, *CW VI*, p. 248.

19 "I found myself feeling very strongly"—Orwell, "As I Please," *Tribune*, February 4, 1944, *The Complete Works of George Orwell XVI: I Have Tried to Tell the Truth 1943–1944* (Secker & Warburg, 2001), 2416, p. 88.

20 "It was my purpose"—Warburg, p. 9.

20 "It shows us the heart"—Quoted in Miriam Gross (ed.), *The World of George Orwell* (Weidenfeld & Nicolson, 1971), p. 144.

20 "I warn everyone"—Orwell, *CW VI*, p. 227.

20 "If I had not been angry"—Orwell, "Why I Write," *CW XVIII*, 3007, p. 320.

21 "To me your book"—Quoted in Crick, p. 363.

21 "It is a most encouraging thing"—Orwell, Review of *The Communist International* by Franz Borkenau, *New English Weekly*, September 22, 1938, *CW XI*, 485, p. 204.

21 "Civilisation is bound to perish"—Borkenau, p. 257.

21 "continued to proclaim"—Wadhams, p. 42.

22 "literature of disillusionment"—Orwell, "Arthur Koestler," *Tribune*, September 11, 1944, *CW XVI*, 2548, p. 393.

22 "is one of those men"—Orwell, Review of *The Mysterious Mr. Bull* by Wyndham Lewis and *The School for Dictators* by Ignazio Silone, *New English Weekly*, June 8, 1939, in *CW XI*, 547, p. 355.

22 "a form of Socialism"—Orwell, "Inside the Whale," *CW XII*, 600, p. 102.

22 "a mechanism for explaining"—Orwell, Review of *The Civil War in Spain* by Frank Jellinek, *The New Leader*, July 8, 1938, in *CW XI*, 462, p. 174.

23 "his speech though delivered"—Orwell diary entry, March 16, 1936, in *CW X*, 294, p. 456.

23 "Mosley will bear watching"—Orwell, *CW V*, p. 197.

23 "had an almost irresistible fascination"—Orwell, "Inside the Whale," *CW XII*, 600, p. 101.

23 "tolerated and even defended"—Orwell, *CW IX*, p. 213.

23 "The formula 2 + 2 = 5"—Eugene Lyons, *Assignment in Utopia* (George G. Harrap & Co., Ltd., 1938), p. 240.

24 "The peculiar horror"—Orwell, Review of *Power: A New Social Analysis* by Bertrand Russell, *The Adelphi*, January 1939, in *CW XI*, 520, pp. 311–12.

24 "I was guilty"—Lyons, p. 628.

24 "So many weary"—Ibid., p. 635.

CHAPTER 2: UTOPIA FEVER

25 "What fun it must have been"—Orwell, Review of *My Life: The Autobiography of Havelock Ellis, Adelphi,* May 1940, *CW XII,* 617, p. 155.

25 "A map of the world"—Oscar Wilde, *The Soul of Man* (privately printed, 1895), p. 43.

25 "permanent happiness"—Orwell (as "John Freeman"), "Can Socialists be Happy?," *Tribune,* December 24, 1943, *CW XVI,* 2397, p. 39.

25 "some central-heated"—Ibid., p. 42.

25 "Whoever tries to imagine"—Ibid., p. 43.

26 "Happiness is notoriously"—Orwell, "Politics vs Literature: An Examination of *Gulliver's Travels*," *Polemic,* no. 5, September-October 1946, *CW XVIII,* 3089, p. 427.

26 "some dismal Marxist Utopia"—Orwell, *The Complete Works of George Orwell I: Down and Out in Paris and London* (Secker & Warburg, 1997), p. 121.

26 "On the whole"—Orwell, "The Art of Donald McGill," *Horizon,* September 1941, *CW XIII,* 850, p. 30.

27 "quiet, yet observant"—Frances Elizabeth Willard, "An Interview with Edward Bellamy," *Our Day,* vol. 4, no. 24, December 1889.

27 "nervous, dyspeptic"—Sylvia E. Bowman, *Edward Bellamy* (Twayne Publishers, 1986), p. 62.

27 "Let us bear in mind"—Edward Bellamy, "Letter to the People's Party," *The New Nation,* October 22, 1892, quoted in Kenneth M. Roemer, *The Obsolete Necessity: America in Utopian Writings 1888–1900* (Kent State University Press, 1976), p. 21.

27 "I am particularly desirous"—Quoted in Bellamy, p. xxxi.

27 "debated by all"—Quoted in Franklin Rosemont, "Bellamy's Radicalism Reclaimed," in Daphne Patai, ed., *Looking Backward, 1988–1888* (University of Massachusetts Press, 1988), p. 158.

27 "I suppose you have seen or read"—Fiona MacCarthy, *William Morris: A Life for Our Time* (Faber & Faber, 1994), p. 584.

28 "an exceedingly remarkable book"—Leo Tolstoy, diary entry, June 30, 1889.

28 "the latest and best"—J. R. LeMaster and James D. Wilson (eds.), *The Mark Twain Encyclopaedia* (Garland Publishing, Inc., 1993), p. 69.

28 "Bellamy is the Moses of today"—Jean Pfaelzer, *The Utopian Novel in America, 1886–1896* (University of Pittsburgh Press, 1984), p. 48.

28 "a child of the Bellamy ideal"—John Bew, *Citizen Clem: A Biography of Attlee* (Riverrun, 2017), p. 390.

28 "Bellamy's *Looking Backward* in reverse"—Harry Scherman, quoted in Eugene Reynal letter to J. Edgar Hoover, April 22, 1949.

29 "the solidarity of the race"—Edward Bellamy, *Looking Backward 2000–1887* (Oxford University Press, 2007), p. 78.

29 "with some impatience"—Edward Bellamy, "How I Came to Write *Looking Backward*," *The Nationalist*, May 1889.

29 "the sober and morally-minded"—Pfaelzer, p. 44.

29 "You have taken on an impossible task"—Quoted in Adam Roberts, *The History of Science Fiction* (Palgrave Macmillan, 2006), p. 132.

29 "a cloud palace," "stumbled over"—Bellamy, "How I Came to Write *Looking Backward*."

29 "intended, in all seriousness"—Bellamy, *Looking Backward*, p. 195.

29 "the logical outcome"—Bellamy, p. 68.

30 "all Socialist thought"—Orwell, "What Is Socialism?," January 31, 1946, *CW XIII*, 2876, p. 60.

30 "the hygiene, the labour-saving devices"—Orwell, Review of *An Unknown Land* by Viscount Samuel, *The Listener*, December 24, 1942, *The Complete Works of George Orwell XIV: Keeping Our Little Corner Clean 1942–1943* (Secker & Warburg, 2001), 1768, p. 254.

30 "festering mass"—Bellamy, *Looking Backward*, p. 189.

31 "The only safe way"—William Morris, *Commonweal*, vol. 5, no. 80, June 22, 1889.

31 "deep-seated aversion"—Quoted in Milton Cantor, "The Backward Look of Bellamy's Socialism," Patai (ed.), p. 21.

31 "saw the world with new eyes"—Bowman, p. 4.

31 "the inferno of poverty"—Pfaelzer, p. 46.

31 "some plan"—Bowman, p. 6.

31 "Hard to live"—Ibid., p. 8.

32 "an impending social cataclysm"—Bellamy, *Looking Backward*, p. 11.

32 "When I came to consider"—Quoted in Cantor, Patai (ed.), p. 33.

33 "In the radicalness of the opinions"—Edward Bellamy letter to William Dean Howells, June 17, 1888, quoted in Pfaelzer, p. 43.

33 "the followers of the red flag"—Bellamy, *Looking Backward*, p. 148.

33 "a hideous, ghastly mistake"—Ibid., p. 191.

33 "the belief that the truth"—Orwell, "Writers and Leviathan," *Politics and Letters*, Summer 1948, *CW XIX*, 3364, p. 289.

34 "A vast conspiracy"—Pfaelzer, p. 121.

34 "not only aroused"—Quoted in Rosemont, Patai (ed.), pp. 162–63.

34 "Edwardina"—Quoted in Pfaelzer, p. 36.

35 "the obvious, necessary"—Edward Bellamy, *Equality* (William Heinemann, 1897), p. 14.

35 "What a pity"—Quoted in Rosemont, Patai (ed.), p. 191.

35   "books on the twentieth"—*The Literary World,* July 19, 1890, quoted in Roemer, p. 7.

36   "The frontier has gone"—Frederick Jackson Turner, "The Significance of the Frontier in American History," 1893.

36   "a counterblast"—Quoted in Warren W. Wagar, "Dreams of Reason," in Patai (ed.), p. 113.

36   "cockney paradise"—MacCarthy, p. 584.

36   "a sort of goody-goody"—Orwell, "Can Socialists Be Happy?," *CW XVI,* 2397, p. 40.

37   "we should most of us be very unhappy"—C. R. Attlee, *The Social Worker* (G. Bell & Sons, Ltd., 1920), p. 141.

37   "Have they got it all right"—Jerome K. Jerome, "The New Utopia," *Diary of a Pilgrimage* (J. W. Arrowsmith, 1891), p. 265.

37   "one language, one law, one life"—Ibid., p. 276.

38   "Memory is the principle"—Edward Bellamy, *Dr. Heidenhoff's Process* (D. Appleton, 1880), quoted in Rosemont, Patai (ed.), p. 151.

38   "rending the veil of self"—Edward Bellamy, "To Whom This May Come" in *The Blindman's World and Other Stories* (Houghton Mifflin, 1898), quoted in Wagar, Patai (ed.), p. 112.

38   "Do you begin to see"—Orwell, *CW IX,* p. 279.

38   "rather painful reading"—Orwell, Review of *The Soul of Man Under Socialism* by Oscar Wilde, *Observer,* May 9, 1948, *CW XIX,* 3395, p. 333.

38   "may demand the impossible"—Ibid., p. 334.

CHAPTER 3: THE WORLD WE'RE GOING DOWN INTO

39   "The future, at any rate"—Orwell, Review of *Journey Through the War Mind* by C. E. M. Joad, *Time and Tide,* no. 8, 1940, *CW XII,* 635, pp. 178–79.

39   "As it is if I start in August"—Orwell letter to Jack Common, May 22, 1938, in *CW XI,* 443, p. 149.

39   "stop thinking"—Quoted in Crick, p. 367.

40   "We called him Marx"—Eileen Blair letter to Norah Myles, January 1, 1938, *The Lost Orwell,* compiled and annotated by Peter Davison (Timewell Press, 2006), p. 72.

40   "rather a dull country"—Orwell letter to John Sceats, November 24, 1938, *CW XI,* 504, p. 237.

40   "a thin disguise for jingo imperialism"—Orwell, Review of Lewis and Silone, June 8, 1939, *CW XI,* 547, p. 354.

40   "fascising"—Orwell letter to Herbert Read, March 5, 1939, in *CW XI,* 536, p. 340.

40   "that if Fascism wins"—E. M. Forster, *Two Cheers for Democracy* (Harcourt, Brace & Co., 1951), p. 23.

40   One of his favourite quotations—Orwell, Review of *The Tree of Gernika* by

G. L. Steer and *Spanish Testament* by Arthur Koestler, *Time and Tide,* February 5, 1938, *CW XI,* 421, p. 113.

40   "Fascism after all"—Orwell letter to Geoffrey Gorer, September 15, 1937, *CW XI,* 397, p. 80.

40   "Fascism and so-called democracy"—Orwell letter to Amy Charlesworth, August 30, 1937, *CW XI,* 393, p. 77.

40   He even planned—see Orwell letter to Herbert Read, January 4, 1939, *CW XI,* 522, p. 313.

41   "the future must be catastrophic"—Orwell, War-time Diary, June 8, 1940, *CW XII,* 637, p. 181.

41   "the feeling of futility"—Orwell, Review of *Personal Record 1928–1939* by Julian Green, *Time and Tide,* April 13, 1940, in *CW XII,* 611, p. 145.

41   "But the dugout"—Eileen Blair letter to Marjorie Dakin, September 27, 1938, *CW XI,* 487, p. 205.

41   "a stifling, stultifying world"—Orwell, *CW II,* p. 69.

41   "It is a corrupting thing"—Ibid., p. 70.

41   "Who spies with jealous, watchful care"—Orwell, *CW IV,* p. 168.

42   "money pricsthood"—Ibid., p. 46.

42   "thousand million slaves"—Ibid., p. 166.

42   "packs a world of lies"—Ibid., p. 58.

42   "Of course you are perfectly right"—Orwell letter to Julian Symons, May 10, 1948, *CW XIX,* 3397, p. 336.

42   "silly potboilers"—Orwell, Notes for My Literary Executor, March 31, 1945, *CW XVII,* 2648, p. 114.

42   "a revolutionary in love with 1910"—Cyril Connolly, *Horizon,* September 1945, reprinted in Meyers (ed.), p. 199.

43   "people then had something"—Orwell, *The Complete Works of George Orwell VII: Coming Up for Air* (Secker & Warburg, 1997), p. 109.

43   "as if I'd got X-rays"—Ibid., p. 26.

43   "The world we're going down into"—Ibid., p. 157.

43   "the things that you tell yourself"—Ibid., p. 238.

43   "It's a ghastly thing"—Ibid., p. 156.

43   "throw sulfuric acid"—Orwell, *CW IX,* p. 180.

44   "new kind of men"—Orwell, *CW VII,* pp. 168–69.

44   "She had not a thought"—Orwell, *CW IX,* p. 69.

44   "Celluloid, rubber"—Ibid., p. 24.

44   "I dislike big towns"—Orwell letter to Stanley J. Kunitz and Howard Haycraft, April 17, 1940, *CW XI,* 613, p. 148.

44   "Only a little while"—Orwell, *CW IV,* p. 258.

44   "We swim in it"—Orwell, *CW VII,* pp. 15–16.

45   "It was our thought"—*New York Times,* October 31, 1938.

45   "covering up the truth"—Quoted in Rich Heldenfels, " 'War of the Worlds' still vivid at 75," *Akron Beacon Journal,* October 26, 2013.

45 "The complexity of modern finance"—Hadley Cantril, *The Invasion From Mars* (Princeton University Press, 1940), p. 154.

46 "so many things we hear"—Ibid., p. 158.

46 "cannot tell lies"—Orwell, Review of *The Invasion From Mars* by Hadley Cantril, *New Statesman and Nation,* October 26, 1940, in *CW XII,* 702, p. 279.

46 "The nation as a whole"—Quoted in Jefferson Pooley and Michael J. Socolow, "The Myth of the *War of the Worlds* Panic," Slate, October 28, 2013.

46 "The evident connection"—Orwell, Review of *The Invasion From Mars, CW XII,* 702, p. 280.

46 "the perfect demonstration"—Quoted in Howard Koch, *The Panic Broadcast: Portrait of an Event* (Little, Brown & Company, 1970), p. 93.

46 "You are not going out of your mind"—Patrick Hamilton, *Gas Light* (Constable & Company, Ltd., 1939), p. 42.

46 "a lunatic asylum"—Orwell, *CW VI,* p. 152.

46 "mentally deranged"—Orwell, *CW IX,* p. 258.

47 "Am I really mad?"—Iulia de Beausobre, *The Woman Who Could Not Die* (Chatto & Windus, 1938), p. 85.

47 "the idea that I've got to abandon them"—Orwell letter to Jack Common, September 29, 1938, *CW XI,* 489, p. 212.

47 "the vulgar lie"—Orwell, Review of *The Novel To-Day* by Philip Henderson, *New English Weekly,* December 31, 1936, in *CW IX,* 342, p. 534.

47 "does not seem to be so very different"—Orwell, Review of *Assignment in Utopia* by Eugene Lyons, *New English Weekly,* June 9, 1938, in *CW XI,* 451, pp. 160–61.

48 "Everything within the state"—Benito Mussolini speech at La Scala, Milan, October 28, 1925.

48 "Brown Bolshevism"—Franz Borkenau, *The Totalitarian Enemy* (Faber & Faber, 1940), p. 13.

48 "simply the bludgeon"—John Strachey, *The Coming Struggle for Power* (Victor Gollancz Ltd., 1932), p. 266.

48 "The two regimes"—Orwell, Review of *The Totalitarian Enemy* by Franz Borkenau, *Time and Tide,* May 4, 1940, *CW XII,* 620, p. 159.

48 "The sin of nearly all leftwingers"—Orwell, "Arthur Koestler," *CW XVI,* 2548, p. 394.

48 "This book is subtitled"—Orwell, Review of *Franco's Rule* (anonymous), *New English Weekly,* June 23, 1938, in *CW XI,* 456, p. 167.

48 "Groping along darkened streets"—Muggeridge, pp. 316–17.

48 "bitched buggered and bewildered"—Ethel Mannin letter to Orwell, October 30, 1939, in *CW XI,* 575, p. 413.

49 "It taught me two things"—Orwell, "My Country Right or Left," *CW XII,* 694, p. 271.

49 "objectively pro-Fascist"—George Woodcock et al., "Pacifism and the War: A Controversy," *Partisan Review,* September-October 1942, *CW XIII,* 1270, p. 396.

49 "dishonest"—"As I Please," December 8, 1944, *CW XVI,* 2590, p. 495.

49 "The intellectuals who are at present"—Orwell letter to Victor Gollancz, January 8, 1940, *CW XII,* 583, p. 5.

49 "cold war"—Orwell, Review of *Arrival and Departure* by Arthur Koestler, December 9, 1943, *CW XVI,* 2389, p. 19.

49 "bored, bewildered"—Orwell, Review of *War Begins at Home,* ed. Tom Harrisson and Charles Madge, *Time and Tide,* March 2, 1940, *CW XII,* 594, p. 17.

49 "this bloody war"—Orwell letter to Geoffrey Gorer, January 10, 1940, *CW XII,* 585, p. 6.

49 "I find that anything outrageously strange"—Orwell, *CW V,* pp. 100–101.

50 "brilliant and depressing"—Orwell, "Notes on the Way," *Time and Tide,* April 6, 1940, *CW XII,* 604, p. 124.

50 "He is looking only on the black side"—Orwell, Review of *The Thirties* by Malcolm Muggeridge, *New English Weekly,* April 25, 1940, *CW XII,* 615, p. 150.

50 "With this craving for facts"—Muggeridge, p. 262.

50 "nihilistic quietism"—Orwell, "Words and Henry Miller," *Tribune,* February 22, 1946, *CW XVIII,* 2906, p. 118.

50 "labels, slogans" and "Good novels"—Orwell, "Inside the Whale," *CW XII,* 600, p. 105.

51 "moving into an age"—Ibid., p. 110.

51 "the literary history"—Ibid., p. 105.

51 "always on the side of the underdog"—Orwell, "Charles Dickens," *CW XII,* 597, p. 55.

51 "It is the face of a man"—Ibid., p. 56.

51 "I should doubt whether"—Ibid., p. 47.

51 "To be a lover of Dickens"—*The Dickensian,* vol. 36, no. 256, September 1, 1940, reprinted in *CW XII,* 627, p. 167.

52 For the next four years—see Wadhams, p. 130.

52 "Everything is disintegrating"—Orwell, War-time Diary, June 10, 1940, *CW XII,* 637, p. 182.

53 "We shall at any rate"—Orwell letter to James Laughlin, July 16, 1940, *CW XII,* 659, p. 219.

53 "ARM THE PEOPLE"—Orwell letter to the editor, *Time and Tide,* June 22, 1940, *CW XII,* 642, p. 193.

53 "an Ironside"—Warburg, p. 36.

53 "A Counter-Revolutionary Gangster Passes"—*Daily Worker,* August 23, 1940.

53 "How will the Russian state"—Orwell, War-time Diary, August 23, 1940, *CW XII,* 677, p. 241.

54 "cultural blue-prints"—*Tribune,* August 16, 1940, *CW XII,* 655, p. 213.

54 "I don't think anyone need fear"—Ibid., p. 214.

54 "Reality has outdone fiction"—H. G. Wells, *Experiment in Autobiography* (Gollancz, 1934), p. 501.

54 "I could imagine an English Fascism" and "The novel does not set

out"—Quoted in Andy Croft, *Red Letter Days: British Fiction in the 1930s* (Lawrence & Wishart, 1990), p. 230.

55   "a horrible brainless empire"—Orwell, Review of *Mein Kampf* by Adolf Hitler, *New English Weekly,* March 21, 1940, *CW XII,* 602, p. 117.

55   "year of the Lord Hitler 720"—Murray Constantine, *Swastika Night* (Gollancz, 2016), p. 11.

55   "We can create nothing"—Ibid., p. 121.

55   "would have no vitality"—Orwell, *CW IX,* p. 281.

56   "a little soft dark fat smiling thing"—Constantine, p. 100.

56   "There is not the whole width of the Empire"—Ibid., p. 80.

56   "remarkable in its insight"—Orwell, Review of *Take Back Your Freedom* by Winifred Holtby and Norman Ginsbury, *Time and Tide,* August 24, 1940, *CW XII,* 678, p. 243.

56   "Action. Isolation. Order."—Winifred Holtby and Norman Ginsbury, *Take Back Your Freedom* (Jonathan Cape, 1939), p. 27.

56   "a more gentlemanly Hitler"—Orwell, Review of *Take Back Your Freedom, CW XII,* 678, p. 242.

56   "We must have emotion"—Holtby and Ginsbury, p. 58.

56   "Many who had found thinking"—Muggeridge, p. 241.

56   "prisoner of power"—Orwell, Review of *Take Back Your Freedom, CW XII,* 678, p. 242.

57   "Is this true"—Holtby and Ginsbury, p. 71.

57   "felt enormously at home"—Cyril Connolly, *The Evening Colonnade* (David Bruce & Watson, 1973), p. 383.

57   "They'll behave like this" and "they preserved the ordinary pattern"—Orwell, "London Letter," *Partisan Review,* Summer 1945, *CW XVII,* 2672, p. 164.

57   "Please sir"—Orwell, War-time Diary, September 21, 1940, *CW XII,* 691, p. 267.

57   "Of course we were painting"—Inez Holden, *It Was Different at the Time* (John Lane, The Bodley Head, 1943), p. 69.

58   "How much rubbish"—Orwell, War-time Diary, June 14, 1940, *CW XII,* 637, p. 184.

58   "Apparently nothing"—Orwell, War-time Diary, June 3, 1940, *CW XII,* 632, p. 176.

58   "We cannot beat Hitler"—Orwell, "Our Opportunity," *The Left News,* no. 55, January 1941, *CW XII,* 737, p. 346.

58   "written in simple language"—Searchlight Books advertisement, quoted in Crick, p. 402.

58   "a land of snobbery and privilege"—Orwell, The Lion and the Unicorn (Searchlight Books, 1941), *CW XII,* 763, p. 400.

58   "bound together"—Ibid., p. 401.

58   "the *privateness* of English life"—Ibid., p. 394.

58   "the only really positive"—Wadhams, p. 120.

59   "George has written a little book"—Eileen Blair letter to Norah Myles, December 5, 1940, *The Lost Orwell,* p. 80.

59 "We are in a strange period of history"—Orwell, "The Home Guard and You," *Tribune,* December 20, 1940, *CW XII,* 725, p. 311.

59 "soft-boiled intellectuals"—Orwell, *The Lion and the Unicorn, CW XII,* 763, p. 427.

59 "Here was somebody"—*Arena: George Orwell.*

59 "The revolution in England"—Bew, p. 256.

59 "a querulous man who was ailing"—Fyvel, p. 121.

CHAPTER 4: WELLS-WORLD

60 "In the early twentieth century"—Orwell, *CW IX,* p. 196.

60 "I doubt whether"—Orwell, "Wells, Hitler and the World State," *Horizon,* August 1941, *CW XII,* 837, p. 539.

60 "fearful, moral, morbid questions"—*Arena: George Orwell.*

60 "he might write"—Jacintha Buddicom, *Eric and Us: A Remembrance of George Orwell* (Leslie Frewin, 1974), p. 39.

60 Orwell's very first published story—"A Peep into the Future," *Election Times,* no. 4, June 3, 1918, *CW X,* 32, pp. 48–50.

61 "so disappointed"—Buddicom, p. 15.

61 "I have to overwork"—H. G. Wells, *H. G. Wells in Love* (Faber & Faber, 1984), pp. 34–35.

61 "the Man Who Invented Tomorrow"—Norman and Jeannie Mackenzie, *The Time Traveller: The Life of H. G. Wells* (Weidenfeld & Nicolson, 1973), p. 400.

61 "this wonderful man"—Orwell, "Wells, Hitler and the World State," *CW XII,* 837, p. 540.

61 "a sort of parricide"—Ibid., p. 539.

61 "The Socialist world"—Orwell, *CW V,* p. 176.

61 "the 'progressives'"—Orwell, "Inside the Whale," *CW XII,* 600, p. 106.

62 "lies in that regard"—H. G. Wells, *A Modern Utopia* (Penguin, 2005), p. 13.

62 "vindictive resentment"—Wells, *Experiment in Autobiography,* p. 104.

62 "nothing more than"—Ibid., p. 102.

63 "I had done practically everything"—Ibid., p. 288.

63 "a match that man has just got alight"—Quoted in Mackenzie, p. 87.

63 "H. G. Wells is a man of genius"—Quoted in ibid., p. 108.

63 "When Wells in his lamp-lit room"—James Gleick, *Time Travel: A History* (4th Estate, 2017), p. 5.

63 "the first well-executed"—Mark Hillegas, *The Future As Nightmare: HG Wells and the Anti-utopians* (Oxford University Press, 1967), p. 34.

63 "It's rather pleasant"—Wells letter to Sarah Wells, October 13, 1895.

64 "It did not take us long"—Quoted in Mackenzie, p. 116.

64 "I make use of physics"—Quoted in ibid., p. 117.

64 "world of cooling stars"—Review of *Mind at the End of Its Tether* by H. G. Wells, *Manchester Evening News,* November 8, 1945, *CW XVII,* 2784, p. 360.

64 "I had realised"—Wells, *Experiment in Autobiography,* p. 516.

64 "the philosopher who masquerades"—Quoted in Sherborne, p. 108.

65 "able-bodied, clean-minded men"—H. G. Wells, *The War of the Worlds* (Penguin Classics, 2005), p. 157.

65 "Everyone who has ever read"—Orwell, Review of *The Iron Heel* by Jack London, etc., *CW XII,* 655, p. 211.

65 "gigantic glass hive"—H. G. Wells, *The Sleeper Awakes* (Penguin Classics, 2005), p. 71.

65 "our contemporary world"—Wells, *Experiment in Autobiography,* p. 645.

65 "idiotic slang"—Wells, *Sleeper,* p. 190.

65 "to print permanent memories"—Ibid., p. 154.

66 "nightmare of capitalism triumphant"—Ibid., p. 8.

66 "It suffers from vast contradictions"—Orwell, *CW V,* p. 188.

66 "worn-out dreams"—Wells, *Sleeper,* p. 202.

66 "monstrous crowds"—Ibid., p. 79.

66 "the impulse of passionate inadequacy"—Ibid., p. 212.

66 "The hope of mankind"—Ibid., p. 170.

66 "For this year"—Quoted in Sherborne, p. 153.

67 "The old local order"—Wells, *Utopia,* p. 33.

67 "the keystone"—Wells, *Experiment in Autobiography,* p. 643.

67 "sober forecasting"—Ibid., p. 646.

67 "designed to undermine"—Quoted in Sherborne, p. 147.

67 "Generally the fault"—Quoted in David C. Smith, *H. G. Wells: Desperately Mortal: A Biography* (Yale University Press, 1986), p. 100.

68 "Well, the world is a world"—H. G. Wells, *Anticipations of the Reaction of Mechanical and Scientific Progress Upon Human Life and Thought* (Chapman & Hall Ltd., 1902), p. 317.

68 "one of the most remarkable men alive"—Quoted in Mackenzie, p. 162.

68 "an explorer of a new world"—Quoted in ibid., p. 170.

68 "Heaven defend us"—Quoted in Sherborne, p. 219.

68 "voluntary noblemen"—Wells, *Utopia,* p. 86.

68 "imaginary laws"—Ibid., p. 23.

68 "strange and inhuman"—Ibid., p. 14.

69 "like a well-oiled engine"—Ibid., p. 117.

69 "There will be many Utopias"—Ibid., p. 245.

69 "We all want to abolish"—Orwell, "Can Socialists Be Happy?," *CW XVI,* 2397, pp. 39–40.

69 "struggle, danger and death"—Orwell, Review of *Mein Kampf* by Adolf Hitler, *New English Weekly,* March 21, 1940, *CW XII,* 602, p. 118.

69 "The difference between us"—Quoted in Smith, p. 167.

69 "besetting sin"—Attlee, p. 138.

69 "counterblast to one of the heavens"—E. M. Forster, *The Collected Tales of E. M. Forster* (Alfred A. Knopf, 1947), pp. 7–8.

69 "Science, instead of freeing man"—Quoted in P. N. Furbank, *E. M. Forster: A Life (1879–1970)* (Secker & Warburg, 1979), p. 161.

70 "several thousand"—Forster, p. 145.

70 "What was the good"—Ibid., p. 156.

70 "Progress had come to mean"—Ibid., p. 186.

70 "terrestrial facts" and "absolutely colourless"—Ibid., p. 183.

70 "confused, tedious"—Wells, *Experiment in Autobiography*, p. 660.

70 "He has neither the patience"—Quoted in Mackenzie, p. 206.

70 "plan for the reconstruction"—H. G. Wells, *Socialism and the Family* (A. C. Fifield, 1906), p. 6.

71 "Many writers, perhaps most"—Orwell, "As I Please," *Tribune,* December 6, 1946, *CW XVIII,* 3131, p. 511.

71 "Wells watered down"—Orwell letter to Julian Symons, *CW XIX,* 3397, p. 336.

71 "The return to complete sanity"—Wells, *Experiment in Autobiography,* p. 668.

72 "a wave of sanity"—Ibid., p. 666.

72 "he suffers from a messianic delusion"—H. L. Mencken, "The Late Mr. Wells," in *Prejudices: First Series* (Jonathan Cape, 1921), p. 28.

72 "there was, among the young"—Orwell, *CW V,* p. 129.

72 "My boom is over"—Quoted in Mackenzie, p. 319.

72 "from nebula to the Third International"—Quoted in ibid., p. 327.

73 "amazing little man" and "very refreshing"—H. G. Wells, *Russia in the Shadows* (Hodder & Stoughton, 1920), p. 138.

73 "What a narrow petty bourgeois!"—Quoted in Sherborne, p. 259.

73 "never desist"—H. G. Wells, *Men Like Gods* (Cassell & Company, Ltd., 1923), p. 289.

73 "fear-haunted world"—H. G. Wells, *The Dream* (Jonathan Cape, 1924), p. 152.

73 "a huge glittering vehicle"—Orwell, *CW V,* p. 193.

74 "a memorable assault"—Ibid., p. 189.

74 "started out as a parody"—*Paris Review,* no. 23, Spring 1960.

74 "I feel that the nightmare"—Aldous Huxley letter to George Orwell, October 21, 1949, in Grover Smith (ed.), *Letters of Aldous Huxley* (Chatto & Windus, 1969), p. 605.

74 "I am writing a novel"—Aldous Huxley letter to Kethevan Roberts, May 18, 1931, ibid., p. 348.

74 "a rather horrid, vulgar little man"—Aldous Huxley letter to Robert Nichols, January 18, 1927, ibid., p. 281.

74 "Men no longer amuse themselves"—"Spinoza's Worm" in *Do What You Will* (Chatto & Windus, 1929), quoted in Hillegas, p. 115.

75 "Utopias appear much more realisable"—Aldous Huxley, *Brave New World and Brave New World Revisited* (Chatto & Windus, 1984), p. 3. Original passage is in French.

75 "just to know the worst"—Quoted in Aldous Huxley, *Brave New World* (Vintage, 2007), p. xx.

75 "City of Dreadful Joy"—Aldous Huxley, *Jesting Pilate* (Chatto & Windus, 1926), p. 267.

75   "It is all movement and noise"—Ibid., p. 284.

75   "What's the point of truth"—Huxley, *Brave New World and Brave New World Revisited*, p. 201.

76   "a taste for words"—Quoted in Sybille Bedford, *Aldous Huxley: A Biography: Volume One: 1894–1939* (Chatto & Windus, 1973), p. 92.

76   "There is no power-hunger"—Orwell, "Freedom and Happiness," *Tribune*, January 4, 1946, *CW XVIII*, 2841, p. 14.

76   "the quite natural interaction"—Orwell, *CW V*, p. 83.

77   "had stayed human"—Orwell, *CW IX*, p. 172.

77   "The birds sang"—Ibid., p. 230.

77   "If there is hope"—Orwell, *CW IX*, p. 72.

77   "Vague New World"—Quoted in Bew, p. 236.

77   "a Brave New World"—Muggeridge, p. 24.

77   "some kind of Aldous Huxley *Brave New World*"—Orwell, *CW IV*, p. 97.

77   "degenerate art"—Cyril Connolly, "Year Nine," collected in *The Condemned Playground*, p. 158.

77   "I fear, wasn't best pleased with it"—Aldous Huxley letter to Harold Raymond, March 19, 1932, Grover Smith, p. 359.

77   "a great disappointment"—Quoted in Peter Edgerly Firchow, *The End of Utopia: A Study of Aldous Huxley's* Brave New World (Associated University Presses, 1984), p. 135.

77   "Bible of the impotent genteel"—Quoted in ibid., p. 59.

77   "one of the most brilliant"—H. G. Wells, *The Shape of Things to Come* (Gollancz, 2017), p. 354.

78   "an ultra-left revolutionary"—Mackenzie, p. 394.

78   "the most effective transmitting instrument"—Wells, *Experiment in Autobiography*, p. 797.

78   "never met a man"—Ibid., p. 806.

78   "Come and see us again"—Ibid., p. 819.

78   "Russia had let me down"—Mackenzie, p. 381.

78   "a disgruntled inspector-general"—Ibid., p. 403.

79   "It gives in one eddying concentration"—*New York Times Magazine*, April 17, 1927.

79   "decaying fragments"—Ibid.

79   "a mess of a film"—Mackenzie, p. 391.

79   "every scientific advance"—Orwell, Reply to J. F. Horrabin, *Tribune*, May 19, 1944, *CW XVI*, 2467, p. 186.

79   "It never occurred to Mr. Wells"—Orwell, Review of *Film Stories* by H. G. Wells, *Tribune*, June 21, 1940, *CW XII*, 640, p. 191.

79   "all-round trustification"—Orwell letter to Brenda Salkeld, June 1933, *CW X*, 176, p. 317.

80   "partly because"—Orwell, *CW IX*, p. 197.

80   "The failure of mankind"—Kingsley Martin, *Editor: A Second Volume of Autobiography 1931–45* (Hutchinson & Co., 1968), p. 107.

80 "old, tired and shrivelled"—Quoted in Mackenzie, p. 424.

80 "I have no gang"—Quoted in ibid., p. 413.

80 "Time to Go"—Ibid., p. 445.

CHAPTER 5: RADIO ORWELL

81 "All propaganda is lies"—Orwell, War-time Diary, March 14, 1942, *CW XIII*, 1025, p. 229.

81 "excellent company"—Anthony Powell, *To Keep the Ball Rolling Volume II: Messengers of Day* (Heinemann, 1978), p. 24.

82 "that screaming little defective"—Orwell, "Wells, Hitler and the World State," *CW XII*, 837, p. 537.

82 "Wells is too sane" and "since 1920"—Ibid., p. 540.

82 "intellectual brutality" and "a human being"—Orwell letter to Stephen Spender, April 15, 1938, in *CW XI*, 435, p. 132.

82 "one of those unusual beings"—George Woodcock, *Orwell's Message 1984 and the Present* (Harbour Publishing, 1984), p. 124.

82 The argument at Langford Court—The most reliable account of the dinner is in Inez Holden's diaries, reprinted in Crick, pp. 429–30.

82 "an amusing evening"—Crick, p. 430.

82 "solve all the ills"—Orwell, "The Rediscovery of Europe," *The Listener*, March 19, 1942, *CW XIII*, 1014, p. 213.

82 "foolish generalisations"—H. G. Wells letter to *The Listener*, April 9, 1942, ibid., p. 218.

82 "I don't say that at all"—Quoted in Sherbone, p. 333.

83 "two wasted years"—Orwell letter to Philip Rahv, December 9, 1943, *CW XVI*, 2390, p. 22.

83 "strange boring nightmare"—Orwell, "English Writing in Total War," *New Republic*, July 14, 1941, *CW XII*, 831, p. 530.

83 "all complacent optimists"—H. V. Morton, *I, James Blunt* (Methuen & Co., Ltd., 1942), p. 58.

83 "Lord Murdoch and General Pointer do not exist"—Robin Maugham, *The 1946 MS.* (War Facts Press, 1943), p. 45.

83 "good flesh-creeper"—Orwell, "Review of Pamphlet Literature," *New Statesman and Nation*, January 9, 1943, *CW XIV*, 1807, p. 301.

83 "Only the mentally dead"—Orwell, "London Letter," *Partisan Review*, March–April 1941, *CW XII*, 740, p. 355.

84 "We must remember"—Connolly, *The Condemned Playground*, p. 273.

84 "the practice of lying"—Orwell, Review of *An Epic of the Gestapo* by Sir Paul Dukes, *Tribune*, September 13, 1940, *CW XII*, 686, p. 258.

84 "so unspeakable"—Orwell, Review of *The Lights Go Down* by Erika Mann, *Tribune*, August 23, 1940, *CW XII*, 676, p. 238.

84 "the horrible political jungle"—Orwell, Review of *Never Come Back* by John Mair, *New Statesman and Nation*, January 4, 1941, *CW XII*, 741, p. 359.

84 "expected to sell his honour"—Orwell, "Confessions of a Book Reviewer," *Tribune*, May 3, 1946, *CW XVIII*, 2992, p. 302.

84 "easily bored"—Anthony Powell, *To Keep the Ball Rolling Volume I: Infants of the Spring* (Heinemann, 1976), p. 139.

84 "sadism"—Orwell, *Time and Tide*, August 9, 1941, *CW XII*, 840, p. 542.

85 "the nightmare atmosphere"—Orwell, *Time and Tide*, January 25, 1941, *CW XII*, 751, p. 375.

85 "a sort of concentrated essence" and "power to reassert"—Orwell, *Time and Tide*, December 21, 1940, *CW XII*, 727, p. 315.

85 "Rat Soup"—Orwell, "As I Please," *Tribune*, December 31, 1943, *CW XVI*, 2398, p. 46.

85 "less terrifying"—Orwell, "London Letter," *CW XII*, 740, p. 354.

85 "a constant scramble"—Orwell, War-time Diary, September 7, 1940, *CW XII*, 685, p. 254.

85 "getting glimpses"—Orwell, War-time Diary, October 19, 1940, *CW XII*, 698, p. 277.

86 "By the middle of 1941"—Orwell, "In Defence of P. G. Wodehouse," *The Windmill*, no. 2, July 1945, *CW XVII*, 2624, p. 60.

86 Orwell enjoyed retelling—Orwell, War-time Diary, July 6, 1941, *CW XII*, 829, p. 525.

86 "switched from one line"—Orwell, *CW IX*, p. 189.

86 "Within two years"—Orwell, War-time Diary, May 18, 1941, *CW XII*, 803, p. 501.

86 "not merely"—Crick, p. 356.

87 "The British Government"—Orwell, "Poetry and the Microphone," *The New Saxon Pamphlet*, no. 3, March 1945, *CW XVII*, 2629, p. 79.

87 "The peculiarity of the totalitarian state"—"Literature and Totalitarianism," May 21, 1941, *CW XII*, 804, p. 504.

87 "the Liars' School"—Coppard and Crick, p. 177.

87 "There is no victory in sight"—Orwell, War-time Diary, August 28, 1941, *CW XIII*, 849, p. 23.

88 "If liberty means anything"—Orwell, "The Freedom of the Press," *CW XVII*, 2721, p. 2560.

88 "an enormous pyramidal structure"—Orwell, *CW IX*, p. 5.

88 "to *diminish* the range of thought"—Ibid., p. 313.

88 "you cannot make a meaningless statement"—Orwell, "As I Please," *Tribune*, August 18, 1944, 2534, p. 338.

89 "There are areas where"—Orwell, "As I Please," *Tribune*, April 4, 1947, *CW XIX*, 3208, p. 118.

89 "The bigger the machine"—Orwell, "Poetry and the Microphone," *CW XVII*, 2629, p. 80.

89 "I believe that the B.B.C."—Orwell, "London Letter," *Partisan Review*, July–August 1941, *CW XII*, 787, p. 472.

89 "going through a London fog"—Wadhams, p. 105.
89 "for being so ignorant"—J. B. Clark, BBC memo, January 19, 1943.
89 "inherently totalitarian"—Orwell, "As I Please," April 7, 1944, *CW XVI*, 2450, p. 147.
89 "put on your thinking-cap"—Z. A. Bokhari memo to Orwell, September 23, 1941, *CW XIII*, 846, p. 12.
90 "university of the air"—George Orwell, *The War Broadcasts*, ed. W. J. West (Gerald Duckworth & Co. Ltd., 1985), p. 13.
90 "Few people are able"—Orwell, "Poetry and the Microphone," *CW XVII*, 2629, p. 79.
90 "I suppose during every second"—"Voice," August 11, 1942, *CW XIII*, 1373, p. 459.
91 "Crocuses now full out"—Orwell, War-time Diary, March 27, 1942, *CW XIII*, 1064, p. 249.
91 "Its atmosphere is something"—Orwell, War-time Diary, March 14, 1942, *CW XIII*, 1025, p. 229.
91 "The thing that strikes one"—Orwell, War-time Diary, June 18, 1942, *CW XIII*, 1231, p. 366.
91 "He was never quite sure"—Wadhams, p. 132.
91 "And now Comrade Orwell"—"Pacifism and the War: A Controversy," *CW XIII*, 1270, p. 395.
91 "kept our propaganda"—Orwell letter to George Woodcock, December 2, 1942, *CW XIV*, 1711, p. 214.
91 "We were listening to 'Germany Calling' "—Wadhams, p. 128.
91 "I think he thought"—*Arena: George Orwell*.
92 "It doesn't need the eye"—Orwell, "As One Non-Combatant to Another (A letter to 'Obadiah Hornbooke')," *Tribune*, June 18, 1943, *The Complete Works of George Orwell XV: Two Wasted Years 1943* (Secker & Warburg, 2001), 2138, p. 144.
92 "Nowadays"—Orwell, War-time Diary, April 1942, *CW XIII*, 1124, pp. 288–89.
92 "If George and I didn't smoke so much"—Crick, p. 432.
92 "the typical figure"—Orwell, *Macbeth* adaptation, BBC Eastern Service, October 17, 1943, 2319, pp. 280–81.
93 "probably the most devastating"—Orwell, "Can Socialists Be Happy?," *CW XVI*, 2397, p. 40.
93 "an extraordinarily clear prevision"—Orwell, "Politics vs Literature," *CW XVIII*, 3089, p. 427.
93 "He couldn't see"—Orwell, "Too Hard on Humanity," *The Listener*, November 26, 1942, *CW XIV*, 1637, p. 161.
93 "Orwell never completely lost faith"—*Observer*, January 29, 1950, reprinted in Meyers (ed.), p. 298.
93 "remarkably dreary"—Orwell, "Can Socialists Be Happy?," *CW XVI*, 2397, p. 40.

93 "A certain smugness"—Orwell, "Review of an Unknown Land," *CW XIV*,1768, p. 254.

94 "a very remarkable prophecy"—Orwell, talk on Jack London, BBC, March 5, 1943, *CW XV*, 1916, p. 5.

94 "a very poor book"—Ibid., p. 6.

94 "a Socialist with the instincts"—Orwell, Introduction to *Love of Life and Other Stories* by Jack London, 1945, *CW XVII*, 2781, p. 355.

94 "I am first of all a white man"—Andrew Sinclair, *Jack: A Biography of Jack London* (Weidenfeld & Nicolson, 1978), p. 108.

94 "one of Nietzsche's blond-beasts"—Jack London, "How I Became a Socialist," *The Comrade*, March 1903.

94 "You have mismanaged the world"—Joan London, *Jack London and His Times: An Unconventional Biography* (Doubleday, Doran & Company, Inc., 1939), p. 308.

94 "his gladiator body"—Jack London, *The Iron Heel* (Everett & Co., 1908), p. 195.

94 "*1984* as it might have been penned"—Earle Labor, *Jack London* (Twayne, 1974), p. 114.

95 "In reading it one does not"—Joan London, p. 315.

95 "one of the best statements"—Orwell, "Jack London," Forces Educational Broadcast, Light Programme, BBC, October 8, 1945, *CW XVII*, 2761, p. 303.

95 "Intellectually he knew"—Introduction to *Love of Life and Other Stories*, *CW XVII*, 2781, p. 354.

95 "streak of brutality"—Orwell, talk on Jack London, *CW XV*, p. 6.

95 "understanding of the primitive," "better prophet" and "You might say"—Ibid., p. 7.

95 "the vision of a boot crashing down"—Orwell, *The Lion and the Unicorn*, *CW XII*, 763, p. 396.

96 "a warning"—London, *The Iron Heel*, p. 4.

96 "The diary would be reduced to ashes"—Orwell, *CW IX*, p. 29.

96 "in our own lifetime"—Orwell, *CW IX*, p. 162.

96 "leaving a few records behind"—Ibid., p. 163.

96 "daringly opens up"—Icke and Macmillan, p. 13.

97 "Orwell is much more optimistic"—Earl G. Ingersoll (ed.), *Waltzing Again* (Ontario Review Press, 2006), p. 116.

97 "have a framing device" and "Optimism is relative"—Jesse Kinos-Goodwin, "We are reading 1984 wrong, according to Margaret Atwood," CBC, May 9, 2017.

97 "We are, as a people"—Wells letter to George Bernard Shaw, April 22, 1941.

97 "the clearest insistence"—Wells letter to *British Weekly*, June 26, 1939, quoted in Mackenzie, p. 420.

98 "By some time in 1944"—Orwell letter to Rayner Heppenstall, August 24, 1943, *CW XV*, 2247, p. 206.

98 "I should think"—Eileen Blair letter to Orwell, March 21, 1945, Belong, *CW XVII*, 2638, p. 99.

98 "On no occasion"—Orwell letter to L. F. Rushbrook Williams, September 24, 1945, *CW XV,* 2283, p. 251.

98 "He is transparently honest"—Rushbrook Williams, confidential annual report on George Orwell, August 7, 1943.

98 On the day he left—see Elizabeth Knights' account in interview transcript for *Arena: George Orwell.*

99 "for the first time, I saw"—Orwell, "Looking Back on the Spanish War," *CW XIII,* 1421, p. 503.

99 "the very concept of objective truth," "controls not only the future"—Ibid., p. 504.

99 "that shifting phantasmagoric world"—Ibid., p. 505.

100 "truly grave"—Emperor Hirohito, October 26, 1943.

100 "If you are a man"—Orwell, *CW IX,* p. 282.

100 "The nightmare feeling"—Orwell, "The Last Man in Europe," *CW XV,* 2377, p. 368.

100 "Is it perhaps childish"—Orwell, "Looking Back on the Spanish War," *CW XIII,* 1421, p. 505.

CHAPTER 6: THE HERETIC

101 "I know that I have"—Yevgeny Zamyatin, "Letter to Stalin" (1931), in *Soviet Heretic,* trans. Mirra Ginsberg (Quartet, 1991), p. 305.

101 "I am interested in that kind of book"—Orwell letter to Gleb Struve, February 17, 1944, *CW XVI,* 2421, p. 98.

101 "it is not a book of the first order"—Orwell, "Freedom and Happiness," *CW XVIII,* 2841, p. 13.

101 "partly plagiarised"—Orwell letter to Warburg, November 22, 1948, *CW XIX,* 3495, p. 471.

101 "proves that these ideas"—Alex M. Shane, *The Life and Works of Evgenij Zamjatin* (University of California Press, 1968), p. 140.

101 "the idea of *1984*"—Isaac Deutscher, "*1984*—The Mysticism of Cruelty," in Raymond Williams (ed.), *George Orwell: A Collection of Critical Essays* (Prentice-Hall, 1974), p. 120.

102 "look out for this book"—Orwell, "As I Please," *Tribune,* January 24, 1947, *CW XIX,* 3158, p. 26.

102 "my most jesting"—Zamyatin, "Autobiography" (1922), in *Soviet Heretic,* p. 4.

102 "robs people of individuality"—Zamyatin, "Contemporary Russian Literature" (1918), in *Soviet Heretic,* p. 44.

102 "the victory of the many"—Yevgeny Zamyatin, *We,* trans. Natasha Randall (Vintage, 2007), p. 42.

103 "sharp, black, piercing"—Ibid., p. 191.

103 "festive rockets"—Ibid., p. 193.

103 "When you are moving fast"—Zamyatin, "On Literature, Revolution, Entropy, and Other Matters" (1923), in *Soviet Heretic,* pp. 111–12.

103   "I never *explained*"—Shane, p. 92.

103   "mathematically infallible happiness"—Zamyatin, *We*, p. 3.

103   "Every station bookstall"—Brian Moynahan, *Comrades 1917: Russia in Revolution* (Little, Brown, 1992), p. 5.

103   "like a machine"—Ibid., p. 119.

103   "ancient sickness"—Ibid., p. 67.

104   "a rather weak and episodic plot"—Orwell, "Freedom and Happiness," *CW XVIII*, 2841, p. 14.

104   "machine-equal"—Zamyatin, *We*, p. 158.

104   "Because reason should win"—Ibid., p. 203.

104   "one of the literary curiosities"—Orwell, "Freedom and Happiness," *CW XVIII*, 2841, p. 13.

104   "Perhaps the most interesting"—Yevgeny Zamyatin, "Autobiography" (1922), in *Soviet Heretic*, p. 4.

104   "Gogol was a friend"—Zamyatin, "Autobiography" (1924), in *Soviet Heretic*, p. 5.

104   "He also finished"—Zamyatin, "Autobiography" (1929), in *Soviet Heretic*, p. 9.

105   "an eternal rebel"—Gleb Struve, *25 Years of Soviet Russian Literature (1918–1943)* (George Routledge & Sons, Ltd., 1944), p. 22.

105   "In those years"—Zamyatin, "Autobiography" (1929), in *Soviet Heretic*, p. 10.

105   "If I have any place"—Zamyatin, "Autobiography" (1922), in *Soviet Heretic*, p. 4.

105   "When the smoke"—Zamyatin, "Moscow–Petersburg" (1933), in *Soviet Heretic*, p. 144.

105   "Yesterday, the thesis"—Zamyatin, "Tomorrow" (1919), in *Soviet Heretic*, p. 51.

105   "Eternal dissatisfaction"—Ibid.

106   "works *only* for the distant future"—Zamyatin, "Scythians?" (1918), in *Soviet Heretic*, p. 22.

106   "a kind of unofficial minister"—Zamyatin, "Maxim Gorky" (1936), in *Soviet Heretic*, p. 250.

107   "The writer who cannot"—Zamyatin, "I Am Afraid" (1921), in *Soviet Heretic*, p. 57.

107   "You really do have to be an acrobat"—Quoted in Martin Amis, *Koba the Dread* (Vintage, 2003), p. 168.

107   "True literature"—Zamyatin, "I Am Afraid" (1921), in *Soviet Heretic*, p. 57.

107   "amenable, quick-witted"—Martha Weitzel Hickey, *The Writer in Petrograd and the House of Arts* (Northwestern University Press, 2009), p. 137.

107   "mechanical, chemical"—Zamyatin, "H. G. Wells" (1922), in *Soviet Heretic*, p. 259.

107   "Most of his social fantasies"—Ibid., p. 287.

107   "*We*, by the author of this essay"—Ibid., p. 290.

108   "a poor conventional creature"—Orwell, "Freedom and Happiness," *CW XVIII*, 2841, pp. 14–15.

108 "strange and irritating"—Zamyatin, *We,* p. 8.

108 "wanted someone, anyone"—Ibid., p. 187.

108 "the choice for mankind"—Orwell, *CW IX,* p. 275.

108 "Happiness"—Zamyatin, *We,* p. 59.

108 "After twice two is four"— Fyodor Dostoyevsky, *Notes from Underground* and *The Double* (Penguin, 2009), p. 32.

108 "Freedom is the freedom to say"—Orwell, *CW IX,* p. 84.

109 "It is this intuitive grasp"—Orwell, "Freedom and Happiness," *CW XVIII,* 2841, p. 15.

109 "seems to me to form"—Orwell letter to Warburg, March 30, 1949, *CW XIX,* 3583, p. 72.

109 "the monster"—Ayn Rand, *Anthem* (Cassell & Company, 1938), p. 134.

109 "a world of the future"—Robert Mayhew (ed.), *Essays on Ayn Rand's* Anthem (Lexington Books, 2005), p. 119.

109 "a grisly forecast"—Ibid., p. 56.

109 "It is so very personally mine"—Ibid., p. 24.

110 "To be free"—Rand, p. 141.

110 "Work hard, increase production"—*THX 1138* (dir. George Lucas), 1971.

110 "the way I see LA right now" and "It's the idea that we are all living in cages"—Quoted in John Baxter, *George Lucas: A Biography* (HarperCollins, 1999), p. 104.

110 "the genius of Ayn Rand"—Sleevenotes, Rush, *2112* (Anthem Records, 1976).

110 "any collectivist mentality"—J. Kordosh, "Rush. But Why Are They in Such a Hurry?," *Creem,* June 1981.

111 "Each morning"—Zamyatin, *We,* pp. 12–13.

111 "give readers the impression"—Mayhew (ed.), p. 26.

111 "Look at all these things"—*The Lego Movie* (dir. Phil Lord and Christopher Miller, 2014).

112 "It is important"—Gleb Struve letter to *Tribune,* January 25, 1946, *CW XVIII,* 2841, p. 16.

112 "This novel is a warning"—*Les Nouvelles littéraires,* no. 497, April 23, 1932.

112 "if the Church told me"—Quoted in D. J. Richards, *Zamyatin: A Soviet Heretic* (Bowes & Bowes, 1962), p. 43.

112 "Zamyatin simply could not"—Hillegas, p. 105.

112 "The collective 'We' "—Mayhew (ed.), p. 139.

113 "But, I-330"—Zamyatin, *We,* p. 153.

113 "hopelessly bad"—Shane, p. 27.

113 "ridiculing and humiliating"—Ibid., p. 59.

113 "certain themes cannot"—Orwell, "The Prevention of Literature," *Polemic,* January 1946, *CW XVII,* 2792, p. 378.

114 "They all merge"—Zamyatin, "Paradise" (1921), in *Soviet Heretic,* p. 65.

114 "Everything was levelled"—Zamyatin, "Moscow-Petersburg," in *Soviet Heretic,* p. 153.

114 "In the old days"—Victor Serge, *Memoirs of a Revolutionary* (NYRB, 2012), p. 308.

114 "the first year"—Arendt, *The Origins of Totalitarianism*, p. 537.

115 "voted whatever was required"—Serge, p. 308.

115 "Facts are stubborn"—Quoted in Max Eastman, *Artists in Uniform* (G. Allen & Unwin, 1934), p. 87.

115 "Zamyatin's crime"—Ibid., p. 85.

115 "a mean libel"—Struve, p. 130.

116 "it becomes possible"—Zamyatin, "Letter to Stalin," in *Soviet Heretic*, p. 308.

116 "death sentence"—Ibid., p. 309.

116 "I know that, while I have been"—Ibid., p. 308.

116 "I did not like to find Gorky"—Wells, *Experiment in Autobiography*, p. 310.

116 "Dozens of people"—Zamyatin, "Maxim Gorky," in *Soviet Heretic*, p. 254.

117 "Nothing remained"—Lyons, pp. 494–95.

117 "There isn't a single thinking adult"—Serge, p. 312.

117 "to treat the present"—Crossman (ed.), p. 208.

117 "ringing and fizzy"—Zamyatin, *We*, p. 92.

CHAPTER 7: INCONVENIENT FACTS

118 "As soon as fear"—Orwell, "Notes on Nationalism," *Polemic*, no. 1, October 1945, *CW XVII*, 2668, p. 154.

118 "I am writing a little squib"—Orwell letter to Struve, *CW XVI*, 2421, p. 99.

118 "a genuine effort"—Orwell, "As I Pleased," *Tribune*, January 31, 1947, *CW XIX*, 3167, p. 38.

119 "It is too like"—Ibid., p. 37.

119 "the only column ever written"—Wadhams, p. 139.

119 "a sort of totalitarian world"—Orwell, "As I Please," *Tribune*, May 12, 1944, *CW XVI*, 2467, p. 183.

119 "The fallacy is to believe"—Orwell, "As I Please," *Tribune*, April 28, 1944, *CW XVI*, 2460, p. 172.

120 "It is intolerable"—Orwell, *CW IX*, p. 267.

120 "by all odds the most debated"—Daniel Kelly, *James Burnham and the Struggle for the World: A Life* (ISI Books, 2002), p. 97.

120 "very prescient"—Orwell, "The Christian Reformers," *Manchester Evening News*, February 7, 1946, *CW XVIII*, 2877, p. 65.

120 "The theory of the managerial revolution"—James Burnham, *The Managerial Revolution: What Is Happening in the World* (John Day Company, Inc., 1941), p. 75.

121 "living in a world"—Ibid., p. 173.

121 "contempt for the common man" and "trying to spread the idea"—Orwell, "As I Please," *Tribune*, January 14, 1944, *CW XVI*, 2404, p. 61.

121 "Nor have I ever stated"—James Burnham letter to *Tribune*, March 24, 1944, ibid., p. 62.

121 "We could all be true prophets"—Orwell reply to Burnham, ibid., p. 64.

121 "in such a way"—Orwell, *CW IX*, p. 41.

121 "Orwell business"—Kelly, p. 118.

121 "piece of shallow naughtiness"—Orwell, Review of *The Machiavellians* by James Burnham, *Manchester Evening News,* January 20, 1944, *CW XVI*, 2407, p. 74.

121 "a sort of fascinated admiration"—Orwell, "Second Thoughts on James Burnham," *Polemic,* no. 3, May 1946, *CW XVIII*, 2989, p. 275.

121 "Burnham sees the trend"—Ibid., p. 280.

122 "three great super-States"—Orwell, "As I Please," *CW XVI*, 2404, p. 61.

122 "huge, invincible, everlasting"—Orwell, "Second Thoughts on James Burnham," *CW XVIII*, 2989, p. 283.

122 "primal traitor"—Orwell, *CW XIX*, p. 14.

122 "the longing for a just society"—Orwell, "Catastrophic Gradualism," *C. W. Review,* November 1945, *CW XVII*, 2778, p. 344.

122 "One does not establish"—Orwell, *CW IX*, p. 276.

122 "No theory, no promises"—James Burnham, *The Machiavellians: Defenders of Freedom* (Putnam & Company, Ltd., 1943), p. 182.

122 "We are interested solely in power"—Orwell, *CW IX*, p. 275.

122 "each is in effect"—Ibid., p. 206.

122 "If the sort of world" and "If one simply proclaims"—Orwell letter to Noel Willmett, May 18, 1944, *CW XVI*, 2471, p. 191.

123 "only through absolute clarity"—Burnham letter to *Tribune, CW XVI*, 2404, p. 62.

123 "Only if we recognize"—F. A. Hayek, *The Road to Serfdom* (George Routledge & Sons, Ltd., 1946), p. 10.

123 "the source of the mortal danger"—Ibid., p. 84.

123 "The word truth itself"—Hayek, p. 76.

123 "Each writer" and "a tyranny probably worse"—Review of *The Road to Serfdom* by F. A. Hayek and *The Mirror of the Past* by K. Zilliacus, *Observer,* April 9, 1944, *CW XVI*, 2451, p. 149.

123 "completely unacceptable politically"—Orwell letter to Gollancz, March 19, 1944, *CW XVI*, 2437, p. 127.

124 "I am highly critical"—Crick, p. 254.

124 "I think the choice of pigs"—Ibid., p. 456.

124 "Imagine old Joe"—Inez Holden quoted in *CW XVI*, p. 266.

124 "that this is the right point of view"—Crick, p. 458.

124 "Unpopular ideas"—Orwell, "The Freedom of the Press," *CW XVII*, 2721, p. 254.

125 "I knew that anyone"—Orwell letter to Gollancz, March 14, 1947, *CW XIX*, 3191, p. 78.

125 "Perhaps even Orwell's morale"—Warburg, p. 47.

125 "robot bombs"—David C. Smith, p. 473.

125 Inez Holden overheard—Stefan Schimanski and Henry Treece (eds.),

Leaves in the Storm: A Book of Diaries (Lindsay Drummond, Ltd., 1947), pp. 241–45.

125 "blitzed"—Orwell letter to T. S. Eliot, June 28, 1944, *CW XVI*, 2496, p. 269.

125 Orwell believed he was sterile—see Rayner Heppenstall's account in Coppard and Crick, p. 114.

125 "I hate London"—Wadhams, p. 147.

125 "grossly wrong"—Orwell, "London Letter," *Partisan Review*, Winter 1944–45, p. 411.

125 "It seems to me"—Ibid., pp. 413–15.

126 "Every time one goes off"—Orwell, "As I Please," *Tribune*, December 1, 1944, 2586, p. 487.

126 1943 Mass Observation report—Orwell, "Survey of 'Civvy Street,'" *Observer*, June 4, 1944, *CW XVI*, 2484, p. 249.

127 "A harmful truth"—Michael Scammell, *Koestler: The Indispensable Intellectual* (Faber & Faber, 2010), p. 160.

127 "Truth is what is useful"—Arthur Koestler, *Darkness at Noon*, trans. Daphne Hardy (Vintage, 2005), p. 182.

127 "Lost Week-end in Utopia"—Crossman (ed.), p. 82.

127 his friend Eva Striker—Ibid., p. 78.

127 "Who will ever forget"—David Cesarani, *Arthur Koestler: The Homeless Mind* (William Heinemann, 1998), p. 175.

127 "Of course I'm guilty!"—Orwell, *CW IX*, p. 245.

128 "All the confessions that are uttered here"—Ibid., p. 266.

128 "one is imprisoned"—Review of *Darkness at Noon* by Arthur Koestler, etc., *New Statesman and Nation*, January 4, 1941, *CW XII*, 741, p. 358.

128 "The horror which No. 1"—Koestler, p. 18.

128 "would be ready to believe"—Conquest, p. 113.

128 "an almost perfect specimen"—Orwell, Review of *Darkness at Noon*, *CW XII*, 741, p. 358.

128 "The Gletkins"—Koestler, p. 183.

128 "It was almost normal"—Orwell, *CW IX*, pp. 26–27.

129 Yevgeny Zamyatin's old friend—Conquest, p. 122.

129 "How could the immortal, collective brain"—Orwell, *CW IX*, p. 290.

129 "Rubashov remarked jokingly"—Koestler, p. 97.

129 "We persecuted the seeds of evil"—Ibid., p. 83.

129 "oceanic sense"—Ibid., p. 204.

129 "Even the victim" and "We make the brain perfect"—Orwell, *CW IX*, p. 267.

130 "shallow"—Orwell, "Arthur Koestler," *CW XVI*, 2548, p. 400.

130 "quasi-mystical belief"—Ibid., p. 399.

130 "Perhaps some degree"—Ibid., p. 400.

130 "an unworthy squib"—Orwell, Review of *Twilight Bar* by Arthur Koestler, *Tribune*, November 30, 1945, *CW XVII*, 2808, p. 406.

130 "That was a bloody awful review"—Scammell, p. 265.

131 The two accounts of this meeting—see Ernest Hemingway, *True at First Light*

(William Heinemann, 1999), pp. 139–40, and Paul Potts in Coppard and Crick, p. 257.

131 "After years of war"—Orwell, "Creating Order Out of Cologne Chaos: Water Supplied from Carts," *Observer,* March 23, 1945, *CW XVII,* 2641, p. 107.

131 "I really don't think I'm worth the money"—Eileen Blair letter to Orwell, March 21, 1945, *CW XVII,* 2638, p. 96.

131 "I don't think you understand"—Ibid., p. 99.

132 "It was a most horrible thing"—Orwell letter to Anthony Powell, April 13, 1945, *CW XVII,* 2656, p. 124.

132 "I don't think he looked after her"—*Arena: George Orwell.*

132 "To walk through the ruined cities"—Orwell, "Future of a Ruined Germany: Rural Slum Cannot Help Europe," *Observer,* April 8, 1945, *CW XVII,* 2654, p. 122.

132 "the whole idea of revenge"—Orwell, "Revenge Is Sour," *Tribune,* November 8, 1945, *CW XVII,* 2786, p. 362.

132 If war criminals were herded—Orwell, "As I Please," *Tribune,* January 12, 1945, *CW XVII,* 2603, p. 19.

133 "barbarous" and "participate at secondhand"—Orwell, "As I Please," *Tribune,* November 15, 1946, *CW XVIII,* 3115, p. 483.

133 "another turn"—Ibid., p. 484.

133 "anti-Jew propaganda"—Orwell, "The Last Man in Europe," *CW XV,* 2377, p. 269.

133 In early drafts—George Orwell, *Nineteen Eighty-Four: The Facsimile of the Extant Manuscript,* ed. Peter Davison (Secker & Warburg, 1984), pp. 29–31.

133 "entirely spurious"—Orwell, *CW V,* p. 103.

133 "pushed out of skilled jobs"—Orwell, "As I Please," *Tribune,* December 10, 1943, *CW XVI,* 2391, p. 23.

133 "Something, some psychological vitamin"—Orwell, "Antisemitism in Britain," *Contemporary Jewish Record,* April 1945, *CW XVII,* p. 70.

133 "is power hunger tempered by self-deception"—Orwell, "Notes on Nationalism," *CW XVII,* 2668, p. 142.

134 "the power of holding two contradictory beliefs"—Orwell, *CW IX,* p. 223.

134 "moral effort"—Orwell, "Notes on Nationalism," *CW XVII,* 2668, p. 155.

134 "by people who know"—Orwell, "Antisemitism in Britain," *CW XVII,* p. 70.

134 "It is obvious"—Ibid., p. 65.

134 "an ability to believe stories"—Ibid., p. 66.

135 "Nobody is searching for the truth"—Orwell, "As I Please," *Tribune,* December 8, 1944, *CW XVI,* 2590, p. 495.

135 "a deterioration in mental efficiency"—Irving L. Janis, "Groupthink," *Psychology Today,* November 1971.

135 "The general uncertainty"—Orwell, "Notes on Nationalism," *CW XVII,* 2668, p. 148.

135 "There can be no doubt"—*Daily Mail,* June 5, 1945.

136 "second hand version"—Bew, p. 333.

136 in a 1943 poll—David Kynaston, *Austerity Britain 1945–51* (Bloomsbury, 2008), p. 43.

136 "In the face of terrifying dangers"—Orwell, "London Letter," *Partisan Review,* Summer 1945, *CW XVII,* 2672, p. 164.

136 "I was wrong on several points"—Orwell, "London Letter," *Partisan Review,* Fall 1945, *CW XVII,* 2719, p. 246.

136 "no one was more surprised"—Bew, p. 348.

136 "that queer, dramatic, dreamlike day" and "the temporary head"—Mollie Panter-Downes, "Letter from London," *New Yorker,* August 4, 1945.

137 "the fundamental decencies of life"—Bew, p. 233.

137 "in accordance with the native genius"—Ibid., p. 235.

137 "brings to the fierce struggle"—Michael Foot, *Aneurin Bevan 1897–1960* (Victor Gollancz, 1997), p. 233.

137 "the invisible man"—*Tribune,* March 30, 1945.

137 "a recently dead fish"—Orwell, War-time Diary, May 19, 1942, *CW XIII,* 1182, p. 331.

137 "colourless"—Orwell, "London Letter," *CW XVII,* 2719, pp. 248–49.

137 "Some of the generals"—Lord Attlee, "The Man I Knew," *Observer,* January 31, 1965.

137 "As a sign of the vitality of democracy"—Orwell, "The British General Election," *Commentary,* November 1945, *CW XVII,* 2777, p. 340.

137 "I just thought the alteration"—Orwell letter to Roger Senhouse, March 17, 1945, *CW XVII,* 2635, p. 90.

137 "To me this single sentence"—Warburg, p. 51.

138 "the destruction of the Soviet myth"—Orwell, Preface to the Ukrainian Edition of *Animal Farm,* March 1947, *CW XIX,* 3198, p. 88.

138 "It is a sad fable"—Graham Greene, *Evening Standard,* August 10, 1945, reprinted in Meyers (ed.), p. 196.

138 "a sort of fairy story"—Orwell letter to Leonard Moore, March 19, 1944, *CW XVI,* 2436, p. 126.

138 "the tops"—Orwell letter to Rayner Heppenstall, January 25, 1947, *CW XIX,* 3163, p. 32.

138 "To say that I was horrified"—Margaret Atwood, "George Orwell: Some Personal Connections," reprinted in *Curious Pursuits,* p. 333.

138 "sinister enchanter"—Orwell, *CW IX,* p. 17.

138 "some kind of invisible influence"—Orwell, *The Complete Works of George Orwell VIII: Animal Farm* (Secker & Warburg, 1997), p. 53.

139 "theoretical possibility"—Orwell, *Nineteen Eighty-Four: The Facsimile,* p. 309.

139 "They all remembered"—Orwell, *CW VIII,* p. 53.

139 "ALL ANIMALS ARE EQUAL"—Ibid., p. 90.

139 "Are you certain"—Ibid., pp. 43–44.

139 "But you could prove nothing"—Orwell, *CW IX,* 38–39.

139 "Ah, that is different"—Orwell, *CW VIII*, p. 55.

139 "Thou watchest over all"—Ibid., p. 63.

139 "Four legs good"—Ibid., p. 21.

140 "though she lacked the words"—Ibid., p. 59.

140 "the huge and simple question"—Orwell, *CW IX*, p. 96.

140 "Once it went sad in the middle"—Wadhams, p. 159.

140 "never liked being associated"—Coppard and Crick, p. 195.

140 In September 1941—Crick, p. 395.

140 Foreign translations—See Paul Potts in Coppard and Crick, p. 253.

140 "I have been surprised"—Orwell letter to Philip Rahv, April 9, 1946, *CW XVIII*, 2966, p. 231.

140 some bookshops had mistakenly racked it—See Susan Watson in Coppard and Crick, p. 220.

141 "looking more like a monkey on a stick"—Orwell, "As I Please," *Tribune*, January 7, 1944, 2401, p. 55.

141 "I belong to the Left"—Orwell letter to Katharine, Duchess of Atholl, November 15, 1945, *CW XVII*, 2795, p. 385.

141 Orwell had told A. J. Ayer—Wadhams, p. 168.

141 "the danger of this kind of perfection"—William Empson letter to Orwell, August 24, 1945, reprinted in Crick p. 492.

141 "the mushiest and most maudlin"—Mayhew (ed.), p. 153.

141 "to hell with it"—Orwell letter to Dwight Macdonald, December 5, 1946, *CW XVIII*, 3218, p. 506.

141 "reaching the exhaustion"—Kingsley Martin, *New Statesman and Nation*, September 8, 1945, reprinted in Meyers (ed.), p. 197.

141 "hunger, hardship and disappointment"—Orwell, *CW VIII*, p. 87.

142 "all the seeds of evil"—Orwell, "Catastrophic Gradualism," *CW XVII*, 2778, p. 343.

142 "The most encouraging fact"—Introduction to *British Pamphleteers*, vol. 1, edited by Orwell and Reginald Reynolds, 1948, *CW XIX*, 3206, p. 109.

142 "If people think"—Orwell letter to Macdonald, *CW XVIII*, 3218, p. 507.

142 "In England you can't get paper"—Orwell, "London Letter," *CW XVII*, 2719, p. 249.

143 A Mass Observation survey in June—Kynaston, p. 69.

143 "The mood of the country"—Orwell, "London Letter," *CW XVII*, 2719, p. 246.

143 "enormous economic blitz," "Almost the only thing," "In England, as elsewhere"—Panter-Downes, "Letter from London," *New Yorker*, September 1, 1945.

143 "all too topical"—Orwell, Review of *That Hideous Strength* by C. S. Lewis, *Manchester Evening News*, August 16, 1945, *CW XVII*, 2720, p. 250.

143 "This is not a moment"—Orwell, Review of *Mind at the End of Its Tether*, *CW XVII*, 2784, p. 359.

143 "the kind of world-view"—Orwell, "You and the Atom Bomb," *Tribune*, October 19, 1945, *CW XVII*, 2770, p. 321.

144 "that the fear inspired"—Orwell, "Toward European Unity," *Partisan Review*, July–August 1947, *CW XIX*, 3244, p. 163.

CHAPTER 8: EVERY BOOK IS A FAILURE

145 "To mark the paper"—Orwell, *CW IX*, p. 9.

145 "wouldn't have been so gloomy"—Quoted in Christopher Hollis, *A Study of George Orwell: The Man and His Works* (Hollis & Carter, 1956), p. 207.

145 "civil wars, bomb outrages"—Orwell, "Old George's Almanac," *Tribune*, December 28, 1945, *CW XVII*, 2829, p. 462.

145 "My God, Orwell *is* a gloomy bird!"—Coppard and Crick, p. 204.

145 "To-day it seems quite possible"—Huxley, *Brave New World and Brave New World Revisited*, p. 13.

146 "Our twentieth century is the century of fear"—Albert Camus, *Neither Victims nor Executioners*, trans. Dwight Macdonald (World Without War Publications, 1972), p. 19.

146 "No thoughtful person"—Orwell, "London Letter," *Partisan Review*, Summer 1946, *CW XVIII*, 2990, p. 288.

146 "the best informed"—Michael Meyer, "Memories of George Orwell," in Gross (ed.), p. 133.

146 "we talked of melancholy subjects"—Christopher Sykes, *New Republic*, December 4, 1950, reprinted in Meyers (ed.), p. 308.

146 "We were all anti-Communist"—Malcolm Muggeridge, *Like It Was: The Diaries of Malcolm Muggeridge* (Collins, 1981), p. 199.

146 "an irresistible attraction"—David Cole letter to *Tribune*, July 27, 1945, *CW XVII*, 2691, p. 203.

147 "no one should be persecuted"—Orwell letter to George Woodcock, January 4, 1948, *CW XIX*, 3329, p. 254.

147 "Antisemitism ... is simply not the doctrine"—Orwell, "As I Please," *Tribune*, January 28, 1944, *CW XVI*, 2412, p. 81.

147 "It is only that I feel"—Orwell letter to Anne Popham, March 15, 1946, *CW XVIII*, 2931, pp. 153–54.

147 "What I am really asking"—Orwell letter to Anne Popham, April 18, 1946, *CW XVIII*, 2978, p. 248.

147 "smothered under journalism"—Orwell letter to Dorothy Plowman, February 19, 1946, *CW XVIII*, 2903, p. 115.

147 "It will probably be an awful job"—Orwell letter to Popham, March 15, 1946, *CW XVIII*, 2931, p. 153.

148 "At various dinners"—Wadhams, p. x.

148 "labour-saving colonies"—Orwell, "On Housing," *Tribune*, January 25, 1946, *CW XVIII*, 2881, p. 77.

148 "One is never alone"—Orwell, "Pleasure Spots," *Tribune*, January 11, 1946, *CW XVIII*, 2854, p. 31.

148 "conveyor-belt process"—Orwell, "The Prevention of Literature," *CW XVII*, 2792, p. 378.

148 "The atom bombs are piling up"—Orwell, "Some Thoughts on the Common Toad," *Tribune*, April 12, 1946, *CW XVIII*, 2970, p. 240.

148 His description of an archetypal junk shop—Orwell, "Just Junk—But Who Could Resist It," *Evening Standard*, January 5, 1946, *CW XVIII*, 2842, pp. 17–19.

148 "the power of holding"—Orwell, "In Front of Your Nose," *Tribune*, March 22, 1946, *CW XVIII*, 2940, p. 162.

149 "To see what is in front of one's nose"—Ibid., p. 163.

149 "the way in which the concern"—Coppard and Crick, p. 204.

149 "The point is that the relative freedom"—Orwell, "Freedom of the Park," *Tribune*, December 7, 1945, *CW XVII*, 2813, p. 418.

149 "swindles and perversions"—Orwell, "Politics and the English Language," *Horizon*, April 1946, *CW XVII*, 2815, p. 425.

149 "orthodoxy, of whatever colour"—Ibid., p. 427.

150 "there is some lie"—Orwell, "Why I Write," *CW XVIII*, 3007, p. 319.

150 "It is bound to be a failure"—Ibid., p. 320.

150 "as shabby and dirty as ever"—Orwell, "London Letter," *Partisan Review*, Summer 1946, *CW XIII*, 2990, p. 289.

151 "miserable, hostile old bugger"—Wadhams, p. 181.

151 "They are most annoying"—Orwell letter to David Astor, October 9, 1948, *CW XIX*, 3467, p. 450.

151 "not worth a bomb"—Orwell letter to Tosco Fyvel, December 31, 1947, *CW XIX*, 3322, p. 241.

151 "I have at last started"—Orwell letter to Humphrey Slater, September 26, 1946, *CW XVIII*, 3084, p. 408.

151 "It just seemed depressingly lacking in hope"—Wadhams, p. 180.

152 "one of those people"—Orwell, "Politics vs Literature: An Examination of *Gulliver's Travels*," *CW XVIII*, 3089, p. 418.

152 "One ought to be able"—Orwell, "Benefit of Clergy: Some Notes on Salvador Dalí," June 1, 1944, *CW XVI*, 2481, pp. 237–38.

152 "This book is on my side"—Orwell, "Writers and Leviathan," *CW XIX*, 3364, p. 288.

152 "picking out a single hidden truth"—Orwell, "Politics vs Literature," *CW XVIII*, 3089, p. 418.

153 "the brief Communist dictatorship"—H. G. Wells, "My Auto-Obituary," *Strand Magazine*, vol. 1041, January 1943.

153 "He was so big a figure"—Orwell, "The True Pattern of H. G. Wells," *Manchester Evening News*, August 14, 1946, reprinted in *The Lost Orwell*, p. 139.

153 "I told you so"—H. G. Wells, "Preface to the 1941 Edition," *The War in the Air* (Penguin, 1941), p. 9.

153 "In the United States there is more money"—Review of *Spearhead*, ed. James Laughlin, *Times Literary Supplement*, April 17, 1948, *CW XIX*, 3380, p. 316.

153 "The *Uncle Tom's Cabin* of our time"—Quoted in Rodden, *The Politics of Literary Reputation,* p. 44.

153 "good bad book"—Orwell, "Good Bad Books," *Tribune,* November 2, 1945, *CW XVII,* 2780, p. 348.

153 Edmund Wilson—*New Yorker,* September 7, 1946.

153 "the satire deals not"—*New Republic,* September 2, 1946.

154 "No one is patriotic about taxes"—Orwell, War-time Diary, August 9, 1940, *CW XII,* 667, p. 229.

154 "fairy gold"—Wadhams, p. 151.

154 "Fairly much a leftist"—Allene Talmey, "Vogue Spotlight," *Vogue,* September 15, 1946.

154 "The Americans always go one better"—Orwell, *CW IV,* p. 262.

154 "anti-American"—Connolly, *The Evening Colonnade,* p. 383.

154 "It ought to be realised"—*The English People, CW XVI,* 2475, p. 220.

154 "a truly remarkable book"—Review of *Native Son* by Richard Wright, etc., *Tribune,* April 26, 1940, *CW XII,* 616, p. 152.

155 "The world of the American novelist"—Review of *Sun on the Water* by L. A. G. Strong, etc., *Tribune,* April 12, 1940, *CW XII,* 610, p. 143.

155 "It is difficult to go anywhere"—Orwell, "As I Please," *Tribune,* December 3, 1943, *CW XVI,* 2385, p. 13.

155 "This anglophile"—Richard McLaughlin letter to *Tribune,* December 17, 1943, ibid., pp. 14–15.

155 "The Nazis, without admitting it"—Arendt, p. 451.

155 "It is clear"—*New Statesman and Nation,* November 2, 1946, quoted in Kynaston, p. 134.

155 "To be anti-American nowadays"—"In Defence of Comrade Zilliacus," August–September(?) 1947, *CW XIX,* 3254, p. 181.

155 "Americophobia"—Orwell, Review of *The Nineteen-Twenties* by Douglas Goldring, *Observer,* January 6, 1946, *CW XVIII,* 2843, p. 21.

155 "I don't, God knows"—Orwell letter to Gollancz, March 25, 1947, *CW XIX,* 3200, p. 90.

156 "Everybody in England"—Kynaston, p. 191.

156 "unendurable"—Orwell letter to Dwight Macdonald, April 15, 1947, *CW XIX,* 3215, p. 128.

156 "to the north and east"—Orwell, *CW IX,* pp. 85–86.

157 "I had the feeling that they had spoilt it"—Orwell to Mamaine Koestler, January 24, 1947, *CW XIX,* 3159, pp. 27–28.

157 "He is too fond of apocalyptic visions"—Orwell, "Burnham's View of the Contemporary World Struggle," *New Leader,* March 29, 1947, *CW XIX,* 3204, p. 102.

157 in a 1947 letter—Orwell letter to Dwight Macdonald, April 15, 1947, *CW XIX,* 3215, pp. 126–28.

157 "a huge secret army"—Orwell, "Burnham's View of the Contemporary World Struggle," *CW XIX,* 3204, pp. 100–101.

157   "a doctor treating"—Orwell, "Toward European Unity," *CW XIX*, 3244, p. 163.

157   "mental disease"—Orwell, "As I Please," *Tribune*, November 29, 1945, *CW XVIII*, 3126, p. 504.

157   "individual freedom"—Quoted in Scott Lucas, *The Betrayal of Dissent: Beyond Orwell, Hitchens & the New American Century* (London: Pluto, 2004), p. 27.

157   "If one could somewhere"—Orwell, "Burnham's View of the Contemporary World Struggle," *CW XIX*, 3204, p. 103.

158   "very dark"—Orwell, "Toward European Unity," *CW XIX*, 3244, p. 167.

158   "As time goes on"—Orwell, "As I Please," January 17, 1947, *CW XIX*, 3153, p. 19.

158   "a ghastly mess"—Orwell letter to Warburg, February 4, 1948, *CW XIX*, 3339, p. 264.

158   "I don't like talking about books"—Orwell letter to Warburg, May 31, 1947, *CW XIX*, 3232, p. 149.

158   "rivetted from the start" and "would have taken"—"Mrs. Miranda Wood's Memoir," *The Complete Works of George Orwell XX: Our Job Is to Make Life Worth Living 1949–1950* (Secker & Warburg, 2002), 3735, p. 301.

159   "He almost seemed to enjoy it"—Coppard and Crick, p. 231.

159   "like a fool"—Orwell letter to Tosco Fyvel, December 31, 1947, *CW XIX*, 3322, p. 240.

159   "I really felt"—Orwell letter to Celia Kirwan (née Paget), May 27, 1948, *CW XIX*, 3405, p. 345.

159   "with a peculiar feeling of happiness"—Orwell, "Notes from Orwell's Last Literary Notebook," *CW XX*, 3725, p. 203.

159   "violently and not too old"—Orwell, "How the Poor Die," *Now*, no. 6, November 1946, *CW XVIII*, 3104, p. 463.

160   "probably forgotten"—Wadhams, p. 197.

160   "because the body swells up"—Orwell, *CW IX*, p. 106.

160   In hospital, Orwell tallied—"Things not foreseen in youth as part of middle age," notebook entry circa May 1948, *CW XIX*, 3402, p. 340.

160   "I suppose with all these drugs"—Orwell letter to Julian Symons, April 20, 1948, *CW XIX*, 3386, pp. 321–22.

161   He wondered if there was some medical explanation—Orwell diary entry, March 30, 1948, *CW XIX*, 3374, p. 307.

161   "impossible and undesirable"—Orwell, "Writers and Leviathan," *CW XIX*, 3364, p. 292.

161   "to push the question"—Ibid., p. 291.

161   "Conclusion: must engage"—Orwell, Preparatory notes for "Writers and Leviathan," 1948, *CW XIX*, 3365, p. 294.

161   "Gissing's novels"—Preparatory notes for "George Gissing," 1948, *CW XIX*, 3407, p. 353.

161   "a chronicler of vulgarity"—Orwell, "George Gissing," May–June 1948(?), *CW XIX*, 3406, p. 352.

162 "a world of force and fraud"—Orwell, "Such, Such Were the Joys," *CW XIX,* 3409, p. 370.

162 "irrational terrors"—Ibid., p. 383.

162 "exactly like a fat"—Orwell, *Nineteen Eighty-Four: The Facsimile,* p. 223.

162 "It was possible, therefore"—"Such, Such Were the Joys," *CW XIX,* 3409, p. 359.

162 "Whether he knew it or not"—*New Yorker,* January 28, 1956, reprinted in Meyers (ed.), p. 78.

162 "totalitarians"—Hilary Spurling, *The Girl from the Fiction Department: A Portrait of Sonia Orwell* (Penguin, 2003), p. 68.

163 "What surprised me mostly"—Interview transcript from *Arena: George Orwell.*

163 "a book doesn't exist"—Orwell letter to Julian Symons, January 2, 1948, *CW XIX,* 3325, p. 249.

163 "It was a cold, blowy day"—Orwell, *Nineteen Eighty-Four: The Facsimile,* p. 3.

163 "spontaneous demonstrations"—Orwell, *CW IX,* p. 24.

163 "voluntary subscriptions"—Ibid., p. 59.

163 "Christian Pacifists"—Orwell, *Nineteen Eighty-Four: The Facsimile,* p. 37.

164 "Thus, the Party rejects"—Orwell, *CW IX,* p. 225.

164 "a deliberate and sadistic" and "worth a cool million"—Fredric Warburg's Report on *Nineteen Eighty-Four,* December 13, 1948, *CW XIX,* 3505, p. 480.

164 "slightly underfed"—*New York Times,* January 5, 1948, quoted in Bew, p. 451.

164 An opinion poll—Kynaston, p. 248.

164 he had previously offered to write a piece for Tosco Fyvel—see Coppard and Crick, p. 216.

165 "So far, in spite of the cries"—Orwell, "The Labour Government After Three Years," *Commentary,* October 1948, *CW XIX,* 3461, p. 442.

165 "caused more resentment"—Ibid., p. 439.

165 "it is doubtful whether we can solve"—Orwell, "As I Please," *Tribune,* November 15, 1946, *CW XVIII,* 3115, p. 483.

165 While Orwell was living in Islington—see Paul Potts, *To Keep a Promise* (MacGibbon & Kee, 1970), p. 71.

165 "The essence of being human"—Orwell, "Reflections on Gandhi," *Partisan Review,* January 1949, *CW XX,* 3516, p. 8.

166 Warburg thought so—See Warburg, p. 102.

166 "Everything is flourishing"—Orwell letter to David Astor, December 21, 1948, *CW XIX,* 3510, p. 485.

CHAPTER 9: THE CLOCKS STRIKE THIRTEEN

167 "My new book"—Orwell letter to Julian Symons, February 4, 1949, *CW XX,* 3541, p. 35.

167 Eileen wrote a poem—See Sally Coniam, "Orwell and the Origins of *Nineteen Eighty-Four,*" *Times Literary Supplement,* December 31, 1999.

168 "it was never possible nowadays"—Orwell, *CW IX*, p. 9.

168 "a beastly book"—Orwell letter to Jacintha Buddicom, February 14, 1949, *CW XX*, 3550, p. 42.

168 "an awful book really"—Orwell letter to Celia Kirwan (née Paget), February 13, 1949, *CW XX*, 3549, p. 41.

168 "a good idea ruined"—Orwell letter to Anthony Powell, November 15, 1948, *CW XIX*, 3488, p. 467.

168 "I am not pleased"—Orwell letter to Warburg, October 22, 1948, *CW XIX*, 3477, p. 457.

168 "an expensive hobby"—Orwell letter to George Woodcock, January 12, 1949, *CW XX*, 3521, p. 16.

168 "it isn't a book I would gamble on"—Orwell letter to Warburg, December 21, 1948, *CW XIX*, 3511, p. 486.

168 "made me spew"—Orwell letter to Brenda Salkeld, August 1934, *CW X*, 204, p. 347.

168 "was a good idea"—Orwell letter to Leonard Moore, 3 October 1934, *CW X*, 209, p. 351.

168 "any life when viewed"—"Benefit of Clergy," *CW XVI*, 2481, p. 234.

169 "that I was idling"—Orwell, "Notes from Orwell's Last literary Notebook," *CW XX*, 3725, p. 204.

169 "schoolboyish sensationalism"—*Times Literary Supplement*, June 10, 1949, reprinted in Meyers (ed.), p. 256.

169 "This is amongst the most terrifying"—Fredric Warburg's Report on *Nineteen Eighty-Four*, *CW XIX*, 3505, p. 479.

169 "I cannot but think"—Ibid., p. 481.

169 "Orwell has done what Wells never did" and "ought to be shot"—David Farrer's Report on *Nineteen Eighty-Four*, December 15, 1948, *CW XIX*, 3506, p. 482.

169 "as though it were a thriller"—Orwell letter to Roger Senhouse, December 26, 1948, *CW XIX*, 3513, p. 487.

170 "We hope you might be interested"—Eugene Reynal letter to J. Edgar Hoover, April 22, 1949.

170 "mucked about"—Orwell letter to Leonard Moore, March 17, 1949, *CW XX*, 3575, p. 67.

170 Warburg estimated—See Warburg, p. 110.

170 "No wonder everyone hates us so"—Orwell, Diary, April 17, 1949, *CW XX*, 2602, p. 92.

171 "Don't think I am making"—Orwell letter to Warburg, May 16, 1949, *CW XX*, 3626, p. 116.

171 "exhausted Dickens disastrously"—Orwell, Review of *Dickens: His Character, Comedy and Career* by Hesketh Pearson, *New York Times Book Review*, May 15, 1949, *CW XX*, 3625, p. 115.

171 "about as good a novelist"—Notes for "Evelyn Waugh," 1949, *CW XX*, 3586, p. 79.

171   "a sort of grown-upness"—Orwell letter to *Wiadomsci*, February 25, 1949, *CW XX*, 3553, p. 47.

171   "They would get hold of five kilograms"—Ibid., p. 95.

171   "a novel of character"—Fredric Warburg's Report on His Visit to Orwell, June 14, 1949, *CW XX*, 3645, p. 132.

172   "frightful cigarettes"—*Daily Mirror*, December 14, 1954.

172   "an inexhaustible rocket fuel"—John Lehmann, quoted in Spurling, p. 53.

173   "With a round Renoir face"—Stephen Spender, journal entry, December 24, 1980, in *New Selected Journals 1939–1995*, ed. Lara Feigel and John Sutherland with Natasha Spender (Faber & Faber, 2012), p. 586.

173   "My own father had died"—Spurling, p. 27.

173   "meanwhile take care"—Orwell letter to Sonia Brownell, April 12, 1947, *CW XIX*, 3212, p. 124.

173   "so-called humanism"—Spurling, p. 77.

173   "a bag of wind"—Orwell letter to Warburg, October 22, 1948, *CW XIX*, 3477, p. 457.

174   "I'm good at spotting people"—Orwell, *CW IX*, p. 128.

174   "her youth and prettiness"—Spurling, p. 93.

174   "atmosphere of hockey-fields"—Orwell, *CW IX*, p. 12.

174   "only a rebel"—Ibid., p. 163.

174   "It was characteristic"—Orwell, *Nineteen Eighty-Four: The Facsimile*, p. 101.

175   " 'Who cares?' "—Orwell, *CW IX*, p. 161.

175   "The Nazis explained"—Randall Swingler, "The Right to Free Expression," *Polemic*, no. 5, September-October 1946, *CW XVIII*, 3090, pp. 433–34.

175   "The ideal subject"—Arendt, p. 622.

175   "In an ever-changing, incomprehensible world"—Ibid., p. 500.

175   "dual standard of thought"—Orwell, "The Last Man in Europe," *CW XV*, 2377, p. 368.

176   fifty thousand TV licences—Kynaston, p. 305.

176   "some kind of mental instability"—Quoted in Gordon Bowker, *George Orwell* (Hachette Digital, 2003), p. 162.

176   "I would like to reassure"—Joe Moran, *Armchair Nation* (Profile, 2013), p. 27.

176   "The only person"—Arendt, p. 444.

176   "asleep or awake"—Orwell, *CW IX*, p. 29.

176   "infallible and all-powerful"—Ibid., p. 216.

176   "His portrait is seen"—Crossman (ed.), p. 191.

176   "the insoluble mystery," etc.—Boris Souvarine, *Stalin: A Critical Survey of Bolshevism*, trans. C. L. R. James (Secker & Warburg, 1939), p. xiii.

176   "The chief qualification"—Arendt, p. 456.

177   "Does he exist" and "As long as you live"—Orwell, *CW IX*, p. 272.

177   "Fantasmagoric effect"—Orwell, "The Last Man in Europe," *CW XV*, 2377, p. 368.

177   "Everything melted into mist"—Orwell, *CW IX*, p. 38.

177 "faded away"—Ibid., p. 44.

178 "in the place where there is no darkness" and "Winston did not know"—Ibid., p. 27.

178 "predestined horror"—Ibid., p. 146.

178 "impending death"—Ibid., p. 158.

178 "the working-out of a process" and "The end was contained in the beginning"—Ibid., p. 166.

178 "In this game that we're playing"—Ibid., p. 142.

178 "Don't deceive yourself"—Ibid., p. 251.

178 "He was the tormentor"—Ibid., p. 256.

178 "a wave of admiration"—Ibid., p. 182.

178 "priest of power"—Ibid., p. 276.

179 "lifted clean"—Ibid., p. 172.

179 "as though their two minds"—Ibid., p. 19.

179 "writing the diary"—Ibid., p. 84.

179 "There was no idea"—Ibid., p. 268.

179 "how to discover"—Ibid., p. 201.

179 "This drama that I have played out"—Ibid., p. 281.

180 "A government based on terrorism"—Muggeridge, *The Thirties*, p. 208.

180 "victory after victory"—Orwell, *CW IX*, p. 281.

180 "in the long run probably"—Orwell, "The Prevention of Literature," *CW XVII*, 2792, p. 374.

180 "We control matter"—Orwell, *CW IX*, p. 277.

180 "How many fingers"—Ibid., p. 264.

180 "a kind of arithmetic [*sic*] progression"—*New Republic*, March 16, 1953, reprinted in Meyers (ed.), p. 315.

181 "The object of persecution"—Orwell, *CW IX*, p. 276.

181 "The moral to be drawn"—Orwell's Statement on *Nineteen Eighty-Four*, *CW XX*, 3636, p. 134.

181 "Mankind was living"—London *Times*, June 8, 1949.

181 "with cries of terror"—*New York Times Book Review*, July 31, 1949.

181 "I read it with such cold shivers"—John Dos Passos letter to Orwell, October 8, 1949, *CW XX*, 3698, p. 194.

181 Several booksellers told Warburg—See Muggeridge, *Like It Was*, p. 331.

181 "too terrible a novel"—E. M. Forster, quoted in Warburg, p. 116.

181 "a glorious book"—Arthur Koestler letter to Orwell, August 26, 1949, *CW XX*, 3681A, p. 328.

181 "profoundly important"—Huxley letter to Orwell, October 21, 1949.

181 "the novel which should stand"—Margaret Storm Jameson quoted in George Orwell, *Nineteen Eighty-Four With a Critical Introduction and Annotations by Bernard Crick* (Clarendon University Press, 1984), p. 96.

181 "Reading it in a Communist country"—Quoted in Publication of *Nineteen Eighty-Four*, *CW XX*, 3643, p. 129.

182 "the type of state"—Hansard, HC Deb, July 21, 1949, vol. 467, col. 1623.

182 "I thought *Nineteen Eighty-Four* was a frightful, miserable, defeatist book"—Wadhams, p. 205.

182 "barely distinguishable"—Orwell, *CW IX*, p. 205.

182 "Behind Stalin"—Forster, *Two Cheers for Democracy*, p. 61.

182 "the totalitarian danger"—*Frankfurter Rundschau*, November 5, 1949, reprinted in Meyers (ed.), p. 281.

182 "Orwell, actually"—*New Leader*, June 25, 1949, reprinted in Meyers (ed.), p. 264.

182 "his book reinforces"—*Life*, July 4, 1949.

182 "required reading"—*Evening Standard*, June 7, 1949.

182 "sickness"—*Masses and Mainstream*, August 1949, reprinted in Meyers (ed.), p. 274.

182 "cynical rot"—Ibid., p. 275.

182 "filthy book"—*Pravda*, May 12, 1950, reprinted in Meyers (ed.), p. 282.

183 "blank hopelessness"—Quoted in Publication of *Nineteen Eighty-Four, CW XX*, 3643, p. 128.

183 "if I was going to smear somebody"—Orwell letter to Mr. Shaw, June 20, 1949, *CW XX*, 3650, p. 139.

183 "some very shame-making publicity"—Orwell letter to Richard Rees, July 28, 1949, *CW XX*, 3669, p. 154.

183 "will pretend to be much more"—Orwell's Statement on *Nineteen Eighty-Four, CW XX*, 3636, p. 134.

183 "NOT intended as an attack on socialism" and "I do not believe"—Orwell's Statement on *Nineteen Eighty-Four, CW XX*, 3636, p. 136.

183 "didn't do two pennorth of good"—Warburg, p. 119.

184 "Having read Mr. Orwell's *Nineteen Eighty-Four*"—*NBC University Theater: Nineteen Eighty-Four*, NBC, August 27, 1949.

184 "kinetic"—*New York Times*, June 12, 1949.

184 "shocking"—Fredric Warburg's Report on His Visit to Orwell, *CW XX*, 3645, p. 131.

184 "Orwell was totally unfit"—Jeffrey Meyers, *Orwell: Wintry Conscience of a Generation* (W. W. Norton & Company, 2001), p. 304.

184 "slightly macabre"—Muggeridge, *Like It Was*, p. 354.

184 "Her body seemed"—Orwell, *CW IX*, p. 143.

184 "He said he would get better"—Spurling, p. 96.

184 "the astonishing selfishness"—Review of *The Two Carlyles* by Osbert Burdett, *The Adelphi*, March 1931, *CW XI*, 103, p. 197.

185 "skin and bone"—Wadhams, p. 210.

185 "There was a kind of rage"—Muggeridge, *Like It Was*, p. 368.

185 "A silence fell"—George Woodcock, *The Crystal Spirit*, p. 45.

186 "fast, clear, gray prose"—*New Statesman and Nation*, January 28, 1950, reprinted in Meyers (ed.), p. 296.

186 "the wintry conscience"—Ibid., p. 294.

186 "the greatness and tragedy"—*Observer,* January 29, 1950, reprinted in Meyers (ed.), p. 297.

186 "exceptional concordance"—Ibid., p. 296.

186 "how the legend of a human being"—Muggeridge, *Like It Was,* p. 376.

186 "everyone else—above all Pritchett"—Quoted in Cesarani, p. 347.

186 "She had persuaded herself"—Spurling, p. 99.

186 "She blamed herself"—Wadhams, p. 211.

PART TWO

CHAPTER 10: BLACK MILLENNIUM

189 "If that is what the world is going to be like"—*Daily Mirror,* December 13, 1954.

189 "the production and message"—Memo, D. K. Wolfe-Murray to Director of Television Broadcasting, December 16, 1954.

189 "the subject of the sharpest controversy"—*New York Times,* December 17, 1954.

189 "horrible play"—*Daily Mirror,* December 16, 1954.

190 "cold eyes stared"—*Films and Filming,* September 1958, quoted in Jason Jacobs, *The Intimate Screen: Early British Television Drama* (Clarendon Press, 2000), p. 138.

190 "It was so awful"—*Daily Mirror,* December 13, 1954.

190 "Never has anything more vile"—*Daily Express,* December 14, 1954.

190 "a nauseating story"—*Daily Mirror,* December 13, 1954.

190 "a picture of a world"—*Daily Mirror,* December 17, 1954.

190 "A Million NIGHTMARES"—*Daily Express,* December 14, 1954.

190 "pander to sexual and sadistic tastes"—*Daily Mirror,* December 15, 1954.

190 "Listeners!"—*The Goon Show,* "Nineteen Eighty-Five," BBC Home Service, January 4, 1955.

191 "probably acquire"—Bernard Hollowood, "On the Air," *Punch,* December 22, 1954, quoted in Rodden, *The Politics of Literary Reputation,* p. 279.

191 "if someone had written a novel in 1910"—*Daily Express,* December 14, 1954.

191 "the beastliness of Communism" and "probably arose"—*Daily Mail,* December 14, 1954.

191 "the lowest essence"—*Guardian,* December 22, 1954.

191 "a typical brain-washing letter"—*Guardian,* December 29, 1954.

191 "an ideological superweapon"—Isaac Deutscher, "*1984:* The Mysticism of Cruelty," reprinted in Williams (ed.), p. 119.

192 "marginal"—London *Times,* December 16, 1954.

192 The Secker & Warburg hardback—for sales figures see Warburg, pp. 114–15.

192 "Kipling is the only English writer"—Orwell, "Rudyard Kipling," *Horizon,* February 1942, *CW XIII,* 948, p. 157.

192 "Some of the words he coined"—Nigel Kneale, "The Last Rebel of Airstrip One," *Radio Times*, December 10, 1954.

192 "[*Flair*] is a leap into the Orwellian future"—Mary McCarthy, "Up the Ladder from Charm to Vogue," July-August 1950, reprinted in *On the Contrary* (Heinemann, 1962), p. 187.

192 "what the late George Orwell"—Hansard, HC Deb, November 2, 1950, vol. 480, col. 353.

192 "a very remarkable book"—Quoted in Taylor, p. 419.

193 "I thought it was a term of affection"—Hansard, HC Deb, June 18, 1956, vol. 554, col. 1026.

193 "the book written by the late Mr. George Orwell"—Hansard, HL, February 7, 1951, vol. 170, col. 216.

193 "Orwell was *really*"—Spender, *World Review,* June 1950.

193 "the man who tells the truth"—Lionel Trilling, "George Orwell and the Politics of Truth," reprinted in Williams (ed.), p. 79.

194 "It is chiefly for the sake"—Arendt, p. 601.

194 "In the past every tyranny"—Orwell, Review of *Russia Under Soviet Rule* by N. de Basily, *New English Weekly,* January 12, 1939, *CW XI,* 524, p. 317.

194 "distorted the meaning of epithets"—Crossman (ed.), p. 261.

194 "Dickens is one of those writers"—"Charles Dickens," *CW XII,* 597, p. 47.

195 "probably had more to do"—Hansard, HC Deb July 21, 1960, vol. 627, col. 770.

195 "no slander is too gross"—A. L. Morton, *The English Utopia* (Lawrence & Wishart, Ltd., 1952), p. 212.

195 "realisation of Utopia"—Ibid., p. 213.

195 "shrieking into the arms"—*Marxist Quarterly,* January 1956, reprinted in Meyers (ed.), p. 290.

195 "Marxist English, or Pamphletese"—Orwell, "As I Please," *Tribune,* March 17, 1944, *CW XVI,* 2435, p. 124.

195 "a Freudian sublimation—Deutscher in Williams (ed.), p. 130.

195 "*1984* is in effect"—Ibid., pp. 131–32.

196 "perhaps more than any other nation"—Golo Mann in Meyers (ed.), p. 277.

196 "Because it is both difficult"—Czeslaw Milosz, *The Captive Mind* (Penguin Classics, 2001), p. 42.

196 "the most hated writer"—John Rodden, *Scenes from an Afterlife: The Legacy of George Orwell* (ISI Books, 2003), p. 71.

196 "make allowances"—*Life,* March 29, 1943.

196 "the secret Ministry of Cold War"—Frances Stonor Saunders, *Who Paid the Piper? The CIA and the Cultural Cold War* (Granta, 2000), p. 59.

197 "Indifference to objective truth"—Orwell, "Notes on Nationalism," *CW XVII,* 2668, p. 148.

197 "a word that can be uttered"—Orwell, *CW IX,* p. 321.

198 "Friends, freedom has seized the offensive!"—Peter Coleman, *The Liberal*

Conspiracy: The Congress for Cultural Freedom and the Struggle for the Mind of Postwar Europe (Free Press, 1989), p. 32.

198 "the Noncommunist left"—Arthur M. Schlesinger Jr, *The Vital Center: The Politics of Freedom* (Da Capo, 1998), p. 148.

198 "George Orwell, with his vigorous good sense"—Ibid., p. 147.

198 "Western man"—Schlesinger, p. 1.

198 *Tribune* and *Partisan Review*—For details see Saunders, pp. 162–63, 166.

199 "that bunch of homeless Leftists"—Arthur Koestler, *The Yogi and the Commissar and Other Essays* (Jonathan Cape, 1945), p. 107.

199 "I was made an unwitting 'accomplice'"—Dwight Macdonald, *Discriminations: Essays & Afterthoughts 1938–1974* (Grossman, 1974), p. 59.

199 "it was rather fortunate that Orwell died"—Conor Cruise O'Brien, *Listener,* December 12, 1968, reprinted in Meyers (ed.), pp. 345–46.

199 "deviate very little" and "retain the spirit"—Daniel J. Leab, *Orwell Subverted: The CIA and the Filming of Animal Farm* (Pennsylvania State University Press, 2007), p. 85.

200 "the mood of the book"—Ihor Szewczenko letter to Orwell, April 11, 1946, *CW XVIII,* 2969, p. 236.

200 "fanatic intellectual"—Ibid., p. 79.

200 "apparent inference"—Ibid., p. 83.

201 "a bitter satire"—Quoted in David Sylvester, "Orwell on the Screen," *Encounter,* March 1955.

201 "hit the jackpot"—Quoted in David Hencke and Rob Evans, "How Big Brothers Used Orwell to Fight the Cold War," *Guardian,* June 30, 2000.

201 "a failure aesthetically"—Sylvester.

201 "Did she approve"—*Today's Cinema,* December 28, 1954.

201 "the most devastating anti-Communist film"—Saunders, p. 459.

201 "I think we agreed"—Ibid., p. 297.

202 "freely adapted" etc.—*1984* (dir. Michael Anderson, 1956).

202 "Will Ecstasy Be a Crime"—Poster for *1984.*

202 "The change seemed to me to show" and "the type of ending"—*Daily Mail,* February 27, 1956.

203 "expressed his wholehearted and enthusiastic approval"—Celia Kirwan report on visit to Orwell, March 30, 1949, *CW XX,* 3590A, p. 319.

203 "a list of journalists & writers"—Orwell letter to Celia Kirwan, April 6, 1949, *CW XX,* 3590B, p. 322.

203 "It isn't very sensational"—Orwell letter to Celia Kirwan, May 2, 1949, *CW XX,* 3615, p. 103.

203 "The whole difficulty"—Orwell letter to Richard Rees, May 2, 1949, *CW XX,* 3617, p. 105.

203 "very tricky"—Orwell letter to Richard Rees, April 17, 1949, *CW XX,* 3600, p. 88.

204 "publicity agents of the USSR"—Orwell, "London Letter," *CW XIII,* 2990, p. 291.

204   "Members of the present British government"—Orwell's Statement on *Nineteen Eighty-Four, CW XX*, 3636, p. 135.

204   "I have been obliged at times"—Randall Swingler, "The Right to Free Expression," annotated by Orwell, *Polemic*, no. 5, September–October 1946, *CW XVIII*, 3090, p. 442.

204   "some kind of Russian agent"—*Lost Orwell*, pp. 147–48.

204   "calamitous"—Orwell, "Burnham's View of the Contemporary World Struggle," *CW XIX*, 3204, p. 103.

204   "vaguely disquieting"—Orwell letter to George Woodcock, March 23, 1948, *CW XIX*, 3369, p. 301.

204   "advanced communist views" and "he does not hold with the Communist Party"—Stephen Bates, "Odd Clothes and Unorthodox Views: Why MI5 Spied on Orwell for a Decade," *Guardian*, September 4, 2007.

205   "I always knew he was two-faced"—Ros Wynne-Jones, "Orwell's Little List Leaves the Left Gasping for More," *Independent on Sunday*, July 14, 1996.

205   "The man of conscience"—Foreword by Alexander Cockburn in John Reed, *Snowball's Chance* (Roof Books, 2002), p. 7.

205   "I am a great admirer"—Wynne-Jones.

205   "I always disagree"—Orwell letter to Richard Rees, March 3, 1949, *CW XX*, 3560, p. 52.

206   "the use of false information"—Ted Morgan, *Reds: McCarthyism in Twentieth-Century America* (Random House, 2004), p. 566.

206   "self-appointed thought police"—*New York Times*, August 27, 1952.

206   "Americanism with its sleeves rolled"—Richard H. Rovere, *Senator Joe McCarthy* (Methuen & Co., Ltd., 1960), p. 12.

206   "the chink in our shining armour"—Richard M. Fried, *The McCarthy Era in Perspective* (Oxford University Press, 1990), p. 136.

206   "Burnham thinks always"—Orwell, "Burnham's View of the Contemporary World Struggle," *CW XIX*, 3204, p. 105.

207   "the existence of a vast"—Richard Hofstadter, *The Paranoid Style in American Politics* (Vintage, 2008), p. 14.

207   "He abandons Communism intellectually"—Crossman (ed.), pp. 224–25.

207   "group-advancement"—Carol Brightman (ed.), *Between Friends: The Correspondence of Hannah Arendt and Mary McCarthy, 1949–1975* (Secker & Warburg, 1995), p. 5.

207   "In five years"—Swingler and Orwell, "The Right to Free Expression," *CW XVIII*, 3090, p. 443.

207   "In the USA the phrase 'Americanism'"—Orwell's Statement on *Nineteen Eighty-Four, CW XX*, 3636, p. 134.

208   "It is difficult, if not impossible"—Quoted in David M. Oshinsky, *A Conspiracy So Immense: The World of Joe McCarthy* (Oxford University Press, 2005), p. 187.

208   "He knew that big lies"—James Reston, *Deadline: A Memoir* (Random House, 1991), p. 215.

208   "came out of the McCarthy period"—Ibid., p. 219.

208 "Don't join the book-burners"—Quoted in Morgan, p. 447.

209 "Whether or not my ideas on censorship"—Quoted in Ray Bradbury, *Fahrenheit 451: 60th Anniversary Edition* (Simon & Schuster, 2012), p. 189.

209 "true father, mother, and lunatic brother"—Ibid., p. 167.

209 "Whereas twenty years ago"—Kingsley Amis, *New Maps of Hell: A Survey of Science Fiction* (Penguin, 2012), pp. 70–71.

209 "A Startling View of Life in 1984"—George Orwell, *Nineteen Eighty-Four* (Signet Books, 1950).

210 "*1984* is already on the way out"—Walsh, reprinted in Meyers (ed.), p. 293.

210 It has even been claimed—See Rodden, *The Politics of Literary Reputation*, p. 211.

210 "if you engaged in any kind"—Raymond Williams, *Politics and Letters: Interviews with New Left Review* (Verso, 1981), p. 384.

CHAPTER 11: SO DAMNED SCARED

211 "It is difficult to imagine"—Stephen Haseler, *The Death of British Democracy: A Study of Britain's Political Present and Future* (London: Paul Elek, 1976), p. 221.

211 "On my trips through Russia"—Buckley, p. 252.

211 "The sad reminders"—Geoff MacCormack, *From Station to Station: Travels With Bowie 1973–1976* (Genesis, 2007), p. 93.

211 "You see Roy"—Roy Hollingsworth, "Cha-Cha-Cha-Changes: A Journey with Aladdin," *Melody Maker*, May 12, 1973.

212 "There is a great sense of crisis"—Benn diaries, December 7, 1973, in *Against the Tide: Diaries 1973–76* (Hutchinson, 1989), p. 220.

212 "because I deeply believed"—Quoted in Stephen Dorril and Robin Ramsay, *Smear!: Wilson and the Secret State* (London: 4th Estate, 1991), p. 230.

212 "a gradual chilling"—Richard Eder, "Battle of Britain 1974," *New York Times*, February 24, 1974.

212 "A country rent apart"—Patrick Cosgrave, "Could the Army Take Over?," *Spectator*, December 22, 1973.

213 "I'm an awful pessimist"—Charles Shaar Murray, "Tight Rope Walker at the Circus," *New Musical Express*, August 11, 1973.

213 "*1974: der Countdown für 1984 hat begonnen*"—*Merkur*, vol. 28, no. 10, 1974.

213 "It is a shock to realize"—Richard N. Farmer, *The Real World of 1984: A Look at the Foreseeable Future* (David McKay Co., Inc., 1973), p. vii.

213 "Never before in history"—Jerome Tuccille, *Who's Afraid of 1984?* (Arlington House, 1975), p. 3.

213 "The term Orwellian"—Burgess, *1985*, p. 18.

214 "the most famous"—Nicholas von Hoffman, "1984: Here Today, Here Tomorrow?," *Washington Post*, June 17, 1974.

214 "If he had lived"—Mary McCarthy, "The Writing on the Wall," *New York Review of Books*, January 30, 1969.

214 "if he does not set down his thoughts"—Sonia Orwell, "Unfair to George," *Nova*, June/July 1969.

214 Even as the ultra-McCarthyite John Birch Society—see Lucas, *The Betrayal of Dissent*, p. 39.

214 "a fink"—Saul Bellow, *Mr. Sammler's Planet* (Alison Press, 1984), p. 42.

214 "this trash can't withstand the storms"—Bruce Franklin, "The Teaching of Literature in the Highest Academies of the Empire," in Louis Kampf and Paul Lauter (eds.), *The Politics of Literature: Dissenting Essays on the Teaching of English* (Pantheon Books, 1972), p. 116.

215 "the common man"—*Omnibus: George Orwell: The Road to the Left* (BBC, 1971).

215 "Oh, where will you be"—Spirit, "1984" (Ode Records, 1969).

215 "We don't want no Big Brother scene"—John Lennon, "Only People," *Mind Games* (Apple, 1973).

215 "If we don't get our thing together"—Rare Earth, "Hey Big Brother" (Rare Earth, 1971).

215 one of Lee Harvey Oswald's favourite books—See *The Official Warren Commission Report on the Assassination of President John F. Kennedy* (Doubleday & Company, Inc., 1964).

215 "it was almost impossible"—*The Prisoner File* (Channel 4, 1984).

216 "the way we're being made into ciphers"—Warner Troyer interviews Patrick McGoohan for the Ontario Educational Communications Authority, March 1977.

216 "the holiday camp, the doodle-bug"—Orwell, Review of *The Unquiet Grave: A Word Cycle* by Palinurus, *Observer*, January 14, 1945, *CW XVII*, 2604, p. 21.

216 "Questions Are a Burden to Others" etc.—*The Prisoner* (ITV, 1967–68).

216 "You still have a choice!"—*The Prisoner*, "A Change of Mind."

216 "If you insist on living a dream"—*The Prisoner*, "Dance of the Dead."

216 "Number Two: It doesn't matter which side runs the Village"—*The Prisoner*, "The Chimes of Big Ben."

217 "usefully divert the violence of youth" etc.—*Privilege* (dir. Peter Watkins, 1967).

217 "Two superstars of their time"—Quoted in Peter Doggett, *The Man Who Sold the World: David Bowie and the 1970s* (Bodley Head, 2011), p. 254.

218 "I could have been Hitler in England"—Cameron Crowe, "Ground Control to Davy Jones," *Rolling Stone*, February 12, 1976.

218 "You always felt you were in *1984*"—Steve Malins, "Duke of Hazard," *Vox*, October 1995.

218 "For a person who married" and "To be quite honest"—Ben Edmonds, "Bowie Meets the Press: Plastic Man or Godhead of the Seventies?," *Circus*, April 27, 1976.

219 "a backward look at the sixties and seventies"—Nicholas Pegg, *The Complete David Bowie* (Titan, 2011), p. 333.

219 "I had in my mind" and "staggered through"—Ibid., 68.

219 "That was *our* world"—Paul Du Noyer, "Contact," *Mojo*, no. 104, July 2002.

219 "not, in my view, a very good novel"—Burgess, p. 91.

219 "It is better to have our streets"—Ibid., p. 93.

219 "Rats the size of cats"—Orwell, *CW VI*, p. 54.

220 "Oh dress yourself my urchin one"—David Bowie, *Diamond Dogs* (RCA, 1974).

220 "a heavy vibe"—Buckley, p. 185.

221 "the warnings from right and left" and "It is very difficult"—Eder, "Battle of Britain, 1974."

221 "conceptualizes the vision"—Quoted in Doggett, p. 211.

221 "Power, Nuremburg"—Quoted in Pegg, p. 555.

221 "World Assembly building"—Sketch for Hunger City film, 1974, reprinted in *David Bowie Is* (V&A Publishing, 2013), p. 135.

221 "diabolical"—Richard Cromelin, "David Bowie: The Darling of the Avant-Garde," *Phonograph Record,* January 1972.

222 "Really I'm a very one-track person"—Robert Hilburn, "Bowie Finds His Voice!," *Melody Maker,* September 14, 1974.

222 "media artist"—Cameron Crowe, Playboy Interview, *Playboy,* September 1976.

222 "a very medieval, firm-handed"—Crowe, "Ground Control to Davy Jones."

222 "You've got to have an extreme right front"—Anthony O'Grady, "Dictatorship: The Next Step?," *NME,* August 23, 1975.

222 "my whole life would be transformed"—Buckley, p. 231.

222 "a theatrical observation"—Quoted in ibid., p. 253.

223 "a formidable vigilante group" and "We are not Fascists"—*Daily Express,* February 1, 1974.

223 "committed to a left-wing programme"—"Firm Action for a Fair Britain," Conservative Party general election manifesto, February 1974.

223 "scrubbing our minds clean"—Andy Beckett, *Pinochet in Piccadilly* (Faber & Faber, 2003), p. 173.

223 "more open-minded"—Quoted in ibid., p. 84.

223 "All right"—Quoted in ibid., p. 85.

224 "the only outcome"—Quoted in Dominic Sandbrook, *Seasons in the Sun: The Battle for Britain, 1974–1979* (Allen Lane, 2012), p. 129.

224 "Today, because of the strikes"—Maugham, pp. 31–32.

224 "the Communist Trojan horse" and "Perhaps the country might choose"—Quoted in Beckett, p. 196.

224 "the militants of the neo-Marxist left"—Lord Chalfont, "Could Britain Be Heading for a Military Takeover?," London *Times,* August 5, 1974.

224 "apprehensive patriots"—Dorril and Ramsay, p. 265.

224 "Although I don't for a moment"—Benn diaries, August 22, 1974, in *Against the Tide,* p. 220.

225 "What is certain"—London *Times,* May 8, 1975.

225 "looking at the faces of the Junta"—Benn diaries, January 20, 1976, in *Against the Tide,* p. 501.

225 One leaked dossier—See Dorril and Ramsay, p. 258.

225 "all these fears of bureaucracy"—Philip Whitehead, *The Writing on the Wall: Britain in the Seventies* (Michael Joseph, Ltd., 1985), p. 216.

226 "you do not pit Hamlet"—Robert Moss, *The Collapse of Democracy* (Temple Smith, 1975), p. 277.

226   "It is a cold world"—Ibid., p. 35.

226   "cold war liberal"—Haseler, p. 10.

226   "all the gobbledegook"—Ibid., p. 199.

226   "a national-socialist member"—Rhodes Boyson (ed.), *1985: An Escape from Orwell's 1984: A Conservative Path to Freedom* (Churchill Press, 1975), p. ix.

226   "It's much more frightening"—*Radio Times,* September 19, 1977.

227   "It is a satire"—Howard Brenton, *Plays: One* (Methuen, 1986), p. 108.

227   "The Justice Department Is Watching You"—*2000 AD,* Prog 1984, May 31, 2016.

227   "I think progress is the biggest enemy on Earth"—Troyer interview, March 1977.

227   "no one creates utopias anymore"—Martin Amis, *The War Against Cliché: Essays and Reviews 1971–2000* (Vintage, 2002), p. 117.

228   "improbable tyranny"—Burgess, p. 102.

228   *Look Forward in Mild Irritation*—Clive James, *From the Land of Shadows* (Jonathan Cape, 1982), p. 104.

228   "everything seemed ready"—Martin Amis, *The War Against Cliché,* p. 116.

228   "the nightmare world of *A Clockwork Orange*"— Margaret Thatcher, speech to Conservative Party conference, October 13, 1978.

228   "the Big Brother state"—Margaret Thatcher, speech to Conservative rally in Darlington, April 23, 1979.

228   "Novels don't care"—Ibid., p. 120.

228   "Look, you know what happened to Winston"—The Jam, "Standards," *This Is the Modern World* (Polydor, 1977).

228   "Now it's 1984"—Dead Kennedys, "California Über Alles" (Optional Music, 1979).

228   "In 1984!"—The Clash, "1977" (CBS, 1977).

                          CHAPTER 12: ORWELLMANIA

229   "Orwell was floating around"—Jack Mathews, *The Battle for Brazil* (Applause, 1998), p. 45.

229   "Information Purification Directives" etc.—"1984" (Chiat/Day, 1983).

229   "thunderclap"—Walter Isaacson, Steve Jobs (Little, Brown, 2011), p. 162.

230   "kick[ing] around phrases"—Steve Hayden, " '1984': As Good As It Gets," *Adweek,* January 30, 2011.

230   "They said it would be irresponsible"—Adelia Cellini, "1984: 20 Years On," *Macworld,* January 2004.

230   "people in bar rooms" and "No commercial"—Nancy Millman, "Apple '1984' Spot: A Love/Hate Story," *Advertising Age,* January 30, 1984.

230   "Will Big Blue dominate"—Isaacson, p. 169.

231   "a B-grade interpretation"—Millman.

231   "THERE IS ONLY ONE YEAR LEFT!"—Nat Hentoff, "The New Age of No Privacy," *Village Voice,* February 1, 1983.

231 "casting its appraising eye"—*Village Voice*, February 1, 1983.

231 "almost as much impact"—Geoffrey Stokes, "The History of the Future," *Village Voice*, February 1, 1983.

231 "Orwell's decade"—Günter Grass, *Headbirths, or The Germans Are Dying Out* (Secker & Warburg, 1982), p. 67.

231 "If you don't have an opinion"—Michael Robertson, "Orwell's 1984— Prophecy or Paranoia?," *San Francisco Chronicle*, December 19, 1983.

231 "black plague"—Quoted in Leopold Labedz, "Will George Orwell Survive 1984?," *Encounter*, June 1984.

231 "We can't control everything."—John Ezard, "Big Brother Looks Ready for Big Business in 1984," *Guardian*, December 28, 1983.

232 "the Ministry of Nightlife"—*The New Show* (NBC, 1984).

232 "WAR IS PEACE"—Reprinted in Rodden, *The Politics of Literary Reputation*, p. 234.

232 *TV Guide* figured—*TV Guide*, January 18, 1984.

232 "Big Brother meets the band with the Big Balls"—*Musician*, March 1983.

232 "The Orwell/Animal Farms/1984"—Quoted in Ezard.

232 "Can we be allowed to forget"—James Cameron, "All Together Now," *Guardian*, January 3, 1984.

232 "a kind of Orwellian nightmare"—*Spectator*, January 7, 1984.

232 "the already hackneyed analogies"—Hansard, HC, January, 25, 1984, vol. 52, col. 1001.

233 "thinking about all the George Orwell jokes"—Reprinted in Rodden, *The Politics of Literary Reputation*, p. 235.

233 "As a forecaster"—*The Futurist*, December 1983.

233 "proved wrong"—Isaac Asimov, "It's Up to the Scientists . . . to Refute Orwell's *1984*," *Science Digest*, August 1979.

233 "According to Orwell"—Reprinted in Rodden, *The Politics of Literary Reputation*, p. 257.

233 "a dirty little scoundrel"—Orwell, "Benefit of Clergy," *CW XVI*, 2481, p. 237.

233 "Big Brother's screaming"—Oingo Boingo, "Wake Up (It's 1984)" (A&M, 1983).

233 "I never read Orwell's book"—*New York Times*, January 1, 1984.

234 "I believe"—Cathy Booth, "1984—The Year of the Book," UPI, January 1, 1984.

234 "I do not believe"—Orwell's Statement on *Nineteen Eighty-Four*, *CW XX*, 3636, p. 136.

234 "I am not in the prediction business"—Robertson.

234 "*never* has any single man"—George Steiner, "Killing Time," *New Yorker*, December 12, 1983.

235 "I've fucked up my life"—David Plante, *Difficult Women: A Memoir of Three* (Victor Gollancz, Ltd., 1983), p. 99.

235 "spouted Orwell like a fountain"—*Variety*, April 25, 1984.

235 "the *Star Wars* or *2001: A Space Odyssey*"—*Photoplay*, December 1984.

235   "We had to guarantee" and following quotes—Author interview with Michael Radford.

236   "You know, this really is frightening"—Fiona Kieni, "John Hurt on *Nineteen Eighty-Four*," *Metro Magazine*, no. 65, 1984.

237   "We were lumbered"—*Guardian*, October 11, 1984.

238   "general knowledge that was in the atmosphere"—Terry Gilliam, Charles Alverson & Bob McCabe, *Brazil: The Evolution of the 54th Best British Film Ever Made* (Orion, 2001), p. 12.

238   "*Brazil* came specifically"—Salman Rushdie, "An Interview with Terry Gilliam," *Believer*, March 2003.

238   "The Ministry needs terrorists"—Gilliam, Alverson and McCabe, p. 157.

239   "purges and vaporisations"—Orwell, *CW IX*, p. 48.

239   "somewhere in the twentieth century"—*Brazil* (dir. Terry Gilliam, 1985).

239   "We used a lot of the same locations"—Interview with Radford.

239   "*1985*"—Mathews, p. 93.

239   "a stoned, slapstick *1984*"—Quoted in ibid., p. 144.

239   "To me, the heart of *Brazil*"—Rushdie, "An Interview with Terry Gilliam."

239   "Quite obviously they tend to stimulate"—Orwell, "Personal Notes on Scientifiction," *Leader Magazine*, July 21, 1945, *CW XVII*, 2705, p. 220.

240   "a super state type of hero"—"Are Comics Fascist?," *Time*, October 22, 1945.

240   "people who don't switch off the news"—Alan Moore and David Lloyd, *V for Vendetta* (DC, 1990), p. 5.

240   Moore's long list of influences—Alan Moore, "Behind the Painted Smile," Warrior #17, March 1, 1984, reprinted in ibid., p. 267.

241   "nightmarish future England"—Ibid., p. 108.

241   "it would take something"—Ibid., p. 6.

241   "the wariness"—Margaret Atwood, "What *The Handmaid's Tale* Means in the Age of Trump," *New York Times*, March 10, 2017.

241   "silently at odds"—Atwood, *Curious Pursuits*, p. 335.

241   "speculative fiction"—Ingersoll (ed.), p. 161.

242   "There is more than one kind of freedom"—Margaret Atwood, *The Handmaid's Tale* (Vintage, 1996), p. 34.

242   "I would not include anything"—Margaret Atwood, "Haunted by *The Handmaid's Tale*," *Guardian*, January 21, 2012.

242   "normal intercourse"—Orwell, *CW IX*, p. 319.

242   "a political act"—Ibid., p. 133.

243   "a refugee from the past"—Atwood, *The Handmaid's Tale*, p. 239.

243   "Let's say it's an antiprediction"—Atwood, *New York Times*.

243   "I understood him up to a point"—*Time*, November 28, 1983.

244   "one of the most disgusting books"—Christopher Norris (ed.), *Inside the Myth: Orwell: Views from the Left* (Lawrence and Wishart, 1984), p. 81.

244   "Normally, to speculate"—Norman Podhoretz, "If Orwell Were Alive Today," *Harper's*, January 1983.

244 "the sort of well-heeled power worshiper"—Christopher Hitchens and Norman Podhoretz, *Harper's*, February 1983.

244 *National Review*—See Robert C. de Camara, "Homage to Orwell," *National Review*, May 13, 1983; E. L. Doctorow, "On the Brink of 1984," *Playboy*, February 1983.

244 *Tribune* published—See *Tribune*, January 6, 13, 20, 27, 1984.

244 "a year of hope"—*Guardian*, December 31, 1983.

245 "tomb-robbers"—Neil Kinnock, "Shadow of the Thought Police," London *Times*, December 31, 1983.

245 "we would have been taken so far"—*The Sun*, January 2, 1984.

245 "ideological overkill"—Paul Johnson, *Spectator*.

245 "a grim warning"—Quoted in Michael Glenny, "Orwell's *1984* Through Soviet Eyes," Index on Censorship, vol. 13, no. 4, August 1984.

245 "a fully realistic picture"—Quoted in Labedz.

245 "anti-Soviet agitation"—Glenny.

246 "No one has ever lived in Lilliput"—*Guardian*, January 8, 1984.

246 "How did he know?"—Timothy Garton Ash, "Orwell for Our Time," *Observer*, May 6, 2001.

246 "probably the single Western author"—Quoted in Thomas Cushman and John Rodden (eds.), *George Orwell Into the Twenty-First Century* (Paradigm, 2004), p. 274.

246 "He was the first person"—Glenny.

246 "When I read the story"—Milan Šimečka, "A Czech Winston Smith," *Index on Censorship*, vol. 13, no. 1, February 1984.

247 "The struggle of man against power"—Milan Kundera, *The Book of Laughter and Forgetting*, trans. Michael Henry Heim (Faber & Faber, 1992), p. 3.

247 "an undifferentiated block of horrors"—Kundera, *Testaments Betrayed*, p. 255.

247 "In their talk of forty horrible years"—Ibid., p. 256.

247 "Amalrik is long dead"—Natan Sharansky, press conference, January 29, 1996.

247 "a ritualistic code"—Milovan Djilas, "The Disintegration of Leninist Totalitarianism," in Irving Howe (ed.), *1984 Revisited: Totalitarianism in Our Century* (Harper & Row, 1984), p. 140.

247 "it must show that power"—Françoise Thom, *Newspeak: The Language of Soviet Communism*, trans. Ken Connelly (Claridge Press, 1989), p. 118.

248 "His inner world consisted"—Masha Gessen, *The Future Is History: How Totalitarianism Reclaimed Russia* (Granta, 2018), p. 65.

248 "She took it for granted"—Orwell, *CW IX*, p. 159.

248 "Our society is deeply ill"—Quoted in Gessen, p. 86.

249 "For Orwell the problem"—Labedz.

249 "The worst kind of Big Brother"—Bob Brewin, "Worldlink 2029," *Village Voice*, February 1, 1983.

249 mechanical "brain"—*Tribune*, June 17, 1949, *CW XX*, 3649, p. 139.

249 "smash the old canard"—David Burnham, "The Computer, the Consumer and Privacy," *New York Times,* March 4, 1984.

249 "If Big Brother could just get"—Walter Cronkite, "Orwell's "1984"—Nearing?," *New York Times,* June 5, 1983.

249 "the complaisance, the eagerness"—John Corry, "TV: 1984 Revisited," *New York Times,* June 7, 1983.

CHAPTER 13: OCEANIA 2.0

250 "The stubbornness of reality"—Quoted in Elizabeth Young-Bruehl, *Hannah Arendt: For Love of the World* (Yale University Press, 1982), p. 255.

250 "Orwell feared"—Neil Postman, *Amusing Ourselves to Death* (Methuen, 1987), p. viii.

250 "In the Huxleyan prophecy"—Ibid., p. 160.

251 "I loved living in a world"—Andrew Smith, *Totally Wired: On the Trail of the Great Dotcom Swindle* (Simon & Schuster, 2012), p. 295.

251 "dilution and cheapening"—*Estate of Orwell v. CBS,* 00-c-5034 (ND Ill).

251 "asleep or awake"—Orwell, *CW IX,* p. 29.

251 "Orwell understood the difference"—Bernard Crick, "Big Brother Belittled," *Guardian,* August 19, 2000.

252 "The world of *Nineteen Eighty-Four* ended in 1989"—Garton Ash.

252 "*Nineteen Eighty-Four* is about power out of control"—*Independent,* March 1, 2003.

252 "Oceania (the US and Britain)"—*Guardian,* December 31, 2002.

252 "Orwellian euphemisms"—David Fricke, "Bitter Prophet," *Rolling Stone,* June 26, 2003.

252 "The war is waged"—*Fahrenheit 9/11* (dir. Michael Moore, 2004).

252 "there is a war on"—Orwell, *CW IX,* p. 60.

252 "the reality-based community"—Ron Suskind, "Faith, Certainty and the Presidency of George W. Bush," *New York Times Magazine,* October 17, 2004.

253 As a popular slogan put it—Daniel Kurtzman, "Learning to Love Big Brother/ George W. Bush Channels George Orwell," SFgate.com, July 28, 2002.

253 "'Orwell' has been used"—Scott Lucas, *Orwell* (Haus, 2003), p. 138.

253 "Shakespeare doesn't have the moral authority"—John Rodden, *Every Intellectual's Big Brother: George Orwell's Literary Siblings* (University of Texas Press, 2006), p. 159.

254 "*V* was designed to warn"—Mihir Bhanage, "Never thought V would become a symbol of global rebellion," TNN, March 1, 2017.

254 "Orwell imagined a huge change"—Philip Roth, "The Story Behind 'The Plot Against America,'" *New York Times,* September 19, 2004.

255 "Any time there's a new invention"—Author interview with Charlie Brooker for *Empire,* London, July 7, 2016.

255 "not the advancement of science"—Huxley, *Brave New World and Brave New World Revisited,* p. 8.

255 "The Ministry didn't do this to us"—*Fahrenheit 451* (HBO, 2018).

255 "Maybe Apple's '1984' ad" and "wasn't a rupture"—Rebecca Solnit, "Poison Apples," *Harper's*, December 2014.

255 "SECRETS ARE LIES"—Dave Eggers, *The Circle* (Penguin, 2014), p. 303.

255 "a new and glorious openness"—Ibid., p. 491.

256 "What happens to us"—Margaret Atwood, "When Privacy Is Theft," *New York Review of Books*, November 21, 2013.

256 "warned us of the danger"—Edward Snowden, *Alternative Christmas Message*, Channel 4, December 25, 2013.

256 As President Obama—Press conference, California, June 7, 2013.

256 "very Orwellian"—*All In With Chris Hayes*, MSNBC, June 10, 2013.

256 "So, Are We Living in 1984?"—Newyorker.com, June 11, 2013.

256 "So George Orwell was wrong"—Tilman Baumgaertel, "'I am a communication artist': Interview with Nam June Paik," Rhizome.org, February 5, 2001.

256 "completely, irredeemably, outrageously wrong"—Peter Huber, *Orwell's Revenge: The 1984 Palimpsest* (Free Press, 1994), p. 235.

256 "the proles do the watching"—Ibid., p. 228.

257 "a development that promises"—George Orwell, *Nineteen Eighty-Four*, with an introduction by Thomas Pynchon (Penguin, 2003), p. xxv.

257 "We have entered the age"—Huxley, *Brave New World and Brave New World Revisited*, p. xxi.

257 "from Lisbon to Vladivostok"—Quoted in Snyder, p. 82.

258 "If the state so wishes"—Quoted in Gessen, p. 249.

258 "show business and propaganda"—Peter Pomerantsev, *Nothing Is True and Everything Is Possible: Adventures in Modern Russia* (Faber & Faber, 2015), p. 7.

258 "the very language and categories"—Ibid., p. 77.

258 "Versionland"—*Guardian*, September 15, 2018.

258 "They don't require belief"—Anne Applebaum, "A Warning from Europe: The Worst is Yet to Come," *The Atlantic*, October 2018.

259 "the hottest literary property in town"—*Hollywood Reporter* online, April 3, 2017.

259 "the clock is already striking thirteen"—Variety.com, March 21, 2017.

259 "It went from zero" and following quotes—Author interview with Robert Icke and Duncan Macmillan, London, July 5, 2018.

259 "how do you begin to talk about?"—Icke and Macmillan, p. 17.

260 "How do we know the Party fell?"—Ibid., p. 95.

260 "What year is it?"—Ibid., p. 80.

261 "The people are not going to revolt"—Ibid., p. 89.

261 "I think dad would've been amused"—*Daily Record*, February 26, 2017.

261 "a continuous frenzy"—Orwell, *CW IX*, p. 220.

261 "something cruel"—Orwell, "As I Please," *Tribune*, March 24, 1944, *CW XVI*, 2441, p. 133.

262 "may quit relying"—Robertson.

262 "crying hysterically"—Orwell, *CW IX*, p. 14.

263 "The People Believe What the Media Tells Them They Believe"—Nicholas Thompson and Issie Lapowsky, "How Russian Trolls Used Meme Warfare to Divide America," Wired.com, December 17, 2018.

263 "I believe the biggest risk"—Andrew Marantz, "Reddit and the Struggle to Detoxify the Internet," *New Yorker*, March 19, 2018.

263 "One of the biggest challenges"—*My Next Guest Needs No Introduction with David Letterman*, Episode 1, Netflix, 2018.

263 "the Ministry of Truth with ML systems"—Twitter, @alexstamos, October 7, 2017.

264 *The Washington Post* calculated—At https://www.washingtonpost.com /graphics/politics/trump-claims-database.

264 "Truth isn't truth!"—*Meet the Press*, NBC, August 19, 2018.

264 "Many dangerous ideas"—Dee Rees in Philip K. Dick, *Philip K. Dick's Electric Dreams* (Gollancz, 2017), p. 54.

264 "What you're seeing"—Donald Trump speech to Veterans of Foreign Wars convention, July 24, 2018.

265 "The party told you to reject"—Orwell, *CW IX*, p. 84.

265 "one is reminded of what Orwell got right"—Adam Gopnik, "Orwell's '1984' and Trump's America," Newyorker.com, January 27, 2017.

265 "I am willing to believe"—"Looking Back on the Spanish War," *CW XIII*, 1421, p. 504.

266 "If men continue to believe"—*Life*, July 4, 1949.

AFTERWORD

267 "2 + 2 = 5"—Orwell, *CW IX*, p. 303.

267 "I think you need that moment"—Author interview with Michael Radford.

267 "spirit of Man"—Orwell, *CW IX*, p. 282.

268 "power of facing unpleasant facts"—Orwell, "Why I Write," *CW XVIII*, 3007, p. 316.

268 "To read this novel"—*Partisan Review*, July 1949, reprinted in Meyers (ed.), p. 270.

268 "for the future, for the unborn"—Orwell, *CW IX*, p. 9.

268 "are not indestructible"—Orwell, "The Freedom of the Press," *CW XVII*, 2721, p. 258.

INDEX

NOTE: George Orwell is also referred to as GO in this index.